Philosophy and Philosophers

PHILOSOPHY AND PHILOSOPHERS

A P Bhardwaj

MD PUBLICATIONS PVT LTD
NEW DELHI
www.mdppl.com

Published by :

MD Publications Pvt Ltd
"MD House", 11, Darya Ganj,
New Delhi - 110 002
Phone : +91-11- 45355555
E-mail : contact@mdppl.com
Website: www.mdppl.com

ISBN : 978-81-7533-340-6

Published and Printed by Mr. Pranav Gupta on behalf of **MD Publications Pvt Ltd** at Repro India Limited.

PREFACE

Philosophy is a well coordinated and systematised attempt at evaluating life and the universe as a whole, with reference to first principles that underlie all things as their causes and are implicit in all experience. It is an impartial approach to all problems and aspects of life and existence, and its studies are not devoted merely to the empirical world, not confined to investigation of the mind and its behaviour, as in psychology; not given over merely to casuistry and ethology, as in the normative science of morality and ethics; not taken up with the consideration of civic duties and problems of administration and constitution, as in the case of politics; not concerned with the solution of problems and techniques of adjusting and ordering and discovering the origin and organisation and development of human society, like economics and sociology; but are adapted for an exhaustive treatment of the basic presuppositions of each and every one of these, as also of what is other than and beyond all these, that on which all these are ultimately founded and which is the ground of all knowledge and experience in general.

Philosophy is a rational enquiry into the forms, contents and implications of experience. It is an attempt at a complete knowledge of being in all the phases of its manifestation in the various processes of consciousness. Philosophy is a necessary means for the possession of the higher knowledge of the Self. Philosophy is a general exposition of the ultimate concepts, meanings and values of the things of the universe, by a resort to their final causes which range beyond the reach of the senses. Philosophy soars above empiricality, though it takes the help of empirical concepts and categories for the sake of proclaiming to the world the truths declared by intuition. No philosopher would deny the profound importance of Greek philosophy, nor the value in reading their works, but that doesn't mean the boundaries and methods of the discipline were set in stone two-and-a-half millenia ago. Many have in fact changed considerably since its inception, although its general concerns remain. 'Love of wisdom' is certainly a commendable principle, but not a working definition for the contemporary specialty. Philosophers aim to reject dogmatic, authoritarian or purely rhetorical approaches to philosophical questions and seek instead to proceed by means of arguments that can be critically assessed. We value lively critical conversation, where people with different views engage respectfully with one another in a common effort to advance their understanding. This book has been prepared keeping in mind the needs and scope of philosophers, students, researchers and for all those associated with the subject philosophy.

I am very thankful to Mr. Pranav Gupta, Director of MD Publications Pvt Ltd, New Delhi, for his kind cooperation and support for this book.

A P Bhardwaj

Contents

1

Cartesian Dualism and Philosophical Revolution

Introduction

The aim is to make a start at sorting out some of these competing views and thus to make clear what precisely is at stake when we ask what minds are. We shall see that the issues are rarely clear-cut. This is scarcely surprising. Puzzles posed by the investigation of minds are some of the deepest in philosophy. In the end we may find no proffered solution entirely satisfactory. Even if that is so, we shall at least have a better understanding of the attractions and liabilities inherent in different ways of regarding minds.

Having said this, I want to head off one natural line of response. A common attitude toward philosophy is that philosophers never answer questions, but merely pose them. Scientists, in contrast, are in the business of delivering answers. Questions the answers to which elude science, questions that seem scientifically unanswerable, are often dismissed as 'merely philosophical'. It is but a short step from this deflationary depiction of philosophy to the notion that where philosophy is concerned, there are no settled truths: every opinion is as good as any other.

This conception of philosophy and its relation to science is inadequate and naïve. What eludes science need not be unsettled. The state of the universe immediately before the Big Bang, for instance, might be forever unknowable. We are evidentially cut off from that state. It would be absurd to conclude, however, that there was no such state, or that every claim about its character is just as good as every other. Similarly, from the fact that there has been little agreement among philosophers as to the status of minds, it does not follow that minds have no definite status or that 'anything goes' when discussing the mind.

As we shall see in the chapters ahead, questions that arise in the philosophy of mind are rarely susceptible to straightforward empirical answers. An empirical question is one decidable, at least in principle, by experiment. Although experimental results tell against some conceptions of mind, most competing traditional accounts of mind are consistent with whatever empirical evidence we now possess or might conceivably possess in the future. The philosophical question concerns what we are to *make* of this evidence. And here our guide cannot be science. Science provides a loose framework for representing empirical findings, but no strictly scientific principles tell us how to interpret or make sense of those findings. For that, we must turn to 'common sense' and to philosophy. This does not mean that we must advance specifically philosophical theories in sorting through empirical evidence. Rather, the activity of sorting through scientific findings and reconciling these with ordinary experience, and with a constellation of beliefs we have adopted on the basis of other findings, is a kind of philosophizing: philosophers are not the only philosophers. Card-carrying philosophers are merely those who do their philosophizing self-consciously.

Descartes's Dualism

Let us take as a starting point an influential conception of mind advanced by René Descartes (1596–1650). Descartes held that minds and bodies are 'substances' of distinct kinds that, in the case of living human beings, happen to be intimately related. This dualism of substances (subsequently labeled Cartesian dualism) nowadays strikes most philosophers and scientists interested in the mind as hopelessly misguided. Until quite recently, it was widely supposed that the source of the notorious mind-body problem stemmed from the acceptance of the Cartesian picture: a solution to the problem could be had by rejecting dualism. As we shall see, this diagnosis has not panned out. Nevertheless, we can begin to develop an appreciation of the mind-body problem by examining Descartes's approach to the mind.

As a preliminary, let us note some *prima facie* differences between mental and material objects and states. First, material objects are spatial; they occupy a location in space and exhibit spatial dimensions. Mental objects – thoughts and sensations, for instance – are apparently non–spatial. What is the size and shape of your desire for a Whopper? Is your thinking of Vienna triangular? Such questions seem to make no sense.

You might think of sensations – some of them at least - as having spatial locations. A pain in your left big toe is, after all, in your left big toe. (Does this mean it is big-toe-shaped?) But is this quite right? Consider the phenomenon of 'phantom pain', a phenomenon well known to Descartes and his contemporaries. Amputees often seem to undergo experiences of pains in their amputated limbs. Your big toe could be amputated, yet you still might continue to experience the very same kind of throbbing pain you experienced prior to its amputation, and this pain might seem to you to be in a region at the end of your foot formerly occupied by your big toe. This suggests that although we experience pains and other sensations *as* occurring in various bodily locations, it need not follow that experiences occur *at* those locations. Following Descartes, we might say that an experience of pain-in-your-left-big-toe is a *kind* of experience. Such an experience differs in quality from an experience of pain-in-your-right-big-toe. There is no reason to think – and indeed good reason not to think that such experiences must be located where they are felt to be located or even that they have any location at all.

Mental states, then, unlike material states, appear to be distinctively non-spatial. This, at any rate, is Descartes's conclusion. A second important difference between the mental and the material is qualitative. Think of the qualities of your experience of a pain in your big toe. You may find these qualities difficult to describe, but that need not affect your awareness of them. Now ask yourself whether you could ever expect to encounter these qualities in a material object. A neuroscientist observing your nervous system while you are experiencing pain will observe nothing qualitatively resembling your pain. Indeed, this possibility seems to make no sense.

The point can be summed up as follows. The qualities of conscious experiences appear to be nothing at all like the qualities of material objects. They are apparently altogether unlike the qualities of any conceivable material object. The natural conclusion to draw is that mental qualities differ in kind from material qualities. Thus, mental qualities are not qualities of material objects.

A third distinction between the mental and the material is partly *epistemological* – that is, it concerns the character of our knowledge of such things. The knowledge you have of your own states of mind is direct and unchallengeable in a way that your knowledge of material objects is not. Philosophers sometimes put this by saying that we have 'privileged access' to our own states of mind. Descartes himself believed that this knowledge was incorrigible: your thoughts about your current states of mind could not be false. He believed, as well, that the contents of our own minds were transparent to us. In consequence:

(a) (Transparency) if you are in a particular state of mind, you *know* you are in that state; and

(b) (Incorrigibility) if you believe that you are in a particular state of mind, you *are* in that state.

The Cartesian notion that the mind is transparent strikes us nowadays as excessive. Freud long ago convinced us that much in the mind can be consciously inaccessible, and cognitive scientists routinely assume that mental states and operations are frequently inaccessible to consciousness. Social psychologists have delighted in showing us that we are often poor judges as to what we believe or want. We can accept all this, however, without jettisoning Descartes's central insight. The access we have to our own states of mind is distinctive, if not infallible. You entertain thoughts and experience pains self-consciously. I can only infer the occurrence in you of such goings-on. Your access to your own states of mind is direct and unmediated; my access to your states of mind is invariably indirect.

We might put this by saying that states of mind are 'private'. They are 'directly observable' only by the person (or creature) having them; outsiders can only infer them from their material effects. You can tell me what you are thinking, or I can guess it from the expression on your face. Neuroscientists might eventually be able to infer what you are thinking by observing patterns of neurological activities in your brain. Our observations of your mental life, however, are never direct in the way yours appear to be.

The situation is very different for material objects and their properties and states. If mental items are necessarily private, material things are necessarily public. When it comes to a material object, or the state of a material object, if you are in a position to observe it, then anyone else could observe it as well by taking up your observational position. The asymmetry of access we find in the case of minds is entirely absent. Again, this suggests that minds and material bodies are very different kinds of object. Descartes offers an explanation for this difference: minds and material bodies are distinct *kinds of substance*. A mental substance possesses properties not possessible by any material substance, and a material substance possesses properties no mental substance could possess. Indeed, according to Descartes, there is no overlap in the properties possessed by mental and material substances.

Before taking up Descartes's view in more detail, let us chart the three differences between the mental and the material we have just isolated. For the present, however, let us accept them as they stand and notice what follows.

Substances, Attributes and Modes

Descartes supposes that the world is made up of substances. A substance is not, as the term might suggest, a kind of stuff like water, or butter, or paint.

Material Bodies	***Minds***
Spatial	Non-spatial
Material qualities	Distinctively mental qualities
Public	Private

Fig. 1.1

Descartes, following tradition, regards substances as individual, self-standing objects. The desk at which I am now writing is, in this traditional sense, a substance, as is the pen I hold in my hand, the tree outside my window, and the bird nesting in its branches. These substances are complex: each is composed of other substances, their parts. My desk is made up of pieces of wood, organized in a particular way. Each of these pieces of wood (and each of the screws holding them together) is a substance in its own right. Similarly, the pen, the tree, and the bird are all made up of parts that are themselves substances. And of course these substances are themselves made up of distinct substances. Substances, note, are individuals – 'particulars' in the jargon of philosophers – as distinct from classes or kinds of thing. This bird and this tree are substances, but the class of birds is a class, not a substance; beech and oak are species of substance, not substances.

Substances are to be contrasted, on the one hand, with non–substantial individuals, and, on the other hand with properties. Non–substantial individuals include 'concrete' items such as events and 'abstract' entities such as sets and numbers. An event (a particular chicken's crossing a particular road at a particular time, for instance) could be regarded as a dated, non–repeatable particular. In this respect, events resemble substances. Just as two exactly similar peas in a pod are nevertheless distinct peas, so your reading this sentence now is one event, and your reading the very same sentence tomorrow is a distinct event. Events are not substances, however, but changes that substances undergo. Finally, substances and events are concrete particulars as distinct from 'abstract entities' like the set of cows or the number two.

Properties are *had* or *possessed* (or 'instantiated') by substances. Think of an ordinary substance, a particular red billiard ball. You can distinguish the ball's *redness* from its *sphericity* and its *mass*. In so doing, you consider three of the ball's properties. But you can also distinguish the ball, as *possessor* of these properties, from its properties. On the view I am associating with Descartes, this ball is a substance that possesses a number of properties including redness, sphericity, and a particular mass. Properties and substances are inseparable. You could not peel off an object's properties and leave the bare substance. Nor could properties float free of substances. Some philosophers have argued that substances are nothing more than collections or *bundles* of properties. This is not Descartes's view, however, and it is not a view that I should want to defend.

I have mentioned substances and properties. Descartes in fact speaks not of properties but of 'attributes' and 'modes'. An attribute is what makes a substance the kind of substance it is. A material (or physical; I shall use the terms interchangeably) substance is a substance possessing the attribute of extension: an extended substance. Extension is, roughly, *spatiality*. Thus, a material substance is one that occupies a definite spatial region and possesses a definite shape and size. The particular shape and size possessed by material substances are *modes* of extension, ways of being extended. What we would ordinarily think of as properties of everyday material objects are, for Descartes, *modes of extension.*

On this conception, a billiard ball's sphericity is a mode of extension; its sphericity is the way it is shaped. What of the ball's color? Here Descartes contends that the distinctive visual experience we have when we look at a red billiard ball does not resemble the feature of the ball that produces this experience in us. That feature might be the texture of the ball's surface, a texture that reflects light in a particular way. Texture – the arrangement of micro-particles making up an object's surface – is a mode of extension.

The metaphysics of Cartesian Dualism

Descartes puts the attribute-mode distinction to work by supposing that each kind of substance possesses a distinctive attribute. A material substance is a substance possessing the attribute of extension. A mental substance, in contrast, is a substance possessing a very different attribute, the attribute of *thought*. Descartes gives the term 'thought' a broader sense than we do today. Anything we in everyday life would count as a state of mind – a sensation, an image, an emotion, a belief, a desire – Descartes regards as a mode of thought, a *way of thinking*. (In another respect, Descartes's conception of thought is narrower than ours. He appears not to countenance the possibility of unconscious thoughts.)

We can now begin to understand Cartesian dualism. Bodies are material substances possessing the attribute of extension. Minds, too, are substances, but not material substances. Minds possess the attribute of thought. One more step is required to yield dualism. Every substance possesses exactly one attribute. If a substance possesses the attribute of extension (and so is extended in particular ways), it cannot possess the attribute of thought. If a substance possesses the attribute of thought (and thus possesses various modes of thought: feelings, images, beliefs), it cannot possess the attribute of extension. Thought and extension mutually exclude one another. It follows that no extended substance thinks, and no thinking substance is extended. Minds are thinking substances and bodies are extended substances, so minds are distinct from bodies.

Descartes embraces this conclusion, but he does not deny that minds and bodies are, as they clearly seem to be, intimately related. Think for a moment, as Descartes does, of the mind as the *I*: the ego, the self. You are related in an especially intimate way to a particular body, your body. When your finger comes too near the flame of a candle you feel pain. When my finger goes near the flame, in contrast, *you* feel no pain, though I do. When you decide to get up and walk across the room, it is your body that moves, not mine. To be sure, you can control my body. You can ask me to get up and walk across the room, or order me to do so at gunpoint, or tie a rope around me and *drag* me across the room. In so doing, however, your decision affects my body only indirectly, only by way of some movement of *your* body. Movements of your own body (your tongue and vocal cords, or your limbs) seem, in contrast, largely under your immediate voluntary control.

Let us pause briefly and take stock. Descartes holds that the world consists of two kinds of substance: material substances and mental substances. Material substances are extended and unthinking; mental substances think, but are unextended. Each mental substance bears an especially intimate relation to some particular material substance. (Or at any rate this is the arrangement with which we are most familiar. According to Descartes, it is at least possible for a mental substance to persist after the demise of the material substance to which it was intimately related: the self might survive the death of the body.) Mental and material substances, although utterly distinct, causally interact. Your body responds to your plans and decisions. Your mind receives signals from your body in the form of sensory experiences that provide you with information about the state of your body and, indirectly, the state of the world outside your body. The world causally impinges on your mind by way of your senses: your eyes, ears, nose, and your sense of touch.

The Cartesian picture is simple to spell out. Imagine that you sit on a tack planted in your chair by a malicious practical joker. Your sitting on the tack (a material event involving a pair of material objects, the tack and your body) gives rise to a distinctive sensation of pain (a mental event). This sensation or feeling in turn generates another mental event, a desire to leap upwards, and this desire brings about a leaping.

Cartesian dualism fits nicely with common sense. We see ourselves as *having* bodies, but as *distinct* from our bodies in at least the following sense. We can apparently conceive of our bodies changing dramatically, or ceasing to exist altogether, while we continue to exist. True, we speak of ourselves as 'having minds' – and, for that matter, we speak of changing our minds. But while you can perhaps imagine your body's being destroyed while you remain, it is less clear that you could coherently imagine your surviving the demise of your mind or self. You can imagine that you or your mind ceases to exist while your body continues to exist (in a vegetative state, perhaps), but that is another matter. Moreover, you might be able to imagine cases in which you swap bodies. This is a not uncommon occurrence in science fiction. But it seems to make no sense to suppose that you could swap minds or selves. 'Changing your mind' is not a matter of exchanging one mind for another, but a matter of revising your beliefs. When a chastened Scrooge becomes 'a new person', he does not swap selves, but alters his attitudes.

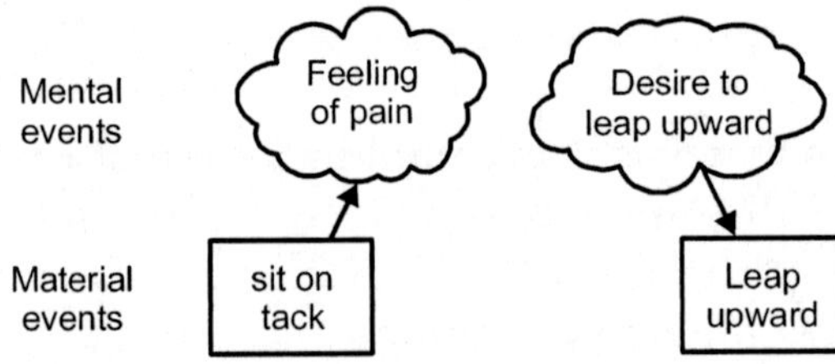

Fig. 1.2

In addition to fitting well with a commonsense conception of ourselves, Cartesian dualism also promises a reconciliation of our scientific picture of the world with ordinary experience. Science tells us or at any rate physics tells us that the world consists of minute, colorless particles jumbled together to form familiar middle-sized objects. Our experience of the world is quite different. Your visual experience of the red billiard ball is not an experience of a colorless spherical jumble. Sounds are vibrations in a medium (air or water, for instance). Yet your experience of a performance of an Offenbach overture differs qualitatively from anything science seems likely to turn up in its investigation of the physical world. Dualism makes sense of this apparent bifurcation. Material bodies are nothing more than collections of minute, silent, colorless objects interacting in space. Such interactions, however, produce in the mind 'Technicolor' experiences with lively qualities that differ from the qualities of any material object.

Qualities of our experiences (at bottom, modes of thought) seem to differ dramatically from the qualities of material bodies (modes of extension). Despite these apparent differences, however, Descartes holds that experiential qualities and material qualities co-vary. One result of this co-variation is that qualities of experiences can serve as reliable signs or indicators of qualities of material objects and events. Red objects look red not because they are made up of red particles, but because (let us suppose) they have a particular kind of surface texture. Red objects share this texture, or at any rate share properties that structure light so as to produce, in observers, experiences of redness.

Mind-body Interaction

We seem, then, following Descartes, to be in a position to account for apparent qualitative differences between our experiences and objects experienced, and for our capacity to 'read off' qualities of the world from qualities of our experiences. Further, we can accommodate our own everyday view of ourselves as housed in, but in some way distinct from, our bodies. All this is to the good. Unfortunately, Cartesian dualism comes at a price, a price few philosophers have been prepared to pay.

The difficulty is one that was immediately obvious to Descartes's contemporaries, a difficulty that Descartes himself understood keenly. Central to Descartes's view is the idea that minds and bodies causally interact. But if minds and bodies are utterly different kinds of substance, it is hard to see how such causal interaction could occur. Minds or selves, you will recall, are immaterial thinking but unextended substances. Material bodies, in contrast, are extended but unthinking. How could entities of such wholly different kinds affect one another causally? How could an event in an immaterial mind bring about a material effect? How could a physical event beget a change in an immaterial mind? The metaphysical distance Descartes places between minds and material bodies seems to preclude causal contact.

A Cartesian might bite the bullet here and contend that causal relations between a mental and a material substance are *sui generis* that is, mental-material causation is not a species of causation of the sort we encounter in the material world, but something unique. This strategy leads us from the frying pan into the fire. Modern science is premised on the assumption that the material world is a causally closed system. This means, roughly, that every event in the material world is caused by some other material event (if it is caused by any event) and has as effects only material events. (The parenthetical rider allows us to leave room for the possibility of uncaused, spontaneous events.) We can reformulate this idea in terms of explanation: an explanation citing all of the material causes of a material event is a complete causal explanation of the event.

The notion that the material world is causally closed is related to our conception of natural law. Natural laws govern causal relations among material events. Such laws differ from laws passed by legislative bodies. A natural law is exceptionless: it cannot be violated in the way a traffic law can be violated. An object that behaves in an odd or unexpected way nevertheless perfectly conforms to natural law. Evidence that an object's behavior violates a given natural law is evidence that what we had thought was a law is not.

Return now to Descartes's supposition that minds are non-material substances capable of initiating events in the material world. This supposition obliges us to give up the idea that the material world is causally self-contained. To see why this is so, imagine how causal interaction between mental and material substances might work. Suppose your mind acts on your body by instigating changes in a certain region of your brain. Descartes himself believed that minds were linked to bodies by way of the *pineal gland*, a small structure near the center of the brain. Minute alterations in the motions of particles in the pineal gland radiated throughout the body via the nervous system, producing muscular contractions and, ultimately, overt bodily motions. Let us pretend Descartes was right. Your pineal gland is made up of micro-particles that operate in accord with physical law. If your mind is to initiate a causal sequence in your pineal gland, then it will have to affect in some way the behavior of these micro-constituents. Its influencing the behavior of micro-constituents, however, would appear to require violation of the laws governing the micro-constituents, an impossibility if we take the material world to be causally self-contained and laws of nature to be inviolable.

You might imagine that the mind could act on the body without violating laws governing its material constituents. Perhaps, as the quantum theory suggests, laws governing those constituents are ultimately probabilistic or statistical in character. Imagine that a micro-system's being in a certain state, *S 1*, causes the system subsequently to go into state *S 2*, but only with a certain probability: there is a 35 per cent probability that a particular micro-system in state *S 1* will go into state *S 2* (during a certain period of time). Now, imagine that you – a mental substance – decide to wave to a friend. You initiate a particular change in your body by making it the case that a particular *S 1* micro-system in your pineal gland goes into state *S 2*. (We might imagine that when the constituents of such states 'line up' in this way, the result is a signal sent to your right arm that causes a series of muscle contractions and ultimately a waving motion of your arm. Here you have decided to wave, and subsequently wave.) In this way, you, a mental substance, seem capable of making yourself felt in the material world without in any sense *violating* laws governing material bodies.

Consider a sequence of tosses of a fair coin, one that lands heads about half the time. When you toss the coin on a particular occasion, you snap your thumb in a characteristic way sending the coin tumbling through the air in a trajectory that leads it eventually to land on the ground, heads side up. We can suppose that there is a completely deterministic basis for the coin's landing as it does on this occasion: given features of the coin, the character of the movement of your thumb, the location and composition of the surface on which the coin lands, and so on, the coin is bound to land heads. Of course, we are ignorant of all these factors. We can only guess how the coin will land on each toss. We express our ignorance by saying that on any given occasion, the probability that the coin will land heads is 50 percent.

Imagine now an outsider who occasionally intervenes in the system by focusing a strong electromagnetic beam on the coin, ensuring that it lands heads. The outsider might do this infrequently and in a statistically undetectable manner: when we evaluate the relative frequency with which the coin landed heads over a long series of tosses, that frequency approaches 50 percent. The outsider, then, intervenes, but in a way that does not alter the statistical likelihood that the coin will land heads whenever it is tossed, and does not reveal itself when we examine the coin's behavior. Perhaps this is how the mind affects the body.

This example misses the mark. It misconstrues the nature of statistical or probabilistic causation as this might be thought to apply to the basic constituents of the material world. If probabilities are written into fundamental laws of nature, these probabilities are not the result of our ignorance in the face of the complexity of physical systems, nor do they simply express statistical frequencies. The probabilities are, as it were, *built into* the fundamental entities. In the imaginary case we are considering, it is an intrinsic – built in – feature of an *S 1* micro-system that it is 35 percent likely to go into state *S 2*. This does not imply that 35 percent of *S 1* systems go into *S 2*. It is consistent with our imaginary law that the relative frequency of *S 1* to *S 2* transitions is much less or much greater than 35 percent. In fact, it is possible, although of course highly unlikely, that no *S 1* system ever goes into state *S 2*.

If we imagine a force from outside nature intervening in a physical transaction governed by a statistical law, then we must imagine the force as somehow altering the probabilities that hold for the physical system in question: if the probabilities are not affected, then it is hard to understand what the alleged intervention amounts to. But if these probabilities are built into the system, then their being altered would amount to a 'violation' of physical law.

To grasp this point, it is important to see that the kinds of statistical law thought to govern the elementary constituents of the world exclude so-called hidden variables. That is, the probabilistic character of these laws is not due to the intervention of some factor the nature of which we might be ignorant. It is, rather, irreducible, ineliminable, grounded in the nature of the elementary entities themselves. If the mind intervenes in the operation of the material world in a way that is statistically undetectable, it does not follow that no 'violation' of physical law has occurred. Genuine intervention would require minds to affect in some way the propensity of particular *S 1* systems to go into state *S 2*. And that would necessitate alterations in the character of *S 1* systems, alterations the occurrence of which would constitute 'violations' of natural law.

Here is another possibility. Although mental events do not alter *S 1*, they can, on occasion, prevent *S 1* from manifesting itself by going into *S 2* – in the way you might prevent a fragile vase from shattering when it is struck with a hammer by swathing the vase in bubble wrap. Selective 'blockings' of this sort, if suitably fine-grained and strategically placed, might account for the effects of thoughts on bodily goings-on. It is hard to see how this could work without violating our conception of the material world as causally self-contained, however.

Of course, it is possible that immaterial minds *do* intervene in the material world. It is possible that the material world is not in fact causally closed and that natural law *is* subject to contravention. The argument against Cartesian dualism is not that minds do not intervene, so dualism must be false. Such an argument would beg the question against Descartes. The argument, rather, is founded on considerations of plausibility. If we accept Cartesian dualism, we must suppose that immaterial minds sometimes intervene in the operation of the material world. This conflicts with a fundamental presumption of modern science, a presumption we have excellent independent reasons to accept. To the extent that we regard the intervention of non-material minds in the material world as implausible, we should regard Cartesian dualism as implausible.

An argument of this sort is scarcely conclusive. Metaphysical arguments rarely are. We might fairly ask, however, who bears the burden of proof here. The Cartesian dualist offers us an account of mind that fits nicely with much of what we believe about our world and with everyday experience. The account has the disadvantage of implying something we have little reason to believe, and many reasons to doubt. It is up to the Cartesian, then, to show that competing accounts of mind suffer equally serious defects. We shall be in a better position to evaluate the Cartesian's prospects when we have examined the alternatives.

2

Medieval Philosophy
Augustine, Aquinas and Ockham

Introduction

It would be wrong to conclude that thinkers in the medieval period merely slavishly reiterated Christian dogma. There exists a tension in medieval philosophy between reason and faith (from the Latin *fidere,* to trust). The distinction, if there is admitted to be one at all, between the reason of philosophy and the faith of theology is that between, respectively, the insights of natural knowledge derived from the natural cognitive powers of the intellect and senses, and the insights of supernatural knowledge derived from divine revelation. The distinction between philosophy and theology in the Middle Ages was often not clear; generally it can be said that whereas philosophy embodied rational arguments based on premises derivable from naturally occurring powers of thought and the logical working out of those premises (particularly from the philosophers of the ancient world, especially Aristotle), theological arguments were based on divine Christian premises derived from God in particular from the Bible and the opinions of the Church Fathers as collected in Peter

Lombard (*c.*1100-60), *Four books of sentences.* Christian thought insisted that reason must succumb to the deliverances of faith or religious belief where the two are irreconcilable.

It is characteristic of the dominant intellectual framework of the scholars of the universities of the medieval period called scholasticism to try to reconcile the demands of rational philosophy and the demands of theological faith. The dissolution of scholasticism at the end of the Middle Ages really amounts to the increasing triumph of reason over faith; instead of Christian faith being the standard by which rational arguments were to be judged, arguments were increasingly followed wherever they led. Reason in scholasticism was often used as a tool for supporting and deepening the understanding of what was already believed to be true as a matter of religious faith. After all, it is reasonable to suppose that even if some true beliefs are accepted as true without sufficient argument, it might still be possible to provide a rational justification for those true beliefs.

It was also thought that some truths were beyond the reach of rational demonstration, but that this was not detrimental to these truths, since their acceptance depended on religious faith. Belief in truths of faith influenced rational arguments by affecting the premises considered, and by judging the truth of the conclusions reached. If a valid argument leads to a conclusion which is false, in this case, according to religious faith we know that at least one of the premises must be false. However, the strain of combining reason and faith eventually led to the separation of philosophy and theology; the attempt had been made to fit philosophy in as a rational, but limited, path to religious truth, but in the end it tended to undermine the body of theological dogma.

The source of medieval theological doctrine was the Bible and the Church Fathers; the problem presented to medieval thinkers was how to reconcile beliefs from these sources with the beliefs and logical arguments derived from Plato and Aristotle, and the attempts of Arabic and Jewish thinkers from the tenth century to the twelfth century to combine Plato and Aristotle. This reflects the high opinion which was held of work from the ancient world; throughout the medieval period, ancient philosophy was a source of authority which toward the end of the period was used to oppose new arguments in philosophy and science. Nearly all medieval philosophical literature takes the form of either commentaries on previous works (especially Aristotle), or disputes *(quaestio disputata)*, where a question would be raised and opposing solutions and objections considered and eventually reconciled.

During the period from the second century to the fifth century AD, while the Roman Empire remained intact, Platonism and Neoplatonism had the upper hand in Christian thought; this is apparent in the works of St Augustine. The greatest Neoplatonists were Plotinus (AD 205–270), his disciple Porphyry (AD 233–304), and later Proclus (*c.* AD 410–485). St Augustine adopted, but profoundly modified, Platonism in the service of Christianity, to which he converted in AD 386 at the age of thirty-two. But with the break-up of the Roman Empire in the fifth century, Western Europe and the eastern parts became separated, and from the sixth century to the eleventh century we enter the Dark Ages.

During the Dark Ages nearly all serious intellectual activity ceased in Western Europe, although it continued in the eastern provinces conquered by the Arabs. From the fifth century onwards little of Plato was known directly in Western Europe, and the full corpus of his works did not re-emerge until the end of the Middle Ages; apart from in the work of John Scotus Erigena (*c.*810–*c.*877) Neoplatonism as such was also not rediscovered until the late twelfth and thirteenth centuries, but its influence seeped in from around the fifth century from the Arabs and the works of Pseudo-Dionysius, who was falsely thought to be the Athenian converted by St Paul. Only the works of Aristotle on logic remained known throughout the Middle Ages, thanks largely to translations and commentaries by the Roman philosopher Boethius (*c.* AD 480–524); but in the latter part of the twelfth century other works of Aristotle were rediscovered, revealing the ambitious system of metaphysics, science, and ethics.

In contrast to the period before the lacuna of the Dark Ages, after that period it was Aristotelian philosophy, rather than Platonic philosophy, which dominated Western European thinking. It was during the period from the twelfth century to the fourteenth century that the tensions between reason and faith intensified, and this gave way to the progressive weakening, from the fourteenth century, of the scholastic attempts to harmonize the two. The spread of new ideas continued, aided by the invention of printing in the fifteenth century. Intellectual changes were matched by the disintegration of the medieval social order; the increased disrespect for ecclesiastical authority and the rise of the rival power of the nation state undermined the unity of Christendom. The door was open for the Protestant Reformation of the sixteenth century and the greater importance of the conscience of the individual and direct understanding of Christianity. Philosophy became increasingly autonomous after the fourteenth century, and the gap between philosophy and theology was never again closed. By the end of the medieval period both Christianity and Aristotelianism, as the authoritative storehouses of correct opinions, were being replaced by a different vision of intellectual and moral advancement in the light of new philosophical and scientific ideas.

Given such a long period as the Middle Ages, it is unsurprising that it is possible here to make only a small selection of its thinkers. Apart from the thinkers discussed, among other important figures are Abelard (1079–1142), St Anselm (1033–1109), St Bonaventure (1221–74) and Duns Scotus (*c.*1266–1308). Augustine, Aquinas and Ockham are chosen here as representative of different important aspects of the period; they might be said to embody respectively medieval philosophy's inception, its consolidation, and the beginning of its dissolution. Their views on the place of reason and faith can roughly be summarized as follows: for Augustine there is no fundamental distinction because reason depends on divine help to grasp eternal truths; for

Aquinas there is a distinction on the basis of the natural and the divine but the two are complementary and to a degree overlapping; for Ockham reason and faith are distinct and have no overlap.

Augustine

Augustine (AD 354–430) was born in Thagaste and died in Hippo, both places in North Africa. Intellectually he straddles the gap between the philosophers of ancient Greece and those of medieval Christian Europe; he lived through the decline of the Roman Empire, which led to the Dark Ages. The eventual historical outcome in the eleventh century was the increased dominance of Christianity. Augustine's mother, Monica, was a Christian, but initially he did not accept the faith and adopted Manichaeanism, which embodied some elements of Christianity among elements from other religions. At the age of seventeen he became a student of the University of Carthage where he became a teacher of rhetoric and, while there, lived a life of extravagant pleasure including sexual pleasure which was to contrast starkly with his later monkish life. In AD 383 he moved to teach in Rome; following financial problems, he accepted a teaching post in Milan, where he greatly augmented his knowledge of ancient Greek philosophy, in particular Neoplatonism. In Milan he was impressed by the teachings of Ambrose, Bishop of Milan.

Augustine converted to Christianity in AD 386, and was baptized the following year. He was then determined to enter the Church and renounced worldly pleasures. Initially Augustine found no difficulty in reconciling the dominant intellectual position of his day, Neoplatonism, with the demands of Christian scripture; later he began to see greater problems in reconciling their basic concepts. He soon founded his own monastic community in Thagaste; but this lasted only a couple of years through his being forced into the Catholic priesthood. Augustine eventually became Bishop of Hippo in AD 396. He never left North Africa for the last thirty-nine years of his life. In AD 410, Rome was sacked by the Goths; in 429 the Vandals crossed to North Africa from Spain and laid siege to Hippo; Augustine died in 430, aged seventy-five, a short time before Hippo fell.

The character of Augustine's thought is distinctly religious, rather than purely philosophical; the discussion of certain philosophical problems is not that of the disinterested academic, but has the overriding purpose of identifying the path to the attainment of blessedness or beatitude. This does not mean that what is true is crudely identified with whatever makes one happy; it is rather the other way around: knowledge of truths will make one happy. It is assumed that the wise man and the happy man are one, and knowledge of truths is part of the attainment of wisdom. The question of whether we can know truths is generally assumed to be answered positively; the chief question is how we can attain that knowledge. The overall religious purpose is two fold: first, to show how we can become closer to God; secondly, to emphasize the importance of God by showing how everything is closely dependent on God. A problem of particular concern to Augustine is how we come to know the universal necessary eternal truths described by Plato and the Neoplatonists. First, however, Augustine sets about demolishing the sceptic who asserts that no knowledge at all is possible. He points to a range of things we clearly know to be true, which the sceptic cannot possibly deny. He is not aiming to use these known truths as the axiomatic foundation of the rest of knowledge, rather, if any of the examples are admitted as known truths, then knowledge is possible, and the absolute sceptic refuted.

(a) We know the law of non-contradiction, whereby if something is true, it cannot also be the case at the same time that the opposite is true.

(b) I know that I exist. "If I err, I exist" *("Si fallor, sum").* This anticipates Descartes' *cogito;* but it is not used in the same way; Augustine is not concerned to use it to prove the existence of the external world.

(c) Appearances cannot in themselves be false; I know infallibly what my subjective experiences are, how things appear to me: my "seemings". I can know infallibly what *seems* to be the case; it is my judgement, which goes beyond what seems to be the case, which introduces the possibility of falsehoods.

(d) We clearly, even from the sceptic's point of view, have the capacity to doubt; so we know at least one truth: there is doubting.

(e) We obviously know with certainty mathematical and geometrical truths.

(f) We do not just know abstract principles, we also know real existences. We know that we exist, that we are alive, and that we understand these facts. Augustine points out that even if our experience is really a dream, we nevertheless still know we were alive. We are also conscious that we will certain things.

These bulwarks against scepticism are in one way or another derived from introspection independently of the errors of the senses. Augustine does not dismiss the senses as wholly deceptive. From the fact that we can sometimes err in our sense-based judgements (for example if we judge that a stick which appears bent in the water really is bent), and can on any particular occasion err, it does not follow that the senses cannot ever support true beliefs. That the senses deliver truths less certain than those of mathematics does not mean the senses do not deliver truths at all. However, Augustine supports the Platonic view that the lack of certainty and the relativity of judgement (the same thing can appear different to different people) that beset the senses make the objects of sense not suitable objects for true knowledge or knowledge proper. The true objects of knowledge the truths we can know with greatest certainty are truths that are universal, necessary, and eternal; this is the highest form of knowledge, and sensory knowledge the lowest. This means that these eternal truths have to be found within the mind independently of sensory experience.

The problem arises of how eternal truths and our knowledge of eternal truths are to be accounted for. The sensible world does not provide us with the required immutable concepts and truths; the human mind or soul, although immortal, is also temporal and mutable. Augustine agrees with Plato that, just as transient truths are accounted for by the mutable objects of the sensible world, so universal necessary eternal truths are accounted for by their being truths about eternal and immutable real objects. Moreover, these eternal objects, and the truths concerning the relations of the concepts of these objects, are independent of the human mind; they are truths that we discover, which we cannot alter, and which are thereby objective and common to all capable of reasoning. Such objects immaterial impersonal essences referred to by Plato as Forms, are identified by Augustine as ideas in the eternal, immutable mind of God they are the content of the divine mind. Such divine ideas provide both truly objective fixed concepts and necessary truths by being the objects of necessary judgements. Augustine, like Plato, has no facility to account for the necessity of some truths which does not involve realism, requiring there to be eternal objects to which those truths correspond; he is unable to account for such necessary truths merely on the basis of the logical relations between concepts, but thinks that such truths require eternal objects which the eternal truths are true of eternally.

Such necessary truths are available to us in the areas of mathematics and geometry, but they are also possible in moral and aesthetic judgements. The divine ideas provide perfect objects for the concepts of number and geometrical forms; they also provide objective standards for moral judgements concerning good and evil, and aesthetic judgements concerning what is, or is not, beautiful. We do not find perfect unity in our experience (we always find things with parts which are thereby both one and many); we do not find absolute goodness or evil or perfect beauty in our experience. We do not find these things in themselves exemplified in the sensible world; but nor are they mere constructions of the human mind. Rather, the divine ideas in God's mind are the absolute eternal standards by which all else is judged, and which are assumed in our judgements.

The problem remains of how such eternal truths are accessible to the non-eternal human mind. We have certainly been granted reason by which we are able to form true or false judgements not derivable from sense-experience. But reason alone is not enough to account for our knowledge of eternal truths. The human mind, in seeking eternal truths, is seeking something beyond, and superior to, the mutable and temporal mind, and to know such truths we need help. Such help emanates from God in the form of "divine illumination"; and as an illuminator God is present in us as He is present in all things. All knowledge in Augustine is seen as a form of seeing. Just as the senses see independent objects when they are illuminated by the sun, so reason or intellect "sees" eternal truths when illuminated by the divine light. This does not mean that in apprehending eternal truths we have direct access to God's nature that is possible only after death, if at all. We do not intellectually see God or the mind of God when we know eternal truths. It is unclear whether the illumination implants the concepts constituting necessary truths in our minds, or whether it simply enables us to recognize which judgements are eternal and necessary it could indeed function in both ways. Perhaps the best interpretation is to say that God does not directly infuse our minds with the absolute concepts which constitute eternal truths, rather such concepts are latent in the mind as copies of the archetypes in God's mind; divine illumination enables us to see intellectually which are the eternal and necessary truths that are latent in our souls, and so to recognize them as eternal and necessary. The latent concepts, and the eternal truths connecting them, are in *memoria;* in this way ideas can be in the mind without the mind being aware of those ideas. This accords with our use of "memory" only in that it refers to ideas that can be in the mind without our being always aware of them; it refers in Augustine, most importantly, to the *a priori* content of minds, which is not literally a remembrance of things past. Nevertheless the theory is close to Plato's account of our possessing *a priori* knowledge through reminiscence.

Eternal truths are, of course, independent of and irrefutable by sense-experience. So the true objects of knowledge are objective eternal objects which depend on there being ontologically appropriate eternal objects in the divine mind. Knowledge of eternal truths is granted by a combination of natural human reason and supernatural divine illumination. To benefit from such illumination we have to turn towards God. This precludes the possibility of making a distinction between natural reason and divine faith, for both are always needed and mixed in the search for knowledge. This again emphasizes the dependence of all things on God, in this case our capacity to know eternal necessary truths.

The immateriality of the soul and its superiority to the body mean that Augustine has great difficulty accounting for perceptions through the corporeal organs. The superior nature of the soul's mode of existence involves the view that it cannot be affected by the inferior corporeal organs. At first he suggests that the mind uses the sense organs as a tool. Later he tries to account for our awareness of changes in our corporeal senses by the mind attending to or noticing such changes; but it is difficult to see how, in this case, some causal influence of the corporeal sense organs on the mind can be avoided.

Augustine uses the existence of eternal truths as proof of the existence of God. Leibniz in the seventeenth century presents a similar argument. The argument starts by getting one to admit that there are eternal truths immutable necessary truths, forced on human beings. The only way to account for there being such necessary inescapable truths is their objective existence as truths in an eternal mind. We serve and are closer to God in so far as we contemplate eternal ideas in the mind of God. This, however, is not all that is required; we also need a spiritual purification goodness in order to approach God.

Aquinas

Thomas Aquinas (1225–74) was born of a noble family at Roccasecca, Italy. From the age of five he began studying at the Benedictine abbey of Monte Cassino. In 1239 he went on to the University of Naples, where he studied the seven liberal arts of grammar, logic, rhetoric, arithmetic, geometry, music, and astronomy; while at Naples he entered the Dominican Order. His entry into this Order, with its emphasis on poverty and evangelism, was opposed by his family to such an extent that he felt the need to escape to Paris; but while on the road to Paris, he was abducted by his elder brother and locked up in the family castle at Monte San Giovanni. He was later held prisoner in Roccasecca for over a year. His family was unable either to strip him literally of his Dominican robes, or to persuade him to renounce the Order. While he was imprisoned his brothers sent him a seductress; but he drove her from the room with a burning brand, and the event merely reinforced his commitment to chastity. Eventually his family relented and he returned to the Dominican Order, first at the University of Paris in 1248, then at Cologne under Albert the Great. During this time he became deeply versed in the works of Aristotle.

He returned to Paris in 1252 for advanced study, and he lectured there in theology until 1259. The next ten years of his life were spent at various Dominican monasteries near Rome; in 1268 he returned to teach again at the University of Paris. In 1272 he went to teach at the University of Naples; but ill-health forced him to stop work. In 1273 he had a mystical vision which caused him to regard his intellectual work as worthless he consequently ceased work on the massive *Summa theologiae*. In 1274 he was journeying to Lyon for a meeting of the church council, but had to rest at Fossanova, not far from his place of birth, owing to illness; there he died in 1274. Aquinas' character seems to have been one of imperturbability, and there is no doubting his sharpness of intellect. After his death the teaching of Aquinas and Thomism formed the official doctrine of the Dominicans, and this was adopted by some other Orders, but it was in general relatively neglected by the Catholic Church. However, in the nineteenth century Aquinas was commended by Pope Pius IX as the premier figure of Catholic philosophy and theology. Aquinas' thought owes a great deal to Aristotle, and he attempts to reconcile the central tenets of Aristotelian philosophy with Christian dogma; these attempts deal with issues like the nature of God, our means to salvation, and our understanding of the nature of creation. Aquinas' thought begins with the presupposition that the universe is, at least partly, intelligible to finite human intellects: the structures and laws of the universe can be understood. Aquinas hatches a compromise between the conclusions derived from our natural cognitive faculties (the senses and reason of secular philosophy), and conclusions derived from divine revelation (the faith of divine theology). One could dismiss one or the other as worthless, or say that each one ultimately depends on the other, as Augustine does; Aquinas however maintains the distinction, and says that they are two generally autonomous ways of looking at the same object, namely God. Whereas our natural cognition works "from below" to know God through His effects as the creator of the world, divine revelation supernatural cognition works "from above" to know God as cause. Thus faith *(fides)* and scientific knowledge *(scientia)* are sharply distinguished not by object, but by method. Both are cognitive processes involving the assent of the intellect to truths; but whereas faith requires the addition of the will in order to believe truths with certainty, scientific knowledge requires no such application of will since the intellect either intuitively "sees" truths immediately, or argues validly to establish truths from intuitively known premises. Within theology we can make a distinction between supernatural and natural theology: respectively, truths revealed about God and other elements of Christian doctrine which depend on divine revelation (grace, which derives from the Latin *gratia,* meaning favour), and those that can be known through natural powers of cognition. There is also an overlap of truths: some truths are both revealed and known through being provable by natural cognition. In this sense natural theology is part of supernatural theology. So the totality of truths grasped by the human mind has three parts.

(A) That which is believed *only* in virtue of divine illumination or revelation.

(B) That which is believed by divine revelation *and* is known by being provable by natural cognition.

(C) That which is known by natural cognition.

Ideally a conflict will never arise between the deliverances of the revelations of faith, and the proofs of natural reason; but in the latter we are fallible, and a conclusion derived from reasoning that conflicts irreconcilably with a properly understood truth of faith shows that we have made a mistake in our reasoning. But we have, ideally, a twofold route to some Christian truths. Natural cognition is made up of the senses and the intellect, and of these the senses are primary both genetically and logically for knowledge of existing things and for possession of abstract ideas; all the materials of our intellectual faculty our ideas are abstracted ultimately from the senses. The intellect is involved in forming judgements about what we perceive: that what we perceive really exists, that it has certain properties and that it is a certain kind of thing. The intellect also engages in abstract reasoning. The senses see *X;* the intellect actively judges *X* as *X;* the intellect goes on to understand and think of *X* when it is not perceived. The intellect goes beyond the sensory experience in forming a judgement, which is an affirmation or denial of some truth; this goes beyond the mere fact of one's having a certain experience. The sensible aspects of particular things (red, sweet, warm, etc.) are given through sense-perception alone; but the intelligible aspects of particular things (that they exist, that they actually have certain properties and are certain kinds of things) are derived not from the passive association of the ideas of senses alone, but in conjunction with an active synthesizing and interpretative intellect, which forms from the ideas of sense complex conceptions and hypotheses. The intellect forms concepts—universal ideas of things by abstracting general ideas from sense-experience; the intellect thinks of the nature of those things and how they are connected to other things by understanding those general concepts. Aquinas follows Aristotle closely in not supposing that essences (the "whatness" of things) can exist apart from individual things; philosophically speaking, there is no *universale ante rem,* that is, essence before or apart from individual things; rather, essence is *universale in re,* present in individual things, in the sense that real things are real substances and are always compounded of two elements.

(a) Essence *(essentia, quidditas, natura)*. This is "whatness"; viewed epistemologically through a definition it tells us *what* a thing is.

(b) Existence (*esse,* which is a form of the Latin verb "to be"; but *esse* is also used as a noun). This is the fact *that* a thing is.

The difference between a mere essence *(quidditas)* and real substance is existence *(esse)*; existence is what turns, by being "added" to it, a merely potential essence into an actual individual substance. This is the primary move from potentiality to actuality: mere potential existence to actual existence. Once a certain essence is actualized, there is a further process of change from potential to actualization as the essence brought into existence strives to fulfil its potential within its kind; an acorn (an actual acorn, but potential tree) will grow into a tree (an actual tree). The terms above in (a) and (b) roughly correlate with the following:

(a) potential *(potentia,* potency);

(b) actuality *(actus,* act).

The difference between essence and potentiality is partly one of generality; to speak of essence is to imply some determinate potentiality: a certain "so-and-so"; whereas to speak of potentiality is to suggest mere possibility: some "so-and-so" or other. Anything that is not logically impossible has potentiality in the second sense.

To know the *essence* of something is to know its real definition, the essential features without which a thing would cease to be the kind or sort of thing it is. The *accidental* features that an individual kind of thing has are those features which it can lose or gain while remaining the same kind of thing. It is most important to note that Aquinas thinks that in giving a definition of the essential nature of an individual, he is giving a *real* definition; that is, the definitions are not a function of the way we conceptually happen to divide up the world, rather the definitions, if true, reflect accurately the way the world divides itself up.

The distinction between essence and existence is also a *real* distinction. That is not to say we ever encounter in the world pure existence or pure essence, but the distinction is real in the sense of being independent of human cognition; it is not a distinction projected onto the world by the mind. For to say *what* something is is one thing, but to say *that* it is, is another; we can know what a dog is the essence "dogness" without committing ourselves to affirming either the existence or non-existence of dogs. Another way of putting this is to say that essences have no existential import. This is true for all entities except God; He alone has existence as part of His essence. For all other beings, existence *(esse)* is something added to essence added to a mere determinate potentiality by God; thus all things depend ultimately on God. Essence and existence are never found in separation; nothing simply *is,* a thing always is a *determinate kind* of thing; to be is to be a "so-and-so"; to be is always a determinate *way* of being. The obvious limitation of individual substances is explained by essences receiving *esse* and at the same time limiting that *esse* to a certain way of being. In God the *esse* is unlimited, and also eternal; there are no limits to God's being; He has "fullness of being".

For Aquinas as a Christian, unlike for Aristotle, the existence of things cannot be taken for granted but requires explanation. Aristotle thought that the world exists eternally, and that any change in the world is not a change from absolute non-existence (nothing) to absolute existence or vice versa, but a change either of an accident, or from one form of substantial being to another. For example a substantial change occurs when a tree ceases to be a tree and becomes ash when it is burnt. For Aquinas the very fact of existence itself is a problem; given that nothing, except God, has existence as part of its essence, an explanation beyond the essences of things is required to explain why anything *is* at all; that explanation derives from God the creator who adds *esse* to essences. Apart from God, no essence is fully actualized. In God's case, the positive essence is fully actualized. God does not merely actualize His divine essence; He actualizes it all the way, so to speak. If we take any other entity, we will always have an entity which has potential within its kind its essence will not be fully actualized; there will be aspects of its essence that it does not fully exemplify.

God's absolute perfection is to be identified with His complete actualization of His positive divine essence He is pure act *(actus purus);* He contains no unactualized potential of His positive divine essence. The relation between essence and existence, and between potency and actuality, applies to any substance whatsoever. It must not be supposed that all real substances must be material or corporeal; not only material things have *esse.* The analysis of material things introduces another pair of terms,

(i) form *(morphe);*

(ii) matter *(hyle).*

This gives a hylemorphic theory of material substance. In the case of material substances, potential corresponds to matter; the matter is potentially a "so-and-so", and is actualized as an individual separable thing of a certain kind by taking on a certain form; that form is actualized in that matter. However, pure matter *(materia prima)* would be completely ineffable; it would by definition possess no character, no whatness. Only by the addition of form in act in the matter does it become a determinate "so-and-so"; matter as a mere determinable is not possible, although we can understand what we mean when we talk of it. The notion of pure potentiality as pure matter is impossible as something that exists it would indeed be a contradiction but it is intelligible conceptually. Indeed, pure potentiality cannot in any case exist. The soul is the form of human beings; and souls are individuated by the matter of the body of which they are the soul. But pure forms can exist, as well as material substances, when certain non-material essences receive *esse.* What Aquinas has in mind here seems to be a three-level hierarchy of being.

(1) Corporeal substances. These are matter and form; they are perishable and finite.

(2) Incorporeal limited substances. These are pure form—spiritual entities, which although imperishable are finite. The kinds of entities Aquinas has in mind here are the separated soul and angels.

(3) Incorporeal unlimited substance. This is pure act; all aspects of the positive essence receive existence *(esse)*. This is, in fact, God who alone exists necessarily, since in Him alone His way of being must be conceived as including existence; in Him no distinction can be made between the essence He has and His existence, for He necessarily completely actualizes His essence, all the positive aspects of the divine essence there are; there is nothing He is only potentially; there is nothing divinely positive He is not.

The object of human knowledge in intellectual cognition is the discovery of what essence is actualized in any individual. We understand substances in so far as we come to know the essence that is in act is *esse*—in substances. Aquinas holds that for each known truth there must always be something existing *(esse)* that corresponds to that truth. Individual substances are understood by us not as individuals *qua* individuals (individual things as such: features which constitute their particularity), but through knowing that which is general or common in them that defines the nature of the kind in which all the individuals of a certain kind share. Thus we know a dog in so far as we know the real definition of "dog", and hence understand it in its essential dogness; we do not know the dog in its full particularity because the terms we apply always have some generality of application.

An essence is what must be the case for a thing to be *what* it is: that which a thing cannot lack and still be what it is. Thus understanding *what* a thing is its essence is logically independent of the fact *that* a thing is, its existence. I can understand *what* a dog or a Phoenix is independently of *whether* it is. The essence of *X* is given in a set of necessary and sufficient conditions *a, b, c* for *X* to be the kind of thing it is. In this way we can form a real definition: *X* is of a specific kind if, and only if, *a, b, c* are true of *X*. When we are correctly said to know *X*, the aspect of *X* we know is that set of features *X* has in common with all and only other *X*s of the same kind. We would not understand a clock as a *clock* by referring to its colour or the scratch on the face, but in so far as we understand that in virtue of which a clock is a clock: what makes it distinctively a clock and not another kind of thing. We understand the nature of the clock by understanding those common features shared by all and only clocks which define them as clocks. Then what makes a clock or a dog a particular clock or dog cannot be its essence or form, since that is common to all instances of the same kind, but must, Aquinas argues, be its being formed of a quantitatively or numerically different parcel of matter.

With incorporeal or spiritual substances such a method of individuation is clearly inapplicable; he suggests that each incorporeal substance must be individuated by essence; that is, the essence of each soul or angel must be different, so each angel differs in essence as a dog does from a cat; each angel is of a different, and unique, kind. Aquinas strikes a middle course on the question of the reality of universals. Universals are general concepts or categories with which we talk about the world and with which we classify particulars into kinds or sorts. Aquinas adopts a form of moderate realism. He rejects the full realism of Plato, whereby universals exist as real entities in a world of intelligible Forms independently of the world of sensible things. He also rejects conventionalism, whereby universal concepts are mere arbitrary, subjective mental constructs, for which the most that can perhaps be said is that they are made for our convenience. Aquinas compromises: universals are *objective* in being real, extramental and immutable, but they exist in instances of individual kinds of things and cannot exist apart from those instances. Universals or kinds as such exist only in virtue of there being individual actual instances of those kinds. Only individuals exist, but the natures of those individuals radically resemble each other and are understood from this essential common resembling nature as being members of universal classes or species for example, humanity, dogness, justice. Individual material things of the same kind are the same kind in virtue of sharing a substantial form; but that substantial form, although it cannot exist apart from the individuals who share it, is nevertheless something objective in the world, and derives its objectivity from the really existing common nature shared by individuals of the same class. The world divides itself into kinds, so to speak; the kinds are real and there to be discovered, and are independent of our subjective mental classifications. Abstracted forms are derived from individual instances; the logical rules of the combination of such forms are revealed in real definitions; the forms, through real definitions, give concepts which have fixed immutable objective meaning; the forms and their logical combination, known through their concepts, are the proper objects of knowledge. Knowledge of the forms, through real definitions, is derived from sensory experience and the intellectual faculty of abstracting general concepts from the resembling essential nature of instances of individuals of the same sort. Thus although universals do not exist as separate entities, they are objective in reflecting the extramental common defining real natures of individuals.

Ockham

William of Ockham (*c.*1285–1349) was born in the village of Ockham outside Guildford near London. The details of his life are obscure, and often a matter of conjecture. Of his early life nothing definite is known. We know that he was ordained subdeacon in 1306. He became a student at the University of Oxford around 1309 and soon a member of the Franciscan Order. He pursued his studies at Oxford until 1315; from 1315 to 1317 he gave lectures on the Bible and, from 1317 to 1319, lectures on the hugely influential *Four books of sentences* by Peter Lombard. The *Four books of sentences* was compiled around 1150; it brought together the teachings of the early Church Fathers especially St Augustine and it was a cornerstone of Christian theology.

Ockham completed the requirements for the degree of *Magister theologiae,* but he never became a Master occupying the Chair of Theology. This was probably due to the opposition of Lutterell, a keen Thomist, to the appointment of Ockham; Lutterell had been removed from the post of Chancellor of the University by 1322. Lutterell left in 1323 for Avignon, the residence of Pope John XXII; there he set about blackening Ockham's name by accusing him of holding in his *Commentary on the Sentences* heretical and dangerous views. Ockham was summoned to Avignon in 1324 to have his views examined; the examination lasted for three years. Ockham refused to retract his views.

Michael of Cesena, the General of the Franciscan Order, also faced the condemnation of the Pope for his Order's espousal of absolute apostolic poverty. Ockham joined forces with Michael, his superior, and, together with another Franciscan, Bonogratia, they fled from Avignon in 1328, seeking the protection of the German Emperor, Louis of Bavaria. Louis had installed in Rome an antipope who had in return crowned him head of the Roman Empire. Ockham, Michael and Bonogratia joined the new Emperor in Munich, and were ex-communicated from the Catholic Church and their own Order. In 1342 Michael died; in 1347 Louis also died. This left Ockham in an extremely vulnerable position; he sought reconciliation with the Church and his Order. Before any reconciliation could be decided upon, Ockham died in 1349, probably of the prevalent Black Death. He was buried in the old Franciscan church in Munich; but in 1802 his remains were moved to a place that is still unknown.

Ockham may be seen as something of a philosophical Janus, since like that god, his philosophy looks in two opposite directions; it looks back to the Middle Ages, and it looks forward to some of the ideas of the Enlightenment to the empiricism of John Locke (1632–1704) and David Hume (1711–76), and aspects of materialism but the forward-looking characteristics must not be overemphasized; Ockham would have seen himself not as a philosophical revolutionary, but merely as reinterpreting an already established tradition. The chief problem was still to reconcile Aristotle and Christianity. A sharp distinction is found in Ockham's thought between reason and faith. The truths of theology are based on revelation and are a matter of faith, and they are neither provable nor refutable by any process of natural cognition in secular philosophy. Theology retreats to a domain of truths about which natural reason can have nothing to say.

The chief characteristic of the tradition to which Ockham

was heir was realism in its various forms: that the human intellect can discover, in the particular things perceived by sense-experience, a real objective system of universal common essences which become somehow individualized, and which can either have an independent existence from, or exist as a real part of, particular individuals. These essences have an extralinguistic reality over and above *really distinct* from the particular features of individuals which are classified in virtue of the essence as being the same kind. Then from the linguistic connections in meaning between the terms that refer to these real essences we can know necessary truths about an extralinguistic reality. Necessary truths can be known about the world we perceive and about God. The universals we intellectually abstract humanity or horse from particular individuals are not merely arbitrary subjective mental or linguistic constructs, or merely derived from objective particular features of individual things, but have a real ontologically distinct reference in or beyond the world, independent of individuals, or their particular features, whereby such individuals fall into the general class designated by universal terms. In short, the linguistic distinction we make between universal and particular terms has a real ontological counterpart.

The problem of universals what if anything universal terms stand for to which realism is one answer, centres on the problem of the relationship between the universality of concepts and our apparently encountering as independent objects only particulars. Realists would argue that, without a suitable system of real entities for universal terms to refer to, our system of universal terms will be entirely arbitrary, conventional and subjective. This would make any science, which will inevitably be couched in general or universal terms (such as "body", "animal", "heavy"), an arbitrary mental construction among other possible constructions with no objective validity derived from its reflecting an extramental reality; this leaves open the rationally anarchic possibility of a variety of different incommensurable conceptual systems of scientific explanation between which we can have no common grounds or independent standard for a rational choice.

Moderate medieval realism does not go all the way with Platonism, which suggests that universal essences or "whatness" such as humanity, horseness, justice can exist as Forms quite independently of all particular individuals which are grouped together in virtue of those universal essences. Moderate realism follows Aristotle in maintaining that in some way there is a real distinction in the world between the common universal essence and the individuating characteristics of particular things sharing that essence. Moderate realism holds that, although the common universal essences of individuals and those individuals cannot be found existing in separation, the distinction between universal essences and particular individuals which can be made in thought nevertheless reflects a real distinction in things in the world. The same common nature or essence is really distinct from things in respect of what makes them particular, as it exists in all the particulars of the same sort, and it is this that makes them the kind of things they are.

The forward-looking aspect of Ockham's philosophy resides in his rejection of realism and his alternative explanation: his rejection of the reality of a world of intelligible, literally common, essences or forms ontologically or really distinct from the characteristics that pick out individuals, and his consequent propagation of nominalism and empiricism. His nominalism and empiricism are closely linked.

Ockham objects to the idea of some literally common nature shared by all and only individuals of the same kind; if this common nature is singular and indivisible, then it cannot be shared by many individuals, and if the common nature is many, then each instance of the many must be singular and itself individual and cannot be shared in common between various individuals.

Ockham does not deny that the world falls into a mind-independent system of natural kinds in this sense he is still a realist. What he denies in his nominalism is that a condition for its being correct to talk about a natural order of kinds of individual things is the positing of common natures or essences, ontologically or really distinct from the individualizing characteristics, and shared by all and only the individual things of the same kind. Moreover, he thinks that such a view is an unnecessary misinterpretation of Aristotle. He denies in this nominalism that universals subsist as ideas in the mind of God prior to their actualization (their receiving *esse*); God is not necessitated even to this extent; He is not constrained to create, if He creates at all, a particular world-system of kinds. There is, therefore, no system of essences whose necessary relations could be known *a priori*.

For Ockham, universality is a property primarily of thoughts, secondarily of language which expresses thoughts, and not of entities or natures distinct from the individual characteristics of things in the world. Universality is the property of a thought, a generalized abstractive cognition, which is entertained in such a way as to be equally truly predicable of, or usable of, more than one individual. Thus the term "city" is used of London, Paris, New York. Ockham's view is roughly equivalent to saying that universals are concepts, along with the commitment that the being of the concepts is as mental states. Nominalism holds that the only thing strictly in common between individuals falling under a universal name is that they all fall under that name.

The question arises as to why we apply the same universal name to many individuals. Ockham's empiricism complements his nominalism by maintaining that there are no literally common real essences graspable by the intellect, but only individuals apprehended by the senses between which we perceive *similarities* in the individuating characteristics, and it is from these albeit objective but nevertheless contingent similarities that we derive the meanings of universal terms and their range of application to a determinate class of individuals. Thus the connotation or meaning of a universal term such as "humanity" is whatever characteristics we perceive as similar between all those individuals whereby we classify them as human. This list of characteristics defines "humanity" and gives us criteria for deciding whether any given individual should be included under that heading; the denotation or reference of the term "humanity" is then just all individual human beings. The meaning of a universal term such as "humanity" is not explained by its denoting a common essence distinct from the characteristics of particular human beings; its meaning is explained by the similar characteristics of a number of individual men, in virtue of which we call them all "men". Talk of something "similar" between many individuals may seem to evoke a common nature again; but Ockham would say that we perceive similarity not by perceiving some literally identical common nature distinct from the individuating characteristics, but in virtue of a resemblance between the characteristics which are part of the natures or features of the individuals themselves.

Thus Ockham denies that there is a metaphysical problem of determining in virtue of what universals are individualized, since there are no such universals to be individuated. Aquinas had suggested that universals are individuated in virtue of their being exemplified in a different parcel of stuff or matter; Duns Scotus (*c.* 1266–1308) rejected this and suggested that beside universal essences what features a thing cannot lack and still be the kind of thing it is there is an individuating essence, the *haecceitas* or individualizing "thisness" of a kind, which gives *this* horse. Ockham, however, has the logical problem of showing how to reduce universal concepts to terms that signify what he regards as the only existents, individuals; and he has the epistemological problem of saying how from experiencing only individuals we form universal concepts.

It should be pointed out that for Ockham the primary carriers of meanings are mental expressions states of mind with which written and spoken expressions become associated by convention. Mental signs mean what they stand for directly; linguistic expressions are signs only conventionally; thus the mental sign for rain is the same for the speaker of any language, but its linguistic expression may be different.

Terms are elements in propositions and they take on different functions depending on the proposition they are in; in particular they acquire a determinate "standing for" *(suppositio)* function. Here we are talking of natural terms or concepts, not the conventional terms of any particular language; the terms *"homme"* and "man" are conventional terms for the same natural sign or concept. Ockham distinguishes between "terms of the first intention" and "terms of the second intention". For example, a singular term such as "Socrates" stands as a natural sign for the *thing* Socrates and is of the "first intention". A universal term such as "species" is of the "second intention" and stands not immediately for things that are not themselves signs, but for other signs that do stand immediately as signs for things. Thus, "Socrates" is a sign for the individual man Socrates; "species" stands not immediately for individual things, but for terms of the "first intention" such as "man", "horse" and "dog"; the term "species" can be predicated of the terms "man", "horse" and "dog", each of which stands for all the members of a different class of individuals, and says of these *terms* that they are all species–terms which are the names of many things. Ockham contends that the realist belief in universal terms standing, albeit obliquely or indirectly, for entities distinct from individual entities is a consequence of confusing the two levels of intentions: terms that stand for things, and terms that stand for terms; that is, talk about things in an object language, and talk about the object language in a metalanguage. If we confuse these two we are tempted to suppose mistakenly that metalinguistic talk is about things.

Nominalism is in accord with the most famous feature of Ockham's thought, "Ockham's razor"; this is a methodological principle designed to keep the number of kinds of entities posited as distinct in the world to a minimum it is a principle of parsimony. Ockham's objection to realism and the positing of real ontologically distinct essences is partly just that they are unnecessary to explain how we come to classify things in a universal manner. Logically what this means is that apparent reference to real abstract entities by universal terms can in principle always be replaced by an analysis of universal terms, so that they refer only to individuals. Thus "man" signifies merely the total disjunction: Socrates, or Plato, or Aquinas, and so on. Relational terms such as "taller" do not denote entities distinct from the individuals to which they apply; in referring to *A* being taller than *B*, we are referring to only two entities, and the truth "*A* is taller than *B*" is reduced to a truth about *A* (*A* is six feet tall) and a truth about *B* (*B* is five feet tall). The only sorts of thing that exist are individuals: individual substances and their individual qualities.

It has been objected that Ockham's criticism of the real distinction between essences and individuals misses the point, for he attacks a position which the most important medieval thinkers such as Aquinas and Duns Scotus never sought to defend. The accusation is that Ockham thought that if the distinction between the common essence of individuals and what constitutes their individuality were to be a *real* distinction, then it must be a distinction between *things* of the same sort, such as exists between any two existing individuals, and that Ockham was led to this assumption by thinking of the attribution of essences as noun-like rather than verb-like. If we think of the attribution of essences or forms as more verb-like than noun-like as in "humanizing", "equinizing" we will see that there is a formal objective extralinguistic distinction being made which is separable in thought and is nevertheless not a distinction between separable individual entities. It is not clear whether this pointing up of the distinction between the grammatically verb-like use of ascribed essences to things, as opposed to naming those same things, is sufficient to maintain that there is a corresponding metaphysical extralinguistic distinction between the common natures and the particular features of individuals.

Moving to Ockham's epistemology, we find that he distinguishes between intellectual acts of apprehension and judgement: apprehension or cognition is awareness on the basis of which a judgement can be made, which is an intellectual assent to the truth or falsity of a proposition. He further contrasts an *intuitive* cognition, on the basis of which one is in a position to make a judgement of contingent fact which is *evident,* and an *abstract* cognition, on the basis of which we are *not* in a position to make an *evident* judgement of contingent fact such contingent judgement will concern whether an object exists or whether it has some contingent property. The objects of these cognitions are the same; what differs is the manner in which they are apprehended; in an intuitive cognition the apprehension of the object is caused immediately by the object apprehended; in an abstract cognition the apprehension of the object is not caused immediately by the object apprehended, but it always presupposes an intuitive cognition of the object at some previous time. From an intuitive cognition of *X,* or *X* as *f,* we can judge *evidently* that it is true that *X* exists, or that *X* is *f.* Once we have an intuitive cognition of *X,* or *X* as *f,* it can be stored in the memory as an acquired capacity *(habitus)* so we can then form an abstract cognition of *X,* or *X* as *f,* which is divorced from *X* existing or not existing, or *X* actually being *f* or not being *f;* but this abstract cognition of *X,* or *X* as *f,* does not put us in the position to make the judgement we might make concerning *X evident.* If I saw you sitting in my study, I would be in a position to form an evident judgement that it is true that you are sitting in my study; if, however, I did not see you, but nevertheless formed from an abstractive cognition the judgement that you were sitting in my study, then the judgement, although it *may* be true, may also be false, and is not in any case evident. Ockham is realist with respect to individual objects and their individual properties in the external world: he does not doubt that in mental acts of intuitive cognition what we directly apprehend is constituted by objects and their properties just as they really are in the external world outside the mind. In intuitive cognition there is no distinction between the way things seem to us and the way they really are; the way they seem is how they are. Ockham holds that we can also have intuitive cognition of introspectively apprehended mental states.

In the natural course of events, if we have an intuitive cognition of *X,* then *X* exists, since *X* is a part of the cause of the cognition of *X;* thus the judgement that *X* exists is evident. However, since it is logically possible, God could produce supernaturally in us the same mental state as a cognitive intuition that is, phenomenologically the same intuition, which is *as if* we were having a real intuitive cognition without the object existing, which would in natural circumstances suffice for the evident judgement that the object exists. But, in fact, God does not normally act like this, although He did so in the case of the prophets.

Ockham's empiricism surfaces in his account of explanations of the natural world. Strictly speaking, science is concerned with necessary universal truths concerning that which must be and cannot be otherwise, expressed in propositions that are proved from self-evident propositions by syllogistic deductive reasoning. But one needs experience even to understand the meaning of the terms in propositions at least those that stand for things even when, once understood, they are self-evident propositions; for to understand the meaning of the terms we need a primary experience of what the terms stand for. For Ockham, as for Locke, there are no innate ideas which could account for this; all our ideas, by association with which words get their meaning, are derived from experience.

Science in a narrow sense includes only necessary provable propositions; and since the existence and nature of the world are in all ways contingent (that which may be true or may be false), it would seem that a science of the world is not strictly possible. In mathematics, geometry, metaphysics and theology, there are truths which are quite independent of whether any world exists or not and these are suitable subjects for scientific knowledge. However, Ockham extends science *(scientia)* to include hypothetical or conditional premises of demonstrations or proofs, and evident contingent judgements made on the basis of intuitive cognitions.

Ockham maintains that God must be supremely unnecessitated, being completely free and completely omnipotent. This leads him to assert that the world is radically contingent in its existence and nature; necessity applies only within thought and language, not to events or things in the world. All that is not self-contradictory is possible; what is actual but not necessary cannot be determined by *a priori* reason or logic alone; reason and logic can determine only what is necessary, impossible and possible, not what is actual and contingent among what is possible. Logically speaking in the world anything could follow from anything else, and the only way to determine what things there are, and how things are connected, is by experience. Ockham does not deny that there are real objective causal connections in nature; the order we appear to see is not merely derived from the conventional use of expressions; he does not deny that there is a natural order in the world that can form the basis for the discovery of universal connections which are the aim of science; what he denies is that these universal connections in fact have any metaphysical necessity which could be discovered through deductive reasoning alone. All those connections between things and events that are not merely analytically true by the definitions which give identifying criteria are radically contingent and can be known to hold only from intuitive cognitions. Thus to have new knowledge of connections which goes beyond what is already assumed in definitions, as is the case with causal connections, we rely on experience. If all connections between things and events were analytic and merely followed from definitions, then working them out would be a purely linguistic matter. Clearly we suppose that most connections are not definitional in this way, in which case the connections can be known to hold only by experience.

Ockham does not tackle the question which was to concern Hume much later, in the eighteenth century, of how we can rationally justify the belief that there is any objective natural system of laws at all—the problem of the "uniformity of nature" or how the evidence from the experience of a finite number of singular instances can ever justify the assertion of universal laws of the form "All *A*s are *B*s" or causal connections of the form "If *A* occurs, then *B* must occur". Ockham thinks that God has, as a matter of fact, so arranged things that we can discover objective regular natural laws; but these laws are only contingently in fact true, and God could have arranged the laws quite differently; He was not bound by any kind of necessity to arrange things the way He actually arranged them. It follows that if the arrangement of things is not a matter of necessity, the discovery of the arranged regularities is not knowable by *a priori* deductive reasoning alone, which can give us knowledge only of necessities (that which must be), impossibilities (that which cannot be) and possibilities (that which may or may not be); rather, we require experience in order to discover what actual contingent (that which is, but need not be) arrangement exists. God maintains the natural order so that we can rely (barring miracles) on *B* always following *A; A* is a sign that *B* will follow, and we can be confident, thanks to God, that *B* will follow. This is not to say that God, and not *A,* is the real cause of *B,* but merely that God chooses to maintain a natural order whereby, albeit contingently, *A* causes *B.*

3

German Philosopher Immanuel Kant and his Philosophy

Introduction

The abandonment of authority as the source of truth leads to a profound search as to the origins and justification of our beliefs. The eighteenth century is marked by many embarking on this search full of hope, confident that human reason has the capacity to provide answers and discover truths. It led many thinkers who were intelligent and honest in their deliberations to scepticism; an inability to see how claims to human knowledge can be justified.

Developments in astronomy, with the work of Copernicus in the sixteenth century, had already begun to undermine the medieval edifice which gave man his defined place in the universe. The Great Chain of Being, with God at its summit, stones at its base, and men and angels in between, was dismembered. The Sun, not the Earth, was the centre of our planetary system, situated in a universe of unthinkable immensity and man was denied his privileged place in it. Newton's synthesis of the astronomy of Copernicus and Kepler, and the terrestrial mechanics of Galileo, gave no one a privileged position; laws of nature are objectively and uniformly true in all places. There was also no need for a God to maintain the activity of the universe since it was relatively autonomous, like a clock, and perhaps only required someone to wind it up periodically; but this diminished God's influence to a point where He could be dispensed with, even if a highly religious man such as Newton did not wish to do so. The religious scientist must now serve God through the humble task of uncovering the wonderful order bestowed upon the universe by the Creator at its inception. However, a tension had now emerged in discoveries that appeared to reveal the magnificent workmanship of God's universe, but that at the same time made belief in God optional, since God's intervention in the universe, except perhaps at the very beginning, of which we knew nothing, was not required in explanation as it had been before.

Out of the Enlightenment we may evolve a criterion separating the religious from the non-religious, a criterion based on a more fundamental notion than the existence and authority of God. This can be based on whether it is thought that the universe has some special place or concern (negative or positive) for human beings. It is a universe unresponsive to all human values, one to which human values are simply not applicable, an amoral universe, that gives rise to the crisis begun for man in the Enlightenment. Some reject this aspect of the Enlightenment and continue in acceptance of God, although for many it can never be quite the same; others embrace the idea of an entirely amoral universe, and suffer the problems of discovering what, if anything, can then have value; still others act merely *as if* the universe still responds to human values; they live under the shadow cast by a figure that has already left the scene.

It would be wrong to think of all the most revolutionary intellectual figures before and during the Enlightenment as free-thinking atheists; some of the most important figures were Copernicus, Descartes, Locke, Spinoza, Newton, Leibniz,

Berkeley, Kant, and all were religious men to varying degrees and in different ways, men often profoundly worried about where their thought seemed inexorably to be taking them; this sometimes forced them to take rearguard action against the consequences of their own thoughts. They all contributed to the complete change in man's world-view, whether they intended to or not.

Kant both benefited from, and went beyond, the Enlightenment. After an initial immersion in the rationalist philosophy of Leibniz, Kant could no longer accept it; under the influence of Hume, and the German Crusius, Kant says he was woken from his dogmatic slumbers. Another powerful influence on Kant was Newton. Before devoting himself to philosophy, Kant had been a scientist; he saw the effect that a Newtonian view of the universe was going to have on morality, God, and our freewill. For if Newtonian views were universally and rigorously applied, they left little place for God, and undermined morality in fundamental ways: a Newtonian universe was an amoral mechanical system in which objective values seemed to have no application; man himself was an entity subject to the universal remorseless laws of nature, whose actions were absolutely determined by events that had already occurred, and which were thereby always outside his control; whatever we may *feel* about the matter, we are not free to choose, and where there is no freedom there is no responsibility for action, and thus there can be no moral evaluations. A tree is not free to choose, despite being alive; so when it falls on someone, the event is neither moral nor immoral, it is amoral, just something that happens. Human actions were now in danger of becoming just things that happen.

Kant tried to respond to all these influences, and reconcile them in a new synthesis. The empiricism of Hume had, it seemed to many, led to scepticism about human knowledge, identity and freedom, and Kant could not accept this. The rationalist view argued that there were innate principles of the understanding or reason with which man could *a priori* comprehend the basic nature of the world, although not the world of appearances, but a real world that lies behind appearances which ultimately explains those appearances. Hume undermined this by showing that these principles either were analytic restating what, in disguised form, had already been assumed or went beyond being analytic and could not therefore be justified by reason alone; but Hume found they could not then be justified by experience either. There was no midway course for empiricism.

Kant set out to show that these views could be reconciled; he tried to show why the true nature of the relationship between experience and the world is such that we can know things about the world of appearances *a priori* truths knowable independently of the evidence of experience although we can have no *a priori* knowledge of a real world beyond appearances. Kant wants to show that we can know certain truths *a priori* which are not trivial logical truths known merely because of their formal structure. We can know the truth "If *p* then *q*, *p*, therefore *q*" *a priori* precisely because we can substitute uniformly any propositions we like for *p* and *q;* but for that same reason such logical deductions can, independently of experience, tell us nothing about the world. Our ability to know them *a priori* derives precisely from the fact that they commit us to nothing about the actual world. Kant thinks he can show how we can know universal necessary truths *a priori* about the world as it appears, although not the world as it is in itself.

Kant draws an analogy between his own revolution in philosophy and that of the Copernican revolution in astronomy, but only in the following respect: Copernicus had dared to suggest that some of the motions of the heavenly bodies were only apparent and were as a result of the motion of the observer. Similarly Kant suggests that some of the properties we ascribe to external objects are a result of constructive mental processes to which appearances have to conform. The philosophy propounded by Kant also attempts to be universally valid in covering all self-conscious rational beings. Kant proposes that our experience involves elements partly contributed by us, and partly by the world; this does not mean our conception of the world is merely subjective in being true only from a particular point of view, or that it is absolutely objective, since the conception of the world cannot be separated completely from ways that we experience the world.

Kant

Immanuel Kant (1724-1804) was born in the Prussian town of Königsberg, into a pietist Lutheran family; there he became Professor of Logic and Metaphysics in 1770, at the age of forty-six.

Kant is frequently seen as almost a caricature of the popular conception of a philosopher; outwardly his life was the very model of the fastidious, studious, self-contained philosophical speculator. There is no doubt that like many original people he was capable of great acts of self-discipline. Yet he was not an unsociable man, or an unentertaining lecturer; he was fond of female company, although he never married. He never ventured many miles from Königsberg. His life is therefore depicted as being, on the whole, dull and uneventful. This may well be true; we should temper this somewhat patronizing conclusion by reflecting that many of us do not have lives a great deal more exciting. Near the end of his life, when he had already been withdrawn from society for some time, Kant's intellectual powers crumbled; he failed to recognize friends, and he was virtually blind; yet those closest to him still had glimpses of his good nature and will power, and of the great philosopher behind the shell of the man that remained.

A discussion of Kant's epistemology and metaphysics naturally centres upon the *Critique of pure reason,* his most complete thinking on these subjects. An additional work on the same subjects is the *Prolegomena.* Kant published many other works on science, aesthetics, and on ethics.

Kant, to some extent, saw himself as solving the errors committed by Hume and Leibniz. Hume's philosophy has been interpreted by some as collapsing into scepticism; central claims for human knowledge, which are logically presupposed by natural science, are found to be unjustifiable on the basis of his empiricist philosophy whereby all such claims must be rationally justified either by pure reason *a priori* or by the evidence of experience *a posteriori*. Neither is found to provide such rational justification, although nature takes care that we nevertheless hold the required fundamental beliefs. Not only did our common-sense beliefs about the world become unsupportable, but the most powerful intellectual achievement of the day, Newtonian mechanics, was also undermined. Newtonian mechanics seemed to give a complete unifying explanation of the workings of the universe; it was revolutionary in regarding the universe not as operating under special laws for different regions, but as being unified throughout under one objective set of laws. Kant saw this as supremely worth defending against Hume's scepticism. Knowledge for Kant, as for Leibniz, had to be necessary and universally valid. Hume undermined this, leaving us with knowledge of the world, in so far as we could have any at all, which was subjective, particular and contingent. The most important basic beliefs about the world could not be justified by reason, but if we examined closely what we actually experienced the information provided by experience they could not be justified by experience either. The most important basic beliefs in question were: the belief that the world operates by necessary causal laws, so we can make inference beyond what we presently perceive to unobserved cases; the belief that there exist independent continuously existing objects; and the belief that there is a continuous self. In short, empiricism, with its adherence to the view that experience must be the sole source of evidence about the world, led to scepticism when it was found that experience in itself, if carefully examined, was not sufficient to justify some of our most basic beliefs about the world.

Kant was convinced both that, contrary to Leibniz, knowledge of the world had always to be concerned with the world of our experience, not a reality beyond appearances, and that, contrary to Hume, the senses were not alone as a means of justifying our knowledge of such a world. The way out of this is to deny that sensation and experience are one and the same. Kant's basic idea is a distinction between form and content; the form of our experience is knowable *a priori,* the content is given *a posteriori,* and only in combination can these provide knowledge of the world. We could not have knowledge of a world other than the experienced one; but sensation alone could not support our claims to knowledge. Sensation is always particular, changing and subjective, and our knowledge claims are general, universal, unchanging and objective. Leibniz was impressed by the power of mathematics; maintaining a distrust of the senses as a source of knowledge that led back to Plato, Leibniz sought a metaphysics that describes the fundamental or underlying nature of the world beyond appearances, which was independent of the evidence of experience, based on a few basic principles; the world of appearances is explained ultimately through the reality that lies behind it; it is this reality which is the metaphysical foundation for all other knowledge of the world. This is not to say Leibniz thought that humans could deduce all scientific laws from *a priori* metaphysical principles; such *a priori* principles are too general and the *a priori* principles and reason describe not appearances but the reality underlying those appearances. Metaphysics seeks to describe what the world must fundamentally be like if it is fully rationally explicable.

Kant thought Newtonian mechanics explained not a reality behind appearances, but those appearances themselves; the question was how this was possible in the light of Hume's attack on our ability to justify through examining our sensations the kind of necessary universal laws Newton proposed, and the application of such laws to experience. It could not be achieved through Leibniz's philosophy, for Hume had also shown that the machinations of pure reason alone could not generate any new knowledge concerning what is actual; a pure logical argument unpacks only items that are already contained in its premises. The finite ability of the human mind may give us the impression that something new is arising; but it is already there; for God there would be no point in doing mathematics, or logic, or playing chess; He would already know all the consequences.

There were other intellectual structures that Kant thought it necessary to defend: Euclidean geometry, absolute space, continuous infinite time, the applicability of mathematics in explaining the world. Underlying Newtonian mechanics especially are the concepts of causality and substance. Each area of human inquiry has its limits; one Newtonian limit consisted in not questioning the existence of matter, but instead concentrating on how all posited matter behaves. But without the establishment in reality of a general concept of an independent, self-subsisting stuff, Newtonian mechanics is left entirely hypothetical: *if* the world is a certain way *then* these are the laws of its behaviour. In addition the justification of general laws as such had to be attempted: universal causality, which allows us to go beyond seeing that this follows that to saying that this always causes that, and so make inferences to cases we have not observed. Hume thought that rational justification for our beliefs could lie only in either reason or experience; but neither reason nor experience could justify our belief in an external world of bodies, substance, causality, or the self of personal identity; we could only show how they in fact arise as natural beliefs in response to the experiences we have. It is just these general concepts or categories that Kant aims to show we are justified in applying necessarily and objectively to the world we experience, although that application could not be justified, or refuted, by experience.

It must be emphasized that Kant thought that in some areas of human inquiry some final answers had been generated. The world did obey Newton's laws, Aristotle's logic said all there was to say about logic; space was Euclidean and three-dimensional, time was classical and stretched like an infinite straight line towards the future and back into the past; causality did apply universally. All these things have been questioned by modern thinking; Einstein questioned Newtonian space, time, and motion; quantum mechanics questioned universal causality; modern logic generated a richer array of theorems, making Aristotelean logic a small fragment of it. Kant was not narrow-minded, but Newton's world-view in particular was so powerful and all-encompassing in its unified explanations of a vastly diverse range of phenomena that to be overwhelmed by its finality was understandable. Nor must we let Kant's adherence to these particular theories detract from his important and revolutionary views.

Kant's *Critique* is, roughly, divided into two parts: the Analytic and the Dialectic; the Analytic includes the Aesthetic. The word "aesthetic" derives from a Greek word *aesthesis* relating to perception by the senses. The special Kantian sense of "Aesthetic" concerns the *a priori* form or order necessarily imposed by our capacity to receive representations our sensibility on the material supplied by the senses. The form or order is *a priori* and necessary, and Kant discovers it by subtraction of both the material of sensation and the concepts contributed by the faculty of understanding. These pure forms of sensible intuition or of experiences turn out to be space and time. The Analytic is largely positive; in it are determined the *a priori* principles of the understanding; we are also shown the proper use of metaphysics in providing the basis for our objective knowledge. The Dialectic is largely negative. We are shown the misuse of metaphysics in using concepts to go beyond what we can possibly experience, to a world of illusion and contradiction; we are also shown why we are prone to be tempted to this kind of speculation. The Aesthetic and Analytic give us a metaphysics of experience; they display what must be the basic features of experience and reasoning. The Dialectic shows how we err when we attempt to extend our knowledge beyond that which it is possible for us to experience.

We now turn to examining some well-used terms in Kant's *Critique*. These divide into three pairs: *a priori/a posteriori*, analytic/synthetic, necessary/contingent. First we distinguish *a priori* statements, which once understood can logically be known to be true prior to, and independently of, the evidence of experience, from *a posteriori* statements, which once understood can logically be known to be true only by the evidence of experience. Analytic statements are true in virtue of the meanings of the terms in the statements and are known to be true merely by understanding the meanings of the terms contained in the statements; synthetic statements cannot be known just by examining the meaning of the terms in the statements. Generally speaking, although it is this that Kant will question, necessary statements (those that must always be true or must always be false) are *a priori* analytic and contingent statements (those that may be true or may be false) are *a posteriori* synthetic. Thus, "All bachelors are unmarried" is *a priori* analytic; we can know it to be true without consulting our experience, nor could any experience refute it, for the meaning of "bachelor" includes "unmarried"; if someone was suggested to us as an example of a bachelor who was married, we would respond by explaining how we define "bachelor", not by seeking empirical evidence. Analytic truths are those truths whose denial is contradictory; the predicate "unmarried" is contained in the concept of the subject term "bachelor". However, "All bachelors admire Kant" may be true, or it may be false; the way we find out is by empirically investigating bachelors; it certainly is not part of the definition of the term "bachelor" that an admiration or otherwise for Kant should come into it, and so it cannot be known to be true *a priori*.

Hume thought that the only necessary propositions were analytic ones (mathematics, for example); but the price we pay for our only pieces of necessary truth is that they are quite empty; they tell us nothing about the world. They simply unravel linguistic definitions. Logical truths such as "not-(*p* and not-*p*)" are known to be true *a priori* precisely because they exhibit a universally valid form which is devoid and independent of content; any proposition could be substituted for *p*, therefore the whole expression can tell us nothing about the actual contingent world. Logic alone can tell us only what is necessary, impossible or possible, not what is actual and contingent: that which is, but might have been otherwise. Hume argues that all our knowledge of the world must come from the senses; but all we can generate from that source is contingent particular statements which cannot support general necessary statements, such as the reality of universal causation, the truth of universal laws, the real existence of an independent constant external world. If we observe *A* followed by *B,* we note that we perceive no necessary connection between *A* and *B,* which is an essential part of the belief that *A* causes *B,* that would justify saying *B* must always follow *A;* but this is the form of universal laws of nature and the basis of any inferences from the observed to the unobserved.

The disagreement between empiricists such as Hume and rationalists such as Leibniz centres on whence our knowledge of the world derives, on what knowledge of truths about the world logically depends, and on the emptiness of analytic propositions. In general, the issue is that of the informativeness of truths knowable independently of the evidence of experience: whether such truths can tell us anything about reality. The rationalists see analytic truths and deductive reasoning as an *a priori* source of knowledge, admittedly not of the ephemeral world just as we experience it, but of the reality behind those experiences. Leibniz has a problem maintaining any *a posteriori* synthetic truths at all, since he thinks all truths concerning underlying reality must ultimately be analyzable into the subject predicate form and be analytic. Unlike the rationalists, the empiricists see analytic truths as empty or trivial statements, which can tell us nothing about the actual contingent nature of the world.

Kant found himself agreeing and disagreeing with both parties. He agrees with the empiricists, and disagrees with the rationalists, that *a priori* analytic truths are empty, and that our knowledge must be of the world we can experience; but he also thinks that we can know necessary and universal *a priori* truths that tell us something about the real or actual world of experience. Kant agrees with the rationalists that not all *a priori* knowledge is empty, but disagrees that this knowledge can be of a world behind appearances. The answer for Kant is the existence of propositions that are synthetic *a priori* and in some way necessary; these truths, knowable prior to the evidence of experience, are irrefutable by any experience, and yet they go beyond the mere meaning of the terms used in expressing them and determine *a priori* certain truths concerning the world as experienced. The necessity and universality of the truth of synthetic *a priori* judgements cannot derive from their being analytic and their denial implying a logical contradiction; they must be necessary and universal truths for some other reason. Kant's positive project, his transcendental philosophy, is to show how it can be possible to know truths *a priori* which are necessarily true of the world as it appears, but which are not necessary by merely being analytic. Such a synthetic *a priori* truth is that every event has a cause.

The term "transcendental" does a lot of work in Kant's philosophy. Generally whatever is transcendental is not derived from, or justifiable or refutable by, experience, yet is applicable to, or is a condition for, all experience. Transcendental knowledge is knowledge not of objects, but knowledge of the necessary *a priori* conditions of our cognition of objects. Kant uses the term to denote the *a priori* factors in our knowledge.

Kant analyzes experience and understanding in order to justify objective knowledge. Intuitions consist of sensations which are necessarily subject to the forms of space and time; sensations are *a posteriori* and space and time are supplied *a priori* by our sensibility or capacity to receive representations; but sensation is not separable from those *a priori* conditions. Space is the form of outer sense, of objects in the external world, whereas time is the form of both outer and inner sense—our inner experience necessarily only involves succession in time. Space and time are the *a priori* forms of our sensibility as a whole. These pure forms of our intuitions are analogous to filters on a camera: the only images formed are ones that have passed through or been subject to the filters. The pure forms of intuition are not empirical: they are not derived *from* experience, rather they are the necessary form *of* all experience. Nor are space and time concepts, for there can be no object (like a table) corresponding to space and time in general. Kant further holds that the pure intuition of space is presupposed by geometry, and that of time is presupposed by arithmetic.

In addition to this, *knowledge,* as opposed to the mere having of experiences, involves the use of the basic concepts or categories of the faculty of the understanding. The knowledge that what we see is a table involves having and applying the concept of a table by a judgement of the understanding, not just seeing something in space and time. Furthermore our understanding *necessarily* operates with certain basic concepts or categories. Knowledge is possible through the conjunction of actual intuitions with the necessary categories of the faculty of understanding. The senses alone are literally thoughtless; the understanding alone is contentless.

A summary of the nature of intuitions, and the relation between them and concepts of the understanding producing knowledge, can be given in the following diagram.

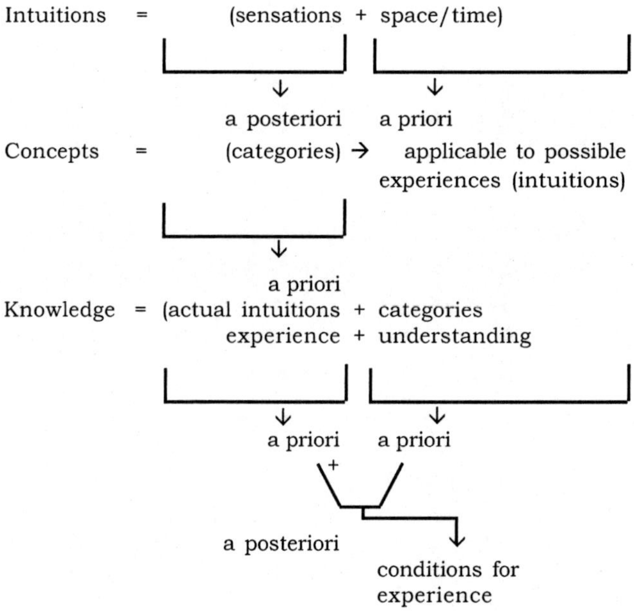

There is a sharp distinction between the intellectual and sensory elements in human knowledge. The mind is active in understanding nature, not a passive receptacle waiting to be filled by experiences. Transcendental philosophy does not give us particular scientific knowledge of the world we experience; but the transcendental deduction shows how we can know the necessary *a priori* elements *presupposed* by such scientific knowledge of the world as experienced. For example, we cannot know *a priori* that *A* is the cause of *B* that is a matter for scientific empirical investigation; but it can be known *a priori* that *B* has some cause that much can be proved by transcendental philosophy.

Kant was well aware of the distinction, said to be confused in the work of some earlier philosophers, between the origin *(quid facti)* of something, and its justification *(quid juris)*. The revealing of the origin or genesis of a truth or belief has to be distinguished from whether the truth or belief can be known *a priori* or *a posteriori*. The origin concerns facts about psychology; the question of whether a proposition is *a priori* or *a posteriori* concerns what logical type the proposition is. Propositions that can be shown to follow deductively from certain logically necessary premises can be known independently of the evidence of experience, since their denial would imply a logical contradiction; but some truths can be known only by consulting the evidence of experience, even if the belief in the truth happens to be psychologically innate. I may have been born with the belief, which is true, that "There are lions in Africa"; but the conditions for the belief being true depend on facts about Africa; knowledge of those facts, and hence knowledge of the truth of the proposition describing those facts, can be justified only by experience of Africa; it could not be proved *a priori* by deductive reasoning or *a priori* by merely understanding the meaning of the terms in the proposition that expresses the belief. To show that something is psychologically *a priori* does not show it to be *a priori* valid or true, still less that its truth is knowable *a priori*.

Kant was not engaged in speculative empirical psychology. If Kant can justify the necessity of the application of the forms of space and time, and the categories, to the world, he will have achieved a great deal. In the first case we have, for example, justified, and explained, applied mathematics; in the second we have justified concepts essential to science, for example, substance, causality, plurality, unity and the like.

Running through Kant's philosophy is a distinction between form and content. The form of experience is knowable *a priori;* the content or filling is given to us and is knowable *a posteriori;* but the two elements are not simply separable. The form of our intuitions is space and time, the forms of our understanding or thought are the categories. In actual intuitions, sensations and space and time are not separable; in actual knowledge, intuitions and categories are not separable. This idea is essential to understanding Kant's transcendental idealism: his notion of objectivity is designed to counter empirical idealism, which is the position that our knowledge is only subjectively valid concerning the content of our own minds.

The "schemata", which are kinds of restricting frameworks, are required to give rules for applying the categories, for the concepts of the understanding in their pure form are never met in intuitions; we must take the pure concepts and form schematisms by which particular intuitions can be identified as falling under pure concepts. If we take the example of the category of substance as that which is always a subject of predication and is never predicated of another subject, the schema of substance is that which is permanent in time while other things change. The schema of necessity is the existence of an object at all times. The schema of causality is the succession of real things according to a rule. Time is presupposed *a priori* in our experiencing things existing simultaneously or successively; and it is indeed temporal existence that is the primary condition to which schemata of the *a priori* imagination must conform. It is the schema which ensures that the categories are applied only to objects of possible experience; the understanding is effectively limited to experience (intuitions of our sensibility) by requiring that the application of the pure concepts is through schemata which involve the *a priori* pure form of inner intuition (time) and outer intuition (space); that is, the categories are limited to objects in time and space. Thus the categories become more than pure or formal logical truths, but come to have objects to which they apply; they come to tell us something *a priori* about the objects of possible experience, that is, possible intuitions. Through the methodological adoption of the mechanism of schemata, reason does not attempt to describe a world beyond or behind all possible experience; in this case it is not a world which is as a matter of fact out of reach of all experience from which we exclude ourselves, but rather a world which is necessarily out of reach of all possible experience. What is denied is "transcendent" knowledge: knowledge of things-in-themselves or, in Kant's terminology, noumena beyond the conditions for all experiences. For example, it can be said to be possible to experience atoms, although in fact they are too small to see (at least with the naked eye); whereas it is impossible that we should experience timelessness or eternity, since all experiences are in time as they involve succession; nor is it possible to conceive of a spaceless world.

We can see the categories as the highest point of a hierarchy of classificatory and ordering concepts. We use the concept "tree", which falls under the concept "plant", which is an "object", which is subsumed under "substance", something that is separable and can remain the same while undergoing certain sorts of changes. We can conceive of a world as experienced to which the lower and more particular concepts do not apply a world without trees, in which the concept "tree" is not applied in our judgements but we cannot conceive of a world to which the concepts of something that can endure through change, universal causality, plurality and unity do not apply. The same applies to the other twelve in the table of categories.

These are the categories with which we must think if we think about the world at all, and they must therefore be presupposed in, apply to, any way the world can appear to us and be involved in all judgement and knowledge.

I
Quantity
Unity
Plurality
Totality

II
Quality
Reality
Negation
Limitation

III
Relation
Substance and accident
Cause and effect
Reciprocity

IV
Modality
Possiblity and impossibility
Existence and non-existence
Necessity and contingency

In the metaphysical deduction of categories, Kant tries to demonstrate how the categories arise from general logic from different kinds of logical judgements. However, Kant's exposition is unusually terse. The judgement "Some S is P" ("Some cows are black') involves concepts; it involves the concept of *plurality,* since it involves two terms, it involves the concept of *reality,* since it states something is.

Perhaps of greater importance to the modern reader is the transcendental deduction, for here we have an argument that attempts to justify the application of categories as such; that there are concepts we necessarily have to apply to experience, whatever these concepts specifically turn out to be. The sense of "deduction" in the transcendental deduction is more akin to a defence in law than an argument in formal logic.

The transcendental deduction runs as follows. The aim of the transcendental deduction is to show not only that there are categories or concepts we necessarily apply to our experience, but also that that experience must be such that in applying the categories we can be said to be making objective judgements, or judgements about objects. The absolutely minimum condition for experiences which are *something to me* is that the experiences are subject to a synthesis such that they are all part of one consciousness. To say that experiences are thus united is equivalent to the condition of apperception, that is, the experiences are possible objects of self-consciousness; it must be possible for the "I think" to accompany all my representations. The "I" here is not empirical self-consciousness; sometimes I reflect, and sometimes I do not; it is the transcendental unity of apperception: the unity given by the mere possibility of my being self-conscious of whatever experiences I have. For this apperception to make sense it is necessary that I am aware of something which is not-self, objects which have a unity and independence of their own, distinct from my self; if they were not thus independent, I would not be engaged in an act of self-consciousness at all. The items on which I reflect in self-consciousness, that is, the items of my consciousness, are not-self and are therefore objects; they have objectivity. Now to reflect at all is to apply concepts; to say, for example, "*x* now", "there are more *x*s than *y*s", "*x* is different from *y*", "*x* again", "*y* has got bigger"; in reflection concepts must be applied, so what presents itself could not be a totally disordered stream of sensation, each item utterly unrelated to any other. In the final step, having shown we necessarily apply concepts, Kant, due to his faith in his metaphysical deduction, thinks he has shown that it must be just those concepts or categories deduced in the metaphysical deduction that we apply.

To sum up: consciousness is a uniting of intuitions, the condition for this is possible self-consciousness; the condition for self-consciousness is awareness of objects, or objective experiences (experiences under categories); the objects of conciousness on which we reflect in self-consciousness are therefore subject to concepts (are objects having order intrinsic to them); and if we must apply concepts, the categories revealed in the metaphysical deduction must be the concepts we apply.

Kant equivocates about the nature of objects, items of which we can claim to be able to make judgements independent of the particular state of the subject. Whether the objectivity granted by the categories as the necessary universally valid conditions for all experience is enough to give us everything we expect of an object, and an objective world, is open to dispute. But the transcendental deduction attempts to justify the application of the categories by all rational consciousnesses, not just the human mind. There cannot be forms of understanding quite different from our own. Kant does allow that there could be forms of sensible intuition other than our own human forms.

Hume correctly thought we could not derive an abiding self from the flux of perceptions open to introspection; but Kant argues that the ability to introspect at all assumes a self or subject which has the experience, for we say, "This is my experience"; it must be possible for the "I think" to accompany all my representations. But I can think only according to the categories; so there can be no experience such that it is not subject in my judgement to the categories, since then there would be experiences of mine which could not be accompanied by "I think", which is impossible. The awareness of self derives from the awareness of our power to unite representations in one consciousness.

This creates for Kant the possibility of objective knowledge of the world; knowledge must include experience, and we necessarily have to apply the categories which give the form of that experience.

Whereas Kant's argument may have justified the application of necessary conditions for experience some set of categories or other it is not clear that he has justified the application of all and only those categories he lists in particular; that would follow only if we accepted the metaphysical deduction.

This has led some to update the categories but maintain their necessity; it has led still others to update them but to abandon their necessity. The second of these positions seems to abandon the point of Kant's transcendental idealism, for then the categories are neither universal (for they apply only to human cognition) nor necessary (not transcendentally necessary but psychological facts). On the other hand, the first position has great difficulty generating categories which at once can be shown to apply necessarily to any comprehensible world, while at the same time avoiding the triviality of being entirely vacuous and non-specific.

Interpretations of Kant's transcendental idealism vary. One view asserts that we have obtained objective knowledge because the categories have been demonstrated to have universal inter subjectivity. Another view suggests that Kant has to show that there is a world of objects existing independent of us in some further sense than the world we experience and know, necessarily conforming to the categories which are not thereby merely arbitrary and subjective. But this destroys Kant's position by asking him to accomplish the impossible. We cannot possibly know that objects in themselves, distinct from how they are experienced or appear to us, are organized according to the categories, but we can know that objects as they appear or the world-as-experienced must be organized according to the categories, since the way objects appear partly depends on ourselves and we must apply the categories in thinking about what we experience. The world, or nature, just is the sum of possible experiences; the world of phenomena. Noumena, or things-in-themselves *(Dinge-an-sich),* are not objects of experience; they stand proxy for a world beyond appearances that is unknowable; this realm is nothing to do with the world as studied by science. Noumenon is not, it must be emphasized, the atomic world, or anything where our lack of actual experience of it is purely a matter of accidental contingent fact. The atomic world exists straightforwardly (or so it seemed in Kant's day) in space and time, even if the laws governing its behaviour are discovered indirectly by its effects; our inability to observe atoms directly is an empirical, not a transcendental, limit to our experience. The appearance/ reality distinction is not between phenomena/noumena, but between the variant/invariant features of our experience. To suggest that we can still look around the edge of all our experiences, dropping our form of cognition, to a world untainted by that form, to see if the categories actually apply, is to attempt what Kant denies is possible, and to abandon precisely the ground from whence the objectivity of the categories arises. The categories which we bring to experience cannot be abandoned, for they are present whenever we have an intelligence capable of self-conscious thought.

Kant says his position supports empirical realism and refutes idealism. Whatever we may think of Kant's arguments, he cannot be defending empirical realism in the form of knowledge of objects devoid of our form of understanding; to think otherwise is to miss the point. If we tried to apply Kant's views to objects totally independent of our, and all intelligent, modes of understanding, Kant could never have hoped to justify the necessary application of categories; there would always be an unbridgeable gap between the way we think and what we think about; we would never be able to show the categories applied to reality in this sense, rather than merely indicating how we have to think about the world. If any conception of reality is inseparable from mind, then there is a possibility of explaining why our basic intellectual structures causality, substance, plurality, and the like must actually apply. The point is that as far as we are concerned, transcendental idealism delivers all that a bald empirical realism supposes to be the case; these two positions are in that sense equivalent and indistinguishable. A logically or transcendentally inescapable perspective is equivalent to an objective view. Universal objectively valid knowledge, invariant with, and not requiring qualifying reference to, the state of the subject, is squared with the argument that there cannot be a perspectiveless world-view of things-in-themselves through the establishment of the categories and forms of intuition as transcendentally necessary and objective for all possible appearances in being invariant with the experiencing subject. There is then no perspectiveless position from which the rational perspective itself can be checked; if the perspective is thereby universal it is also necessary and objective and independent of the individual subjective perspective.

This is not the only interpretation of Kant's position, and Kant himself was not entirely consistent or clear; he plainly felt uneasy about it. Kant sometimes speaks as if noumena are the unknowable causes of our experiences.

Kant attacks in the Dialectic the possibility of knowledge transcending experience and its *a priori* form or conditions to attempt to gain knowledge of unconditioned noumena, a perspectiveless view of things-in-themselves. Kant is setting the necessary presupposition of all human knowledge and so marking the bounds of legitimate inquiry. The Dialectic is the logic of illusion. That is not to say that we cannot think beyond the bounds of possible experience; we can form concepts for example of substance to think about that which exists beyond our possible intuitions, and so outside space and time; but knowledge is not possible.

Noumena are unknowable; we can speak of noumena only negatively: we can say what they are *not* as compared to phenomena that we can experience, since we can say that none of our concepts can be positively applied to characterize noumenon. It is indeed unclear if we can legitimately talk of either noumenon in the singular or noumena in the plural, since the first involves the category of unity and the second that of plurality. Whatever is the case, noumenon, or the thing-in-itself, is reality in the sense of being independent of all conceptual determinations which apply necessarily to the world as experienced; and, since all knowledge involves applying concepts, things-in-themselves are unknowable.

Illusory metaphysics which aims at knowledge has three main subjects: God, and proofs for the existence of God; freedom, which connects with cosmology; immortality, which connects with the soul. Metaphysical speculation which aims at knowledge of truths concerning these subjects has been endless, fruitless and contradictory. In contrast to physical science, disputes seem undecidable. As Kant says, it has involved "deluding the adventurous seafarer ever anew with empty hopes, and engaging him in enterprises which he can never abandon and yet is unable to carry to completion". Kant wants to show why this is so, and put an end to it. This is the overall aim of Kant's "critical philosophy".

Kant sets about this demonstration in the Antinomies. The strategy is, after taking some matter about which we illegitimately aim to know, to present a pair of equally logically compelling arguments from which are derived a thesis and antithesis which are mutually exclusive and collectively exhaustive alternatives. The conclusions cannot both be true, but we have no way of knowing which is true and which false. The proof of the thesis and antithesis is by *reductio ad absurdum:* showing that denying an assertion leads to an impossibility, thus demonstrating the truth of the assertion. Kant presents four Antinomies: first, the finitude or infinitude in space and time of the universe; secondly, the finite or infinite divisibility of substance; thirdly, whether there is freedom or no freedom; fourthly, whether there exists an absolutely necessary being or not. These matters are undecidable by human reason, since we are presented with equally convincing conclusions which are mutually contradictory. However, to agree that the Antinomies show this, we would have to accept the arguments for each thesis and antithesis in each Antinomy as equally valid; unfortunately their quality is variable.

Hegel (1770–1831) was to suggest that the opposing conclusions of Kant's Antinomies indicate not the limits of human reason, but the need for a synthesis which somehow encompasses the conflicting conclusions as to the nature of reality.

Arguments for the existence of God are classified in three ways: physico-theological, cosmological, ontological. The physico-theological is basically the argument from design, whereby, if an orderly clock needs a clockmaker, the world surely needs a worldmaker. Hume had attacked this argument on the grounds that if the clock/world analogy was weak, then the world might not need a maker; if the analogy was strong, then the worldmaker was no better than a clockmaker, and need not be a God at all. The cosmological argument harks back to the ancient unmoved-mover argument of a first cause required to start the universe off; this is already implicitly undermined in the Antinomies. The most significant attack is upon the ontological argument. Here God's existence is said to be deducible from the concept of God; God is perfection, it is more perfect to exist than not to exist, therefore the perfect being must exist. Kant's refutation of this proof rests on arguing that "existence" is not a descriptive predicate adding anything to the meaning or concept of a subject, so that to say something exists does not therefore attribute an additional property to a subject at all; rather it merely says that there is something to which the concept of the subject applies. We do not add an additional property, after we have listed all the attributes of Kant, by saying Kant exists; rather it is to say that all the properties of Kant shortness, thin body, philosopher, etc. actually have an instance.

Kant was concerned that he had, in a sense, done his job of providing necessary metaphysical foundations too well; especially with reference to the universally valid application of causality to phenomena, it seemed as if there was no place left for human freedom. Kant replies through an analysis of the self. Although the world of phenomena may be determined by the causal laws of physics and transcendental concepts, the noumenal world beyond experience is not. Kant's answer is to posit a noumenal-self, or transcendental-self, which is "outside" the phenomenal world; man viewed as noumenon can therefore act freely according to the moral law. The transcendental-self is the only transcendental object we have access to; here our perspective and a perspectiveless view become one and the same; the distinction between appearance and reality can be eliminated. This explanation of freedom leaves too many questions in obscurity to be satisfactory; moreover, because the moral law governs the operation of the noumenal-self, it fails to explain how we could ever act wrongly. If it is maintained that the operation of the noumenal-self originates totally spontaneously, then it amounts to nothing more than a reassertion of belief in freewill. In any event Kant's call upon the transcendental world should, on his own account, be illegitimate, as this world is unknowable, and its causal interaction with the phenomenal world impossible, since the concept of causality cannot apply to it.

Kant does leave some positive function to the ideas of unconditioned reason; they can be regulative of our inquiries, even if concrete knowledge of truths cannot directly be derived from them. If we treat the ideas of unconditioned reason as unobtainable aims, they may act as injunctions. For example, the idea of determining if the world has a beginning in time is not something we can settle by pure reason, nor could any empirical inquiry determine the answer; but the question of the universe's temporal origin requires us to keep searching for ever greater understanding of the universe's origin.

We can summarize the philosophy of Kant in the following way. Kant starts from the problem of justifying the objectivity and necessity of the form of intuitions and the concepts we apply to the world. Their necessity and objectivity seem unjustifiable by the raw sensations of experience alone or because their rejection would involve logical contradiction. The world for us can be nothing but the sum total of possible appearances, and the form given to those appearances applied to the raw sensations is the product of our minds; appearances, but not things-in-themselves, have to conform to the form given to them by our understanding; these forms are objective and necessary because they are that to which all appearances must conform if there are awareness and judgements concerning those appearances; these forms are universally valid for all rational beings. Thus they are objective because they apply to all worlds conceivable to us, and to rational beings in general, and so are independent of the subjective contributions of any individual minds. The world as noumenon is the world considered as other than how it can ever appear to us; such a world beyond all possible appearances is unknowable; it is a world in which the *a priori* form produced by our intellect is not valid, since it is the world as it is independent of all appearances, beyond possible experience. The function of philosophy is not to provide us with knowledge of the nature of reality as a whole or in itself how the world might be beyond how it can possibly appear to us but with knowledge of the *a priori* form or structure of those appearances themselves. Nor can philosophy lay down *a priori* the scientific laws of nature; but it can justify the presuppositions that the scientific empirical inquiry into the laws of nature involves. Philosophy studies the only thing it can: the necessary and universal *a priori* form of the world as it appears to us; the *a priori* forms are necessary and objective because they are how any rational minds must think; the forms are therefore applicable to any conceivable world, that is, to all that is a possible appearance to us.

4

Linguistic Philosophy of Wittgenstein

Introduction

There are, however, some common concerns and connections between the earlier and later philosophies. The most obvious of these are the concern with language, the drawing of linguistic boundaries, and the idea that we are led into philosophy and philosophical problems through misunderstanding the nature of language. We should not "solve" the problems of philosophy in their stated form, or on their face value, but should first see whether the problems are a result of our being fundamentally misled by language. Wittgenstein wishes to jolt us out of the traditional way of approaching philosophical problems, not so as to provide yet more in the way of "solutions", but so that we may look at the problems themselves in a manner whereby we see why they do not require such "solutions". Much philosophy rests on a confusion about the way language acquires its meaning, and many philosophical problems are really pseudo problems or are misconceived.

Wittgenstein also opposes the idea that philosophy is a kind of super-science in either its methods or its problems.

He objects to the picture of philosophy as being just like science except for the fact that it pushes the search for explanations and justifications deeper, presenting philosophical theories and hypotheses. If we examine carefully the matters discussed in philosophy, we will discover something peculiar and illegitimate about them, and in the later philosophy this will be manifest chiefly in comparing the use of language in philosophy with other uses.

In the *Tractatus* philosophical or metaphysical propositions are ruled out all at once in virtue of their involving meaningless linguistic signs. Since philosophical propositions do not conform to what is *essential* to a proposition being meaningful, they cannot be meaningful. There is an essential way that propositions are meaningful: it is supposed that propositions are meaningful because of something they all have in common; that is, if, and only if, certain conditions are met can a linguistic expression or sign be said to be meaningful. There are necessary and sufficient conditions that any linguistic expression must satisfy if it is to be meaningful; if it fails to satisfy these conditions, then a putative linguistic expression or proposition is meaningless. The essential condition for meaningfulness given in the *Tractatus* is the picturing relation with the world: a genuine proposition is an arrangement of names that pictures a possible fact and is ultimately constituted out of names whose meanings are the objects they stand for in the world. That the propositions of philosophy do not satisfy the essential condition means that philosophy and its "problems" are disposed of in one blow as meaningless.

The *Philosophical investigations* involves a very important shift in approach. If anything binds together the later philosophy, it is *anti-essentialism.* Essentialism amounts to the view that the reason for regarding a group of distinct things as of the same kind is that they have a distinguishing set of features shared by all and only members of that group. Thus we might define an "automobile" as "a self-propelled vehicle suitable for use on a street or roadway". Wittgenstein opposes essentialism generally, and in particular in the attempt to demonstrate that there must be some single way that all instances of meaningful language ultimately have their meaning, which therefore explains or accounts for the meaningfulness of the whole of language. There is no essential feature in virtue of which all language is meaningful. The key to the later philosophy is perhaps the attack on essentialism in general, and about meaning in particular. One attempt to give an account of the essence of language that language consists ultimately of names of objects is given in the *Tractatus* itself. A *part* of language may consist of names of objects, but it is not the essence defining common feature of all language.

The anti-essentialism of the *Philosophical investigations* has far-reaching consequences. It may seem that in rejecting the view that language has an essential way of being meaningful Wittgenstein is giving up all hope of disposing of philosophical problems in virtue of their expression being meaningless. In a sense this is true, although an expression might be meaningless in virtue of not being meaningful in *any* of the different ways it might be meaningful. However, anti-essentialism cuts both ways: it has the consequence that there is no way of dismissing philosophical expressions as wholly meaningless because they do not satisfy what is essential for meaningfulness, but it also has the consequence that because there is no single universal way that expressions are meaningful, there is no way of claiming that philosophy concerns itself with the one true, correct, or real meaning of expressions as opposed to the vagaries of their meaning outside philosophy for example, their ordinary meaning. That there is no single universal criterion for meaningfulness suggests that all philosophical talk cannot be dismissed as wholly meaningless; but it also entails that there is no universal hidden, but perhaps discoverable, standard of meaningfulness in virtue of which one meaning could be picked out as the true meaning which takes precedence over other meanings in other contexts.

It is important to bear in mind the revolutionary nature of Wittgenstein's later thought. The attempt to fit his later thought into the philosophical tradition will result only in distortion and fundamental misunderstanding. There is a great temptation to take Wittgenstein as presenting new solutions and theories for traditional philosophical puzzles; but if we do this we misunderstand what he is about, and come away with a diminished view of his achievement because, viewed as traditional philosophy, what he says may seem deeply unsatisfactory and even beside the point. The later work offers ways of stopping before we begin to step on the road that leads to the traditional problems of philosophy by revealing something about how language acquires its meaning. If this is to be consistent it must avoid philosophizing as it is traditionally thought of. For this reason some have said that in his later thought Wittgenstein is not doing philosophy at all; indeed, Wittgenstein says that his philosophy is "one of the heirs of the subject which used to be called 'philosophy'". The point is that it is possible to talk *about* philosophy without *doing* philosophy in the traditional sense.

Wittgenstein is adamant that he is not putting forward philosophical theories or explanations, but rather assembling reminders as to the actual use of language. Some have argued that the assembling of reminders of actual usage of language in different contexts is without philosophical significance; but this objection assumes that there is something beyond, or other than, the employment or function or use of language in particular contexts, in virtue of which it acquires its meaning, and from which *the* true meaning could be determined independently of the use in particular contexts. If there were something beyond, and other than, the actual concrete usage of language in different contexts which determined the essential meaning of expressions, then we might ignore the usage in different contexts and concentrate on the real essential meaning of expressions. Wittgenstein argues that there is nothing hidden beyond the meaning involved in the exact description of the usage of expressions in different contexts which would give the real meaning; and there is nothing in common between the various usages in different contexts which we could pick out as the essential meaning of words and concepts.

The negative part of Wittgenstein's project is to show why none of the ways that have been suggested in which language essentially has meaning are correct. There have been various suggestions as to how language essentially has its meaning: for example, terms get their meaning ultimately by naming objects, or by ostensive definitions whereby we are shown examples of what terms mean, or by the association of terms with mental images or ideas. When a feature or set of features is suggested as necessary and sufficient for meaning, Wittgenstein cites instances where these features are not present, and yet we still regard the language as meaningful. The positive part of the project is to describe the different ways that expressions are used in different contexts, which is the same as showing the various meanings that expressions can have.

The *Philosophical investigations* aims to make explicit that philosophy involves using language in ways that are *different* from their normal employment, also that philosophy does not pick out some essential core meaning of expressions. One aim of the later philosophy is not primarily to correct philosophical language, but to show that philosophical usage is radically different from ordinary usage; in that case, what we mean by certain expressions in a philosophical context will be different from what we mean in an ordinary context; and there is no external standard to which we could refer to establish which of the various meanings in different contexts is the only correct one. The generation of many of the problems of traditional philosophy for example, skepticism relies on supposing that the meanings given to the concepts studied are the correct ones, or at least that talk of *the* single correct meaning makes sense.

In traditional philosophy there is the semblance of an attempt to solve problems and really get to the bottom of matters, whereas really there are, in different areas, always frameworks and presuppositions which keep the problems alive indeed keep them as problems while in other contexts outside philosophy such "problems" do not even arise.

One of the chief characteristics of traditional philosophy is to seek ultimate explanations and justifications beyond the point at which they can make sense and even arise. That this is not manifestly impossible is only because we do not really take such a step, but bracket off some area in virtue of which the philosophical problems can be stated and solutions offered. For example, in applying universal Cartesian doubt to discover the indubitable foundations of knowledge, we omit to doubt the meaning of the words used to express the universal doubt, without which questions of doubt and knowledge would not arise at all. The supposedly universal doubt of the Cartesian sceptic inconsistently assumes that we know the meaning of the language in which the processes and arguments leading to such doubt are expressed. The later philosophy of Wittgenstein makes these implicit assumptions explicit, and thereby demonstrates that our seeking after ultimate explanations and justifications outside contexts within which they can arise is impossible or non-sensical. There cannot be such explanations for they would either involve something further that would itself require explanation although this may not be immediately apparent or step into an area where the request for explanation does not arise. One of Wittgenstein's slogans is that "Explanations come to an end". The import of this is that there comes a point at which our attempts to explain and justify have to stop, and beyond which the question of justification can no longer arise. But we do not stop at something that finally explains all the rest, we stop at something which cannot be given further explanation: at the perimeter of the framework within which asking the questions in that context makes sense. Explanation has to stop and we have to be content with a *description*.

This does not mean that in the special sciences, such as physics, we cannot explain one thing in terms of another, and push this procedure to profound depths. Philosophy asks certain kinds of questions that sometimes look like questions in the special sciences, but they are not; they often seek to question the very framework in which providing explanations and solving problems could make sense, and so they go beyond the point where explanations can be given or are required. If we do not notice differences in the meaning of the expressions we use in different contexts, we will be tempted to think that we are doing exactly the same kind of thing in each context. If we are explaining *X,* we can do so in terms of *a, b, c;* and we can perhaps further explain *a, b, c.* In explaining anything we are involved in a web of interrelated elements which are used in explaining one another; but it makes no sense to try to step outside everything, and ask for an explanation of the whole thing. Explanations of why something is so require contexts within which asking for explanations makes sense. Eventually we will reach a point at which to ask for explanations in a given context has to end: further explanations will fail either because they are question-begging, or because they involve something further that itself requires explanation. There is in any case no framework of explanation accounting for or justifying the practices of all other explanatory frameworks, although the frameworks may be logically interconnected. And even if there were such a super-framework, it would also require explanation. This important idea applies to meaning: expressions have meaning in their use in various contexts, and it makes no sense to ask what is their real meaning stripped of what would be said to justify their meaning as employed in various actual contexts.

Moreover, what philosophy is concerned with is seeking logical *justifications* or *reasons,* not, as in the sciences, causal explanations. It is of course possible to give logical justifications or reasons for what we do or say in various contexts; but traditional philosophy often seeks justifications or reasons in ways and in contexts, or outside all contexts, where we can no longer provide them. It seeks to answer the question of what rational justification we have to go on, as we have been doing in certain contexts beyond the point at which such justifications need or can be given; and the attempt to do so merely generates philosophical conundrums which further entangle the philosopher in fruitless theorizing. For example, Wittgenstein himself in the *Tractatus* sought to give an ultimate reason for the meaningfulness of language in terms of its consisting of names of simple or unanalyzable objects.

That there are sometimes *causal* explanations for why we do what we do is not in dispute; but to give a causal explanation is not to say we are *justified* in doing what we do. I might, for example, believe it to be true that 1,574×6,266=9,862,684, and give a causal explanation for having this belief as resulting from a sharp blow on the head received while a child; but that would not give any justification for the belief that the multiplication is true or should be thought so by others. What we require is a justification for the belief that the multiplication is true in terms of some appropriate evidence from which the conclusion can be seen to follow logically or by which it is supported. For example: this was the result I got with my pocket calculator. We might go on further and ask why we believe the calculator reliable. Again we are asking for the evidence we have used, from which the conclusion follows, to be displayed; we are not asking for a causal explanation. An appropriate answer to the question would not be in terms of my brain being in a particular causally produced state, or my being brought up in a particular way, for that would not give us a reason for believing the calculator reliable. I may judge that *p* is true; a causal explanation for my making that judgement could be given; but that would not answer the question of whether I had a valid reason for thinking *p* true; for that I would have to present evidence for judging *p* true; and that would involve some kind of appropriate *logical* connection between the evidence or reasons and the conclusion that *p*. To suggest otherwise is to confuse causal power and logical validity. I can be causally determined to arrive at a conclusion without the conclusion rationally following from any available evidence; conversely a conclusion may rationally follow from the available evidence without any causal process guaranteeing that I draw it. An example of the latter case is someone saying, “But after all this evidence, you can’t say that”, followed by the quip “I just did”.

Wittgenstein's point is that the giving of reasons or justifications must come to an end, and what we can use as evidence or justification must be available to us to use as evidence or justification, and not be something hidden. But such justification must reach something that does not require further logical justification, and beyond which the seeking of logical justification becomes senseless. At this point we hit bedrock. This line of thought applies, for example, to the justification of belief. In the same way an explanation or an account of the meaningfulness of language must come to an end with something available to us which can be given in explanation, with reference to which we can justify or give reasons for the meanings that words and other linguistic expressions have, but beyond which no further justification is required or can be given.

This attempt to stand completely outside the totality of the patchwork of contexts it might be pictured as a collection of many overlapping circles in which justification can be given, and to give reasons for everything at once, is prevalent in the various areas of philosophy. We find it in the area of giving an account of how language gets its meaning and also in the area of what we can be said to know. We are seeking to answer the question of what rational justification we have for saying that certain words have a meaning, and what right we have to say that we know certain things. What justification have we for saying that certain words have, or have not, a meaning? What justification have we for saying we understand the meaning of a word? What justification have we for saying that we do, or do not, know some particular truths? Again, that there are necessary causal conditions for our making claims (such as having brains, having been born, etc.) is not in dispute; nor does what Wittgenstein says rival such causal accounts. What is at issue is whether we can give logical justifications for such claims; we require evidence that in some way supports the truth of the conclusions, and not just a causal explanation for why we in fact make those claims.

Wittgenstein replaces essentialism about meaning with what might be termed linguistic instrumentalism: an account of the phenomenon of language eventually ends at a description of what we do, and the meanings of the concepts language involves can be explained or justified as being the way they are only from within language, not by something else that lies beyond or behind language. Wittgenstein says in the *Philosophical investigations* "Think of the tools in a tool-box.

The functions of words are as diverse as the functions of these objects." Wittgenstein shows how the attempt to justify the meaningfulness of language as a whole fails, because the use of factors outside language always presupposes some linguistic competence, and so does not succeed in grounding the *whole* of language. He also shows that such external ultimate justification is not in any case required for meaningful language. The negative side of Wittgenstein's work attacks various attempts to justify the meaning that expressions have in virtue of something extralinguistic that purports to give a complete explanation or justification for language having the meanings and concepts it has. If the view opposed by Wittgenstein were established, we might discover the real meaning of expressions beyond their meanings acquired and justifiable within certain contexts. The accounts of language that Wittgenstein opposes involve giving a single unified account of how all language ultimately gets its meaning; it is supposed that all the various manifestations of language have an essence, or single logic, in virtue of which its expressions ultimately have or acquire their true meaning. Three cases Wittgenstein considers are as follows:

(a) the theory of the *Tractatusi*

(b) ostensive definition

(c) mentalism.

(a) The heart of the *Tractatus* theory is that whatever the surface appearance of language, on analysis it consists entirely of names which mean the objects for which they stand. There is an obvious problem with the *Tractatus* view that the ultimate constituents of language are names, and the meaning of a name is its object: the problem is that Wittgenstein was unable to give any examples of simple names or objects of the required indestructible unchanging simplicity which would guarantee the meaningfulness of language. If the objects named are complex and hence capable of destruction, and the object is the meaning, then the meaningfulness of language cannot be assured. Moreover, if the objects are hidden and not available readily for us to use in any justification of what we mean, it is difficult to understand in what sense they can be said to explain the meaning of words or be used to justify our understanding of their meaning. Also, naming is merely one of a multitude of functions language can perform and is an activity that presupposes an understanding of what naming something is.

(b) If we are asked to give the meaning of a word we might give some kind of account of its meaning in words in a verbal definition; but this would be of any use only if we understood the meaning of the words used in the given definition. Some have thought that if this process is not to go on indefinitely and language is to talk about the world, not just words, we must step outside language. This is said to be done through ostensive definitions that is, by showing. If we take the word "dog" for example, we might learn the meaning of the word through someone uttering the word "dog", in the presence of a dog, and perhaps pointing at the dog. Such understanding of the meaning of words could then be used to build up verbal definitions within language. Wittgenstein does not question that such ostensive teaching of language takes place. What he objects to is the idea that such teaching is sufficient to underpin our understanding of language as a whole. Ostension is systematically ambiguous, so we must understand the significance of, or what is intended in, the situation in which ostensive definitions are given, and such understanding is not accounted for by ostension itself. For us to understand that we are meant to be learning a general name like "pencil", and not a particular name like "Fred", already presupposes some linguistic understanding in this case the distinction between particular and general names not accounted for by mere ostension. For this reason ostensive definitions cannot be the ultimate explanation for how language gets its meaning, for ostensive definitions leave some linguistic understanding unexplained; they do not explain how we get from no language at all to some language. Children and foreigners learn some aspects of language by ostensive definition; but such ostension works only because they already have some linguistic understanding,

(c) Another view is that to understand the meaning of a word involves associating it with a mental image or idea in the mind. Insuperable difficulties arise for this view even if we set aside the obvious objection that what an image of, say, justice would consist in is entirely baffling. Suppose we try to use this theory to explain our understanding of the word "red". I come across an object and I am deciding whether or not to call it red. The mentalistic account suggests that what happens is that I call up the image I have of red, compare it with the colour of the object, and decide whether they are the same; if they are the same the object is correctly called red. But how is this to be done? It is no use my merely *having* the image of red; I must be able to call up the correct image. However, being able to call up the right image involves recognizing which image, among others, is that of red; but such recognition was exactly what we set out to explain. My ability to call up the right image is not explained by my comparing it with another image, because how am I to call up the correct image in that case? Wittgenstein is not denying that we do sometimes use images, and that we may use them to identify things; what he denies is that the reference to images can be the foundation for our understanding of all language, for it already presupposes the kind of understanding it was meant to explain.

Wittgenstein generally objects to the idea that understanding the meaning of a word is constituted by being in some kind of special mental state. The meaning of words does not rest on our mentally intending a meaning. If we say, "Alan understands what is meant by a crescendo", we are not supposing that there must be thoughts running through

Alan's head which constitute this understanding. If this were the case we would say that he ceases to understand what it means when he is asleep or distracted by some other thought. Mental processes are neither necessary nor sufficient for many other cases, such as "knowing", "remembering", "believing".

Wittgenstein's aim is not to deny that many of the ways which are mistakenly proposed as accounting for or explaining the meaning of language as a whole could not be used to account for or explain what we mean within parts of language; what he denies is that there is a single unified account or explanation in terms of something external to language as a whole. This means that the answer to the question "What justifies the meanings and concepts we have in our language as a whole?" is "Nothing does". There is no standard external to the *agreed use* of an expression in the language by which our usage can be further justified. The question cannot be answered any other way because any justification would already involve understanding and taking for granted that we did understand the meaning of certain expressions and concepts. So there is nothing outside all language which gives such a total or complete justification for language being as it is.

This complements Wittgenstein's denial that he is presenting overarching justificatory philosophical theories about language or indeed about any other philosophical matter. By posting reminders of the diversity and multiplicity of the uses of language, he hopes to show that such overarching theories cannot be produced.

It may be thought that if we correctly call a collection of things or activities by the same name, then they *must* have something in common in virtue of which they are things or activities of that kind; they must have a set of features which they, and only they, share; they must have an essence. Such an essence could be characterized by a definition which gives necessary and sufficient conditions or features for being a particular kind of thing: necessary because anything of that kind must have those features; sufficient because anything with those features will be of that kind so something is an *X* if and only if it satisfies a certain set of conditions or has a certain set of features. Wittgenstein thinks this is a mistake. If we try to define a concept in this way, we will be unable to give conditions that are at once both necessary and sufficient. Wittgenstein asks us to consider games, and points to the difficulty involved in giving the essence of games: something that they all have in common in virtue of which they are all games. There is no such essence. There are of course resemblances; but there is no single defining set of features that runs through them all. We characterize them all as games in virtue of a series of various overlapping resemblances; these Wittgenstein calls "family resemblances" and likens to the way that we notice various resemblances between members of the same family.

In the case of language, what we have is not a common defining essence across all uses of language in virtue of which we count something as language, but "a complicated network of similarities overlapping and criss-crossing" between various linguistic activities. There is also a network of logical relations between different linguistic activities which enables us to speak of the whole system of *language* as such.

In the *Tractatus* there was a single essential nature to language and a single boundary between sense and nonsense; in the later philosophy of the *Philosophical investigations* we have a patchwork of related languages with internal boundaries and although they may change, the ignoring of them produces confusion the sum total of which constitutes our whole language. Wittgenstein refers to the variety of kinds of ways that language can be used and the functions it can have as "language-games". Outside the boundary of *all* language-games collectively, we do not have language at all, but nonsense.

Wittgenstein is not denying that we can lay down special technical definitions, in science, say; but this is not the way words acquire meaning or their meaning is understood in ordinary language. Once we begin to use a word or concept in normal contexts the definition will break down, and be outgrown, as we extend the application of the concept.

The notion of "family resemblance" applies to the characterization of language itself. Wittgenstein draws an analogy between language and games, and so refers to language-games. But the resemblance between games and language is only partial. He uses the term language-game sometimes to apply to parts of actual language, sometimes to restricted or different imaginary languages, and sometimes to the whole of human language. He is of course concerned not with any particular human language (like English or German), but rather with features of human language in general. Examples of language-games Wittgenstein gives are, among others, giving and obeying orders, describing, storytelling, joking, asking, praying, speculating. Each language-game has a "grammar" which describes, but does not explain, the possible ways that concepts can be combined within the game. We are making a grammatical, not an empirical, point, if we say, "Every measuring rod has a length"; its denial would be ungrammatical, and it is impossible in a different way from a physical impossibility.

Wittgenstein's position is that there is nothing that underlies the whole of language which explains its meaning. Language forms a patchwork of logically related activities which, unlike games, more than merely resemble one another: they are interrelated. Thus we may *order* someone to answer a *question*. The justification for saying that words have a certain meaning does not reside in some single mode of justification and cannot reside in something postulated that is hidden from view beyond language. What justifies the meaning of a word, so far as it *can* be justified, to be of any use to us in giving a justification, must not be something hidden (as the *Tractatus* suggests) but something open to view. If we are to give a logical justification for a word having a certain meaning, it must be in terms of features that are open to view and not hidden. What is hidden is not available to us, and so could not be used in giving a justification of our understanding of the meaning of linguistic expressions. What is available to view is the various ways that language is *used* or employed in different contexts. If we want to give the meaning of a word, the best we can do is to *describe the use* of the word in various contexts; eventually there is no further justification for the use we can give. Ultimately we describe, saying: *that is* how we use it.

If we were asked, "How many goals have been scored in this chess game?", the question would not pose a problem which needs to be solved on its face value, like "How many goals have been scored in this football match?"; rather, we would explain the rules of chess, and that "goal" is "ungrammatical" (in Wittgenstein's sense of the term) in this context. So it is with language-games; propositions are ungrammatical in involving words transferred from a context in which they have a use to a context where they are inappropriate, that is, they have no use. Many philosophical problems are a result of not noticing the transference of a word from one context where it has a use to another where it does not have a use. For example, we may transfer talk of "mechanism" or "object" in a physical context to the context of talk about minds. We produce nonsense by trying to transfer talk outside any and all linguistic frameworks.

It is important to note that Wittgenstein is not giving a "use theory of meaning", as if the use *explains* the meaning; the use in various contexts just *is* the meaning; meaning and use are identical. There is no single feature common to all the various uses to which language can be put; there is a multiplicity of uses. It is not as if the meaning of a word were one thing and its use another; a word gets its meaning in its being used in particular ways. Ultimately the meaning of a word does not determine its use; rather, the use of a word is its meaning; and without a certain sort of use the word does not have a meaning which could determine its use.

However, not every difference in use entails a difference in meaning, so is it right to identify meaning and use? What is involved here are matters of degree; we do not have to suppose that expressions which we regard as having the same meaning must have identical common uses which are *the* use; that would be to revert to the kind of essentialism Wittgenstein rejects; all that we need suppose is that there is sufficient overlap in use for us to say the meaning is the same. Analogously it is perfectly correct to say a mallet and a plane are both carpentry tools because of what is done with them and the contexts in which they are used, even though their use is not identical. If the uses to which a word was put failed to overlap at all, we would say that we have a word with different meanings, for giving a description of how we would use the word in various situations is what the meaning of the word amounts to. If words failed to overlap by the criteria (whatever they turn out to be) which determine their correct application that is, uses that are recognized by others—we would then be likely to say that the words each had a different meaning. That a word has a meaning at all depends on there being *some* agreement in use. But the point at which a change of meaning occurs is not necessarily clear-cut. Here Wittgenstein gives up the *Tractatus* requirement of definiteness of meaning.

A good analogy is with money; something becomes money through the way it is used. That something is money consists in what people are willing to do with it, such as take it in exchange for goods and services as virtually everyone else is willing to do. It was soon found to be unnecessary for coins to be made from gold or even to be backed by gold. It is not something intrinsic to the coin which constitutes its being money. If this is doubted we have only to think of the way cigarettes became money during the Second World War and at other times; cigarettes being money was a matter of the way they were used.

To understand the meaning of a word is to be able to participate in using the word appropriately in a language-game. To use a word or other linguistic expression in a language-game is in turn to be involved with using language in a certain "form of life" certain natural activities and behaviour which arise from human needs, interests and purposes. Language is autonomous in the sense that its justification must lie within it, but is nevertheless evolved from human practices and human needs. At the basic level it is agreement in these practices the agreement as to how to go on that makes meaningful language possible but does *not* justify that meaning. That is, the form of life is not what justifies our saying that certain words have such-and-such a meaning; but that we naturally go on in certain ways is what makes agreement in use hence meaning possible. The form of life is what we have to "accept as given"; it involves the most basic features of the human condition which stem from the fundamental facts about human nature and the world, "the common behaviour of mankind". That certain fundamental things are unavoidable features of human beings, and that we share needs and interests, is what enables agreement as to ways of going on in certain situations to get going in the first place. These common needs and interests and our agreement to go on naturally in certain ways are what makes agreement as to use possible. That these ways of going on are often unavoidable means that they are not open to choice; they are not arbitrary; they are simply what we do in a given situation, and lie beyond being justified or unjustified. It is possible that we could go on differently, but in fact in certain ways we do not: we agree.

We can no more ask for rational justification for the givens of human life, or say that they are unjustified, than we can ask for a rational justification rather than a causal explanation for a tree falling on us. Rational justification, once we have exhausted all the ways in which we can justify our doing something in such-and-such a way, must come to an end in a description. To lay to rest our philosophical search for ultimate foundations, we have to come to see that certain of our human activities for example, deriving one proposition from another are ultimately groundless and not justified, but *also* that they are not the kinds of activities that can be further grounded or justified; therefore their lacking such a grounding is not a deficiency in those activities. Such ways of going on are neither justified nor unjustified, rather they are fundamental facts about human nature and the way humans agree to go on in various situations. That there is no rational justification does not show that what we do is irrational or confused, it could be simply non-rational: what we do. In this it is possible to see some similarity between Hume and Wittgenstein: they agree that rational justification has its limits, and what we are left with are the most basic things that human beings cannot help doing; and it now makes no sense to ask for rational justification for matters that are not a product of reasoning at all.

The possession of our most basic concepts such as inferring, recognizing, assent and dissent is not something that can be further explained or justified, because any explanation would *presuppose* those concepts or some others. There is a great diversity of practices or language-games and each involves basic concepts which it is senseless to question; it is senseless because without taking those concepts for granted as "given", the kinds of justifications that take place within the language-games could not even arise. Having these concepts means we can take part in the language-game or practice; but if one does not have them, then the possession of those concepts cannot be further justified by anything else within the language-game, for that would already involve accepting the basic concepts the language-game involves. If the use of expressions within two practices is sufficiently different that is, there is little or no overlap in use then it is not that we disagree in our judgements involving these concepts; rather, we are simply saying something else. Wittgenstein says the practice, or language-game, and the form of life of which it is a part, is given. It is not given in the sense of being a self-evident logical foundation; it is given in the sense that there is no further justification for the whole practice, for justification only makes sense within practices. The form of life which involves a language-game is neither reasonable nor unreasonable. That is not to say that up to a point the normally accepted bedrock of a language-game cannot alter, but there are limits, for beyond a certain point we will say not that we are dealing with a different linguistic practice, but rather that we are not dealing with a language at all. If we cannot identify any part of some behaviour as manifesting the possession of any of our concepts such as assent and dissent then we will say that what we are witnessing is not language at all. It might be thought that the meaning of a word could be finally settled and justified as being such-and-such by citing a rule for its use. We can first note there is no such rule-book for ordinary language; but even if there were it would not help. Any rule can be interpreted in an indefinite number of ways. Suppose I am asked why I interpret a rule in a certain way. I could go on to cite a further rule which says how the original rule is to be interpreted. But suppose I am then asked why I interpret the further rule in a certain way. Eventually this process must come to an end and I will have exhausted all justifications; I will have to say: "This is what we do", which gives a description, not a justification. It makes perfect sense to say that one can act correctly, in accordance with a rule follow a rule even though one can give no justification for why one acts that way and interprets it thus. Following a rule amounts to acting in a customary way in specific cases. In the end it is not rules that determine the meaning of words but use of words that determines the rules for use that we might formulate; the rules for use do not exist prior to what we do with the words in the language. That a certain rule can be "interpreted" substituting one rule for another in a certain way eventually depends upon there being an agreed natural particular way of going on, perhaps after some kind of natural response to training. Some examples will illustrate these points.

(i) We might give a justification for saying *X* is red by comparing *X* against a colour-chart. How would we know that what we had identified on the chart as red was red? We might say it was because "red" was printed there. But how would we know we were using the chart correctly? A mental colour-chart would have the same problem. We have reached bedrock; we have the capacity to identify the colours of things thanks to the way we naturally respond to certain training. No rational justification can be given as a whole for our adopting classification by colour-concepts.

(ii) Suppose we asked someone to accept the simple logical theorem *modus ponens:* "If *p* then *q, p,* therefore *q*". Here "*p*" and "*q*" stand for any propositions you like. What further justification could be given of this? If a person cannot see this, then it is not clear how we could go on to offer further justification as to why, given "(if *p* then *q*) and *p*", he should logically infer "*q*". The person has parted company with us even before the game of logic begins; he is playing a different game. Even if something further could be offered in justification, we would have to come to an end in a natural way of going on. For a rule does not say of itself how it must be interpreted.

(iii) Wittgenstein gives the following example. Suppose we are given the following table or schema where the letters can be used as orders as to how we should move about:

a →

b ←

c ↑

d ↓

We are then given an order, *aacaddd*. We look up in the table the arrow corresponding to each letter; we get:

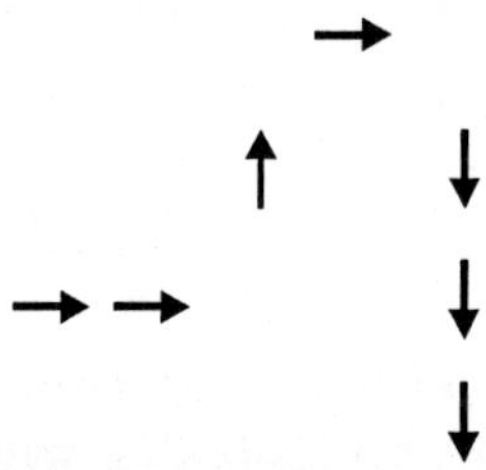

suppose someone read not straight across the table but diagonally instead? Thus he or she would proceed to read the table according to the following schema:

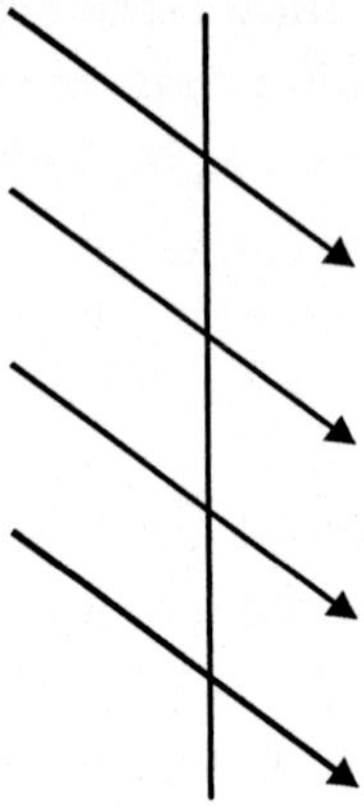

And there are many other possible schemata. What could we do? Construct another table on how to read the first? But this cannot go on indefinitely; eventually one simply has to gather or catch on to what is wanted, and no further justification can be given, for *any* rule can be variously interpreted.

We cannot be compelled to do logic and use language in a certain way unless we already take for granted a framework within which disputes about the correct way of going on can arise. The meaning of the rules is generated by the way they are used; we then impose the truth or falsity of a statement is possible, then we must mean the same by the statement. That we mean the same will be determined by agreement in use. Take the statement that "*x* is *F*"; that two people can be in disagreement as to the truth of this statement presupposes that the meaning of "*F*" for the two people is the same; whether it is the same is established by how the two people use or apply "*F*" in particular contexts. Disagreement as to whether "*x* is red" is true or false presupposes an agreement over what we mean by "red". This brings us to Wittgenstein's "private language argument". Wittgenstein argues that language is communal in nature: it depends upon agreement in use within a community. If it were possible to construct a logically private language then this would refute Wittgenstein's view. We must note that such a case must be *logically* private, so that it is impossible for anyone else to understand the language; that is, it must be untranslatable into any other language. Such a case is where we supposedly give names to our private sensations by a sort of "inner" ostensive definition; by this is meant the association of a word with a private mental image which is then the meaning of the word. This is a special case of the meaning of a word being the object for which it stands. Suppose that I keep a diary, and write down "*S*", intending it to stand for a certain sensation; I then aim to write down "*S*" on subsequent occasions when the sensation occurs. How can I tell that I am applying "*S*" correctly on subsequent occasions? One suggestion might be that I could call up from memory the original sensation and check that in applying "*S*" to my current sensation I am applying it correctly. But how do I know that I have called up the right sensation from my memory? Do I go on to check that memory against a further memory? But in that case I have got no further, as the same problem would arise. Without there being some kind of independent objective check as to whether I am applying "*S*" correctly, we cannot speak of being correct or incorrect at all, since there is no distinction between merely seeming right and being right. No consequences follow from my applying the word in one way rather than another; it cannot clash with any established use; and so it is not proper to speak of "*S*" being correctly or incorrectly used. Hence, "*S*" has not been given a meaning; a logically private naming of sensations is not possible. This may imply that no logically private language is possible. The philosophical import of Wittgenstein's views derives to a large extent from two important connected ideas:

(I) That there is no essence to language: there is no single way that words and other linguistic expressions acquire their meaning by reference to something external to language.

(II) That the meaning of a word and other linguistic expressions varies with their use in particular contexts or practices.

These two points together have the effect of undermining much of traditional philosophy and its problems. They attack the idea that philosophy can establish and study the true or real meaning of certain words which express concepts. There is no independent absolute standard from which the question of *the* correct meaning could be judged or arise, since words and other linguistic expressions have meaning only in their use in actual or concrete human practices. If we attempt to step outside all cases where an expression is actually used, then it ceases to have any meaning, and the question of a meaning being correct does not arise.

Traditional philosophy tends to claim that it is examining the real meaning of "knowledge", and other concepts, as opposed to their meaning in ordinary usage. But there are no grounds for claiming that the philosophical meaning is superior. The sceptic claims that we do not have knowledge in situations where it is perfectly obvious that according to ordinary usage we do have knowledge but it is in ordinary usage that the meaning of "knowledge" is established; therefore the sceptic's meaning of "knowledge" is different.

Wittgenstein is not saying that the ordinary usage of these concepts is unalterable. The point is that there is no way of establishing that a term has only one correct meaning, disregarding the meaning arising from the ordinary employment of the term. If a term ceases to be applied in any of the cases where it normally has a use, then we will say that it has at least altered its meaning. To argue that this fact is philosophically unimportant relies on the idea that there is some single correct meaning of words which is their true meaning established in all cases by something other than their actual function or use. Philosophers use words in ways different from their ordinary use. Wittgenstein posts reminders that words do have other than philosophical uses and that if philosophers uses the words in ways they would never be used in ordinary contexts, then he must mean something different by them. Concepts have different meanings in different contexts, and no one context can claim to be superior to the rest in giving the single correct meaning of the concept. The denial of this supposes that there is more to the meaning of a word or linguistic expression than the description of how it is used, functions, or is applied in a given context; it supposes that somehow, behind the description of how an expression is used, there is something else by which we can identify its real or essential meaning. The view that posits something else giving the real meaning of a term beyond the meaning resulting from a term's actual agreed use is the view that Wittgenstein rejects.

What becomes of the traditional problems of philosophy? Why does Wittgenstein have so little to offer in the way of traditional philosophical solutions? The answer to this is that Wittgenstein's account of language means that many of the traditional problems of philosophy disappear as problems. The problems we are referring to are such as "our knowledge of the existence of the external world", "our knowledge of the existence of other minds", "that we cannot really know that someone is in pain, but can only infer it from their behaviour"; and such problems involve concepts such as "knowledge", "being", "object", "I", "proposition", "name". Given that traditional philosophy cannot claim the right to say it has identified the true or real meaning of these terms, Wittgenstein makes explicit the fact that they have a use in circumstances in which there are no problems of the sort characterized by philosophy. There is a perfectly good sense in which we do know whether other people have minds, and whether they are in pain, and we can describe the circumstances in which we employ the words involved. If it is said that we do not really *know* in such cases, then we must say, precisely because there is an attempt to exclude the use of "know" in circumstances central to establishing its use and hence its meaning, that "know" must be being used in a different sense from normal. The meaning of a concept such as "know" is its use in appropriate circumstances; therefore it makes perfect sense to say that we know in those circumstances. There is nowhere beyond a description of actual agreed use from where we could say that it is wrong to speak of knowledge in those cases. If we do not mean by "knowledge" what we mean in cases where "knowledge" is most normally used, then what do we mean by it?

What the sceptical position is supposed to show is that correctly establishing the satisfaction of the criteria of application of a term *"X"* does not show that anything actually corresponds to the theoretical or ontological assumptions that are normally involved in the application of *"X"*. The sceptic about knowledge does not doubt that we in fact clearly distinguish cases of knowing from not-knowing in the sense of consistently applying "know" in certain circumstances and withholding it in others; but this fails to show that the cases where we are linguistically correct (by the normal criteria of our language) in applying "know" can be justified as cases of knowing. The reply to this is that if the cases in which we normally use the word "know" are not what we *mean* by "know", then it is not clear what the sceptic can mean when he says that in ordinary cases we do not "know". The sceptic must mean we do not "know" (giving some special sense to this word), which is to construe "know" independent of its ordinary use. But then the proposition "I know in circumstances *abc*" cannot be logically contradicted by the proposition "You do not in circumstances *abc*". Otherwise it would be like saying that "I fight in circumstances *abc*" is logically contradicted by the proposition "You do not jump in circumstances *abc*". We may also take the view that if the sceptic fails to pick up on publicly established criteria for the usage of terms, then he does not mean anything at all by " ", since it has no use. And even if he does give a new meaning to " " (perhaps by definition, or by indicating the criteria which have to be satisfied for its use), the onus is on the sceptic to show why it is that we should accept his radically different use (hence different meaning) as the one that should be satisfied before anything can count as knowing instead of the one we all normally accept.

5

Ayer and Popper Positivism and Falsificationism in Philosophy

Introduction

A common historical and intellectual connection is the Vienna Circle; this was a group that met in Vienna during the 1920s and 1930s and developed the philosophy of logical positivism, which was intent on setting philosophy on a sure footing so that the scope of its tasks was clear. Logical positivism, by way of a theory of meaning, involves the elimination of much of traditional philosophy, in particular metaphysics and also theology, as literally meaningless. What this amounted to was the view that the investigation of any substantial facts about the world was the province of science alone, not philosophy, which could be concerned only with conceptual elucidation and the linguistic task of precise definition. Both Ayer and Popper attended the meetings of the Vienna Circle, but whereas Ayer initially became a powerful advocate of its views, Popper, although deeply interested, like the Vienna Circle, in the philosophy and methodology of science, was critical of logical positivism. Popper aims to demarcate science from non-science so as to understand better the nature of scientific knowledge. Non-science includes pseudo-science: areas which are not scientific but claim to be so. It does not follow from this that what is non-science, including pseudo-science, is thereby literally meaningless, as logical positivism supposed, or even that it is untrue. Ayer has always had a great interest in the problem of meaning, which Popper regards as a largely fruitless field of philosophical investigation if regarded as an end in itself. What perhaps unites Ayer and Popper, although they are by no means alone in this, is their view that the heart of philosophy is epistemology, and in particular the nature of empirical knowledge.

Ayer

Alfred Jules Ayer (1910–89) was educated at Eton and Christ Church, Oxford; his tutor in philosophy at Oxford was Gilbert Ryle (1900–76). After graduating, he thought of going to Cambridge to study with Wittgenstein; instead he went to study in Vienna in 1932 in order to find out more about the logical positivist philosophy of the Vienna Circle. After a short period in Vienna he returned to Oxford and became a lecturer in philosophy at Christ Church. In 1936 he published *Language, truth and logic.* While we must allow for differences within the logical positivist movement, *Language, truth and logic* states clearly what is essential to the doctrine of logical positivism. In 1940 he joined the Welsh Guards and worked for most of the war in military intelligence. He returned to Oxford in 1945 to become Dean of Wadham College. From 1946 to 1959 he was Grote Professor of the Philosophy of Mind and Logic at University College London. From 1959 until his retirement in 1978 he was Wykeham Professor of Logic in the University of Oxford. In 1970 he was knighted. Although he came to reject the most radical proposals of logical positivism, Ayer remained a close follower of the British tradition of empiricism and logical analysis. It was Wittgenstein's *Tractatus* that set Ayer on the course which led to *Language, truth and logic.* However, the greatest influences on Ayer were Russell and Hume. He continued to admire Bertrand Russell, regarding him as probably the greatest philosopher of the twentieth century; and, like Russell, he was an enthusiastic atheist. Ayer also became interested in the American pragmatists, such as William James (1842–1910). Again, like Russell, Ayer was a passionate advocate of reason, and thought that intellectual honesty demanded that we seek sufficient evidence for any beliefs that might be proposed for acceptance.

The motivation for logical positivism stems from two connected lines of thought: (I) the unity of science, and (II) the elimination of metaphysics. In short, this amounts to the view that really all science forms a single system; it alone is able to give true characterizations of the nature of the world which can in the end be exhaustive. The unity of science means that all branches of scientific inquiry have a common epistemological basis: it is that determining the truth or falsity of scientific theories about the nature of the world depends entirely on an appeal to the evidence of experience and observation. The elimination of metaphysics complements this, because metaphysics commonly supposes there is some way of determining the nature of the world perhaps its real or essential nature beyond appearances other than by an appeal to experience and observation. The apparent assertions by metaphysics about the nature of the world are, according to logical positivism, not true or false, but nonsense literally meaningless. With the elimination of metaphysics as a source of knowledge about the world, science is unified as a system of factual propositions, that is, statements whose truth or falsity and, indeed, meaning depend on their being open to the test of the facts of experience.

Propositions are what is determinately true or false: that is, they are *literally meaningful.* Propositions are what literally meaningful indicative sentences (sentences which grammatically appear to state things) of any particular language express; this is important because sentences of different languages can express the same proposition, as in *it is raining* and *il pleut.* The criterion for a sentence is that it is grammatically well formed, that is a necessary condition for it to be meaningful, otherwise it is mere gibberish, such as "foot a fight will". The logical positivists argue that many grammatically well formed sentences do not express genuine propositions, although being grammatically well formed sentences they may appear to do so. Sentences that appear to express a proposition, whether they do so or not, Ayer calls putative propositions or statements. The logical positivists argue that all genuine propositions are either analytic/ tautologies or verifiable by experience; statements that is, indicative sentences which appear to express propositions which are neither analytic nor verifiable by experience are literally meaningless or nonsense. Sentences and statements that do not express genuine propositions may be meaningful in some other way they may have poetic or emotive significance but they are not *literally* meaningful. If a statement is literally meaningless, then the question of its truth or falsity cannot arise.

It has to be the case that a distinction is made between sentences being meaningful in some broader sense than *literally* meaningful because otherwise the criterion of literal meaningfulness would have no possible application; in order to discover if a statement is analytic or empirically verifiable, we already have to understand what it means.

A sentence expresses an *analytic proposition* if, and only if, its truth or falsity follows solely from the definition of the terms it contains. Thus "All bachelors are unmarried" is analytic, since the predicate "unmarried" is part of the definition of "bachelor"; establishing the truth or falsity of the proposition consists in merely unpacking the definition of its terms. The truth or falsity of analytic propositions depends entirely on the meaning of the symbols in the sentence the proposition expresses. Analytic propositions are true or false, and can be known to be so, *a priori,* that is, independently of the evidence of experience; they are also devoid of factual content as they make no claim about the world; their truth or falsity is compatible with any evidence of experience whatsoever. That which is necessary is that which must be and cannot be otherwise. If an analytic proposition is true, it is *necessarily* true it must be true and cannot be false. If an analytic proposition is false, it is *necessarily* false it must be false and cannot be true. The denial of a true analytic proposition implies a logical contradiction.

A sentence expresses an *empirically verifiable proposition* if, and only if, some possible experience is relevant to determining its truth or falsity. The truth or falsity of such empirically verifiable or factually significant propositions cannot be determined merely by examination of the definition or meaning of the symbols in the sentence the proposition expresses. Thus "The cat is on the mat" is a factually significant proposition; its truth or falsity does not follow from the meaning of the terms it contains it is not an analytic but a synthetic proposition; its truth or falsity can only be determined *a posteriori* by consulting experience. That which is contingent is that which may or may not be: that which could be otherwise. If an empirically verifiable proposition is true, then it is *contingently* true it is true, but could have been false. If an empirically verifiable proposition is *contingently* false, it is false, but could have been true. The denial of an empirically verifiable proposition never implies a logical contradiction.

The two classes of analytic and empirically verifiable statements are mutually exclusive and collectively exhaustive of all literally meaningful statements: they are the totality of genuine propositions. That is, it is a necessary and sufficient condition for a statement to be literally meaningful, and so capable of being true or false a proposition that it be either analytic or empirically verifiable. Put another way, a statement is a genuine proposition if and only if it is either analytic or empirically verifiable, otherwise it is nonsense.

Metaphysics generally attempts to describe the essential structure of reality: what the real world *must* ultimately be like according to intellectual argument, although it may appear otherwise. Plato speaks of fixed "Forms" beyond the flux of experience and space and time, but accessible to the intellect, defining the "whatness" of things; Leibniz speaks of non-spatial "monads" as the indivisible, indestructible substance of the world which remain the same through all natural change; Hegel speaks of the fully real as "The Absolute", the universe as ultimately a self-thinking totality. There are also theological statements asserting the existence and nature of an eternal transcendent God outside space and time.

Metaphysics, with theology, is eliminated as literally meaningless because what it characteristically proffers as propositions are not genuine propositions at all. The need to be clear about what are genuine propositions arises from the fact that we are misled by the surface appearance of statements in metaphysics into thinking they express propositions; but we know they do not express propositions because they do not say anything whose truth or falsity can be determined in the only two ways possible: by their being analytic or by their being empirically verifiable. Metaphysics is disposed of not because it is false, but because it is composed of statements which are largely nonsense; it may appear to be composed of propositions statements that can be true or false but really it is composed of statements incapable of being either true or false because their truth or falsity cannot be established even in principle by the only two ways possible. If we are to say that any of the statements of metaphysics is literally meaningful, then it must be translatable into statements that are analytic or empirically verifiable. However, if a statement is analytic, it tells us nothing about the world, and if it is empirically verifiable, then it ceases to be a metaphysical statement at all, but merely becomes part of the body of scientific theory testable by observation. Neither translation is congenial to the metaphysician who wishes to contend that his statements both say something about the world are factually significant and cannot be settled by empirical verification; but it is impossible, Ayer argues, that both these conditions can be simultaneously satisfied. Indeed, metaphysics often claims to speak of the world behind or beyond the world as it appears. Either a statement says something about the world, in which case it is empirically verifiable, or a statement says nothing about the world; no statement can be about the world and not be empirically verifiable. Therefore metaphysics, which purports to produce truths and refutations of falsehoods about the nature of the world or reality in statements which are empirically unverifiable, is impossible; it produces only literal nonsense. Metaphysics makes only literally meaningless assertions and raises spurious questions; it is, in short, composed of meaningless pseudo-propositions which have the appearances of genuine propositions. It follows that there can in reality be no genuine disputes between metaphysicians: if "*p*" is a metaphysical statement, it is literally meaningless, but then "not-*p*" is also meaningless.

Logical positivism holds that all *a priori* propositions are analytic and, although necessary, are necessary only because they are factually empty: they say nothing about the world, but reveal only the conventional meanings of words. All *a posteriori* propositions are synthetic and contingent, but they are, whether true or false, factually informative: they say something about the world. Contrary to the view of a philosopher such as Kant, there can be no *a priori*, necessary propositions that are synthetic. These considerations can be summarized in the following diagram:

	Analytic/tautological /necessary	Synthetic/contingent
a priori	A	B
a posteriori	C	D

All genuine propositions that is to say, all propositions fall into either, but not both, of the shaded areas: *A* and *D*. No propositions fall into the unshaded areas: *B* and *C*. There are therefore only two classes of genuine propositions:

A: a priori/analytic/necessary.

D: a posteriori/synthetic/contingent.

All statements that fail to fall into the classes *A* or *D* are not propositions at all; they are incapable of being true or false they are not literally meaningful although they may be meaningful in some other way.

Thus, in so far as metaphysics does contain literally meaningful propositions, it consists either of analytic propositions, which tell us nothing about the world, whose truth or falsity can be determined *a priori,* or synthetic propositions, which do purport to tell us something about the world, whose truth or falsity can be determined only *a posteriori.* There is no special class of metaphysical propositions which are at once *a priori* and tell us something about the world: no facts can be known *a priori.*

All the statements of logic, mathematics and geometry express non-empirical, non-factual, propositions, that are *a priori* valid and necessary in virtue of their being analytic or tautologies: their truth depends solely on the meaning of the symbols of which their statements are composed. They are also devoid of factual content; the reason such truths are necessary is just that they do not make any assertions about the world that could be confuted or confirmed by the evidence of experience. We do not have to suppose, in order to explain our *a priori* knowledge of necessary truths, that the truths refer to some realm of entities transcending experience. All *a priori* analytic truths including those of logic, mathematics and geometry are not *about* anything at all, but simply reflect the meaning we have chosen to give to linguistic signs.

Philosophers such as Kant have argued that there is a special class of propositions which are *a priori* synthetic and necessary. Kant accepted that propositions such as "All bachelors are unmarried" are analytic, necessary, their denial implying a contradiction; the concept of the predicate is implicity contained in the concept or definition of the subject, so to assert that someone is a bachelor, but not unmarried, is a logical contradiction. Such propositions, Kant agreed, tell us nothing about the world. However, Kant thought that the propositions of arithmetic and geometry were at once *a priori* and synthetic.

He then felt obliged to construct an elaborate philosophical system in order to explain how this was possible. How could a proposition which is synthetic, so that its denial does not entail a logical contradiction, be true, and be known to be true, *a priori!* It appeared to Kant that arithmetical propositions such as 7+5=12 were known *a priori,* and were necessary truths, and yet were *synthetic* because it was possible to think of 7+5 without thinking of 12. Ayer argues that this is a purely psychological point. Kant's explanation for our knowledge of synthetic *a priori* truths is that they characterize the form we impose on the matter of sensation and so are valid for the world only as it appears. Ayer thinks such an explanation quite unnecessary: the truth of 7+5=12 and the *a priori* knowledge of that truth depend entirely on the conventional definition of the terms in it, and it is thus quite independent of empirical evidence or, *a priori.* The same argument applies to geometrical truths; such truths are not a description of physical space, they merely unravel whatever definition of the terms we started off with. Logical propositions such as "Either *p* or not-*p*" are true regardless of any facts of experience and depend for their truth entirely on the meaning of the signs composing them; they are tautologies because they always come out true regardless of what propositions are substituted in them provided the substitution is done uniformly. It follows that such analytic propositions, although necessary, are trivially true or devoid of factual content. The proposition "either it is raining or it is not raining" tells us nothing whatsoever about the weather, and is true independently of whatever the facts about the weather are; its truth excludes nothing at all.

If it is the case that all *a priori* propositions are analytic, how do we explain the usefulness of logic, mathematics and geometry, and their ability to surprise us? The explanation lies entirely in the limitations of our intellect. In the case of complex analytic propositions we are, as a matter of fact, intellectually incapable of seeing at once all the consequences of the definitions we adopt. To an intellect of sufficient power, the complex prepositional theorems of logic, mathematics and geometry would be of no more interest than *"A=A"* is to us. The interest for us of analytic propositions is that we cannot always see immediately everything that our definitions imply.

This brings us to what for Ayer is the function of philosophy. Philosophy cannot determine the nature of reality, as metaphysics would suggest. Any proposition concerning the nature of reality would be a factual scientific or common-sense proposition whose truth or falsity could be established only by the test of experience and not by philosophy as such. The function of philosophy, once it is demonstrated that metaphysics is literally meaningless, is analysis and clarification. Analysis is a branch of logic and consists of giving precise definitions of concepts, or presenting the logical consequences of definitions, of terms used in science and common sense; thus all the propositions of philosophy are analytic. The function of philosophy is to translate talk of one sort into logically equivalent talk of another sort, an activity which has purely linguistic significance. Philosophy itself can produce no new factual knowledge about the world but can only deduce the logical consequences of propositions whose truth or falsity, if they are not analytic and so devoid of factual content is determined by the facts.

It is important to establish more exactly what is meant by empirical verifiability in order to determine which non-analytic statements are propositions. Such propositions must in all cases be capable of being verified or falsified by experience. It is necessary, however, to make two sets of distinctions here:

(a) verification in practice

(a') verification in principle

(b) "strong" or conclusive verification

(b') "weak" or probabilistic verification.

In both cases Ayer says he adopts the more liberal of the two alternatives, (a') and (b'). The reason for this is that (a) would entail denying as literally meaningful all sorts of empirical propositions because we could not in fact verify them. Thus the proposition "There are mountains on a particular planet on the other side of the galaxy" is not a proposition which I could in fact verify; perhaps it never will be verified; nevertheless we know what *would* verify the proposition; we can conceive of certain logically possible observations which could *in principle* be made which would verify or falsify the proposition. There would be an inevitable tendency for (a) to lead to solipsism whereby my possible knowledge extended only as far as propositions describing my actual private experiences. Adopting (b) would also prove or exclude too much, for no empirical proposition can be *conclusively* verified or falsified; empirical observations can only render the truth or falsity of a proposition more or less probable. One reason for this is that, whatever empirical proposition we take, the conclusion or import we draw from observations relevant to determining the truth or falsity of the proposition will always depend on assuming the truth of certain other propositions describing the circumstances of the observation. But then the truth or falsity of these other propositions describing the initial conditions of the empirical test could themselves, if they are factually significant, be tested by experience, and so on. Also most of the propositions of natural science of the form "All *A* is *B*" would be rendered literally meaningless if we adopted (b) because we could not even in principle examine what is an open infinite class of cases; there may always be cases we have not examined, and there is no way of demonstrating that there are not such cases. In short, Ayer thinks all empirical propositions are *hypotheses* because there is no way of absolutely confirming or refuting such propositions.

Ayer admits that empirical hypotheses do not confront experience singly, but only as part of a system of propositions. Thus if an observation appears to verify or refute a given hypothesis, it is always logically possible for us to refuse to admit to the significance of the observation by modifying the other hypotheses that gave the observation its significance as evidence of a particular sort. Take the proposition "All trees have leaves"; suppose we test the truth or falsity of this proposition by making observations; whatever observations we make, they always depend on certain other empirical hypotheses connecting the observation and the proposition under test; for example, that we are not suffering from an illusion, or we have correctly identified something as a leaf. Some of the logical positivists argued that there is a class of isolated "basic propositions" about which it is impossible for us to be mistaken, and which can be conclusively confirmed or refuted by experience because they refer only to immediate experience. Ayer initially thought that any factually significant proposition involves using general classificatory terms (such as "red") which it is always possible to misapply, and so no factual proposition can be conclusively verified or refuted, since we can always find out we have made a mistake in the light of further evidence.

Thus, according to "weak" verifiability (b'), a genuine proposition a statement capable of being true or false if it is not analytic, is an empirical hypothesis the truth or falsity of which experiences could, in principle, render more or less probable. The purpose of formulating scientific theories is essentially predictive and pragmatic: it is therefore the very meaning of rational behaviour that we adopt those theories and methods which function to enable us to anticipate and control the course of our experiences. The function of theories, and the purpose of testing them, is to produce theories which are more efficient instruments for describing and anticipating experiences. Whether a theory will be successful in this way can be revealed not by *a priori* argument but only by its success in practice, but it is always logically possible that it may fail in cases we have not observed.

The "weak" verification principle thus states that all literally meaningful non-analytic statements are in principle verifiable by being rendered more or less probable by propositions which describe specific experiences; all other statements, apart from analytic ones, are literally meaningless. So all statements which are not analytic propositions and cannot be verified by experience are literally meaningless: they do not express a proposition at all. The verification principle gives a criterion for distinguishing the literally meaningless from the literally meaningful.

The attempt to give a precise formulation of empirical verifiability leads Ayer into difficulty. Ayer's initial version of the "weak" verifiability principle is: a non-analytic statement is a genuine factual proposition and thus not literally meaningless if we can deduce from it, along with certain other statements describing the conditions under which relevant observation could take place, some experiential proposition which refers to actual or possible experience (sense-contents), which cannot be deduced from those other statements alone. This formulation is, however, faulty as it excludes nothing as a literally meaningful proposition. If *N* is any statement you like, even one that is meaningless or metaphysical, and *O* is an experiential proposition, then *O* is deducible from [(if *N* then *O*) and *N*], without being deducible from *O* alone. This means that *N* would, by the criterion, be verifiable and hence a literally meaningful proposition even though it can be any statement at all. If we say that the "other statements" must be themselves factually significant, then we have got no further, since distinguishing factually significant statements was the point of the criterion, and we cannot assume we can distinguish which statements are factual. Ayer tries to rectify this fault, but he does not succeed in discovering a precise formulation that includes and excludes just what he wants.

One way of avoiding such problems would be to adopt the "strong" verification principle (b). In this case it is not just a matter of some empirical evidence being deducible which would be favourable or unfavourable to the truth of a proposition. "Strong" verification demands that the whole content of empirical or factual propositions, when fully analyzed, be expressible in wholly experiential propositions or observation-statements. Indeed, sometimes Ayer does seem to be working with the "strong" verifiability principle, whereby any genuine non-analytic proposition must, if we are to understand it, be translatable into propositions which describe only actual or possible experiences: sense-contents. A statement is then a factually significant proposition if and only if it can be completely defined as a logically equivalent set of purely experiential propositions which entails the original proposition and is entailed by it; the two statements are thus identical. The literal meaning of any factual proposition is then no more or less than a set of propositions describing some actual (categorical) or possible (hypothetical) experiences. The thinking behind this is that understanding the meaning of factually significant statements involves having, at least in principle, access to experiencing the factual conditions under which the proposition which expresses the statement would be true; that is, experience in principle of the truth-conditions of a proposition is required to understand the literal meaning of the statement it expresses. All factually significant propositions, such as "I am now sitting in front of a table", are abbreviations for a complex of propositions describing sense-contents alone. If any part of a statement appears to refer to something that is not even in principle a feature of actual or possible experience, then we can be sure that that part of the statement is without factual significance, and is meaningless unless it is analytic: that part is literal nonsense, what we say is literally "senseless". Only by expressing a non-analytic statement using symbols which wholly stand for sense-contents are we able to make literally intelligible *what* it is we are talking about.

It is surely this "strong" notion of verifiability that leads Ayer to various forms of philosophical analysis and reductionism. Such analyses are epistemological and are ontologically neutral. We find this reduction at work, for example, in his analysis of the concepts of a material object and of causation. In the case of material objects Ayer is led to phenomenalism: statements about material objects, if they are meaningful at all, must be wholly translatable into experiential propositions which do not mention material objects; what we mean when we talk about "material objects" is nothing more than some set of actual or possible sense-experiences. Such a translation defines "material object". This disposes of the problem of the existence of the external world arising from our making inferences from propositions concerning our experiences to propositions referring to material objects, because there is no gap in the end between experiences and material objects: to talk of material objects is just to talk of certain ordered collections of actual or possible experiences, and the set of propositions describing particular sense-contents is identical to a proposition describing a material object. The same analysis applies to causation. Ayer agrees with Hume that "*C* causes *E*" is not a logical relation: if "*C* causes *E*" is a non-analytic, factual, proposition then to assert *C* occurs but deny *E* occurs is never a logical contradiction. To say that "*C* causes *E*" is to say no more than that "whenever *C*, then, under certain circumstances, *E*"; there is nothing further in our experience, and indeed nothing further at all, to which the concept of the "necessary connection" of *C* and *E* could correspond. Causality amounts to no more than the definition "invariable association in a potentially infinite number of possible cases". Generally, to avoid talking literal nonsense one must specify what feature of actual or possible experience the talk describes.

The "self" is also not meaningfully identifiable with any non-experiential soul or mental substance, but is, like a material object logically constructed out of sense-contents. The way in which we think of the minds of others presents problems, however, because we have in principle no access to their sense-contents, but only to their behaviour. This produces an incoherent asymmetry whereby the ascription of mental states to myself is phrased in "mental" sense-contents, whereas its ascription to others is phrased in "physical" or "behavioural" sense-contents.

Logical positivism has a dilemma. The problem with adopting "strong" verifiability is that although it excludes statements that Ayer wishes to regard as literally meaningless, it also excludes statements he would wish to regard as meaningful. Ayer came to think later that the complete reduction of propositions about material objects to sense-contents was not possible, because no finite set of propositions referring to sensory experience was ever logically equivalent to a statement referring to a physical object. No finite set of observation-statements can give the necessary and sufficient conditions which would constitute the truth that *X* is a physical object, since further, logically possible evidence further experiences may show we must have been mistaken. So no finite set of propositions referring to sense-experiences can conclusively verify the proposition that *X* is a material object. Hence the problem with "strong" verifiability is that it implies that most, perhaps all, of the statements of natural science are meaningless. The problem with "weak" verifiability is that although plausibly it permits the statements of science and common sense as literally meaningful, factual, propositions, it fails to exclude those statements which Ayer wishes to regard as metaphysical and meaningless.

Take, for example, the statement "God exists": the same considerations apply to "God does not exist". Ayer wants to say that such an assertion is literally meaningless rather than false. But it is not excluded by the "weak" verification principle, for someone might admit that a particular experience was evidence for or against the existence of God thereby qualifying "God exists" as a literally meaningful proposition without thereby having to admit that what is meant by "God" and "His existing" is wholly exhausted by those evidential experiential propositions. Only by adopting the "strong" verification principle is there hope of identifying "God exists" as literally meaningless and so eliminating it. However, no sophisticated religious believer is likely to admit that what he means by God existing is nothing more than some actual or possible sense-experiences—for example, the observed intricateness and orderliness of nature—even if he might admit it as evidence of God's existence.

Ayer's analysis of apparent ethical and aesthetic statements "statements of value" concludes they are not genuine propositions at all; they are without literal meaning. They are not factual synthetic statements, but rather *expressions* of feelings of approval or disapproval, which may affect others so they feel the same way. Value statements are not about anything they do not even describe the fact that there is a subjective psychological state which constitutes a feeling rather, they are an expression *of* feeling, akin to a cry of pain or grunt of satisfaction. Expressions of value are therefore neither rational nor irrational: they are just a piece of non-rational behaviour.

Since value statements are incapable of truth or falsity, then no two value statements can conflict. If we argue with someone over value, it must be over what are the facts concerning the situation which prompted our feeling.

For the statement "Every genuine proposition must be either analytic or empirically verifiable" appears itself to be neither analytic nor empirically verifiable, in which case it is self-defeating and the "verification principle" is literally meaningless and incapable of truth or falsity. Logical positivism is not the first or the last philosophy to saw off the branch on which it is sitting. One response to this is to say that the principle is not a statement, but a prescriptive rule which we ought to adopt. But the problem with that is there is no way of showing why the rule should be adopted.

Popper

Karl Raimund Popper was born in Vienna in 1902. Although his parents were Jewish, they were baptized into the Protestant Lutheran Church before their children were born. The circumstances in which he was brought up were bookish and intellectual. His father was doctor of law of the University of Vienna and, as well as practising as a lawyer, he was also a scholar. With this background Popper began reading early about philosophical, scientific and political matters. In 1918 he enrolled at the University of Vienna and sampled a wide range of lecture courses, but concentrated his attention on mathematics and physics. After university he taught mathematics and physics in secondary schools. During this time he took a keen interest in left-wing politics, although his later work was greatly concerned with the totalitarian dangers of socialist and Marxist mass collectivization and of the belief in inevitable laws of historical development. His resistance to doctrines claiming access to final truths and dogmatism led him to favour individualism and piecemeal evolutionary social change rather than grand revolutionary change, also tentative solutions to social problems against a background of the greatest possible freedom for the expression of opinion and criticism which is characteristic of an open society. The chief culprits attacked by Popper are Plato, Hegel and Marx.

Popper had contacts with the logical positivism of the Vienna Circle, but he was never a logical positivist, and instead became one of its critics, despite a common interest in the methods of science. The root of Popper's criticism was that questions of meaning were of relatively little importance; what concerned him was the status of theories and their testing. The logical positivists held that, apart from the propositions of logic and mathematics, all literally meaningful statements were empirical and scientific. Popper never held that all non-logical statements that were not scientific were meaningless.

Popper's "criterion of demarcation" was, unlike the logical positivists' criterion, concerned with the distinction not between the meaningful and the meaningless but between science and non-science. Non-science includes pseudo-science, which consists in intellectual activities that claim to be scientific, but are not. Before the Second World War, Popper left Austria, and from 1937 to 1945 he taught philosophy at the University of New Zealand. He came to England in 1946. He remained on the outside of philosophical activities as practised in both Oxford and Cambridge, and received greatest intellectual sustenance from those who were not primarily philosophers such as the art historian E.H. Gombrich and the economist and political theorist F.A. Hayek. In 1949 Popper was made Professor of Logic and Scientific Method at the London School of Economics; and this position he held for the rest of his university career. He was knighted in 1965. Popper's work has been enormously influential in the philosophy of science, and on the methodology of the social sciences. It is possible to identify three important connected strands of thought in Popper's philosophy: (a) the solution of the problem of induction, (b) the problem of demarcating science from non-science, (c) the importance of maximizing criticism and maintaining a "critical attitude" as essential for rationality and vital for the growth of knowledge. The essential nature of philosophy involves the critical questioning of fundamental assumptions that we might otherwise take for granted; this is obviously connected with point (c). Points (a) and (b) are also connected with this because it has been thought that what distinguishes science from non-science is the inductive method: the extent to which the truth of its propositions is derived from and justified by their origin in the facts of experience. The ideal picture that this inductive model of science evokes is its beginning by collecting pure or presuppositionless observations which give the facts, in a passive, unprejudiced, neutral manner; then from the repetition of these observations certain patterns begin to emerge which lead to the framing of universal hypotheses connecting particular observed phenomena; these hypotheses are then, by further experimental tests, proved true, or at least confirmed as highly probable. The aim is to pick out, from the many features repeatedly observed, the necessary and sufficient conditions for the event to be explained; that is, the aim is to identify the cause of the event by identifying that feature of the situation that is always present when the event to be explained occurs and is never present when the event to be explained does not occur. Popper argues, with others, that there are at least two major problems that such a view of science encounters,

(i) The first problem is that there are no presuppositionless, neutral, raw observations free of theoretical content. All observation involves some identifying, and therefore theory-loaded, idea of the nature of the thing observed that already determines and presupposes the kind of thing observed, which therefore necessarily pre-empts any conclusion derived from observation.

To observe at all necessarily involves theoretical presuppositions about what we are observing. We always when observing observe something *as* a so-and-so which carries with it theoretical implications which often take us beyond the bare content of the observation. For example, the assertion "Here is a glass of water" carries with it theoretical assumptions about the behaviour of entities denoted by "glass" and "water", assumptions with implications beyond the evidence of present observations; indeed, Popper says that such a statement is unverifiable, because the universal law-like behaviour implicit in denoting terms such as "glass" and "water" is not reducible to any finite class of experiences. Another point is that when we identify two events as a repetition of the same event, we are necessarily picking out some respect in which they are similar, and ignoring other respects in which they differ; they must differ or they would not be two distinct events. Observations, to be possible at all, always involve the selection, implicitly or explicitly, of certain of the features of our environment and the rejection of others; the possible range of things we could make note of is infinite, so we are forced to be selective. What we choose to observe is guided by theoretical interests.

(ii) The second problem is that of inductive inference; Popper characterizes this as "Hume's problem". In valid deductive reasoning it is not possible for the premises of the argument to be true and the conclusion false; necessarily if the premises of a valid deductive argument are true, then the conclusion is true. To assert the premises and deny the conclusion of a valid deduction is to contradict oneself. A deductive argument involves the claim that the premises present conclusive grounds for its conclusion. Thus if it is the case that "All men are mortal" and "Socrates is a man", then "Socrates is mortal". Inductive arguments are not conclusive in this way: the premises can be true, yet the conclusion false.

The theories of science are characteristically universal propositions of the form "All *A*s are *B*s" which go beyond the evidence of experience; the proposition does not follow from any finite number of observations of *A*s and *B*s which give propositions of the form "Some *A*s are *B*s" for there is no logical contradiction involved in the assertion that the next observed *A* will not be a *B*. From this it follows that no universal scientific proposition can be proved to be true. Scientific laws always transcend experience. The inference from experience to universal laws, or more generally to unobserved instances, is neither a logically valid deductive argument nor an inference that could be justified by experience, for the argument from "inductive inferences have worked in the past" to therefore "inductive inferences will work in the future" is itself an inductive inference, so any such attempted justification would be circular.

An inductive inference could be made valid on the assumption that regularities or uniformities observed in the cases we have observed hold in cases we have not observed. But this assumption is not a logical *a priori* truth such that its denial implies a contradiction or such that it can be justified by experience. We might say that uniformities have been found to hold in all cases we have observed, therefore uniformities will hold in cases we have not observed; but that evidence from cases we have observed can be evidence for cases we have not observed is exactly what the uniformity principle justifies, so such evidence cannot be used to justify the uniformity principle itself.

It will not help to fall back on probability, for we can still ask why we think the observation of certain cases should even make more probable events we have not observed. We can say further that no finite number of observations can make a universal statement of the form "All *A*s are *B*s" more probable by the frequency theory of probability; the class of examined cases is always finite, and the class of unexamined cases is potentially infinite, so that the probability of the universal statement "All *A*s are *B*s" will always approach zero. Even if we restricted the range of our general statement, we could still not be sure that the next, ninety-ninth out of a hundred, *A* will be a *B*, on the basis of observing past *A*s and *B*s, since "*A* and not-*B*" is never a logical contradiction.

Popper rejects induction both as a fruitful method of formulating scientific theories, and as a logic for justifying theories. He claims to have solved the problem of induction, but he does not so much solve it as sidestep the problem; he does not give or seek a justification for induction, rather he substitutes a different scientific methodology that is independent of induction, but does the same job as induction in allowing us rationally to prefer one theory to another on empirical grounds. Popper maintains the empiricist principle that it is only by observation and experiment that we may rationally decide to accept or reject scientific theories. Such decisions cannot be justified *a priori*. This leads on to the heart of Popper's philosophy, and the idea that what distinguishes science from non-science is not induction as a method or a justificatory logic, but that science consists of theories which are both logically self-consistent and such that they can *in principle be falsified or refuted.* Popper uses the terms "hypotheses", "conjecture", "theory" and "scientific law" interchangeably. The logical basis for this is quite simple, and derives from the deductive principle of *modus tollens:*

If *p* then *q,*

not-*q*

therefore, not-*p.*

Roughly this says that if asserting *p* entails asserting *q,* and *q* is false, then *p* is also false. We can substitute in this formula, *H,* standing for some universal scientific hypothesis, for *p,* and *e,* standing for an observation-statement, for *q.* The observation-statement *e* is *deduced* from *H.* We then have the following.

If *H* then *e,*

not-*e*

therefore, not-*H.*

The essential point to notice is that this indicates a logical asymmetry between verification and falsification: while it is the case that no finite number of observations can ever prove the truth of a universal scientific theory, logically only one case is required to contradict a theory's universal assertion in order for it to be falsified or refuted. What is distinctive about scientific theories is not that they can be proved true, or even made more probable, but that they are testable, that is, they can be falsified. So from the universal proposition "All *A*s are *B*s" *(H)*, we can deduce the proposition that "It is not the case that some (even one) *A* is not a *B*" *(e);* if we observe "Some (at least one) *A* is not a *B*" (not-*e*), then it follows purely as a matter of deductive logic that "All *A*s are *B*s" is false (not-*H*). The assertion "All swans are white" is falsified by the observation of a single non-white swan which entails that "Not all swans are white". Thus a theory is falsifiable if and only if there is some observation-statement deducible from it, which, if false, would falsify the theory. A genuine scientific theory must exclude some logically possible state of affairs by specifying more or less exactly what the state of affairs will be: it must not be compatible with all logically possible evidence. More exactly what is deducible from a scientific theory is at least one "basic statement" which is a potential falsifier; such a statement will be a singular observation-statement that refers to some publicly observable event. This excludes pure existential statements of the form "Some *A* is a *B*" from being scientific because they are untestable; no possible evidence can ever refute them as there is, so to speak, always somewhere we have not looked.

Popper was impressed by the contrast between the theories of Marxism and Freudian psychoanalysis on the one hand, and Einstein's theories on the other. According to Popper, Marxists and Freudians saw everywhere confirmation for their theories, whereas Einstein made an effort to formulate a very specific observable prediction which followed from his theory concerning the bending of light, which, if it failed to be upheld by observation, would have refuted the theory. What is at issue here is not the psychological fact, if it is one, of the reluctance of Marxist and Freudian defenders to admit evidence refuting their theories, but rather the nature or logical structure of Marxist and Freudian theories themselves which rendered them immune from falsification. Popper's suspicion was that Marxist and psychoanalytic theories were only "confirmed", and seemed to explain everything, because they were, through reasons of vagueness or devices designed to explain away counter-evidence, irrefutable. Such theories are anathema to the proper critical scientific attitude. That is not to say that Marxist and Freudian theories were meaningless, or even that what they said was untrue, rather the theories were not scientific in that they were highly untestable, that is, difficult, if not impossible, to falsify. The theories were constantly hedged around with caveats or qualifications, so that apparent counter-evidence was no longer a deducible consequence of the theories. For Popper this indicates that the holders of these theories were not adopting the proper critical scientific attitude. But far from pre-scientific myths being meaningless, Popper says they can often be modified to form the basis of later scientific theories and so become testable by experience. A further point concerns a comparison of Newton's and Einstein's theories. Popper argues that despite the fact that Newton's theory can be massively confirmed by observation, this is not enough to establish its truth. He holds the view that discrepancies emerged in Newton's theory, between its predictions and observations, which led to the development of Einstein's competing theory despite the enormous confirmation of Newton's theory. Having explained the *logic* of Popper's philosophy of science, it is necessary to distinguish this from the *methodology* or practice of falsificationism. While the logic of falsification is quite simple, the methodology is a good deal more complex. This arises because, although it is clear what would, logically speaking, constitute the refutation of a scientific theory, determining whether a theory is in fact refuted is quite a different matter. Not only is it the case that there are various reasons why it is difficult to determine if a refutation has taken place, but Popper also acknowledges that there are various ways in which an apparent refutation can always be avoided. These considerations require that we adopt certain *methodological rules* so as to maximize the possibility of scientific progress, although there is no method that can guarantee it. There are various problems that arise in attempting the actual falsification of a theory by critical discussion, observation and experiment,

(i) It is always possible to doubt that the observation we have made is correct we may have made an observational error.

This introduces the problem of the empirical base: if we cannot be certain of the truth of the observation statements we use to test our theories, we cannot be certain our theories are refuted by them. Popper admits that there are no indubitable observation statements; all observation statements themselves have some theoretical content and are open to further testing. But this does not lead to a vicious infinite regress, because although all empirical statements are potentially testable, they can be provisionally or conventionally held as true, and so used to test or falsify theories for which they are potential falsifiers. If they are doubted, further tests can always be carried out. There are no ultimate empirical foundations.

(ii) This problem concerns the fact that scientific theories are always tested in groups. In testing any theory it is necessary that we describe the initial conditions by a set of auxiliary hypotheses; that is, certain other theories are involved which act as assumptions concerning relevant circumstances of the test; these also give the falsifying significance to the observation deduced from a theory. For example, in making an observation we might assume that light travels in a straight line. Thus the falsifying *modus tollens* formula becomes more complex.

If $(H{+}h)$ (hypothesis + Auxiliary hypothesis), then *e*,

not-*e*

---

therefore, not-*H*.

Strictly speaking, all we can say in this complex situation is that some element in the totality $(H{+}h)$ is refuted is shown to be false and that need not be the theory *H* under test, but could instead be one or more of the auxiliary hypotheses *h*. What can be said here is that the auxiliary hypotheses are themselves open to testing.

(iii) Closely connected with point (ii), it is always possible to adopt *ad hoc* hypotheses so as to evade refutation. By *ad hoc* hypotheses is meant hypotheses adopted for no other purpose than to avoid refutation. For example the theory "All bread nourishes" can be immunized against refutation by the example of some poisonous bread in France by tacking on to the proposition "All bread nourishes" the expression "except in France". Another *ad hoc* method of evading refutation is simply to define away apparent counter-evidence; thus if "All *A*s are *B*s" is presented with the evidence of an *A* that is not a *B*, it can be said that if we seemed to observe an *A* that was not a *B*, then it could not have been an *A* that we observed at all; this makes being a *B* part of the identifying definition of an *A*. So we might say a non-white swan is not a swan at all.

The adoption of *ad hoc* hypotheses and definitional manoeuvres Popper regards as intellectually dishonest. We must therefore adopt some methodological rules so as to avoid adopting *ad hoc* hypotheses. Partly this is achieved by the methodological principle that if we modify a theory with the addition of some new hypotheses so as to avoid refutation, there must be some consequences that can be deduced from the original theory and the new additional hypotheses that were not deducible from the original unmodified theory. In other words, the additional or modified hypotheses must form a new hypothesis which is testable in some way the original hypothesis was not: they must be independently testable. Thus we reject as *ad hoc* "All bread nourishes, *except in France*", since it has no new testable consequences which are not also a test of "All bread nourishes"; the reverse is not the case, since there are testable consequences of "All bread nourishes" which are not also testable consequences of "All bread nourishes, except in France".

It is clear that some hypotheses are more testable or falsifiable than others. The theory that "All planets move in loops" (*H*1) is less falsifiable than "All planets move in ellipses" (*H*2), because *H*1 is less specific about what evidence would refute it. To put it another way, *H*1 excludes less than *H* 2: its truth is compatible with a far greater range of possible observations. *H* 2 not only says that the planets move in closed loops, but also specifies the exact kind of loop that is involved. Thus we can say that all the observations that would falsify *H*1 would falsify *H*2 but some observations that would falsify *H*2 would not falsify *H*1; if the planets moved in anything but ellipses, *H*2 would be false, while as long as they still moved in some kind of loop *H* 1 would be true. Popper expresses this point by saying the greater the *information content* of a theory, the more falsifiable it is: it tells us more about the way the world *is* by excluding as being the case more logically possible states of affairs. The information content increases with the set of statements which are incompatible with the theory.

Popper also notes that the falsifiability and the information content of a theory are in inverse proportion to its probability. The information content of a tautology for example, "Either it is raining or it is not raining" is zero, and its probability is at the maximum of 1. The probability of $H2$ ("All planets move in ellipses") being true is far less than the probability of $H1$ ("All planets move in loops") being true because the class of potential falsifiers of $H1$ is a proper subclass of the potential falsifiers of $H2$. For example, "The planets move in a straight line" would falsify both $H1$ and $H2$, but "The planets move in a circle" would falsify $H2$ but not $H1$ because a circle is a kind of loop.

Popper's overall position is then that we make progress in our knowledge, and approach the truth, by a process of trial and error.

Popper gives the following evolutionary view of the growth of scientific knowledge:

$P1 \rightarrow TT1 \rightarrow EE1 \rightarrow P2$

Here $P1$ designates a problem, for which we propose the tentative theory $TT1$; we then try to eliminate false theories by testing them severely and subjecting our theory to critical discussion, $EE1$; then $P2$ is the problem-situation as we emerge from our attempted solution to our problem, and so on. Science makes progress by conjecture and refutation; we learn from our mistakes. We start with problems, not with neutral observation: that is, we start with the failure to explain some phenomenon. No mere observation constitutes a problem; we have a problem only in the light of some existing theory which fails to explain an observation. We try to solve the problem not by proposing the most probable theory for more probable theories have less information content but by proposing bold conjectures or guesses which, because they are highly specific and precise in what they say about the world, are highly falsifiable; we can then test these theories in severe and crucial tests. The tests are severe because what the theory entails is incompatible with a very wide range of possible observations. Intuitively we can see that the severity of a test will increase with its improbability. A new theory will be bold and improbable (unlikely) and its tests severe because it involves rejecting part of the background knowledge of scientific theories of its historical time. For example, Einstein's theory was bold relative to the theoretical background assumptions of its time because it contradicted the background assumption of its time that light travels in straight lines.

It is significant that in Popper's falsificationism the *source* of a scientific theory is totally irrelevant to whether it is scientific or not. A theory is scientific if and only if it is falsifiable; it is quite unimportant whether the theory arises from laboratory observation or an inspirational blow on the head. One method might as a matter of fact be more fruitful as a means of producing good theories than another; but that is irrelevant to the question of whether a statement is scientific or not, and, if it is scientific, how good a scientific theory it is. Science has no mechanical method by which it can make progress; Popper's philosophy gives free rein to imaginative bold speculation. Good science requires just as much imagination as any of the arts. Popper says we do not in fact come to the world as passive or neutral observers, but are born with certain natural expectations or dispositions that operate in the same way as consciously constructed theories. Indeed all animals are in their behaviour acting out innate solutions to problems. But while these innate "theories" might be psychologically *a priori,* that does not mean they are *a priori* valid. The main difference between man and other animals is the extent to which man can allow his theories to die rather than dying himself; man can adopt new theories rather than hanging on to his theories and dying with them. One sees the point of this in considering the way a wasp unremittingly batters at a glass window and so "fails to solve" the "problem" of escaping.

Normally we will not be in the situation of testing one theory in isolation, but will have to choose between a number of competing theories. Even if we find an observation that falsifies a theory we will not reject it unless we have some better theory with which to replace it. Indeed, Popper's methodological rules demand that we do not hastily reject a theory after a single falsifying instance, but only after frequent and rigorous falsification has taken place, and we have a better theory with which to replace it. The choice between competing theories should be made in the following way: theory *T*2 should be preferred to *T*1 if *T*2 solves all the problems that *T*1 solves and it solves the problems *T*1 failed to solve (that is, where *T*1 was refuted), *and* it offers solutions to some additional problems about which *T*1 says nothing, thus allowing the further possibility for refutation. To put it another way, we should choose the theory that explains all the previous theory explains, explains what the previous theory failed to explain, and offers an explanation for further phenomena not explained by the previous theory. The satisfaction of these conditions effectively rules out our new theory being merely the old theory plus some *ad hoc* hypotheses which serve only to avoid the apparent refutations or failures.

Popper's philosophy of science can be summarized in the following way. Knowledge progresses by proposing bold explanatory theories, that is, explanations with a high information content that are highly falsifiable, by subjecting those theories to severe and crucial tests and by the replacement of falsified theories by better theories. We can be said to replace a theory by a rationally preferable, better theory, even if the old theory has not been *conclusively* falsified, when the new theory, provided it has not been falsified, is able to explain all that the old theory explained, and things the old theory failed to explain, and offers as well explanations for things for which the old theory offered no explanation. That is, the better theory *T*2 will contain *T*1 as an approximation. If any falsification of *T*1 would be a falsification of *T*2, but not vice versa, then *T*2 is rationally preferable to *T*1 provided *T*2 has not been falsified. This means we choose the theory which is more falsifiable has more information content provided that theory has not been falsified. We can make our assessment of theories only from the position of the current historical state of critical discussion.

If a theory survives continuous attempts to falsify it by severe tests, it can be said to be highly *corroborated*. That is *not* to say its truth has been conclusively established, or even made more probable. The corroboration of a theory at a certain time is essentially a report on its degree of testability, the severity of the tests to which it has been subjected, and the way it has stood up to those tests. The corroboration of a theory will increase with its falsifiability, provided it is not falsified, because the more falsifiable it is the more severe the tests it can potentially survive. It can then be subjected to further severe tests. Popper is quick to deny that corroboration reintroduces the notion of induction, for he says that the corroboration accorded to a theory does not say anything about its reliability in the future or anything about its future performance. The less the probability of a theory, the higher its degree of potential corroboration can be. A less probable theory can pass more severe tests and so can be more highly corroborated. A theory that has been well corroborated can be *provisionally* accepted. If there is more than one theory covering the same ground, it is rational to choose the best corroborated theory because that has been most severely tested. This again gives an account of rational preference between theories: *T*2 is preferable to *T*1 if *T*2 survives all the tests *T*1 survives, survives the tests *T*1 fails, and goes on to explain further facts which are testable consequences of *T* 2, and if *T* 2 has not yet been refuted.

It is clear from Popper's position that we can never establish that a theory is true. He says that we can never "know" in the sense of conclusively establishing a theory to be true so that there is no possibility of our being mistaken. In this sense Popper is a fallibilist: we can never be certain that we have found the truth. All our theories are conjectures or guesses which are open to testing; we can then perhaps say that some conjectures are better than others because they have stood up to tests better.

Since we are interested in the truth we shall be interested in eliminating a theory which we discover to be false, for that way we might hit upon a theory that is true. Popper is absolutely clear in distinguishing whether a theory *is* objectively true or false as a matter of correspondence, or failure of correspondence, with facts (*p* is true if and only if it corresponds to the facts), from our *knowing* if *p* corresponds to the facts. Popper takes from the logician Alfred Tarski (1902–83) the definition of truth: "'*p*' is true if and only if *p*". Every unambiguous statement is either true or false, and there is no third possibility; but determining *when* a proposition corresponds to the facts is quite a different matter, and Popper thinks we are never in the position to say that we have established or justified the truth of a theory. However, the correspondence definition of truth can act as a regulative principle: it is something we can aim at and get nearer to. Indeed, as the corroboration of a theory increases, it is reasonable to conjecture that we are getting nearer the truth. The extent to which a theory approaches the truth Popper refers to as its *verisimilitude.* Popper derives the notion of verisimilitude from the information content of a theory: the content of a theory *T* is all those propositions entailed by it. The content of *T* can then be divided into its truth-content (the class of all true statements entailed by *T*) and its falsity content (the class of all false statements entailed by *T*). The verisimilitude of *T* is its truth content minus its falsity content. Assuming that theories *T* 1 and *T* 2 are comparable, then *T* 2 has greater verisimilitude than *T*1 if its truth-content is greater than *T*1, but its falsity-content is less than *T*1, or the falsity-content of *T*2 is less than *T*1 but the truth-content of *T* 2 is greater than *T* 1. If more true statements, but not more false statements, follow from *T* 2 than *T* 1, then *T* 2 is nearer the truth.

If *T* 2 entails all the true statements entailed by *T* 1, and *T* 2 entails some true statements not entailed by *T*1, and *T* 2 does not entail more false statements than *T*1, then it is reasonable to say that *T* 2 is nearer the truth than *T* 1 :*T* 2 has greater verisimilitude even if it is false. Thus we can rationally prefer *T* 2 to *T*1 if we are in pursuit of the truth even if *T* 2 is false, provided that the falsity-content of *T* 2 is not too great.

The verisimilitude and the degree of corroboration of a theory are connected. If we compare the corroboration of two theories and determine that all the tests passed by *T* 1 are also passed by *T* 2, and that *T* 2 passes some tests that *T*1 does not pass, and that *T* 2 does not fail more tests than *T*1 failed, then it is rational to prefer *T* 2 to *T*1 because *T* 2 can be conjectured to have greater verisimilitude: it is nearer the truth. *T* 2 will be more testable than *T*1 : it will have a greater information content; it will say more about the way the world is. Although we have not established the truth of *T* 2 indeed, as we are fallible, it is likely to be false we can express a *rational preference* for *T* 2 as being better corroborated than *T*1 and nearer to the truth than *T*1. *T* 2 is more testable and survives more tests than *T*1.

From Popper's acceptance of the correspondence theory of truth it can be seen that he is a metaphysical realist. He thinks that our theories, if true, refer to a reality which is independent of mind and our theories. However, he agrees that such metaphysical realism does not take us very far except as a regulative idea, for we still have to determine when our theories correspond to things as they really are. We cannot "look around" our theories to reality, but can only take to be reality what our best theories in the light of current *critical* discussion and testing say reality is. Popper thinks it unlikely that we will ever discover "the truth" about the world. Popper is opposed in science to instrumentalism, which asserts that scientific theories do not refer to real entities which explain the course of our observations, but are rather useful devices which posit whatever is required without maintaining its reality for predicting accurately the course of our experience. On this view scientific laws are rules rather than truths. Popper also opposes essentialism, which maintains that we can discover an ultimate reality in terms of which everything else is explained. This attitude he sees as stultifying to the pursuit of ever better explanations. Popper takes a middle course in which science is a genuine attempt to explain some real state of affairs which is known or assumed to be true by some other real state of affairs that is unknown and requiring discovery, the truth of which can be tested independently of the phenomena to be explained; but there is no end to the depth to which we can progress in pursuit of explanations.

When Popper talks about "knowledge" he is not referring to finally established, or justified, truths. He also emphasizes that when he talks about "knowledge" he is talking about knowledge in the *objective sense.* He intends by this to make a distinction between any person's subjective knowledge and objective knowledge as it is formulated in language and existent in books and journals in libraries and research institutions open to public inspection and testing. Scientific knowledge is objective in this sense. Objective logical relations exist between statements which are formulated in language, regardless of whether anyone is actually aware of them or not. What individual scientists believe is relatively unimportant compared to the objective growth of knowledge. The error of what Popper terms "belief philosophy" is that it tries to see knowledge as an especially sure kind of belief.

Popper, in fact, makes a distinction between three interdependent worlds: World 1 is the physical world; World 2 is the subjective mental world; World 3 is the objective world of theories, mathematics, literature, art, and the like, within which there exist objective logical relations—objective, that is, in being independent of the awareness of individual minds. The objects of World 3 are developed by World 2 minds, often in response to problems perceived in World 1; but once formulated, they have an objective status transcending the intentions of the individual. Yet it is knowledge in the subjective sense what the individual person can know on which traditionally philosophy has concentrated, the notion being that it is only from what an individual mind can really know that any further knowledge claims can be justified. Yet most human knowledge in the objective sense is not known by anyone in the subjective sense. Human knowledge, especially scientific knowledge, almost entirely consists of knowledge without a knowing subject. Popper's World 3 has some similarities to Plato's realm of objective Forms; however, a vital difference is that Popper's World 3 is by no means fixed, but constantly changes and develops as knowledge grows and progresses through the critical examination of the knowledge we already have.

6

Recent Philosophy and its Consequences

Introduction

There will be no attempt here to discern the detail of trends or tendencies in recent philosophy; but it can at least be said that recent philosophy is extremely diverse in its interests and approaches. There is, no doubt, room for disagreement over which figures should be selected and which omitted; there is no question of this choice being definitive. The people mentioned are discussed in chronological order according to their date of birth, and main works by the philosophers mentioned are given in the bibliography.

Gilbert Ryle

Gilbert Ryle (1900–76) was part of a philosophical movement that held that many philosophical problems arose from a misunderstanding and misuse of ordinary language. One of the ways in which such mis-understandings arise is through what Ryle calls “category mistakes”, whereby we mistakenly take a concept to refer to a certain kind of entity. Generally this leads to mistaken ontological commitments, that is, to the existence of all sorts of entities which we are misled into supposing exist owing to the way we misunderstand our language. Ryle applies this view to his theory of mind: his opposition to mind as a ghostly object-like substance. We take the term "mind" to refer to some special, albeit ethereal, kind of *thing*. But the mind is not any kind of thing; it is not a thing at all; rather, to talk of mind is to refer to certain kinds of behaviour and dispositions to behave.

J.L. Austin

J.L. Austin (1911–60), like Ryle, thought that philosophical problems tended to arise from a misunderstanding of language. Unlike Ryle he did not attempt to replace the systematic philosophies which arose from what he saw as the inattention to fine distinctions of language with a systematic philosophy derived from a view of language purged of such inattention. Austin supposed that philosophy and logic were too ready to ignore the subtle discriminations present in ordinary language. This led to the careful study of shades of meaning manifest in linguistic usage which would be not only a way of avoiding philosophical error but also of interest in its own right.

Stuart Hampshire

Stuart Hampshire (1914-) has put forward a theory of language and knowledge which is relativistic in that the system of concepts which we bring to talk about the world is not absolute or fixed, but depends upon the special interests we bring to the world as human beings and as agents in the world. We cannot detach ourselves as disembodied spectators and so achieve a disinterested view of the world. He rejects the view that the more we know about the causes of our actions the less free we will become; on the contrary, it is the essence of our existence as human beings always to be able to stand back from knowledge of our situation, no matter how detailed, and decide what we then want to do.

Donald Davidson

Donald Davidson (1917–) has been notably influential on certain parts of analytical philosophy in recent years. Much of his work has centred on the philosophy of language, and the implications of this work for various other areas of philosophy, such as the philosophy of mind. In the philosophy of mind he argues for an "anomalous monism" where, although each mental event is identical with a physical event, there are no strict law-like connections between the two different sorts of descriptions of events.

P.F. Strawson

P.F. Strawson (1919–) has been one of the chief opponents of the idea that logic somehow represents in an ideal form the structure of ordinary language. Strawson's investigations into the informal logic of ordinary language led him to what he called "descriptive metaphysics", which aims to lay bare the most basic features of the conceptual system we actually have; that is, those features of our conceptual system which are a historically unchanging core; this is to be contrasted with "revisionary metaphysics", which aims to change or replace the conceptual structure we actually have with a better one. It is from these considerations that Strawson's project has been seen as having an affinity with the Kantian one of making manifest the common core of conceptual presuppositions logically required for our talk about the world; however, in Strawson's case the aim is the less ambitious one of identifying the logical requirements relative to *our* conceptual system, that is, the concepts logically presupposed by our conceptual system, not by any conceptual system whatsoever. For example Strawson concludes that the possibility of a world in which we re-identify various categories of kinds of particular things depends upon the category of material bodies in space and time. Strawson has also written against the correspondence theory of truth: the function of saying "*p* is true" is not to describe *p* as having some special relation with the world, but rather to say that one confirms or endorses *p*.

Thomas S. Kuhn

Thomas S. Kuhn (1922–) was trained as a physicist and has been extremely influential in the philosophy of both the physical and social sciences; in this respect he is second only to Popper. His chief thesis involves suggesting that science is not the tidy rational enterprise it is sometimes represented as being by philosophers. Scientists most of the time engage in "puzzle-solving" or "normal science" within a set of currently unquestioned assumptions about the world which forms a "paradigm" or world-view. The "anomalies" presented by experience are in normal science accommodated within the assumptions defining the paradigm. But eventually the anomalies become too troublesome. The choice of paradigms, the revolutionary movement between them being called a "paradigm shift", is difficult to justify rationally because the standards of rationality, methodology, and what constitutes good evidence are determined within each paradigm. Many have seen Kuhn's view as an admission of relativism because of the rational incommensurability of paradigms, and as an undermining of the rationality of science.

Paul Feyerabend

Paul Feyerabend (1924–) is a philosopher whose training was originally in theoretical physics. His main work has been in epistemology and the philosophy of science. The chief outcome of his work has been to criticize the view that there is something called "the scientific method", and thus to release human investigations into the nature of the world from the presupposition that there is only one rational way of going about such investigations. There is no pure way of describing the world independently of conceptual and theoretical assumptions, which leaves us with the possibility of there being a variety of conceptual systems between which there can be no means of adjudication ultimately independent of all theoretical assumptions. This has led to a view of Feyerabend as a methodological anarchist. But his position is best described as that of a democratic relativist which, he suggests, frees inquiry from the shackles of supposing there is only one correct method of understanding the world.

Michael Dummett

The two most important aspects of Michael Dummett's (1925–) philosophical doctrines are his search for a systematic theory of meaning and his anti-realism. The knowledge we display of the meaning of expressions is based on the implicit knowledge of linguistic principles, and it is the function of a theory of meaning to bring these to light. The proposition central to the notion of anti- realism is the assertion that there are certain classes of statements which are not determinately true or false independently of our means of knowing which they are. This amounts to a denial of the principle of bivalence which says that any statement must be determinately either true or false regardless of whether we can know which it is.

Richard Rorty

Much of Richard Rorty's (1931–) recent work has been concerned with examining the nature of the philosophical enterprise itself. This has led him to question the presuppositions that lie behind much of what he identifies as the philosophical tradition. The philosophical approaches that are chiefly criticized are analytical philosophy and continental phenomenology; philosophy in these traditions he sees as a kind of dead end where there is no possible way of adjudicating between different views. In particular Rorty suggests that the central error of the philosophical tradition of which he is critical is the attempt to hold a mirror up to nature in which is reflected the nature of the world in a way that is ahistorical, spectatorial, and independent of any perspective. But we cannot escape our historical and human perspective. Rorty advocates that we replace traditional "systematic" philosophy, which aims at timelessly true foundations (represented by such figures as Descartes, Kant, Husserl, Russell), with "edifying" philosophy (represented by such figures as Heidegger, Wittgenstein, Dewey, Sartre), whose central job is the freeing and facilitation of dialogue between different areas of human inquiry in the historical context in which they find themselves.

John R. Searle

Much of the work of John R. Searle (1932–) has been in the philosophy of language, but he has also done important work in the philosophy of mind and the philosophical implications of artificial intelligence. Central to Searle's work in the philosophy of language is that of "speech acts" (which partly develops the pioneering work of Austin), which are distinguished by their point or purpose; expressions with similar content fall into different types of speech act depending on what is done with them: whether they are orders, promises, pleas, descriptions, predictions and the like. Searle aims to produce a taxonomy of speech acts.

Saul Kripke

Saul Kripke (1940–) is a philosopher trained in mathematical logic; his work in modal logic has led him to revive a form of essentialism and reintroduce the concept of natural or metaphysical necessity. Necessity is said, especially by empiricists and logical positivists, only to hold among the propositions of mathematics, logic and semantic truths (such as "All bachelors are unmarried"), not among objects or events in the world, and all propositions concerning the actual nature of the world are contingent. Kripke thinks mistaken the view of some philosophers that the *a priori* and the *a posteriori,* and the necessary and contingent, are, respectively, coextensive. The distinctions belong to different philosophical domains: knowledge and metaphysics. There are, Kripke argues, necessarily true statements which cannot be known to be true merely through understanding the meanings of the terms involved, but can be known only through experience *a posteriori.* In particular there are expressions that Kripke calls "rigid designators", which name the same individual in every possible world in which that individual exists, and which form identity statements, such as "The Morning Star is identical with the Evening Star", which are necessary but knowable only *a posteriori.* He reintroduces essentialism: the notion that particular objects and kinds of objects have necessary properties: that is, those properties something must have to be just *that* object or *that sort* of object.

7

Analytical Philosophy of Russell and Wittgenstein

Introduction

Analysis is a process which aims to elucidate complexes by reducing them to their simpler elements and the relations between those elements. This can apply to complex concepts, entities, or philosophical problems. In analytical philosophy, the analysis is characteristically linguistic. It is done through analyzing the language in which a complex philosophical problem, say, is expressed; perplexing complex philosophical concepts are dealt with by resolving the complexes into what are logically equivalent related simple constituents, which can be better understood.

The origins of analytical philosophy lie in work done in the latter half of the nineteenth century and the beginning of the twentieth century on logic and the foundations of mathematics. This work involved the construction of a new and powerfully expressive formal logical symbolism. Much of this work was carried out independently by the German logician Gottlob Frege (1848–1925). The culmination of the work in England was *Principia mathematica* (1910–13), written jointly by Bertrand Russell and Alfred North Whitehead

(1861–1947). The motivation for this work was the rejection of psychologism, and indeed all forms of naturalism, as providing a foundation of mathematical truth; the new view embraced objective logicism concerning mathematical truths. What this amounted to was the attempt to show that mathematics was reducible in principle to the propositions of logic. The philosophical significance of this is that mathematical truths were shown to be independent of human thought, such as structural features of our way of thinking, and were absolutely necessary objective truths. This meant that mathematical truths were, contrary to Kant's view, independent of whether they expressed even essential features of human thought. Nor did such mathematical truths express extremely general empirical facts as John Stuart Mill (1806–73) suggested. Mathematical truths were shown to be necessary and objective because they depend only on certain basic rules of logic which hold independently of mind or the empirical world. The new logical language is formal in that the rules governing its terms are known exactly; it is powerful in that, unlike traditional Aristotelian logic, it is able to express an enormously richer range of meanings. Aristotelian logic, which dealt with the relations between classes, is shown to be only a tiny fragment of the new logic, which could deal with whole propositions and the internal structure of propositions.

Analytical philosophers saw in the new symbolism a way of tackling old philosophical problems. The new logic delivered an ideal or perfect language which was at the same time powerful enough for the formulation of propositions and arguments previously only expressible in ordinary everyday language. Ordinary language developed for purposes which mean it is ill-suited for the expression of philosophical concepts and problems. The precision, clarity and unambiguity that were possible in the new logic promised to give a way of reformulating philosophical problems so that their solution would become apparent, or the original problem would simply disappear as a pseudo-problem this perhaps describes the essence and promise of analytical philosophy. Even those philosophers who did not actually reformulate the propositions of philosophy, and the propositions of science and common sense, into formal symbolism saw that the ordinary language in which the propositions were expressed could be systematically misleading, and that we must logically analyze the propositions into their underlying logically related constituent parts to understand what they really mean, if they are meaningful at all, so better to assess how their truth or falsity might be discovered. This process of analysis chiefly involves revealing the underlying structure, or logical form, of propositions in everyday language so as not to be philosophically misled by the apparent grammatical structure. The apparent linguistic structure can be misleading because it can be taken as mirroring structures in the world; but there is no reason why this is necessarily the case. The *logical form* expresses only what are the essential or common features of apparently different linguistic expressions, thus characterizing all expressions of the same given sort. A simple example is "The flower is red" or "The book is red", which can be expressed as "*a* is *F*" and "*b* is *F*"; the common logical form is "*x* is *F*", or more concisely "*Fx*".

For example, if we take the proposition "I see nobody coming down the road", we might be tempted to think "nobody" functions grammatically as a proper name and names someone, in the same way that in "I see Alan coming down the road", "Alan" functions as a proper name and names someone. If we take the example of the proposition "Numbers can be both odd and even", we might think that "numbers" functions in the proposition in just the same way as "tables" does in "Tables can be both large and small", and so assume that there must exist things called "numbers" in the same way that there exist things called "tables". Philosophical problems might then arise in deciding in what peculiar sense numbers exist.

Often it is the case that the surface grammatical form is not the same as the underlying logical form. In everyday use this rarely matters; but if we are asking philosophical questions, we can be misled not only by ambiguities of sense but also by what the grammatical form apparently implies; we thus misunderstand the philosophical implications or philosophical meaning of the proposition. This misunderstanding can be brought out by revealing the logical form of the propositions, which is to say that all that is ambiguous and grammatically misleading is removed. We then understand what kind of philosophical problem, if any, we are still really confronted with.

Analytical philosophy is characterized by an awareness of the need for self-consciousness in the use of language as the vehicle of human thought about the world. In its less ambitious moods, analytical philosophy has sought to clarify through pre-emptory analysis philosophical problems, and to show that some were only problems at all because we were misled by language, but some philosophical problems remain genuine. In its more ambitious moods, analytical philosophy has sought to show that all philosophical problems are illusory pseudo-problems which originate in our being misled by the language in which they are expressed, resulting in misunderstanding. The former position is more characteristic of Russell and the latter of Wittgenstein. Russell saw the new logic as an ideal language which in philosophy could sometimes replace the vagaries of ordinary language. Wittgenstein saw the new logic as revealing the essential structure of ordinary language itself; ordinary language was in logical order, but this needed to be shown through logical analysis.

The account so far presents mostly the negative or destructive side of analytical philosophy. For philosophers who think that logical analysis reveals all philosophical problems as pseudo-problems, the negative side is all there is. For others there is also a positive or constructive side. If ordinary language is misleading in philosophy, then it has led, among other things, to bad metaphysics. For example, the subject-predicate structure of ordinary sentences has led to our positing the existence of all kinds of puzzling entities apparently denoted by the subject-terms of propositions. In this way we misconstrue the true nature of reality by supposing certain things must exist which need not. The positive side of analytical philosophy is that if we display the true logical form of propositions through a full analysis, rather than disposing of metaphysics, we also produce a true metaphysics: in our new language we *do* reveal the true essential nature of reality, that to which we are ontologically committed whatever else we might suppose is real. The displaying of logical form involves making explicit, behind the apparent structure, what is the implicit but true structure.

Ordinary language contains, chiefly inherent in its structure, implicit metaphysical assumptions. We can either clear these assumptions away and conclude that there are no metaphysical problems left, or we can clear the assumptions away to reveal a true metaphysics: a description of the essential structural features of reality. In Russell and Wittgenstein, in rather different forms, this metaphysics is that of logical atomism. It can be supposed that analysis must come to an end somewhere: if complexes depend, in a general sense, upon related simpler elements, we must, if we are not to embark on an infinite regress, reach ultimate elements which cannot and need not be further analyzed.

Generally speaking, Russell's interest in analysis is epistemological: complexes are better understood and our knowledge of them secured by their analysis into better understood elements with which we are most directly acquainted. Sentences with complex meanings, if they are to be understood, must be composed wholly of constituent atomic meanings which are understood through their reference to atomic entities with which we are directly acquainted. The tendency of Wittgenstein's thinking is metaphysical: he thinks that there simply must be such atomic elements in order to make the understanding of everyday language possible, but not that we need to be directly acquainted with such elements.

We can bring to the surface what is implicit under the grammatical structure of ordinary language: by complete analysis we can reach the ultimate logical form or true structure. Complete logical analysis reveals the logical form, not of any particular proposition expressed in ordinary language, but of the essential structure, or the minimal conditions, for any language capable of representing or describing the world at all. Full logical analysis reveals what must be common to any possible language capable of representing reality; in that way the logical analysis also reveals what must be common to any possible world; it displays the essential nature of reality. Logical analysis is required because we cannot assume that the structure of everyday language reveals the essential nature and ultimate constituents of reality as a whole; for that we must look to the essence of language and leave out what is accidental and inessential. The absolutely minimal structure for any language capable of describing the world or reality at all must also reveal the essential structure of the world or reality itself. It does not reveal contingent features of the world those are to be discovered by science—but it reveals the logically necessary minimal features of any reality or any world by revealing the necessary minimal features of any language capable of representing any reality or world. Philosophy cannot reveal, for example, what are the facts, but it might reveal that the world is ultimately constituted of independent facts. Language has a structure; the world has a structure; the essential structure of language which is the condition for its being capable of mirroring reality at all must be the same as the essential structure of reality, because without this similarity of structure language could not mirror the world at all. What kind of minimal entities a fully analyzed language requires to function meaningfully are the ultimate entities of the universe. What can be represented or described in language pared down to the logical minimum of descriptive power, beyond which it is logically impossible to go, is what must be part of reality; much else may be a reality, but need not be. If language derives its meaning from its relation to the world, then what must be the case about reality, if language descriptive of reality is possible at all, is what is essential or common to all possible real worlds, however else they may differ. But this conclusion can be interpreted variously: it is unclear whether we have revealed the structure of any possible reality or only any reality that is describable.

Russell

Bertrand Russell (1872–1970) was born into an aristocratic family; his father was the son of the first Earl Russell. His life was eventful and often controversial, and he is notable among philosophers, mainly because of his public activities and his social and ethical views, in being extremely well known even outside philosophical circles. He was noted for the analytic sharpness of his intellect and wit. He was a passionate advocate of reason and debunker of superstition; we should seek out evidence for beliefs no matter how much this might mean abandoning beliefs we may wish to be true. He came to recognize the limits of human certainty and the limits on attaining timeless impartial objective knowledge of the world. After his early years Russell was an atheist, and regarded the existence of God and personal immortality as at best mere logical possibility, and belief in God as generally harmful as well as false. The evidence for a belief in the existence of God was totally insufficient and must therefore be regarded as false. As a boy he was educated privately at home. He took an early interest in mathematics, and in 1890 he went up to Trinity College, Cambridge, to study mathematics. He soon became interested in philosophical matters through dissatisfaction with the foundations of mathematics. He became a Fellow of Trinity College in 1895.

In 1912 Wittgenstein came to Cambridge from the University of Manchester to study with Russell the foundations of mathematics. Russell was impressed by Wittgenstein, and was greatly influenced by his early work. Russell was briefly imprisoned for his pacifist activities during the First World War. In 1931 Russell became Lord Russell when he succeeded to the peerage. In 1938 he moved to America, teaching at the University of Chicago and the University of California in Los Angeles. In 1944 he returned to be re-elected Fellow of Trinity College, Cambridge. In 1950 he was awarded the Nobel Prize for Literature. His last substantial philosophical work, *Human knowledge: its scope and limits,* appeared in 1948; but he was disappointed by the poor attention it received; this he put down to the rise of ordinary language philosophy and to

Wittgenstein's later approach to philosophy, which differed sharply from Russell's; he regarded both as largely misconceived. In the last part of his life Russell had an increasingly high public profile by becoming embroiled in social and political issues. His outspoken opinions on private and public morality caused considerable opprobrium to be heaped on him. Russell died at the great age of ninety-eight.

In his early thought Russell swiftly moved through two diametrically opposed philosophical positions: Hegelian absolute or monistic idealism and extravagant pluralistic realism. He then moved to a third view that was supported by a belief in analysis and the process of logical construction: parsimonious pluralistic realism this he held in various forms from then on.

Russell started with Hegelian monistic idealism, which holds that the world is essentially mental and apparently independent facts are really imposed abstractions which cannot really be characterized or understood in isolation, but can be properly understood only in relation to the whole of reality. Initially Russell was a convinced advocate of Hegelianism. But the Hegelian denial of external relations made mathematics impossible, since the terms of mathematics could not then be characterized in isolation. The denial of external relations, and the consequent doctrine of internal relations, amount to a rejection of ultimately independent facts and entities in the universe; any relation between facts is reducible to properties of each fact concerned and ultimately the whole which they form; in this way no fact can be fully conceptually characterized in isolation and the characterization must eventually expand to the only independent and therefore fully real entity: the universe as a whole. It followed from this doctrine that no proposition concerning less than the whole universe could ever be wholly true. Russell rejected monistic idealism, not only because it undermined mathematics, but also because he thought it was plain that propositions were true because they corresponded to individual facts alone by expressing the structure of the relation of the constituent elements of the facts. Monistic idealism also makes any philosophical analysis into intelligible simple or atomic entities impossible, because one cannot understand the constituent elements in isolation but only after one sees how they fit into the whole.

The rejection of monistic idealism moved Russell to a form of extravagant realism where all the apparent references of propositions have being in some extralinguistic way. It involved adopting a form of Platonic realism. This applied to mathematical truths and concepts: the necessary truth of mathematical propositions derived from their describing the timeless relations between immutable entities which do not exist in physical space. But that such things as numbers existed in some Platonic heaven eventually offended Russell's intuitive sense of reality.

This leads to the final position which in various forms Russell held for the rest of his life: parsimonious pluralistic realism. It amounts to the view that the world consists of a plurality of independent elements, but that many apparent entities are "logical fictions" that are really constructs of other simpler elements. Through the notion of logical construction, entities whose existence is doubtful or problematic can be replaced by entities whose existence is more certainly known and better understood. The view applies a version of Ockham's razor: "Whenever possible, substitute constructions out of known entities for inferences to unknown entities." The three important areas to which Russell applies this principle are mathematics, physical objects, and mind. The purpose of this is in part metaphysical and in part epistemological, and it is sometimes difficult to disentangle the two; the former concerns what there is, the latter our knowledge of what there is and these matters are, however, distinct.

As far as knowledge of entities, as opposed to knowledge of truths, is concerned, Russell holds that we can know with greatest certainty the nature and existence of those entities with which we are most directly acquainted; knowledge of the nature and existence of all other entities, where a reduction to entities with which we are directly acquainted is not possible, will involve some kind of inference from those entities with which we are directly acquainted. This inference will involve various degrees of certainty, and our aim should be to see how certain this inference is in various cases. The way of making the belief in certain entities most secure is logically to reduce everything we wish to say about the doubtful entities to propositions concerning entities about which we have less or no doubt. On the one hand this has the epistemological purpose of revealing what justification, if any, we have for asserting the existence of entities with which we are not directly acquainted; on the other hand it might have the metaphysical purpose of suggesting that if statements about entities with which we are not directly acquainted can be reduced without loss of meaning to propositions about entities with which we are directly acquainted, it is the entities with which we are directly acquainted which are the basic elements of the universe. Thus among knowledge of things we must distinguish between "knowledge by acquaintance", where we have knowledge of things by direct awareness of the things concerned, without any intermediary inference or knowledge of truths being involved, and "knowledge by description", where we have no direct awareness of the things concerned, but have knowledge only by inference from direct awareness of intermediary things and knowledge of truths. There is no state of mind in which we are directly aware of the things known by description; all knowledge of such things is really knowledge of truths concerning those things; we never know the actual things themselves. Russell's considered position is that what we can justifiably claim to know about posited entities irreducible to objects of immediate acquaintance is inferred from entities with which we are immediately, non-inferentially, acquainted. Thus we have knowledge by description of such physical objects as tables, which it is possible to doubt exist, through our direct acquaintance with sense-perceptions, which it is not possible to doubt exist. The logical reduction to objects of direct acquaintance does not show necessarily that such reduced entities do not exist; it shows merely that we are not committed to their existence; we can say everything we want to say without mentioning them. If we honestly examine our experience, the objects with which we are directly acquainted are not continuous invariable physical objects but the discontinuous variable immediate data of sense-perceptions and introspection. At one time Russell included ourselves and universals as objects of direct acquaintance. With universals included as objects of acquaintance it is easy to see how propositions could be made up of elements with which we are acquainted. The key general point is that understanding and knowledge of propositions describing entities or states of affairs with which we are not directly acquainted must be composed wholly of elements with which we are directly acquainted.

The following general characterization can be given of Russell's mature philosophy. There are two kinds of truths: logical and mathematical truths, and factual truths. Logical truths are necessary and can be known to be true *a priori,* since the truth of such propositions is independent of any facts about the world; such truths are tautologies; tautologies are true because of their intrinsic logical form and regardless of content. A proposition is a tautology if it always comes out true regardless of the truth or falsity of its constituent parts; because of this it can tell us nothing about the world; it is devoid of factual content, since it remains true regardless of the truth or falsity of any propositions stating facts about the world; such a proposition is "*p* or not-*p*". There is no *a priori* way of proving the existence of anything. The world consists of a plurality of logically independent facts. Factual truths are contingent and can be known to be true only *a posteriori,* through experience, since the truth of such propositions depends on their corresponding to non-necessary facts about the world; such a proposition is "*p* or *q*". If facts are complex, then sentences are true if they express the relation of the constituent parts of the complex facts. All non-logical truths are true in virtue of their accurate correspondence with some independent extralinguistic fact about the world, and are false otherwise; and such facts can logically stand in complete isolation from any other facts and the universe as a whole. Some facts about the world we know directly, without inference, and some only by inference from facts we do directly know. Our knowledge of facts that we do not know directly, if they cannot be logically reduced without loss of meaning to facts that we do know directly, depends on inferences from facts that we do know directly by principles of inference that are non-demonstrative. No deductive or demonstrative relation exists between ultimate matters of fact, since it is logically possible it implies no contradiction that an isolated fact could be the case although the rest of the universe has been extinguished. If deductive relations existed between matters of fact they would be necessarily connected; but, properly analyzed, facts are never necessarily connected. That facts can appear to be logically dependent arises from our putting together two facts as if they were one fact. From "*A* and *B* are men" it logically follows that *B* is a man; but from the truth "*A* is a man" alone we cannot deduce anything whatever about *B*. Russell sharply differentiates between truth and knowledge: between a truth and verification or proof of that truth. Primarily, beliefs, and derivatively propositions, are true in virtue of objectively and correctly corresponding to the facts. A belief or proposition just *is* true if it corresponds to the facts, regardless of whether anyone knows or could know it to be true by its actual verification, and regardless of any other beliefs or propositions thought to be true. The fact in virtue of which a belief or sentence is true is called its verifier. Russell is adamant that there are many true beliefs that no one will ever know to be true; what is true is not limited by our capacity for knowledge of truths and powers of verification. Increasingly he was forced to admit the perspectival nature of our knowledge, and our inability to attain complete certainty, impartiality, and objectivity divorced from our point of view; nevertheless, such an objective point of view should be our aim so we can mirror the world with as little distortion as possible.

Russell clearly rejects both the pragmatist theory of truth, where a proposition is held to be true in virtue of the satisfactory practical consequences in relation to our experiences of its being accepted, and the coherence theory of truth, where the truth of a proposition is dependent on its consistency with other propositions which form a complex system. Truth, apart from in logic and mathematics, consists of a relation to non-linguistic facts that are in general non-human.

In the philosophy of logical atomism Russell argues for a metaphysics in which the world consists ultimately of logically atomic objects or particulars qualified by properties or standing in relation; these are atomic facts; logical relations between atomic facts form complex facts. Particulars are logically independent; there is no logical impossibility involved in saying the universe might consist in one particular. Thus the truth of any complex proposition concerning a complex fact depends on whether it correctly describes the relation of the elements of the complex fact. Complex propositions are compounds which depend for their truth or falsity on the truth or falsity of their constituent parts: they are truth-functional compounds of atomic propositions. So there must be ultimately simple objects whereby analysis comes to an end. The ideal logical language would clearly show what was simple and what complex. The simplest objects are those that can only be denoted by logically proper names; that is, names that have no hidden descriptive content which would imply the objects named have parts. The meaning of a proper name is fully given by an acquaintance with the particular named. Either a logically proper name names a particular or it has no meaning. The simplest of atomic facts would be stated as *"Fa"*, where *"a"* is a logically proper name qualified by a predicate *"F"*, or *"aRb"*, which expresses the relation between atomic objects *a* and *b* which have the logically proper names *"a"* and *"b"*. This gives a logical definition of what particulars would be; whether there are any is another matter.

The only logically proper names which are guaranteed meaning, because they cannot fail to have a reference, seem to be the demonstratives "this" and "that", which refer to the smallest perceptibly distinguishable part of a sense-datum (a minimum sensible); that is, they must refer to an absolutely simple part of the immediate present content of our sense-experience; thus we might have the atomic fact "This is white" if this means the minimal sensible sense-datum of my immediate sense-experience. But a consequence of this would be a vocabulary private to the speaker and shifting in meaning, for "this" and "that" would mean different things for different speakers, and different things for the same speaker at different times, since "this" and "that" refer only to the minimal content of experience at a moment. A molecular proposition is a truth-functional compound of atomic propositions, such as "*Fa* and *Gb*". Such qualified proper names as *"a"* and *"b"* either name an object or are not meaningful at all. Logically proper names do not name physical objects, since they are complex. The names of physical objects might cease to be meaningful if the complex physical object named ceased to exist through its disintegrating; such names can be replaced ultimately by descriptions of atomic facts that describe sense-experience.

Later Russell came to see problems with logical atomism and to think that whether there are atomic facts and objects which are unanalyzable was a question which did not need answering, and the lack of an answer did not detract from the value of analyzing complexes into constituent parts.

Russell maintained a deep respect for the findings of science; whatever doubt we may have about the details of the discoveries of science, he thought that the scientific view of the universe, particularly as derived from the most basic science of physics, was essentially true. The existence and nature of the world or reality are almost entirely non-human, and are quite independent of mind, modes of cognition, or capacity for knowledge. Fundamental features of the world are not in any way dependent on concepts contributed by mind. Most of the universe is governed by laws in which the mind plays no part, and in which mind in particular the human mind occupies only a tiny fragment of space and time. How we know is itself only a small part of what we know; otherwise, Russell says, we would be inclined to think that the mind in some way determined the nature of the world. Russell accepts that there might be things we cannot know. These views fit with Russell's rejection of idealism, including the philosophy of Kant, and also of some tendencies of empiricism.

This connects with Russell's attitude to extreme scepticism, as practised by Descartes. Russell, although initially sympathetic to scepticism because he saw it as a way of discovering certainty, came to think no progress can be made from the starting point of extreme scepticism. He is not an insincere sceptic who would reject beliefs that no one acquainted with the current state of knowledge could seriously doubt; we should accept the best current knowledge of the time unless we have specific reasons for rejecting it. Scepticism can, however, be useful as a methodological device to see how many assumptions can be eliminated as unnecessary, so making our knowledge more secure by eliminating the number of assumptions required to be accepted. This attitude to scepticism amounts to an admission that extreme scepticism cannot ultimately be refuted; but Russell also denies there are any grounds for thinking it true. It is logically possible that the whole universe came into existence five minutes ago with our having false memories apparently of a time before that; everything now is as it would be if the universe had existed before that time there is no way of showing such a hypothesis to be impossible. There would be no way of proving that it did not exist earlier; indeed all the evidence would point the other way. That scepticism cannot be ultimately refuted does not mean that its grounds cannot be minimized; it is just that it is logically possible that it is true. The only way of giving an absolute refutation of any position, including extreme scepticism, is by showing that it involves a logical contradiction and is hence logically impossible; this often cannot be done. But that does not mean any view that cannot be shown to be logically contradictory must be equally believed to be true. Intellectual honesty demands that reasons or evidence for and against should be the overriding consideration in deciding what we do and do not believe. Russell reduces, in his later work, his expectations as to how much certainty is possible. Essentially his view is that absolute certainty of the sort that would satisfy exaggerated scepticism exists only with respect to logical truths (and only then because they are contentless tautologies) and with respect to our awareness of the immediate content of our minds; elsewhere absolute certainty is impossible and doubt logically possible.

Russell was convinced that much bad philosophy was a product of a naive acceptance of the structure or syntax of ordinary language as reflecting the structure of the world. The ambiguity of the vocabulary of ordinary language produces additional but less profound difficulties. Language could display the metaphysical structure of reality the logically basic, or essential, features of the world but only if the language in question were purified of the accidental accretions which lead to unwarranted metaphysical commitments. The purification of ordinary language is carried out by displaying the logical form buried in the grammatical form of ordinary language. Otherwise we find ourselves ontologically committed to some entities having some kind of being which both is problematic and which leads to paradox. The purpose of constructing such an ideal language is to eliminate unnecessary assumptions as to the existence of certain entities by paraphrasing expressions which denote those kinds of entities and seem to presuppose their existence in expressions which do not contain such a presupposition. The question of whether such entities actually exist is not a matter that can be settled by logic alone; but we are not committed by our language to supposing that such entities must exist.

An application of this idea, and of logical analysis, can be seen in Russell's theory of descriptions. Russell assumes that the meaning of a name is to be identified with the object that it denotes; he also assumes that if we have a meaningful declarative sentence, it must be either true or false. Take the proposition "The present King of France is bald", when there is no King of France. This obviously seems to be a meaningful declarative sentence. By a denoting phrase Russell means an expression of the form of "the so-and-so". If a denoting phrase such as "The King of France" functions as a name, and expressions in which the phrase occurs are to be meaningful, we seem to be committed to the existence, in some sense, of an object named by the denoting phrase. Moreover, any proposition in which a predicate is ascribed to a subject would seem to involve the implication that there is an object which the subject term denotes. Indeed decidedly paradoxical results arise where we wish to deny the existence of objects; if "*X* does not exist" is to be meaningful, "*X*" must denote an object, so we seem to have to suppose that *X* after all has being in some way. The way Russell deals with this problem is with his theory of descriptions. He denies that definite descriptions function as names; so for them to contribute to the meanings of propositions in which they occur there need not be objects that they denote. The temptation to assume that there must be an object which a definite description denotes is removed by making explicit the implicit assumption and paraphrasing the propositions so that the definite description does not occur. Thus the full and correct analysis of "The present King of France is bald" is a conjunction of three propositions:

(a) There is a King of France

&

(b) There is not more than one King of France

&

(c) There is nothing which is both King of France and is not bald.

More formally this can be stated as follows:

There is an *x* such that

(a') *x* is now King of France

&

(b') For all *y*, if *y* is now King of France, *y* is identical with *x*

&

(c') *x* is bald.

This shows that although the whole original proposition, "The present King of France is bald", is meaningful, there is thereby no need to find oneself committed to assuming the existence of any object denoted by the subject term of the proposition. The analysis enables us to affirm or deny what was merely assumed, that there exists an object denoted by the subject term of the original proposition. It also maintains the principle that all meaningful declarative sentences must be determinately true or false, because the whole original proposition is false. The whole original proposition is false because (a) is false, that is, (a') is false for every value of *x*, and if one of a set of conjuncts is false, then the whole set is false. If the King of France did exist but was not bald, then the whole original proposition would be false because (c) is false, that is, the conjunction (a') & (b') & (c') would be false for every value of *x*, while (a') & (b') was true for some *x*.

Russell's logical constructionism involves the construction wherever possible of the world from those items with which we are directly acquainted, unless we are forced to do otherwise. This means that entities *X* can be constructed out of entities *Y*. The principle of this *logical* construction proceeds through showing that all sentences about *X*s can be translated without loss of meaning to sentences about *Y*s; the direction of the construction always involves the construction of those entities of whose existence and nature we are most doubtful out of those entities about which our knowledge is least doubtful and most secure. This attempts to give greater security against doubt to beliefs concerning the nature and existence of entities.

Russell applies this idea to mathematical truths; here the aim is to minimize the number of truths that have to be accepted without proof, and the number of entities that need to be postulated. The aim is to show that all mathematical truths can, in principle, be stated in terms derived from logic alone. Mathematics seems to refer to various problematic entities—for example, numbers; but numbers are not empirical entities and do not seem to be in space or time at all. It is extremely unclear, in that case, what sort of being such entities can have. The strategy here is to define numbers in terms of classes: the number one is the class of all classes in which any member is identical with any other member; the number two is the class of all classes of couples, and so on. We must note that the number of members a class has is defined in a non-circular manner using the notion of "similarity" of classes where there is a one-to-one relation which correlates the members of the one class each with one member of the other class. Thus the need to posit problematic entities outside space and time is avoided, and we can think of numbers as classes of classes of unproblematic entities. In the end Russell came to accept reluctantly Wittgenstein's view that mathematics consisted of tautologies; he was reluctant to do this because it destroyed the idea that mathematics was a system of certain discoverable eternal truths about a non-human world beyond the uncertainty concerning the world revealed by the senses. The conclusion is that the interest of mathematics for us derives entirely from our limited intellectual power, and its truths would to a mind of sufficient power be as trivial as 2+2=4.

The same logical constructionism is applied to our knowledge of physical objects and mind. Russell's convictions with respect to our knowledge of the world are basically empiricist, but he accepts certain limitations to empiricism; experience alone is not sufficient to justify many of our non-logical knowledge claims. He accepts that our knowledge of the world must be through experience, while at the same time he holds that certain of the suppositions required for such knowledge, given the range of what we wish to claim to know, cannot be justified by experience. If strict empiricism were followed, we would seriously have to limit our claims to know by being unable justifiably to go beyond the information we strictly immediately experience. Either what we normally claim to know we do not really know, or we must accept certain principles not justifiable by experience in order to claim such knowledge.

Russell accepts the traditional view that we do not directly experience physical objects; rather, we directly and indubitably experience private objects, actual sense-data and possible sense-data—sensibilia—which are not thereby necessarily something mental, and it is from these that physical objects are to be either constructed or inferred. This is because when we say we are perceiving a table, we and other people perceive different things depending on things about us (our position, for example); since there is no reason to show favouritism and say that any one of the perceptions *is* the "real" table (its real shape or colour, for example), what we actually perceive cannot be the real table itself, but must be something else.

Initially Russell adopted a dualism of mind and matter and a triadic structure for our sense-perception. In any act of sense-perception there are said to be three elements: act, content, object. By "act" is meant the subject's act of awareness; by "content" is meant the private sense-data of which the subject is aware; by "object" is meant whatever is the cause of the sense-data. The problem that immediately arises is how one is to justify the belief in the existence of public physical objects if one is never directly aware of them. This problem, along with the fact that the supposed act of awareness, as distinct from what one is aware of, is also never a datum of experience, led Russell to adopt a form of neutral monism. This view accorded, Russell believed, more exactly with modern science. According to this view, neither matter nor mind constitutes the ultimate stuff of the universe (neither are substances); both are logical constructs out of something more fundamental: events. Events are analyzable into qualities in some space-time region, space and time being constructs out of relations between qualities. These events, in so far as knowledge rather than truth is concerned, are identified by Russell with "percepts", which are the immediate data of our experience, but which as possible objects of experience can exist unperceived. In this way both matter (physical objects) and mind can be logically constructed out of percepts, and the only difference between matter and mind consists in the way in which they are collected into related bundles. Objects are constructed out of the class of all actual and possible appearances or aspects; subjects are the class of percepts which constitute a perspective bound together by memory. Roughly we can think of this as "act" and "object" being collapsed into "content".

What I am immediately aware of is a percept in my private perceptual space, which is an event in my brain; but my brain, for me, does not form part of my private perceptual space, although my brain is an object in public neutral space. In saying "I see *X*" I am directly aware of percepts in private perceptual space, the necessary and sufficient conditions for which are brain events in public neutral space, and such events are causally linked in some way to events constituting *X* in public space. Particular percepts which I experience are associated with two places: the place associated with the group of particulars, which is my biography, and the place associated with the group of particulars, which is the "thing" *X;* these are two ways of grouping the same percepts.

With respect to knowledge of the world we are acquainted indubitably without inference only with present private experiences; the problem then arises as to the principles by which we are justified in claiming knowledge beyond the evidence of our immediate experience. We claim to know truths about the past, and the future, and universally valid laws of science. Russell holds that whatever the required principles might be, they cannot be deductive, because no deductive connections hold between matters of fact. The inference from matters of fact with which we are immediately acquainted, if they cannot be reduced without loss of meaning to propositions about immediate experience, must depend on a non-demonstrative principle of inference. Russell is asking what logical justification there can be for beliefs beyond what we immediately experience; he is not asking in what circumstances we are in fact caused to make such inferences and have such beliefs.

We can ask, for example, what is the justification for the belief in material objects that continue to exist unperceived? There is also the problem that inference from "Some *A*s are *B*s" to "All *A*s are *B*s" is never deductively valid, for there is no logical contradiction in supposing that the next observed *A* will not be a *B*. The principle we are seeking to justify such an inference is one that somehow validates the move from things that we have observed to things that we have not observed. Russell ultimately rejects the view that this principle is one of simple enumerative inductive inference: that the more observed *A*s have been *B*s, the more probable it is that the next *A* will be a *B*. He rejects it because it is more likely, if unlimited by common sense, to lead to false beliefs than to true beliefs. Given any finite set of facts, there is, logically speaking, an infinite number of possible theories which will fit the facts, all of which are equally probable. If, however, we start with certain assumptions about the world antecedent to our empirical investigation, then some outcomes, following the empirical gathering of facts, will be more probable than others. These Russell outlines as five "postulates" in *Human knowledge*. These postulates are indemonstrable; if they were logical *a priori* principles, then they would, through being tautologies devoid of content, be unable to fulfil their function of factually describing the world by ruling out certain factual possibilities, going beyond mere logical non-contradiction. On the other hand, such postulates cannot be verified by experience, for they are being presupposed in all empirical reasoning. Although the postulates cannot be proved, Russell's valuing of them is justified by his claim that they distil from obvious cases of scientific practice the details of what is actually assumed in such empirical inquiry. This fits with Russell's general notion of philosophical analysis: the aim is not to speak obscurely about science, and empirical inferences, being a valid practice; the aim is to make clear by analysis exactly what that practice logically assumes. Although the ensuing postulates cannot be proved, we at least know where we stand, and what exactly is being assumed. These postulates in turn mark the limits of empiricism, but limits which Russell in one sense does not overstep because he does not think that the postulates could have other than an empirical justification; the limitation arises from the fact that no empirical justification is possible. He does not suggest that they can be known to be objectively valid by being Kantian *a priori* principles because he does not think the mind can legislate for facts about the world; mind cannot dictate facts to the world.

The problem with empiricism as a theory of knowledge is its inability to justify our knowledge of things which we clearly wish to claim to know; it is unable to do this because it would require, but cannot justify empirically, principles of inference which take us beyond what is justified by private present immediate experiences. Empiricism as a theory of knowledge must have limits, since it will involve some general proposition about the dependence of knowledge on experience, such as "All knowledge is based on experience", which is not itself knowable by experience; so, if true, empiricism cannot be known to be so.

Wittgenstein

Ludwig Wittgenstein (1889–1951) was born in Vienna into a wealthy merchant family; he was the youngest of eight children. Wittgenstein's paternal grandfather had been a wealthy Jewish merchant who had converted to Protestantism. Wittgenstein's mother was a Roman Catholic, and he was brought up in that faith. The house was one of great cultural sophistication, particularly with regard to music, Brahms and Mahler being regular visitors. The attempt was made to tutor the children at home; but this proved a failure academically. At an early age, Wittgenstein showed great aptitude for practical engineering, and constructed a small sewing machine. His poor academic performance meant that he failed to enter Vienna University, and instead went to a technical college in Berlin. He left the college in 1908 and went to the University of Manchester as a student of aeronautical engineering. Naturally his work involved the application of mathematics; this led him to be interested in the foundations of mathematics itself. He asked who had done work in this area and was directed to Bertrand Russell's *Principles of mathematics*. This proved a revelation to Wittgenstein, and he was advised by Frege to study with Russell in Cambridge, which he did in 1912. Although the personalities of Russell and Wittgenstein were frequently at odds, Russell soon developed a deep respect for Wittgenstein's early philosophical and mathematical ideas.

Wittgenstein went to Norway in 1913 and built himself a hut in a remote location in which to continue his work on logic. When the First World War broke out, Wittgenstein enlisted in the Austrian army. He survived the war and was taken prisoner by the Italians. One result of the war was that a new austerity or asceticism characterized his life. Throughout his time in the army he had been completing his first great book, the *Tractatus logico-philosophicus;* this was eventually published in 1921. Since he thought that the *Tractatus* disposed of all the problems of philosophy, he quite consistently gave up the subject. From 1920 to 1926 he was a primary school teacher in rural Austria. Under the influence of discussions with other philosophers, and through dissatisfaction with the *Tractatus,* Wittgenstein resumed his philosophical activity. In 1929 he returned to Cambridge and received a PhD for his *Tractatus*. Around this time Wittgenstein began the transition from his early philosophy to his later ideas.

After returning to Cambridge Wittgenstein was, with Russell's recommendation, awarded a Fellowship at Trinity College. During this time the second, and in many ways quite different, phase of his philosophy in the *Philosophical investigations* developed, although there are connections with his earlier thought.

Wittgenstein was in many ways an extraordinary person. He was a man of lacerating self-criticism, troubled about his own life. He could be extremely difficult, but he elicited great loyalty from his friends. Although cultured, he was relatively unread in the philosophical classics. It is difficult to identify philosophical influences on Wittgenstein; some known influences are Spinoza, Schopenhauer, Kierkegaard (1813–55), William James (1842–1910) and also Frege and Russell. He also admired writers such as Dostoyevsky and Tolstoy. He was driven by his character to think about philosophical problems; good philosophy was not seen by him as something that could be compartmentalized as a professional job distinct from the rest of one's life and the deepest considerations as to how we ought to live; philosophy and wisdom were, or ought to be, interlinked. His thought was profound, and yet he had doubts about the nature, function and value of philosophical thought. He had a deep desire to solve philosophical problems, and not use them as a field for mental exercise.

In order to understand the *Tractatus* it is necessary to give an account of its overall aim, motivation and method. The aim of the book is to draw the limits of the thinkable; and this is the same as drawing the limits of language; beyond those limits the attempt to say things can only produce nonsense. This brings us to the motivation for the book; this can be seen as ethical, or perhaps aesthetic. In the face of that which is "higher", matters concerning ethics, religion, aesthetics and profound questions about the meaning of life, we should stand in silence; the attempt to say things about such subjects offends not only against the logic of what language is capable of saying, but also against a cultured sensibility which refuses to babble futilely in the presence of what is awesome and mystical. The attempt to say things about what cannot be said is worse than silence, not only because it is a waste of time, but also because it leads us to corrupt and destroy the true nature of that of which we speak. This idea accords with the intuition of many that words are somehow inadequate in the face of the things that really matter most the most profound aspects of the human condition and that silence is the only proper response; the attempt to speak only sounds gauche, shallow and tactless.

Much of philosophy has been concerned to tackle philosophical problems head-on by trying to develop answers to the problems as stated. The notion that there are limits to thought and language can be applied to the problems and questions of philosophy itself. Wittgenstein rigorously develops the critical tradition in philosophy. There is some similarity with Kant's assault on transcendent metaphysics. To give a philosophical critique is to describe the logical limits of something, such as knowledge, thought or language. In the *Tractatus* the aim of the critique is to show that the problems of philosophy do not need to be addressed because they are pseudo-problems which arise from illegitimately going beyond logical limits. Thus we should try not to tackle philosophical problems head-on but rather to show that they are not genuine problems; they are necessarily nonsense, and no more require to be answered than "How many goals have been scored in this cricket match?" requires an answer in terms of the number of goals. Philosophical problems are not solved but dissolved.

In Wittgenstein the method used to carry through this critique is deceptively simple: how every and any language acquires its meaning determines the limits of what is meaningful in language. These limits are determined by discovering the essence of language: what all meaningful language must have in common, that without which it would not be meaningful language. Wittgenstein regards the limits of language as the limits of thought; beyond those limits we not only lack any possibility of knowledge, we also reach what is unthinkable. It is vital to realize that Wittgenstein assumes that language at bottom has an essence, a single or unified logic; there is a single universal form of language. There are features common to all and only languages that make them language. Anything that has these features is a language, and anything that is a language has these features. In short, it is possible to define language by a set of features that are together necessary and sufficient for anything to count as language.

Language is considered as the totality of propositions. Propositions are linguistic expressions that can be determinately true or false. What we have to show is the way that words and propositions, the basic units of our language, acquire their meaning. We analyze the essential way that propositions such as "The cat is black" acquire their meaning or sense; all that can be meaningfully said can be expressed in propositions; it follows that we cannot speak, or can speak only nonsense, if we try to use propositions to talk about subjects in which they cannot have a meaning. In short, we must study the way language essentially acquires its meaning in order to show that there are limits to what can be meaningfully expressed in language. That is, the discovery of the necessary and sufficient conditions the essential features in virtue of which any linguistic expression is meaningful entails that anything that fails to satisfy those conditions must be meaningless. The limits of the meaningful mark the limits of genuine propositions, and thus of language.

It must be pointed out that, generally speaking, the propositions in which philosophical problems are stated appear meaningful. But this appearance is an illusion; once we understand the logic of our language, that is, how ultimately and necessarily language becomes meaningful, we will see that such propositions do not accord with what can be meaningful. Russell in the theory of descriptions had shown that certain philosophical problems disappear once we see the underlying logical form beneath the apparent surface grammar. Such insight into the nonsense of the apparent propositions of philosophy reveals itself not immediately, but only after analysis. According to Wittgenstein, it is unnecessary to do this analysis piecemeal; one can show the limits of meaningful language, and that philosophy lies outside those limits, all at once. The aim is to indicate what cannot be said by clearly presenting what can be said; we thus indicate what cannot be said from inside the boundary of what can be said.

Wittgenstein's inquiry is not an empirical one; it is a matter of pure logic; it is a matter of showing how any propositions of any language acquire their meaning by showing in what that meaning essentially consists or must consist when all superficial differences are removed. There is just *one* way all language is meaningful. This involves showing what *must* be the case in the deep structure of language and the nature of the world if meaningful language is to be possible as it obviously is at all. The key to this is to understand that ultimately language gets its meaning from its having a certain relation to the world; apparently meaningful expressions which cannot have that relation are not really meaningful.

If we are able to determine the essential conditions required for meaningful descriptive language, and these derive from something about the world, we have also displayed the essential nature of reality; that is, how any possible world logically must be if any world exists at all. There will of course be all sorts of contingent features about the world which we cannot determine by logic alone; but there must be some essential features that are common to all possible worlds regardless of their contingent differences. The minimal conditions for having a meaningful descriptive language at all reveal the minimal nature of any possible world the substance of the world. Basically this will come down to what is common between the essential structure of meaningful language and the essential structure of the world.

In giving an account of how language gets its meaning, it must be understood that we are looking below the surface structure of language to the hidden deep structure on which its meaningfulness depends. Wittgenstein is saying: if language has meaning, then, as a matter of logical necessity, this, at its deepest level, is how language must be.

Language gets its meaning in virtue of a relation between it and the world. So language that cannot have this relation is meaningless. The starting-point of Wittgenstein's view of language is roughly outlined as follows. The meaning of a word is the object for which it stands; the meaning of a word is the object to which the word refers. Words are basically names. The world is made up of objects, and the relations between objects form facts. Propositions describe the facts by describing how the objects stand in relation to each other. If the relation of the objects expressed in the proposition is the same as the relation of the objects themselves, then the proposition is true, otherwise it is false. What the facts are is quite independent of language or thought; we do not make the facts.

As an account of ordinary language the above seems obviously inadequate. If the meaning of names is their objects, then names referring to objects that cease to exist, or never did exist (such as "Excalibur"), become, or are, meaningless. This means that any proposition containing such names will also be meaningless. Also there are various components of ordinary language that do not seem to be names at all such as "is", "or", "must"—so their meaningfulness is unexplained. The answer to this is that ordinary language hides a complexity that can be revealed by analysis.

Suppose we have a proposition *"p"* asserting "*x* is *F*", but *x* does not exist. If "*x* is *F*" is false just because *x* does not exist, then "*x* is not-*F*" is also false; but it is a principle of logic that propositions *"p"* and "not-*p*" cannot both be false or both true. So what the proposition *"p"* really asserts is that some related complex combination of objects constituting *x* in fact obtains. But although the elements of the complex exist, the described relation between them concealed in the name *"x"* does not hold; *"x"* covertly describes a fact rather than names an object. So "*x* is *F*" is false because part of what it describes, under the guise of the term *"x"*, is false; the complex combination of objects constituting *x* does not obtain, although the constituent objects exist.

We might say "*x* is *F*" is not false but meaningless if *x* does not exist. On Wittgenstein's view of language, if we find a complex expression that contains a name referring to an object that does not exist, then it would seem that the whole expression must be meaningless. If the expression is to be meaningful, then the terms referring to the object that does not exist must really be a description using terms referring to more fundamental objects that do exist and to the relation between them. Then the original whole expression is not meaningless, but simply false, because one of its constituent parts describes a relation between fundamental objects that does not hold, although those objects themselves exist. Because those objects exist, the whole expression referring to them is meaningful, although the relation it describes as holding between them is incorrect.

The implication of this is that proper or *real* names ("simple signs") should refer to simples atomic objects that are logically without parts and so cannot break up if expressions which include names are not to run the risk of being meaningless or nonsense when the object named does not, or ceases to, exist. "Excalibur has a sharp blade" is meaningful whether Excalibur exists or not; so the word "Excalibur" is really a description which must by analysis be eliminated and replaced by names of simple parts, which, if they are not combined in a certain way, means that Excalibur does not exist, but to which the names cannot fail to refer and so have meaning.

If we are not to embark on a regress in which we are unable to guarantee that propositions have a determinate sense, we must reach real names that cannot fail to refer to objects; that is, absolutely simple objects that cannot be described. If the terms of propositions did not ultimately name objects that are not complexes, then any proposition could always fail to have meaning, since it might be constituted of terms that had no reference, and hence no meaning. The only way to guarantee that terms have meaning is that they are ultimately constituted of terms that cannot fail to refer to objects that exist if the world exists at all. This means the objects cannot be complexes, but must be without parts. If they are without parts, they cannot be described but can only be named, for a description is an analysis into constituent parts. This is the only way of guaranteeing that propositions have meaning; otherwise any proposition could fail to have a meaning by containing terms that are ultimately words referring to non-existent entities. Wittgenstein calls these ultimate terms simple or atomic names and their references simple or atomic objects. Thus Wittgenstein gives an account of what must be the case if language is to be guaranteed as meaningful.

This emphasizes the requirement that sense be determinate; propositions must have a definite sense, for a proposition without definite sense could not be said to have a sense at all, and could not be determinately true or false.

Wittgenstein's aim is to produce a theory of language whereby propositions have meaning even when they appear to refer to non-existent objects. If the meaning of words consists in the objects for which they stand, and propositions are made up of words, then, for it to be the case that propositions are guaranteed a sense even when they apparently name non-existent objects, at a deep level it must be the case that language as the totality of propositions consists of names that cannot fail to have meaning by having objects for which the names cannot fail to stand. At the deepest level language, as the totality of propositions, must consist of names of logically simple indestructible objects.

When completely analyzed, the structure of language mirrors the structure of the world. The most basic constituents of language are atomic names which mean their atomic objects; the meaning *(Bedeutung)* of a name is the object to which it refers. Atomic names and objects are, respectively, the simplest constituents of language and of the world. Atomic objects are the substance or form of the world in that they are common to any possible world. These objects are logically atomic: they can only be named and not described, for if they could be described they would consist of a complex combination of elements which would mean they were not simple; but atomic objects are indestructible, permanent and unchanging. Atomic objects are the constant elements of all change and enter into combination with other atomic objects to form a state of affairs or atomic fact *(Sachverhalt)*. The possible ways in which atomic objects can enter into combination with other objects fix the form of such objects, the sum of which ways is the possible states of affairs in which such an object can be an element. This form is the timeless order determining all the possible states of affairs into which it can enter. When we know *(kennen)* an atomic object, it is "given"; we then know all the possible states of affairs into which it can enter; in that sense we then know all other objects and all possibilities. Possible and actual states of affairs, which are arrangements of atomic objects, are depicted by elementary propositions, which are concatenations of atomic names. In elementary propositions atomic names substitute for, or stand proxy for, objects. The totality of existent and non-existent states of affairs is the totality of possible arrangements of atomic objects. Understanding the essence of a proposition means understanding its constituent atomic names which means knowing their atomic objects, and that is to know all possible combinations of those objects: all possible states of affairs or the whole of logical space. An elementary proposition is meaningful or has sense *(Sinn)* in virtue of its describing a possible state of affairs in logical space; it is true if it describes an actual state of affairs and false otherwise. Thus an elementary proposition will be meaningful even when it is false in virtue of its being wholly a concatenation of names which cannot fail to have meaning because they cannot fail to stand for their atomic objects.

The meaning of a name is its reference; but a name does not have a *sense;* a name does not say anything about the world; it does not describe the world, but stands for objects in it; names cannot be true or false. Propositions are true or false; they describe how things stand in the world. Propositions have a sense in that they each describe possible facts in the world; the sense of a proposition is what would be the case if it were true.

The world is the totality of facts. When complex facts *(Tatsachen)* are broken down this ultimately means the totality of states of affairs as described by elementary propositions. The facts are always constituted by rearrangements of the same constant atomic objects. Every proposition which is not an elementary proposition can be analyzed into one, and only one, compound of elementary propositions.

Such elementary propositions consist entirely of concatenations of names. An atomic fact might be that object *a* is to the left of b; we might write this as *"aRb"* where *"R"* stands for the relation between *a* and *b*. But ultimately *"R"*, if it is not a name standing for an object, must be eliminated so we have only atomic names. Indeed, *"ab"* does show the relation of the named objects *a* and *b*. The arrangement of names within the proposition, if it is true, directly *shows* how things are in the world. This is the picture theory of language, whereby the way that language depicts facts in the world ultimately derives from a common logical form: a structural isomorphism between language and the world. Language models or maps the world. How this picturing takes place in propositions is unclear. Even allowing for the spatial *ab* relation, there are more kinds of relations than spatial relation to be depicted. Nevertheless, it can be pointed out that a variety of relations is depicted in other areas, such as that which occurs between a musical score and the music itself. This picturing relation is not apparent for the sentences of ordinary language but holds at a deep level. The idea is that to represent something there must be a one-to-one correlation between elements in the picture and elements in the state of affairs represented; some kind of arrangement or ordering of the elements in the picture shows how the corresponding elements in the world stand to each other. The nature of the ordering of the elements depicted and the nature of the ordering in that which depicts may be different, but the ordering itself is in both as their common *logical form:* the minimum required for picturing to occur at all. It is in virtue of their logical form that propositions are able to depict facts. This minimum universal logical form cannot itself be depicted, since it is what is common to all pictures; to picture logical form alone one would need to stand outside all ways of picturing; but then one could not picture at all.

This picturing theory applies to thoughts; a thought is a proposition; for a thought to be of a possible fact in the world it must, like the proposition, be constituted from an arrangement of psychical elements that correspond to the elements making up the fact in the world. What cannot be stated in a proposition cannot be thought. That which does the representing of a fact is itself a fact, not something other than a fact.

Wittgenstein makes an important distinction between *showing* and *saying.* The thinking here is that ultimately we must reach propositions that simply *show* their sense; their sense is manifest. Proposition *"p" says* that things are so-

and-so. We might attempt to explain the sense of proposition *"p"* by proposition *"q"*; but if *"p"* is to have a sense, we must ultimately reach elementary propositions whose sense simply *shows* itself. In a sense one cannot say what the meaning of a proposition is. If *"q"* does its job of explaining the sense of *"p"* properly, then we have got no further, but have merely re-expressed the same sense. The sense must show itself, and what can be shown cannot be said. Wittgenstein is convinced that the cardinal problem of philosophy has been the attempt to *say* what can only be *shown;* that is, the attempt to explain by saying things which can only be shown; and that can only produce nonsense.

Propositions compounded of elementary propositions are called molecular propositions. Molecular propositions are truth-functions of their elementary propositions: that is, the truth or falsity of whole molecular propositions depends entirely on the truth or falsity of their constituent elementary propositions. Molecular propositions have logical structures which are compounded from elementary propositions by truth-functional logical constants. These truth-functional constants are defined by the way in which they determine the truth or falsity of complex propositions in which they occur. These truth-functional constants, "or" (?), "and" (&), "not" (-), "if...then... " (?), "...if and only if..." (=), are now a standard part of prepositional logic. In addition there is the apparatus of predicate logic, which includes within it prepositional logic, and which takes us "inside" propositions, which involves as logical constants the universal quantifier "all" (?) and the existential quantifier "some" (?). A particular proposition "p", "The chair is red", might be expanded and symbolized as "*a* is *F*" or *"Fa"*, where *"a"* names an individual thing (the chair), and *"F"* is a predicate term (is red). The common structure or general logical form of all propositions like *"p"* can be symbolized as *"Fx"*, where *"x"* is an individual variable (for which constant terms denoting individual things can be substituted) and *"F"* a predicate term. The logical form of the conclusion we can draw, given any one proposition such as "*p*", that is "*Fa*", is expressed in the propositional function.

Take "and" (&) as an example of a truth-functional constant: it is clear that a molecular proposition "*p* & *q*" is true just in that case where both "*p*" is true and "*q*" is true, and is false otherwise. With "not" (-) or negation, for example, we can see that if "*p*" is true, then "-*p*" must be false, and vice versa. The way that truth-functional connectives operate is displayed in truth-tables. For example:

p	-*p*
T	F
F	T

p	*q*	*p* & *q*
T	T	T
T	F	F
F	T	F
F	F	F

The most important point is that all molecular propositions can be analyzed into elementary propositions by truth-functional analysis and that the truth or falsity of the whole original molecular proposition is a function of the truth or falsity of its constituent atomic propositions related by truth-functional connectives.

The essential structure of language, at its various levels of simplicity and complexity derived from analysis and synthesis, mirrors the world. This can be displayed in the diagram opposite, in which the arrows show the direction of analysis. That a proposition describes a possible fact gives the proposition its sense; it describes an arrangement of objects in the world; that the fact is actual or not actual determines the truth or falsity of the proposition. Propositions have a sense even when they are false because they are ultimately a concatenation of atomic names that cannot fail to have meaning because they cannot fail to stand for atomic objects.

The truth of all elementary propositions is logically independent: it is impossible from one elementary proposition to deduce the truth or falsity of any other and impossible for any elementary proposition to contradict another. From the existence of one state of affairs it is impossible to deduce any other state of affairs. If one proposition can be deduced from another, then the proposition from which it is deduced cannot be elementary, but must be a truth-functional compound. One proposition can be deduced from another only if the deduced proposition is contained in the original proposition. For example, "*p*" is deducible from "*p* and *q*", because "*p*" is already contained in the complex proposition "*p* and *q*". A deducible proposition is contained in the proposition from which it is deduced by being a truth-functional component of the complex proposition from which it is deduced. If the individual propositions "*p*" and "*q*" are really elementary propositions, and are not compounds of simpler propositions, then there is no complex for any other proposition to be contained in. This logical independence should show itself clearly in the ideal notation; we can see that if "*p*" and "*q*" are elementary propositions, "*q*" cannot be deduced from "*p*", and vice versa; "*p* and not-*q*" is never a contradiction and "not-(*p* and not-*q*)" is never a tautology.

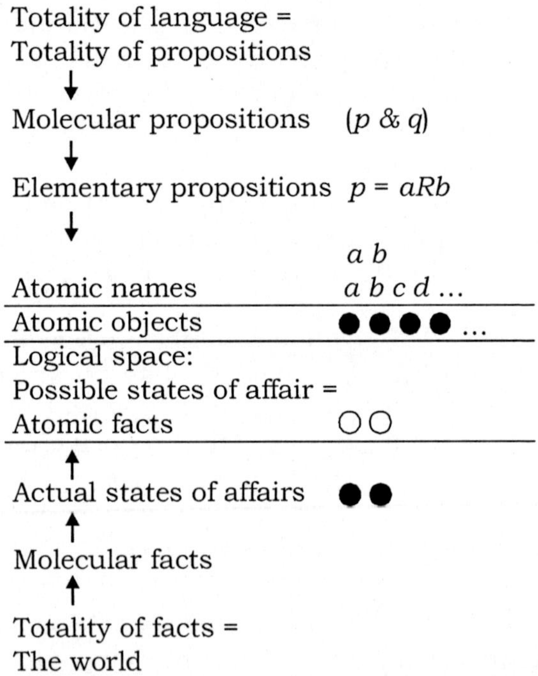

This brings us to logically necessary truths, and contradictions. No elementary proposition can be necessarily true or necessarily false; such propositions are essentially bipolar: true-false, that is, contingent. The only necessarily true propositions are logically necessary truths or tautologies; the only necessary false propositions are contradictions. Necessary truths are necessary because they are truth-functional compounds formed of simpler propositions in such a way that, whatever the truth or falsity of their component parts, the whole proposition is always true. Necessary falsehoods or contradictions are truth-functional compounds formed of simpler propositions in such a way that whatever the truth or falsity of their component parts, the whole proposition is always false. Tautologies say nothing about the world precisely because they are true independently of whatever the facts are about the world which give a truth-value (true or false) to the components of the tautology. Contradictions are false regardless of any facts about the world. Wittgenstein suggests that both tautologies and contradictions are in fact called true or false "propositions" only by courtesy of genuine propositions which are contingently true or false. Tautologies and contradictions are thus senseless *(sinnlos),* but not nonsense *(Unsinn)*. Although tautologies and contradictions say nothing factual about the world, they show the logical structure of the world and language, and show the boundaries within which all propositions which can say anything about the world must fall. They mark the boundaries of factual discourse, and only factual discourse has sense; language gets its meaning from the world, the totality of facts, it cannot therefore say anything about matters outside the world; ethics, values, religion, the meaning of life lie outside the world of facts; they make themselves manifest to us; they show themselves, but we cannot say anything about them. Genuine propositions state possible facts, and can have sense only by doing so, or are tautologies or contradictions. Beyond those boundaries there is only nonsense which does not say anything, but merely shows itself to be nonsense. In short, language gets its entire meaning *from* the world ultimately from names of objects and so language is meaningful only when it states facts *about* the world.

Many problems arise from the *Tractatus,* some of which led to Wittgenstein's later thought. One is the absence of any examples of atomic objects and atomic names. An atomic object must be such that it cannot be described, but only named, and the name is guaranteed to have a reference, and hence a meaning. Russell suggested such real or proper names might refer to the present content of our sense-experience (sense-data): that is, demonstratives such as "this" and "that" are the only logically proper names, which cannot fail to point to the present content of our sense-experience and hence to their reference. But the fleeting nature of such objects of experience means they are not what Wittgenstein wants. A real name should not only have a guaranteed reference, but must also refer to the *same* enduring and unchanging object if its meaning is to be fixed and determinate. But "this" and "that" will mean different things depending on the present content of experience which will vary within the same person and between different people. So Wittgenstein could not share Russell's view. Indeed it seems inevitable that atomic objects are ineffable in that we cannot say anything about them because to say anything about them would be to describe them, and in that case they could not be simple. Wittgenstein's view seems to be that as a logician it is not his job to decide what are atomic objects, atomic names, and the ultimate psychical constituents of thoughts; but it is a matter of logic that there *must be* such things if the propositions of language are to have a sense. We cannot even say of a simple object *a,* that "*a* exists", for the assertion is either meaningless in the case where *a* does not exist, or trivially redundant.

An important problem is the status of the propositions of the *Tractatus* itself. It is not uncommon in philosophy for a philosophical theory or system to cut off the branch on which it is sitting. The attempt to assert and show that some ways are the only ways of being intelligible or knowing things turns out to go beyond those ways and involve just those ways which are said to be unintelligible or unknowable. The point of the *Tractatus* is to put an end to philosophy, or at least all metaphysics, by revealing its propositions to be nonsensical *(unsinnig)*. More generally it reveals what can and what cannot be said; what can be said are the propositions of natural science which are factual: they state facts about the world. This means that about important matters, such as ethics, religion and the meaning of life, nothing can be said, since they are not concerned with facts about the world. It is not that ethics, religion, and the meaning of life are nonsense; what produces nonsense is the attempt to say things about them. But in attempting to make its point it would seem that by its own criteria the propositions of the *Tractatus* itself are just such nonsense. They do not state facts about the world, but say things about the necessary structure of all fact-stating and the necessary structure of the world, which are not themselves further facts about the world. Wittgenstein is aware of this, and declares that one must transcend the propositions of the *Tractatus:* one uses it like a ladder up which one climbs, and which, once used to make clear that metaphysics and the propositions of the *Tractatus* are nonsense, can be thrown away.

Analytic philosophy attempts to clarify, by analysis, the meaning of statements and concepts. Analytic philosophy has been important in the in the English speaking academic world since the beginning of the 20th century. Following Kant a split occurred between Anglo-American academic philosophy and the philosophy practised on the European continent. 'Continental' philosophy took off in an Idealist direction with Hegel, took an existentialist turn via Nietzsche and Heidegger and entered a less certain phase with post-structuralism.

Analytic philosophers on the other hand, saw the German philosopher Gottlob Frege (1848–1925) as the most important thinker since Kant. Frege wanted to put a rigorous logic at the heart of philosophy. He was influential in the philosophy of mathematics, logic and language. He thought that the basis for mathematics could be securely derived from logic and that a rigorous analysis of the underlying logic of sentences would enable us to judge their truth-value.

The British philosopher Bertrand Russell (1872–1970) combined Frege's logical insights with the influence of David Hume's empiricism. Russell thought that the world was composed of 'atomic facts'. Sentences, if they were to be meaningful, had to correspond to these atomic facts. Ludwig Wittgenstein (1889–1951) studied under Russell, his early ideas influenced the Vienna Circle and help form the logical positivism of the 1920's and 30's.

There is a radical break between the early and the later works of Wittgenstein. In his earlier work Wittgenstein saw language as picturing the world, in his later philosophy he understands language by using the metaphor of a game. This change in direction spurred the development of 'Linguistic philosophy', in the mid 20th century. Linguistic philosophers such as Gilbert Ryle (1900–76) thought many of the traditional problems of philosophy could be dissolved by the careful study of language as it is used.

By the 1970's there was a growing dissatisfaction with linguistic philosophy, and philosophers began to show more interest in the philosophy of mind and the application of philosophical methods to wider issues in politics, ethics and the nature of philosophy itself. Richard Rorty (1931–) has used the methods of analytic philosophy to deconstruct its assumptions. Rorty is influenced as much by Heidegger as he is by Wittgenstein, and his approach echoes the ideas of the post-structuralists. It may be that the future will see the concerns of 'analytic' and 'continental' philosophies converge.

8

Behaviorism and Philosophy

Introduction

Materialists deny that the world includes both mental and material substances. Every substance is a material substance. Minds are fashioned somehow from the same elementary components from which rocks, trees, and stars are made. If we take the fundamental particles that make up inanimate objects and arrange them one way, the result is a granite boulder; differently arranged, the outcome is a creature with a mind. The mind is not a separate, non-material entity, but only matter, suitably organized.

Materialism has a long history. Democritus (*c.*460–370 BC) described the world as a fleeting arrangement of atoms swirling in the void. Hobbes (1588–1679) and La Mettrie (1707–1751) regarded mental phenomena as nothing more than mechanical interactions of material components. Nowadays, materialism of one stripe or another is more often than not taken for granted; in David Lewis's words, materialism is *non-negotiable*. In any case, the belief that minds are just brains is evidently widespread. Francis Crick's recent description of this as 'the astonishing hypothesis' flies in the face of my own experience with undergraduate philosophy students, who seem to use 'mind' and 'brain' interchangeably.

Although many philosophers would, if pressed, describe themselves as materialists, materialism comes in different flavors. Disagreements among materialists tend to overshadow their common rejection of dualism. In recent years, dissatisfaction with materialist assumptions has led to a revival of interest in forms of dualism. Surprisingly, much of this interest has been spawned by work in the neurosciences, where difficulties in reconciling characteristics of complex material systems with characteristics of conscious experiences are especially acute.

In this chapter we shall examine one precursor to the contemporary debate: behaviorism. Behaviorism as a philosophical doctrine about the nature of mind differs from behaviorism as a movement in psychology. Philosophical behaviorism is associated with a thesis about the nature of mind and the meanings of mental terms. Psychological behaviorism emerged from an influential conception of scientific method as applied to psychology. This brand of behaviorism dominated experimental work in psychology until the early 1960s when it was eclipsed by the 'information-processing' model, a model inspired by the advent of the computing machine.

The relation between philosophy and the empirical sciences, including psychology, is scarcely straightforward. On the one hand, philosophers of mind have had an important part in shaping conceptions of mentality that guide empirical investigators. On the other hand, philosophers have periodically re-evaluated their theories in light of advances in the sciences. One result is that philosophical influences on the sciences find their way back into philosophy. When this happens, a philosophical thesis can gain an undeserved air of empirical respectability in the minds of philosophers eager to embrace the pronouncements of science.

Philosophers impressed by behaviorism in psychology sometimes failed to appreciate the extent to which the behaviorist conception of mind was the product of a contentious philosophical conception of scientific method. Ironically, the roots of that conception lay in a positivist tradition that many of these same philosophers would have found unappealing. One lesson is that it is a mistake for philosophers of mind to accept uncritically or at face value claims issuing from psychology or the neurosciences.

Historical and Philosophical Background

Until the twentieth century, scientific study of the mind was assumed to revolve around the study of conscious states and processes. Subjects in psychological experiments (most often the experimenters themselves or their students) were trained to 'introspect', and report on features of their conscious experiences. In this milieu, mental imagery and subtle qualities of sensory episodes had a central place.

At the same time, psychologists were concerned to integrate the study of the mind with the study of the brain. It had long been evident that occurrences in the brain and nervous system were intimately related to mental goings-on. The difficulty was to understand precisely the nature of this relation. It is tempting to think that minds (or selves: I shall continue to use the terms interchangeably, without intending to suggest that they are synonymous) are nothing more than brains. Properties of brains, however, seem to differ importantly from properties of minds. When you undergo a conscious experience, you are vividly aware of characteristics of that experience. When we examine a living brain, the characteristics we observe appear to be utterly different.

Think what it is like to have a headache. Now imagine that you are able to peer at the brain of someone suffering a headache. What you observe, even aided by instruments that reveal the fine structure of the brain, is altogether different from what the headache victim feels. Imagine a neuroscientist, intimately familiar with the physiology of headache, but who has never experienced a headache. There is, it would seem, something the scientist lacks knowledge of, some characteristic the scientist has not encountered and could not encounter simply by inspecting the brain. This characteristic would appear not to be a neurological characteristic. When we look at the matter this way, it is hard to avoid concluding that mental characteristics are not brain characteristics: minds are not brains.

If this were not enough, we do well to remind ourselves that we evidently enjoy a kind of 'access' to our conscious experiences that others could never have. Your experiences are 'private'. Your awareness of them is direct and authoritative; my awareness of those same experiences is, in contrast, indirect, inferential, and easily overridden. When you have a headache, form an image of your grandmother, or decide to comb your hair, you are in a position to recognize immediately, without the benefit of evidence or observation, that you have a headache, that you are imagining your grandmother, or that you have decided to comb your hair. I can only infer your state of mind by observing your behavior (including your linguistic behavior: I can inter-rogate you). If mental goings-on are correlated with neurological processes, then I may be able to infer your state of mind by observing your brain. But my access to your mind is still indirect: I infer your state of mind by observing a neurological correlate. I do not observe your state of mind.

All this is exactly what we should expect were dualism true. But dualism, or at any rate Cartesian dualism, apparently leads to a bifurcation of the study of intelligent, sentient agents. We can study the biology and physiology of such agents, but in so doing we ignore their minds; or we can study their minds, ignoring their material composition.

Now, however, we are faced with a difficulty. Science is limited to the pursuit of knowledge concerning objective, 'public' states of affairs. A state of affairs is objective if it can be apprehended from more than one perspective, by more than one observer. The contents of your mind, however, are observable (if that is the word) only by you. My route to those contents is through observations of what you say and do. This appears to place minds outside the realm of scientific inquiry. We can study brains. This might lead us to conclude that particular kinds of neurological going-on are correlated with kinds of mental going-on. Knowledge of such correlations would enable us reliably to infer states of mind by observing brain activity. But we should not be observing or measuring those states of mind themselves, except in our own case.

Privacy and its Consequences

Once we start down this road, we may come to doubt that states of mind as distinct from their physiological correlates are a fit subject for scientific examination. Eventually, the very idea that we are in a position even to establish correlations between mental occurrences and goings-on in the nervous system can come to be doubted. Imagine that every time you have a particular kind of experience every time you see a certain shade of red, for instance, the red of a ripe tomato your brain goes into a particular state, *S*. Further, whenever your brain goes into state *S*, you experience that very shade of red. (You might go into state *S* because you are looking at a tomato, or because you are dreaming that you are looking at a tomato, or because your brain is being artificially stimulated by an implanted electrode with the result that you hallucinate a tomato.) It looks as though there must be a correlation between experiences of this kind and neurological states of kind *S*.

Suppose, now, you observe my brain in state *S*. I announce that I am experiencing a certain shade of red, a shade I describe as the red of a ripe tomato. It might seem that this provides further evidence of the correlation already observed in your own case. But does it? In your own case, you have access both to the mental state and to its neurological correlate. When you observe me, however, you have access only to my neurological condition and my report as to what I am experiencing. What gives you the right to assume that *my* mental state resembles *yours*?

True, I describe my experience just as you describe yours. We agree that we are experiencing the color of ripe tomatoes. But of course this is how we have each been taught to characterize our respective experiences. I have a particular kind of visual experience when I view a ripe tomato in bright sunlight. I describe this experience as the kind of experience I have when I view a ripe tomato in bright sunlight. You have a particular kind of experience when you view a ripe tomato under similar observational conditions. And you have learned to describe this experience as the kind of experience you have when you view a ripe tomato in bright sunlight. But what entitles either of us to say that the experiences so described are exactly similar? Perhaps the experience *you* have is like the experience *I* would have were I to view a lime in bright sunlight! Our descriptions perfectly coincide, but the state of mind I am describing might be qualitatively altogether different from yours.

It would seem, then, that attempts to correlate kinds of neurological goings-on and kinds of mental occurrences boil down to correlations of neurological goings-on and first-person descriptions or reports of mental occurrences. We learn to describe the qualities of our states of mind by reference to publicly observable objects that typically evoke them. And this leaves open the possibility that, while our *descriptions* match, the *states* to which they apply are wildly different qualitatively.

This might seem an idle worry, a purely philosophical possibility. But ask yourself: what earthly reason do you have for thinking that your states of mind qualitatively resemble the states of mind of others? It is not as though you have observed others' states of mind and discovered they match yours. You lack a single example of such a match. Might you infer *inductively* from characteristics of your own case to the characteristics of others? (Inductive inference is probabilistic: we reason from the characteristics of a sample of a population to characteristics of the population as a whole.) But canons of inductive reasoning proscribe inferences from a single individual to a whole population unless it is clear that the individual is representative of the population. If you assume that characteristics of your states of mind are representative, however, you are assuming precisely what you set out to establish.

The problem we have been scouting is the old problem of other minds. Granted that you can know your own mind, how can you know the minds of others? Indeed, once you put it this way, you can see that the problem is deeper than you might have expected. How could you know that others have minds at all? That they have conscious experiences? True, others behave in ways similar to the ways you behave; they insist they have pains, images, feelings, and thoughts. But what reason might you have for supposing that they *do*? You cannot observe others' states of mind. Nor do you have adequate inductive grounds for inferring that they enjoy a mental life from what you can observe about them.

A recent twist on this ancient puzzle introduces the possibility of 'zombies', creatures identical to us in every material respect, but altogether lacking conscious experiences. The apparent conceivability of zombies has convinced some philosophers that there is an unbridgeable 'explanatory gap' between material qualities and the qualities of conscious experience.

You may be growing impatient with this line of reasoning. *Of course* we know that others have mental lives similar to ours in many ways - and different as well: it is also possible to know that. Well and good. But it is hard to see how this confidence could be justified so long as you accept the notion that minds and their contents are private affairs, incapable of public scrutiny.

The Beetle in the Box

Perhaps our starting point is what is responsible for our predicament. Perhaps we have been led down the garden path by a certain conception of mind inherited from Descartes. If we begin to question that conception, we may see our way clear to a solution to our problem, a solution that better fits our commonsense idea that we can know that others have minds and that their minds resemble ours qualitatively.

Wittgenstein (1889–1951), in his *Philosophical Investigations* (1953/1968), § 293, offers a compelling analogy:

> *Suppose everyone had a box with something in it: we call it a 'beetle'. No one can look into anyone else's box, and everyone says he knows what a beetle is only by looking at his beetle. Here it would be quite possible for everyone to have something different in his box. One might even imagine such a thing constantly changing.*

The picture here is meant to resemble the picture of the relation we bear to our own and others' states of mind that we have been taking for granted.

Wittgenstein argues against this picture not by presenting considerations that imply its falsity, but by showing that our accepting it leads to a para-doxical result: if this is the relation we bear to our own and others' states of mind, then we should have no way of referring to them.

Suppose the word 'beetle' had a use in these people's language? If so it would not be used as the name of a thing. The thing in the box has no place in the language-game at all; not even as a something: for the box might even be empty. No, one can 'divide through' by the thing in the box; it cancels out, whatever it is. That is to say: if we construe the grammar of the expression of sensation on the model of 'object and designation' the object drops out of consideration as irrelevant.

What is Wittgenstein's point? You report that your box contains a beetle. Your report is perfectly apt. You have been taught to use the word 'beetle' in just this way. Imagine, now, that the object in my box is very different from the object in your box. If we could compare the objects, this would be obvious, although we could never be in a position to compare them. Suppose now that I report that my box contains a beetle. In so doing, I am using the word 'beetle' exactly as I have been taught to usc it. My utterance, like yours, is perfectly correct.

Suppose, now, we each report that our respective boxes contain a beetle. Is either of us mistaken? No. In the imagined situation, Wittgenstein argues, the word 'beetle' is used in such a way that it makes no difference what is inside anyone's box. 'Beetle', in our imagined dialect, means, roughly, 'whatever is in the box'. To wonder whether your beetle resembles my beetle is to misunderstand this use of 'beetle'. It is to treat 'beetle' as though it named or designated a kind of object or entity. But 'beetle' is used in such a way that 'the object drops out of consideration as irrelevant'.

Wittgenstein's point is not merely a linguistic one. Any thoughts we might harbor that we would express using the word 'beetle' are similarly constrained. Those thoughts turn out not to concern some particular kind of entity. Differently put: if the word 'beetle' does not refer to entities of a particular sort, then neither do thoughts naturally expressible using 'beetle'.

How might the analogy be extended to states of mind? As a child, you react in various ways to your surroundings. On some occasions you whimper and rub your head. Adults tell you that what you have is called a headache. Others are taught to use 'headache' similarly. Does 'headache' designate a kind of entity or state?

Perhaps not. Perhaps when you tell me that you have a headache, you are not picking out any definite thing or private condition at all (think of the beetle), but merely *evincing* your headache. You have been trained in a particular way. When you are moved to whimper and rub your head, you are, as a result of this training, moved as well to utter the words 'I have a headache'. When you ascribe a headache to me, you are saying no more than that I am in a kind of state that leads me to whimper, rub my head, or utter 'I have a headache'. The private qualitative character of that state could differ across individuals. It might continually change, or even, in some cases (zombies?), be altogether absent. The function of the word 'headache' is not to designate a private, qualitatively distinctive entity or episode, however. This 'drops out of consideration as irrelevant'.

Suppose that this account of our use of 'headache' applied

to our mental vocabulary generally. Then mental terms would not in fact be used to designate kinds of entity, or qualitatively similar private episodes, as Descartes would have it. Their role is quite different. And in that case, the question whether the state you designate by 'experience I have when I view a ripe tomato in bright sunlight' qualitatively matches the state I designate when I use the same expression could not so much as arise. To raise the question is to mischaracterize the use of mental terminology, and thus to utter nonsense!

Philosophical Behaviorism

This line of reasoning supports what is often dubbed philosophical behaviorism. (It is dubbed thus by its opponents. Few philosophers routinely so characterized have applied the label to themselves.) The philosophical behaviorist holds that the Cartesian conception of mind errs in a fundamental way. Minds are not entities (whether Cartesian substances or brains); and mental episodes are not private goings-on inside such entities. We are attracted to the Cartesian picture only because we are misled by what Wittgenstein calls the grammar of our language.

So long as we deploy our language in everyday life, we steer clear of philosophical puzzles. Words owe their significance to the 'language games' we play with them. An appropriate understanding of any word (hence the concept the word expresses) requires a grasp of the part or parts it plays in these language games. When we engage in philosophy, however, we are apt to be misled by the fact that 'mind', like 'brain' or 'tomato', is a substantive noun. We reason that 'mind' must designate a kind of entity, and that what we call thoughts, sensations, and feelings refer to qualitatively similar states or modes of this entity. We can avoid confusion only by looking carefully at the way our words are actually deployed in ordinary circumstances.

This prescription is intended by Wittgenstein to apply to philosophy generally. Philosophical problems arise 'when language goes on holiday', when we lose touch with the way words are actually used. In our everyday interactions with one another, we are not puzzled by our capacity to know how others feel or what they are thinking. The philosophical problem of other minds arises when we wrench 'mind', 'thought', 'feeling', 'sensation', and their cognates from the contexts in which they are naturally deployed, put a special interpretation on them, and then boggle at the puzzles that result.

Gilbert Ryle (1900–1976) extends Wittgenstein's point. According to Ryle, the supposition that minds are kinds of entity amounts to a 'category mistake': 'it represents the facts of mental life as if they belonged to one logical type or category when actually they belong to another'. Suppose I show you around my university. We stroll through the grounds; I show you various academic and administrative buildings; I take you to the library; I introduce you to students and members of the faculty. When I am done, I ask whether there is anything else you would like to see. You reply, 'Yes. You've shown me the grounds, the academic and administrative buildings, the library, students, and faculty; but you haven't shown me the *university*. I'd like to see that.' You have made a category mistake. You have taken the term 'university' to designate an item similar to, but distinct from, those items you have seen already.

If you persisted in the belief that 'university' designates such an entity despite failing ever to encounter it, you might come to imagine that the entity in question is 'immaterial'. An analogous mistake, says Ryle, encourages Cartesian dualism. We begin with the idea that minds are entities, distinct from but similar to brains or bodies. When we have trouble locating such entities in the material world, we assume that they must be non-material. We see the mind, to use Ryle's colorful phrase, as the *ghost in the machine*. But minds are not entities at all, ghostly or otherwise, a fact we should immediately appreciate if only we kept firmly before us the way 'mind' functions in ordinary English.

The theoretically interesting category mistakes are those made by people who are perfectly competent to apply concepts, at least in the situations with which they are familiar, but are still liable in their abstract thinking to allocate those concepts to logical types to which they do not belong.

At the risk of confusing matters by piling analogies on top of analogies, an example of Wittgenstein's may help here. Suppose you look into the cab of a locomotive (or the cockpit of a jetliner). You see levers, knobs, buttons, and switches. Each of these operates in a particular way (some are turned, some slide back and forth, some are pushed or pulled), and each has a particular function in the locomotive's (or jetliner's) operation. We should be misled if we assumed that levers or knobs with similar shapes had similar functions. In the same way, the fact that 'mind' is a substantive noun, or that we speak of 'states of mind', should not lead us to assume that 'mind' functions to designate a particular entity, and that states of mind are states of this entity.

If 'mind', like 'university, does not function to name a particular kind of material or immaterial ('ghostly') entity, how does it function? Perhaps we ascribe minds to creatures with a capacity to comport themselves, as we should say, 'intelligently'. A creature possesses a mind not in virtue of being equipped with a peculiar kind of mysterious internal organ, but in virtue of being the sort of creature capable of engaging in behavior that exhibits a measure of spontaneity and a relatively complex organization. For their part, states of mind headaches, intentions, beliefs are possessed by intelligent creatures in virtue of what they do or would do. Your believing that there is a bear in your path, for instance, is a matter of your taking (or being disposed to take) appropriate evasive measures, your assenting (or being disposed to assent) to 'There is a bear on the path', and the like. Your intending to attend the World Series is a matter of your being moved to purchase tickets, arranging for transportation, announcing 'I'm going to the World Series', and so on.

Dispositions

We have noted that behaviorists hold that agents are correctly describable as having states of mind, not only in virtue of what those agents *do*, but also in virtue of what the agents *would do*, what the agents are *disposed* to do. If you have a headache, you may be disposed to whimper, rub your head, seek out aspirin, and announce when prompted, 'I have a headache'. You may do none of these things, however. Imagine, for instance, that you think it ill-mannered to speak of one's afflictions. In that case, although you are *disposed* to behave in particular ways, you do not behave in those ways.

But now we are confronted with a new question. What is it to 'be disposed' to behave in a particular way? What are dispositions? A fragile vase possesses a disposition to shatter. In shattering when struck by a tire iron, for instance it manifests this disposition. A salt crystal possesses a disposition to dissolve in water. In dissolving upon being placed in water, it manifests its solubility. An object can possess a disposition, however, without manifesting that disposition. A fragile glass need never shatter; a salt crystal need never dissolve.

Among other things, dispositions take up the slack between what you do and what you would do. You do, presumably, what you are disposed to do; but you could be disposed to do many things you never do because the opportunity to do them does not arise or because they are overridden by competing dispositions. You might be disposed to act bravely when faced with danger, but pass your life in tranquil surroundings. That need not detract from your bravery. Of course, if you never *manifest* your bravery, we should have no reason to think you brave nor, for that matter, need *you* have any inkling that you possess this virtue. Similarly, we should have no reason to think that a particular unfamiliar substance was water soluble if its solubility were never manifested. You may be disposed to remain steadfast in a dangerous encounter but nevertheless flee because you are disposed, too, to spirit away a threatened companion.

Similarly, a salt crystal disposed to dissolve in water may fail to dissolve if it is subjected to a powerful electromagnetic field.

Behavioral Analysis

In what sense, exactly, does philosophical behaviorism 'tie states of mind to behavior'? Behaviorists hold that assertions concerning states of mind can be translated or analyzed into statements about behavior or dispositions to behave. We have had a taste of this already. If you believe there is a bear in your path, you are disposed to take evasive action, to assent to 'There is a bear on the path', to warn your companions, and the like.

The guiding idea is that if talk about states of mind can be *analyzed* or *paraphrased* into talk about behavior (or dispositions to behave), then talk of states of mind will have been 'reduced to' shown to be nothing more than a shorthand way of talking about behavior (or dispositions to behave). Analysis of this sort amounts to the reduction of something to something else. To see the point, think of a parallel case. We sometimes speak of the average family. The income of the average family in rural areas has declined from what it was a decade ago. Is there an average family? Is there an entity (or, for that matter, a collection of entities) designated by the phrase 'the average family'? That seems unlikely. In this case, we can see how talk about the average family's income might be reductively analyzed into talk about the income of individual families summed and divided by the number of families. The upshot: there is nothing more to the average family than this. If we could analyze away claims about minds and mental goings-on, replacing it with claims about behavior and dispositions to behave, then (so the argument goes) we would have succeeded in showing that there is nothing more to an agent's possessing a mind than the agent's behaving or being disposed to behave in appropriately mindful ways.

What are the prospects for behaviorist-style reductive analyses of states of mind? One worry is that behavioral analyses are open-ended. There is no limit on the list of things you might do or be disposed to do if you harbor the belief that there is a bear on the trail, for instance. What you do will depend on the circumstances, and the circumstances can vary indefinitely in many ways that resist specification in advance. Moreover, it seems clear that among the things you will be disposed to do is to form new beliefs and acquire new desires. Each of these beliefs and desires will require its own behavioral analysis.

This complicates the picture, certainly, but it need not pose an insuperable problem for the philosophical behaviorist. The envisaged analyses could turn out to be nonfinite. We can accept a non-finite reductive analysis provided we can see how it could be extended, even when we would be in no position to do so ourselves.

Another difficulty is less easily dismissed. You see a bear on the path and form the belief that there is a bear on the path. But what you do and what you are disposed to do evidently depends on your *overall* state of mind: what else you believe and want, for instance. And this is so for any state of mind. Suppose you believe that there is a bear on the path, but want to have a closer look (you are curious by nature), or believe that bears are not dangerous, or suppose you have a yen to live dangerously or to impress a companion.

It would seem that your belief is compatible with your behaving or being disposed to behave in *any way at all* depending on what else you believe and what you want. In that case, it looks as though no reductive analysis of states of mind is on the cards. The problem is not just that each of these additional states of mind requires a further behavioral analysis, thus complicating and extending the analytical task. The problem, rather, is that there is apparently no way to avoid mention of further states of mind in any statement of what behavior a given state of mind is likely to produce. It is as though we set out to analyze away talk about the average family only to discover that our analysis reintroduced mention of average families at every turning.

To appreciate the magnitude of the problem, think of your belief that there is a bear on the path. This belief, in concert with the belief that bears are dangerous, and a desire to avoid dangerous animals, may lead you to hurry away. But now imagine that you believe that there is a bear in your path, believe that bears are dangerous, and desire to avoid dangerous animals (your beliefs and desires are as before), but that you believe, in addition, that hurrying away will only attract the attention of bears. In this case, you will be disposed to behave, and behave, very differently.

The example illustrates a general point. Any attempt to say what behavior follows from a given state of mind can be shown to be false by producing an example in which the state of mind is present but, owing to the addition of new beliefs or desires, the behavior does not follow. Nor will it help to try to rule out such cases by means of a general excluder: if you believe that there is a bear on the path, believe that bears are dangerous, and desire to avoid dangerous animals, then, provided you have no further conflicting beliefs or desires, you will be disposed to turn tail. The problem here is that we have reintroduced mention of states of mind in the exclusion clause. And these are precisely what we were trying to analyze away. The analytical project looks hopeless.

Sensation

A committed behaviorist might regard all these worries as pedantic philosophical details. Perhaps it is unreasonable to expect perfect translations of assertions about states of mind into statements about behavior. Perhaps all we need show is that we can *replace* talk of inner goings-on with behavioral talk. Perhaps so doing would mesh nicely with scientific accounts of the activities of intelligent creatures.

This 'verificationist' line of response is likely to be attractive to psychological behaviorists. How reasonable is it? In discussing behaviorism's analytic project, we have focused on kinds of mental state that might seem especially apt for reduction: belief, desire, intention, and the like (the so-called propositional attitudes). What happens when we extend the analytical enterprise to *qualitatively loaded* states of mind? To see why there might be a problem with such cases, consider a concrete example. Imagine that you have contracted a mild case of food poisoning as a result of a visit to a local fast-food emporium. You suffer a variety of symptoms, including nausea. Your feeling nauseous doubtless leads you to behave in various ways and to be disposed to behave in various others. Could this be *all there is* to your being nauseous? The behaviorist analysis apparently leaves out the most salient feature of nausea: its qualitative character! Most of us would find it hard not to believe that this qualitative character is what *leads* us to behave as we do.

Behaviorism opposes the idea that states of mind are inner states that yield behavioral symptoms. But this seems crazy when you think of nausea, headache, or the electric feeling you have when you bump your 'funny bone' or your foot falls asleep. In fact, behaviorism seems to have things backwards when you reflect on any qualitatively vivid state of mind. These can be unpleasant, as in headache or nausea; pleasant, as in feelings of warmth; or both pleasant and unpleasant, as in a child's feeling when being tickled by an older sibling. Analyzing talk of such things into statements about behavior or dispositions to behave apparently omits just what is most important about them.

Is this just more philosophical pedantry? I urge caution here. As we shall see, behaviorists are not alone in wanting to factor out talk of the qualitative character of states of mind. Many materialist philosophers who reject behaviorism reject, as well, the idea that states of mind possess an irreducible qualitative nature. If you are so inclined, you will be in no position to criticize behaviorists on this score.

The Legacy of Philosophical Behaviorism

If the attempt to analyze talk of states of mind into talk of behavior is unworkable, what is left of philosophical behaviorism? It is true, certainly, that our grounds for ascribing states of mind to one another are largely behavioral.

This is an epistemological point, however, a point about what constitutes evidence for our beliefs about one another's mental lives, and a point a Cartesian could happily accept.

What of Ryle's contention that it is a mistake to regard your possessing a mind as a matter of your body's standing in a particular relation to a distinct entity, your mind? And what of Wittgenstein's suggestion that terms used to ascribe states of mind are not used to designate definite sorts of object or episode? Both of these ideas are independent of the behaviorist's analytical project, and both survive in accounts of the mind that are self-consciously anti-behaviorist. Thus, you might suppose that to have a mind is just to possess a particular sort of organization, one that issues in what we should call intelligent behavior. And you might imagine that to possess a given state of mind is just to be in *some state or other* that contributes in a characteristic way to the operation of this organized system.

For the moment, let us simply register behaviorism's lack of concern for the qualitative dimension of states of mind. If your having a headache is solely a matter of your behaving, or being disposed to behave, in a particular way, then the intrinsic qualitative nature of whatever is responsible for your so behaving, or being disposed to behave, is irrelevant. This is explicit in Wittgenstein's beetle in the box analogy.

Intrinsic and Extrinsic Characteristics

Speaking of 'intrinsic qualitative nature', you are bound to ask what exactly this phrase is supposed to signify. The notion of an intrinsic quality is best understood in contrast to the complementary notion of an extrinsic characteristic. (I prefer to contrast *intrinsic* with *extrinsic* rather than *relational*. That two cells bear a certain relation to one another is a relational feature of the cells, but an intrinsic feature of the organism to which they belong.) An intrinsic quality is a quality an object has in its own right. Being spherical is an intrinsic quality of a billiard ball. Being near the center of the billiard table is, in contrast, a non-intrinsic extrinsic feature of the ball. Think of intrinsic qualities as being *built into* objects, extrinsic characteristics as being possessed by objects only in virtue of relations those objects bear to other objects. In the beetle in the box case, imagine that one person's box contains a marble, and another's contains a sugar cube. Then the intrinsic nature of what is in each box differs. And it is precisely this that 'drops out of consideration as irrelevant'.

We can distinguish an object's intrinsic qualitative nature from its dispositionalities or causal powers. The billiard ball has the power to roll across the table, the power to shatter a pane of glass, and the power to reflect light in a particular way. But the ball has, as well, a particular qualitative nature: a particular shape, a particular size, a particular temperature. The relation between an object's powers or dispositionalities and its qualitative characteristics is a subtle business, as we shall see later. For the present, we need only recognize that it seems possible to distinguish an object's qualitative aspects from its causal propensities or powers. And, again, behaviorism regards the intrinsic qualitative nature of states of mind as irrelevant.

One way to put this is to say that according to the behaviorist, states of mind, '*qua* states of mind', lack an intrinsic qualitative nature. Think again of the beetle in the box analogy. Whatever is in the box has some intrinsic qualitative nature. But this nature is irrelevant to its being true that the box contains a beetle *qua* beetle considered solely as a 'beetle'; what the box contains lacks intrinsic qualities.

We noted above that a view of this kind might seem wildly implausible. Surely your headache has an intrinsic qualitative nature, and this is an important part of what makes a headache a headache. These days it is fashionable to put this point by saying that 'there is something it is like' to have a headache. What it is like to have a headache differs from what it is like to have other kinds of conscious experience. Part of what makes a given conscious experience a headache is just this 'what-it's-likeness'.

The denial of all this could strike you as incredible. Yet behaviorists do deny it. And, as we shall see, many other philosophers, philosophers dismissive of behaviorism, deny it as well. These philosophers argue that states of mind owe their identity not to their intrinsic qualitative nature (if indeed they have any such nature at all), but exclusively to their causal powers or, as I prefer, their dispositionalities. We can evaluate such claims only after we have built up an understanding of the underlying metaphysical issues. Before embarking on that project, however, let us look briefly at psychological behaviorism.

Psychological Behaviorism

Philosophical behaviorism is a thesis about the meaning of mental terms and, ultimately, about the significance of mental concepts. Its proponents consider philosophical questions about the nature of mind to be reducible to questions about the character of such concepts. They reason that if we want to know what minds are, we must make explicit what 'mind' and its cognates *mean*. This, they contend, is largely a matter of spelling out how 'mind' and its cognates are used by competent speakers. Minds are whatever answers to 'mind'.

A conception of this sort neatly divides philosophy from psychology. Philosophers are in the business of making clear the subtleties of the conception of mind enshrined in our linguistic practices. Psychologists, and other empirical scientists, investigate the character of the world. Our language carves up the world in a particular way. We can interpret scientific claims only after comparing concepts deployed in those claims with the concepts encoded in ordinary language. When psychologists speak of belief, or emotion, or mental imagery, do they mean what is ordinarily meant by 'belief', 'emotion', 'mental imagery'? To find out, we must see how these expressions function in psychological theories and compare what we find with their use in everyday language.

When we do this, according to philosophers like Wittgenstein and Ryle, we discover that psychology has more often than not made use of familiar terminology in unfamiliar ways. This can lead to a systematic misunderstanding of psychological theses. Wittgenstein put it this way: 'in psychology there are experimental methods and *conceptual confusion*'. 'Conceptual confusion' applies as much to the psychologists' interpretation of their own work as it does to the layperson's grasp of psychological results. We introduce a technical notion using a familiar term. The technical notion may be importantly different from the sense of the term in its everyday use. We then establish truths that pertain to the technical notion. Confusion results when we interpret these as applying to whatever the original term applies to. It is as though we decided to give 'pigeon' a rigorous sense: a four-legged artifact with a flat surface used for supporting objects. We then go on to establish that the common belief that pigeons can fly, mate, build nests, and lay eggs is a myth.

Behaviorism in psychology was spawned not by worries about the significance of mental terms, but by a concern that psychology has an appropriately *scientific* status. On a traditional view of the mind, a view accepted without question by psychologists in the nineteenth century, states of mind are taken to be private states not amenable to public scrutiny. You know the story. While 'access' to your own states of mind is direct, others can only observe their effects on your behavior. If we suppose, as early behaviorists like J. B. Watson (1878–1958) and B. F. Skinner (1904–1990) supposed, that only what is publicly observable is a fit subject for science, we shall exclude states of mind, as traditionally conceived, from scientific consideration. If we suppose, as well, that talk about items not susceptible to public verification is unsavory, or perhaps meaningless, we shall have in effect ruled the traditional conception of mind out of bounds for serious consideration.

We could put this by saying that on the behaviorist conception, minds, conscious experiences, and the like do not exist. Talk of such things reflects only a superstitious past in which the observable characteristics of objects were explained by reference to ghosts and spirits taken to inhabit them. To deny ghosts and spirits – and mental states – is to deny neither that objects and intelligent creatures have complex observable traits, nor that these are susceptible to rigorous scientific explanation. Just as we have put behind us explanations of demented behavior that appeal to possession by evil spirits, so we must put behind us explanations that appeal to private inner occurrences. This is what behaviorists set out to do.

The data for psychological behaviorism are instances of behavior, 'behaviors': what organisms do in response to environmental contingencies. We explain an instance of behavior not by postulating unobservable interior states of mind, but by reference to environmental stimuli that elicit the behavior. The governing model is the simple reflex. You sit in a relaxed position in a chair with your legs crossed. A doctor taps your knee, and your leg bobs in a characteristic way. Here, a bit of behavior, a response – your leg's bobbing is explained by the occurrence of a stimulus my tapping your knee. What connects stimulus and response is an unadorned reflex mechanism. We describe that mechanism exclusively by reference to its role in clear-cut Stimulus-Response (*S-R*) relations.

Behaviorists hold that all behavior, even complex behavior, can be fully explained in *S-R* terms. Complex responses are simply the result of complex stimuli. The job of the psychologist is to provide a systematic accounting of these *S-R* relations. As far as psychology is concerned, the organism is a 'black box', something the psychological nature of which is exhaustively describable by reference to its response to stimuli (Figure 5.1). Black boxes and organisms have an internal structure, something capable of being investigated in its own right. But this is the province of the biologist or the physiologist, not the psychologist.

Behaviorists proscribe mention of inner mechanisms except insofar as these are capable of exhaustive characterization in terms of relations between stimuli (observable inputs) and output responses (observable behavior). Complex organisms are capable of learning – capable, that is, of modifying their *S-R* relations. Again, the mechanism is straightforward. A particular kind of response can be 'reinforced' if its occurrence is 'rewarded'. A rat may not be inclined at the onset of a particular sound - a ringing bell, say – to respond by pressing a bar in its cage. But if, perhaps by accident, the rat, hearing the bell, presses the bar and receives a food pellet, then a barpressing response to the aural stimulus will be reinforced.

Fig. 8.1

We would find it natural to describe the rat as 'discovering a connection' between the bell's sound, pressing the bar, and the receipt of a food pellet. If behaviorists are right, however, such a description must be purely metaphorical. Taken literally, it suggests an inner mental process of the sort behaviorists disdain. Sticking to the purely behavioral facts, we find that the rat presses the bar at the onset of a particular sound and receives a food pellet. Subsequently, the rat's bar-pressing comes to co-vary reliably with the onset of instances of the sound. More precisely: the probability that the rat will press the bar at the onset of the sound increases dramatically. Eventually, the rat presses the bar during, and only during, a period immediately following the onset of the sound. This is, at bottom, what the rat's 'discovering the connection' amounts to.

The Demise of Behaviorism

Behaviorists are committed to the idea that all learning can be explained in terms of simple associative mechanisms. This assumes that complex tasks your learning to play Parcheesi, for instance, or your coming to master English or Urdu can be broken down into simpler tasks, each of which can be explained in something like the way the rat's bar-pressing is explained. In 1959, Noam Chomsky published a review of Skinner's *Verbal Behavior* in which he argued that Skinner's attempts to extend the behaviorist model of learning to the linguistic performances of human beings were hopelessly inadequate. Chomsky claimed that linguistic abilities could not, even in principle, be explained without assuming that human beings possessed a sizable repertoire of complex cognitive structures that governed their use of language.

This attack on central behaviorist themes had a devastating effect on the behaviorist program. Many psychologists had grown dissatisfied with rigid behaviorist doctrines, and were already moving in new directions. Chomsky's review, combined with a growing interest in 'rule-governed' activities generally, sealed behaviorism's fate. Behaviorism was never again to possess the kind of authority it once enjoyed. It became increasingly clear that behaviorism was founded on a view about scientific legitimacy, a view rooted in unappealing philosophical doctrines going back at least to Berkeley. By requiring that every scientifically respectable expression be characterizable in terms of observations that would confirm its application, behaviorists foreclosed modes of explanation that had proved fruitful in other sciences. These modes of explanation distinguished, as behaviorists often did not, between entities postulated to explain observable features of the world and observations that constituted evidence for these entities.

One further difficulty inherent in the behaviorist program is worth mention. Consider the central notion of *behavior*. What constitutes an instance of behavior? When do two 'behaviors' count as instances of the same behavior, and when are they different? Answers to these questions are important. The behaviorist envisages a rigorous pairing of stimuli and response behavior. The model we began with was the patella reflex: your knee is tapped, and your leg bobs. This same response your leg's bobbing happens whenever your knee is tapped. If your leg's bobbing is an example of behavior, then it would seem that behavior is to be understood as bodily motion. Two instances of behavior are the same only in cases when they are instances of the same bodily motion.

Unfortunately, matters are not so simple. Consider the rat's bar-pressing. Suppose that on one occasion the rat presses the bar with its right paw, then later with its left paw. We count these as instances of the same behavior 'bar-pressing behavior' even though the bodily motions differ. Now we have moved away from the basic reflex model. It is relatively easy to envisage a simple mechanism that accounts for your leg's bobbing when your knee is tapped. But the mechanism responsible for a rat's pressing a bar at the onset of a particular sound is not like this. That mechanism connects the onset of a particular sound with a variety of different kinds of bodily motion. What these bodily motions have in common is merely that they each result in the bar's being pressed. And now it looks as though any mechanism behind the rat's bar-pressing behavior must be specified by reference to what we non-behaviorists might blushingly describe as the rat's desires or purposes. Unfortunately, desires and purposes are 'unobservable' states of mind, and so officially out of bounds for the behaviorist.

When it comes to complex human behavior, the situation is worse still. Think of your answering the door when the doorbell rings. Call this door-answering behavior. But there need be no bodily motions in common among instances of this behavior. Sometimes you walk calmly to the door and open it. On other occasions you may trot to the door, or go on tiptoe, or press a button unlocking the door, or, if you are otherwise occupied, merely shout, 'Come in!' Again, it is difficult to imagine that the mechanism connecting the doorbell's ring with your door-answering behavior is a simple reflex mechanism. It looks, for all the world, like a relatively complex state of mind.

Similar considerations hold of the behaviorist notion of stimulus. When we look at what behaviorists count as instances of the same stimuli, we discover that these lack the sorts of common feature the approach would seem to demand. Your 'door-opening behavior' might be elicited by a loud banging on the door, or a soft knock; by the ringing of a doorbell; or by a glimpse through the window of an acquaintance striding up the footpath. These stimuli have little in common beyond being in some respect responsible for your opening the door.

Suppose we cannot come up with a non-circular, independent characterization of 'door-opening stimulus', one that does not invoke the very thing for which it is the postulated stimulus: 'door-opening behavior'. Then it looks as though appeals to such stimuli in explanations of behavior will be trivial. A response is elicited by a stimulus. Which one? The response-eliciting stimulus! This does not mean that the behaviorist contentions that all behavior is explicable by reference to stimulus-response relations and that learning is explicable purely by reference to contingencies of reinforcement of such relations are thereby condemned. It does strongly suggest, however, that the central notions of stimulus and response gain credence only by taking in one another's washing. And if this is so, the theory is uninformative.

Perhaps these worries about the emptiness of behaviorist explanation can be overcome. Even so, there is some reason to suspect that the behaviorist model is fundamentally misguided. Think for a moment of your response to a given stimulus: the appearance of a bear in your path, for instance. Strictly speaking, it would seem not to be the *bear* that elicits your response (whatever it might be), but your *perceiving* or in some way taking note of the bear. If a bear appears in your path, but you remain oblivious to it, you will be unmoved by the bear. Similarly, you may be moved to a bear-avoiding response even if a bear is absent. You may be so moved if, for whatever reason, you *take* there to be a bear in your path.

The example suggests that behavioral responses are determined not by behaviorist-style stimuli, but by our perceptions of those stimuli, their effects on us, or by apparent perceptions of stimuli. The bear's presence explains your behavior only if it leads you to a perception of a bear. This perception mediates your subsequent behavior.

Perceiving (or apparently perceiving) a bear, however, includes a definite mental component. And it was just such mental intermediaries that behaviorism was supposed to eliminate.

None of these reflections yields a knock-down argument against behaviorism. Behaviorists have attempted to respond to worries of the sort we have addressed. I shall not pursue those responses here. Instead, let us push ahead to what may be more promising realms.

Behaviorism also called the learning perspective (where any physical action is a behavior), is a philosophy of psychology based on the proposition that all things that organisms do including acting, thinking and feeling can and should be regarded as behaviors. The behaviorist school of thought maintains that behaviors as such can be described scientifically without recourse either to internal physiological events or to hypothetical constructs such as the mind. Behaviorism comprises the position that all theories should have observational correlates but that there are no philosophical differences between publicly observable processes (such as actions) and privately observable processes (such as thinking and feeling).

From early psychology in the 19th century, the behaviorist school of thought ran concurrently and shared commonalities with the psychoanalytic and Gestalt movements in psychology into the 20th century; but also differed from the mental philosophy of the Gestalt psychologists in critical ways. Its main influences were Ivan Pavlov, who investigated classical conditioning although he did not necessarily agree with Behaviourism or Behaviourists, Edward Lee Thorndike, John B. Watson who rejected introspective methods and sought to restrict psychology to experimental methods, and B.F. Skinner who conducted research on operant conditioning.

In the second half of the twentieth century, behaviorism was largely eclipsed as a result of the cognitive revolution. Though these two schools of psychological thought may not agree theoretically, they have complemented each other in practical therapeutic applications. One notable legacy of behaviorist investigations is cognitive-behavioral therapy, a popular treatment that uses cognitive models alongside behaviorist techniques such as "systematic desensitization" and "contingency management" that have demonstrable utility in helping people with certain pathologies, such as simple phobias, PTSD, and addiction. In addition, behaviorism sought to create a comprehensive model of the stream of behavior from the birth of the human to his death.

9

Daniel Dennett Approach and His Philosophy

Introduction

According to Dennett, a creature's having a mind is strictly a matter of our usefully regarding the creature as having a mind. This amounts, in practice, to our treating the creature as 'one of us': a being with various (mostly true) beliefs about the world and desires for particular states of affairs; a creature that acts reasonably in light of those beliefs and desires. You observe a robin hunting worms in the garden. You explain that is, make sense of the robin's behavior by supposing that the robin is hungry and so seeking food. The robin *believes* that worms are food, *believes* that worms are to be found in the garden, and in consequence *desires* to hunt worms in the garden. The robin, in sum, acts reasonably in light of its beliefs and desires.

In explaining the Robin's behavior by reference to beliefs and desires, you are adopting what Dennett calls the 'intentional stance'. This 'stance' is one we take up in order to *make sense of* and predict the behavior of any creature. Why is that octopus emitting a black inky substance? Because the octopus believes it has been spotted by a predator, wants to protect itself, believes it can do so by placing a dark cloud between it and the predator, and believes that by emitting an inky fluid it will cause a dark cloud to come between it and the predator. Why is this white blood cell enveloping that microbe? Because the cell wants to destroy invaders, believes the microbe is an invader, and so wants to destroy it. For its own part, the microbe wants to invade a red blood cell, believes that it is likely to find a red blood cell by swimming about randomly in the bloodstream, and so swims randomly.

Do Robins, octopodes, and white blood cells *really* have beliefs and desires? Do such organisms *really* behave rationally? Or do they merely behave *as if* they had beliefs and desires (and act reasonably in light of these)? Dennett regards questions of this sort as wrong-headed. Having beliefs and desires amounts to nothing more than being explicable via the intentional stance. If we can make sense of the behavior of a microbe by taking up the intentional stance toward its activities, then the microbe does indeed have beliefs and desires, hence reasons for what it does.

You might object. If this is what having beliefs, desires, and reasons amounts to, then plants must have beliefs, desires, and reasons, too! This elm sinks its roots deep into the soil because it wants to find water and believes that water is likely to be found at greater depths. More startlingly, perhaps, on a view of this sort what is to prevent *artifacts* your desktop computer, or even a lowly thermostat from having beliefs and desires? Your desktop computer is displaying a 'printer is out of paper' alert because it believes that the printer is out of paper, and wants to let you know. The thermostat turns on the furnace because it believes that the room temperature has dropped below 21°C, and it wants to increase the temperature to at least 21°C.

You might concede that although we do talk this way on occasion, we do so merely as a matter of convenience. We can see single-celled organisms, plants, and artifacts as loosely analogous to rational agents in certain ways. Thus, we speak of them *as if* they were like us in those ways. But of course they are not *really* like us. Their behavior is governed by simpler mechanisms. To imagine that they have *really have* beliefs and desires, to suppose that they have *really have* reasons for what they do, is to confuse the metaphorical with the literal.

Dennett insists, however, that ascriptions of beliefs and desires to single-celled organisms, plants, and artifacts are no more metaphorical than is the ascription of beliefs and desires to our fellow human beings. *All there is* to an entity's having beliefs and desires, *all there is* to an entity's acting on reasons, is the entity's *behaving as if* it had beliefs and desires and acted on reasons. In ascribing beliefs, desires, and reasons to organisms or objects, we take up the intentional stance. The intentional stance enables us to make sense of and predict the behavior of whatever falls under it. But it will do this quite independently of whether those entities have an internal makeup resembling ours.

A view of this sort construes the propositional attitudes 'instrumentally'. That is, the correctness of an attribution of beliefs, desires, and reasons for action lies not in its corresponding to some independent fact or state of affairs, but in its serviceability. To the extent that the practice of ascribing propositional attitudes serves our interests enables us to make sense of and predict the behavior of objects with which we interact it is fully justified. To expect anything more, to take a baldly 'realist' line on beliefs, desires, and reasons for action, is to miss the point of the practice.

From Intentional Stance to Design Stance

Your having beliefs, desires, and reasons for action, then, is simply a matter of your being susceptible to descriptions framed in terms of beliefs, desires, and reasons. In deploying such descriptions, we take up the intentional stance. We find this unavoidable in the case of our fellow human beings, and equally unavoidable in attempting to come to terms with the exploits of non-human creatures. In the case of simple organisms, plants, and inanimate objects, we find that we can in most cases dispense with the intentional stance and explain their behavior by working out their *design.* In so doing, we move to what Dennett calls the *design stance*. We make sense of the behavior of objects by regarding them as having been designed or engineered in a particular way to achieve a particular end.

You may describe the behavior of your desktop computer by attributing various beliefs and desires to it, but a programmer is in a position to make sense of the device's behavior by reference to its program. In the same way, a biologist is in a position to explain the behavior of a white blood cell by reflecting on its design from an evolutionary perspective. The design of a desktop computer has a human origin. The design of a white blood cell, or the circulatory system of a frog, or the mechanism that controls the growth of a plant reflects the hand of Mother Nature. Evolutionary pressures ensure that badly engineered mechanisms, those that prove maladaptive, are weeded out.

The design stance does not *replace* the intentional stance. When we arrive at a 'design-level' understanding of a white blood cell or the behavior of a bird protecting her nestlings by feigning injury, we do not *falsify* claims made from the intentional standpoint. On the contrary, we merely offer a deeper, more fine-grained explanation of why such claims hold. Such explanations in many ways resemble functional explanations. But our capacity to deploy the design stance in particular instances does not, according to Dennett, mean that beliefs, desires, and reasons for action are, at bottom, functional states. We adopt the intentional stance when our interest in understanding or explaining the behavior of some entity is largely action oriented when we have an interest in predicting, quickly and without expending much effort, how that entity is likely to behave. If this is our aim, the intentional stance is wonderfully cost-effective. We resort to the design stance only when our interests change and when circumstances make it possible (or desirable) to examine more carefully and systematically mechanisms controlling an entity's activities. An ethologist adopts the design stance in explaining the behavior of a particular species of bird, but a hunter need not, and typically will not.

Psychologists, psychobiologists, sociobiologists, and, in general, cognitive scientists adopt in their various ways the design stance toward human beings. Once again, this is not a matter of rejecting or negating the intentional stance we take up in order to make sense of one another's behavior by appealing to beliefs, desires, and reasons. Nor, on Dennett's view, is it a matter of discovering that beliefs, desires, and reasons are at bottom functional states responsible for behavior. The beliefs, desires, and reasons for action ascribable to us are so ascribable, perhaps, because we have the functional architecture we have. But beliefs, desires, and reasons are not causally potent components of that architecture. In this regard, Dennett and Davidson are in agreement.

What, then, would a design-level description of a human being look like? You can get some idea by reflecting on what scientific investigators tell us about, for instance, the mechanisms of vision, or memory, or language processing. Explanations of such things involve appeals to details of our nervous system components of the retina and optic nerve, for instance in a way that regards these as subserving particular systemic ends. Examples of the design stance taken toward human and nonhuman creatures' capacities abound in psychology and biology textbooks.

This design-level approach is to be distinguished from the line taken by functionalists. Functionalists regard terms designating states of mind appealed to in the intentional stance as, at bottom, designating functional states of creatures to which the terms apply. But in adopting the design stance we in effect take up the intentional stance toward mechanisms we regard as underlying creatures' behavior. We see these mechanisms (as opposed to the creature as a whole) as having ends, and working to achieve them. You might worry too that this imports an unwarranted anthropomorphic element into our fine-grained accounts of creatures' inner workings. You might worry too that the strategy bogs down in a kind of circularity: we explain complex states of mind by positing mechanisms that possess the very features we had hoped to explain. To what extent are these worries well founded?

From Design Stance to Physical Stance

Dennett's idea is that we account for mental phenomena by locating neural mechanisms capable of a design-level description, one that, true enough, involves seeing those mechanisms as working to achieve certain goals. The explanatory process need not stop here, however. We move to explain *these* mechanisms by uncovering simpler mechanisms that make them up. The retina is taken to perform a particular intelligent function, and this is explained by discovering that the retina consists of rods, cones, and assorted other cells that themselves perform intelligent, but more limited, narrowly directed functions. As we analyze systems into component systems in this way, we eventually arrive at a level at which the constituent mechanisms are acutely focused or single-minded. At this level of analysis we might expect to find, for instance, individual cells that do nothing more than detect the presence or absence of a particular chemical substance and notify neighboring cells accordingly.

When we reach this level, we have in effect 'discharged' the design stance and moved to the *physical stance*. We can see how the imagined cell performs its function by examining its chemistry. In this way our investigations are grounded in the non-mental, non-intentional, and the threat of circularity is deflected. Intentionality, that feature of thoughts in virtue of which they are of or about one thing or another, is seen to stem from the biochemistry of organisms enjoying it.

The Emerging Picture

Functionalists regard it as a genuine empirical question whether creatures or artifacts to which we commonly and unhesitatingly ascribe beliefs, desires, and reasons for action do in fact have beliefs, desires, and reasons. The question is one that might be resolved for a given creature by discovering whether that creature sufficiently resembled us functionally. Dennett regards this as a red herring. The having of beliefs and desires is wholly a matter of being so describable. When we regard it as more than that, when we imagine that in ascribing beliefs, desires, and reasons we are identifying components of mechanisms causally responsible for behavior, we run the risk of anthropomorphizing, and thereby missing the gulf between the minds of human beings and the minds of other creatures.

The idea is straightforward. In taking up the intentional stance in ascribing beliefs, desires, and reasons for action we deploy a system of categories that enables us to sort out and predict the behavior of creatures, artifacts, and natural systems. The justification of this practice depends not on its successfully cataloging cogs and levers responsible for the operation of whatever it is we hope to explain, but on its utility. For a great many purposes this is all we need. You explain to a companion what your desktop computer is doing by noting that it *wants* to print a document, *discovers* that the printer is out of paper, and *hopes* to attract your attention by beeping.

The italicized words in the preceding sentence are not, if Dennett is right, used metaphorically: they hold literally of your desktop computer; you are using them in exactly the sense you would use them in describing the behavior of a fellow human being. You would err, however, if you imagined that what goes on *inside* your desktop computer resembles functionally or otherwise what goes on inside a human being. Understanding what makes us tick requires that we descend to the design stance. And when we do this, we begin to notice vast differences between desktop computers, human beings, and other creatures.

In taking up the design stance, we in effect extend the intentional stance to components of intelligent systems. The project is saved from circularity or a bottomless regress by the fact that it is premised on the possibility that we can successively analyze intelligent systems into sub-systems until we arrive at a systemic level the operation of which is, though perhaps physically complex, trivial from a design perspective. Here we move to the physical stance and 'discharge' our higher-level talk of beliefs, desires, and reasons for action. Our arriving at this level, our taking up the physical stance, does not falsify or replace our higher-level intentional stance and design stance assessments, however. To imagine that it does is to lose sight of the utility and economy afforded by the intentional and design stances. This utility and economy provide all the justification we need for deploying them.

Thought and Language

Like most theorists who regard themselves as cognitive scientists, Dennett accepts the idea that human beings and nonhuman creatures process information and internally manipulate *representations* of their surroundings. It is one thing for a creature's behavior to be guided by representations, however, and quite another matter for a creature to appreciate that this is what it is doing. Moreover, there is, Dennett contends, not merely a difference in degree, but a difference in kind between a capacity for representation (something arguably possessed by single-celled organisms and thermostats) and a capacity for *higher-order representation*: representation *of representations* or representation of oneself as representing. Only creatures capable of surveying their own representations (and recognizing these representations as theirs), only creatures capable of taking up the intentional stance toward themselves, deserve to be described as 'thinking'. The behavior of sea slugs and single-celled creatures suggests that they are guided by representations of aspects of their limited worlds, but we need not regard such creatures as capable of thought in the strictest sense. But what of beagles, or dolphins, or chimpanzees? Again, a case can be made for saying that such creatures represent their surroundings. Do they think? They do so only if they represent self-consciously, only if they possess a capacity for second order representation, a capacity to appreciate, hence represent, their representations as representations.

This latter capacity, Dennett believes, emerges with the advent of language. If we accept Dennett's earlier suggestion that thinking includes an ability to manipulate representations self-consciously, then it would follow that thought and language go hand in hand. This is not because language is required as a *medium* for thought. Thinking need not be linguistic or language-like; thought could be non-sentential, or 'pictorial'. The connection between thought and language is less direct. Evolutionary pressures for self-conscious representation are absent until the birth of cooperative communication. Communication provides a mechanism for the sharing of information. More importantly (from an evolutionary perspective), communication provides a way for creatures to turn the possession of information not possessed by others to their own advantage. If I know something you do not know and are unlikely to know unless I tell you, I can trade my information for some benefit, or, if it serves my interests, *mislead* you.

If we look at the evolutionary paths of non-human species, we see that members of those species typically inhabit surroundings in which information obtained by one individual is likely to be obtainable by every other individual. When this is not so, we may find that practices of deception emerge (as when chimpanzees take steps to prevent fellow chimpanzees from discovering a hidden morsel of food). Such practices mandate a degree of representational sophistication that constitutes what might be called 'proto-thought'. This is a stage on the evolutionary road to fully fledged thinking.

Infants and young children may lack the kind of reflective capacities that Dennett considers necessary for genuine thought. In one much-discussed experiment, a child is shown a puppet hiding a toy in a particular place. The puppet goes away and, during its absence, the experimenter, in full view of the child, moves the toy to a new hiding place. The child is then asked where the puppet will look for the toy when it returns. Three-year-olds typically say that the puppet will look in the new hiding place; older children reply that the puppet will look where the toy was originally hidden.

One possible explanation for this disparity is that younger children represent the world, but are unable to represent representations of the world. They are, in consequence, in no position to represent the puppet's imagined representations of the world, and so unable to regard the puppet as falsely representing the toy's location. Predicting that the puppet will look in the new hiding place does not, or so it is claimed, require the child to represent the puppet as having a true representation, hence does not require the child to represent the puppet as representing anything.

The argument implicit in Dennett's line of reasoning is not founded on purely philosophical a priori considerations concerning what suffices for thought. It is rather that when we look below the surface at how other creatures do what they do, we are not tempted in the slightest to imagine that they engage in self-conscious thinking in anything like the sense in which we do. A philosopher or a pet owner might point out that it is still possible that infants, or chimpanzees, or dolphins, or beagles engage in elaborate but secret cogitations. This impression, Dennett suggests, is just the result of deploying the intentional stance over-zealously.

Once we realize this, once we descend to the design stance, we learn that nature has provided much more elegant solutions to problems posed by the environment. Were you to set out to build a nest, you would no doubt first plan a course of action and keep this plan in mind modifying it as necessary as you proceeded with the task. Encouraged by the intentional stance, you might imagine that a bird building a nest operates in much the same way. When we begin to study the behavior of birds more carefully, however, we discover that their elaborate, and in many cases ingenious, solutions to the nest-building problem are the result not of elaborate and ingenious thoughts, but of simpler mechanisms shaped by evolution. The mechanisms are ingenious, certainly, but the ingenuity is Mother Nature's, not the birds'.

Kinds of Mind

Although we are within our rights to describe infants, chimpanzees, dolphins, beagles, sea slugs, even thermostats as having beliefs, desires, and reasons for what they do, we do well to reserve the notion of thought for creatures who, like us, have evolved a capacity for self-conscious representation, a capacity to entertain representations of representations. Does this mean that only creatures resembling us have minds? Not according to Dennett. Having a mind is a matter of being guided by representations. And we have ample evidence that the activities of infants, chimpanzees, dolphins, beagles, and sea slugs are governed by representations of their goals and circumstances. Perhaps this is so even for the lowly thermostat.

Conceding that sea slugs and thermostats have minds, however, is not to concede very much at least, not if Dennett is right about minds. We can still identify vast qualitative disparities among *kinds* of mind. Dennett envisages a hierarchy. At the basic level are primitive 'Darwinian' minds, minds hard-wired to respond in optimal ways to a relatively stable environment. Darwinian minds are possessed by the simplest creatures, those that have evolved clever solutions to problems posed by their circumstances. In the case of Darwinian creatures, the steps from the intentional stance to the design stance and from the design stance to the physical stance can be relatively abbreviated.

At a rung above Darwinian creatures are creatures possessing 'Skinnerian minds' (named in honor of the behaviorist psychologist B. F. Skinner). Skinnerian minds are possessed by creatures capable of learning via operant conditioning trial and error. A creature possessing a Skinnerian mind exhibits a degree of mental 'plasticity' not possessed by simpler Darwinian creatures. A Skinnerian creature can adapt its behavior to changes in its circumstances. In this way, creatures endowed with Skinnerian minds have a hand in shaping themselves to fit their environmental niche. For Darwinian creatures, this role is played exclusively by Mother Nature: Darwinians are shaped wholly by evolutionary pressures.

'Popperian minds' belong to creatures who have managed the trick of representing their environment in a way that enables them to test likely outcomes of distinct courses of action 'in their heads', and so to learn without the attendant risk of potentially lethal errors. Why 'Popperian'? Popperian minds operate on principles reminiscent of those the philosopher Karl Popper takes to lie at the heart of scientific rationality. According to Popper, the success of science as a rational enterprise hinges on scientists' willingness to engage in 'conjecture and refutation'. Theories are conjectured and tested against the evidence. A theory is accepted only insofar as it survives rigorous testing.

A Skinnerian learns from experience, trial and error; a Popperian can learn by anticipating experience. Rats are evidently Popperian. A rat allowed to explore a maze may later put its knowledge of the maze to use in attaining a particular reward. The rat does so by constructing a 'cognitive map' of the maze. Once constructed, this 'map' can be put to advantage in negotiating the maze to obtain a food pellet.

Skinnerian creatures ask themselves, 'What should I do next?' and haven't a clue how to answer until they have taken some hard knocks. Popperian creatures make a big advance by asking themselves, 'What should I think about next?' before they ask themselves, 'What should I do next?'

At the top of Dennett's hierarchy are creatures endowed with 'Gregorian minds' (named not for the Pope, but for the psychologist Richard Gregory). A creature possessing a Gregorian mind, like its Popperian forerunners, is capable of testing hypotheses in its head. The difference is that Gregorian minds are capable of representing *self-consciously*. This opens up new horizons and possibilities not available to Popperians.

Human beings, endowed as we are with language, possess Gregorian minds. We are also, in some measure, Darwinian, Skinnerian, and Popperian. The human nervous system bears the marks of its evolutionary history, exhibiting Darwinian, Skinnerian, Popperian, and Gregorian aspects. Any complex action requires the coordination of all of these elements. We must not, then, conflate kinds of mind with kinds of creature. The brain of a Skinnerian creature, for instance, a creature capable of learning, incorporates Darwinian hard-wired mechanisms, as do sophisticated mammalian brains. A Gregorian creature, one capable of self-reflection, is not *non*-Darwinian, or *non*-Skinnerian, or *non*-Popperian. Rather, Gregorian creatures among terrestrial species, human beings have evolved additional capacities that distinguish their minds from the minds of creatures lacking self-consciousness.

Important differences between Gregorian creatures and the rest are largely invisible so long as we rest content with the intentional stance. We ascribe beliefs, desires, and reasons for action in a way that, wrongly interpreted, makes the minds of non-Gregorian creatures appear to resemble ours. So long as our interest is merely in interacting with and predicting the behavior of such creatures, this attitude is perfectly justified. But when we pursue a deeper understanding of what makes other creatures tick, when we seek to refine our understanding and increase our prospects of predicting and manipulating their behavior, we are bound to look below the surface. When we do, when we descend to the design stance, we discover that differences swamp similarities.

Most notably, we discover that the intelligence of non-human creatures is, in comparison to our own, rigid and 'gappy'. Spot, whose behavior exhibits considerable intelligence in many domains, is unable to arrive at a solution to the problem of how to unwind his leash from a tree. It seems not to occur to dolphins (regarded by some enthusiasts as our intellectual equals) to try to escape tuna nets by leaping over them, although this is something any dolphin might easily do. These gaps appear puzzling only so long as we imagine that other creatures think as we do. The results of careful experimental work suggest otherwise. Thus, impressive as they are, tool-using chimpanzees and ants that engage in 'farming' fungus harvested for food fall short of the Gregorian plateau. Reports of chimpanzees (and other apes) engaging in apparently deceptive practices might suggest that this assessment is overly pessimistic: perhaps chimpanzees have a 'theory of mind' that they put to use in deciding how to interact with their fellows. The intelligence displayed by chimpanzees and other non-human creatures does not call for the Gregorian solution. Indeed, if we interpret chimpanzees as thinking as we do about matters that concern them, then their inability to generalize this thinking in obvious ways will appear baffling.

Consciousness

What of conscious experience: consciousness? Many philosophers of mind regard consciousness as a big deal. According to Dennett, the problem of consciousness what David Chalmers calls 'the hard problem' is a problem of our own making. Our obsession with the qualitative aspect of experience, its 'what-it's-like-ness', has prevented philosophers from appreciating a solution to the mystery of consciousness that is ready to hand.

Dennett's idea is implicit in his discussion of higher-order representation. Representations play an important role in the production of behavior in even the simplest creatures. Consciousness, however, emerges only with the capacity to reflect on these representations, and, as we have seen, this capacity is, according to Dennett, linked to the ability to deploy language. Strictly speaking, then, thought and consciousness are possible only for linguistically endowed creatures. For such creatures, conscious states of mind are not those exhibiting distinctive qualitative or 'phenomenological' features, or those located in some central chamber of the mind, but those that, in competition with other representational elements, assume control of behavior.

Why should this feature be thought to suffice for consciousness? Surely more is required for representation to take on the characteristics of a conscious experience? But according to Dennett, Such questions betray a deep confusion, for they presuppose that what *you* are is something *else*, some Cartesian *res cogitans* in addition to all this brain and body activity. What you are, however, just *is* this organization of all the competitive activity between a host of competencies that your body has developed.

Does this mean that other creatures chimpanzees,

dolphins, beagles are 'zombies', that they do not feel pain, for instance? No; such creatures have pains and assorted other sensory states. What they lack is an additional capacity to reflect on these states. And this lack, Dennett suggests, means that although they may be said to feel pain, they do not 'suffer'. Attempts to model their pains on ours are invariably misleading.

Dennett is aware that in advancing such a view, he is opening himself to attack from pet owners and animal rights activists. He argues, however, that our moral obligation to refrain from needlessly harming other creatures stems not from their possession of a capacity to suffer as we do, but merely from the fact that they, like us, can experience pain. A capacity for pain, however, is to be distinguished from a higher-level capacity, your capacity to reflect that you are in pain. A creature lacking this capacity cannot dwell on its pain, or dread its onset, or be haunted by painful memories. And a capacity for such things underlies the capacity for suffering.

How could one's possession of the capacity for self-reflection affect the *feeling* of pain, the *qualitative* dimension of an experience of pain? Dennett thinks this is the wrong question to ask. Experiential qualities *qualia* are dubious entities, artifacts of an outmoded and discredited Cartesian conception of the mind. We can account for the apparent prominence of these qualities by recognizing that when you are in pain, for instance, you are in a particular kind of state, one that, among other things, leads you to believe that you are in a state with particular qualities. Creatures lacking language lack a capacity for higher-order, reflective thought, hence for thoughts of this sort. Such creatures can be in states functionally resembling our pain states, but they lack the wherewithal to reflect on those states.

Does this imply that such creatures *feel nothing* when they are in pain? The question presupposes what is false, namely that pain states or episodes possess intrinsic qualitative features. They do not at least not if Dennett is right. But this does not mean that non-human creatures do not undergo pain, or that their pains are less intense or distressing than ours. To think that it does is to assume falsely that pains are what they are pains in virtue of their intrinsic qualitative character. *Nothing* possesses an intrinsic qualitative character, however! The fact, if it is a fact, that pain states lack it, then, is entirely unremarkable.

You would not be alone in finding a view of this sort wholly implausible. To his credit, Dennett takes seriously the problem of reconciling the apparent qualitative nature of conscious experience with the character of the material states and episodes that seem to 'underlie' such experiences. As many philosophers like to point out, it is hard to see how these could be reconciled without accepting some form of dualism. One way to see what Dennett is up to is to compare the qualitative dimension of a pain with the qualitative aspect of an after-image. When you experience a round yellowish-orange after-image, nothing material in your vicinity and certainly nothing in your brain need be round and yellowish-orange. Similarly, when you experience a pain as dull and throbbing, nothing need be dull or throbbing. Perhaps this is no more mysterious than our entertaining thoughts of dragons or mermaids when there are no dragons or mermaids.

Searle's Objection

One response to such attempts to analyze away the qualities of conscious experience is to argue, as John Searle has, that the move merely represses a problem without solving it. The argument is simple. Suppose you hallucinate a tangerine-colored geranium on the table in front of you. There need be nothing tangerine-colored or geranium-shaped in your vicinity. But now consider your hallucination itself. We seem to have removed a tangerine-colored or geranium-shaped item from the public, material world and placed it inside your mind. The qualities you seem to find in the 'external world' exist, perhaps, but 'only in your mind'.

Nevertheless, they indisputably exist there: *in your mind*. And this is no help at all if our aim is to advance a fully materialist conception of mind.

We commonly distinguish appearance from reality. When it comes to the mind, however, appearance *is* reality. Suppose we agree that something's merely appearing pink is a matter not of its *being* pink, but of your being in a particular state of mind. We banish the perceived pinkness to the mind. Searle takes Dennett to be attempting a similar move with respect to *experienced* pinkness. But how is *this* supposed to work? Perhaps experienced pinkness is 'merely apparent'.

This means that your experience of pinkness is just a matter of your taking yourself to be experiencing pinkness. And this merely seems to move the troublesome 'phenomenal quality' from a first-order perceptual experience to a second-order experience (just as the quality was originally moved from the external world into the mind). This does not remove the troublesome quality, however. It merely shifts it from one venue to another.

From this it seems to follow that attempts to analyze away the qualities of conscious experiences by attaching them to higher-order mental states your beliefs about the pain you now feel, for instance are bound to fail. We eliminate the problematic qualities from your pain state only by depositing them in your *representations* of your pain state.

We broached these issues in earlier chapters (6 and 9). There we noted that it is vital to distinguish qualities of objects experienced from qualities of experiences. Your visual experience of a red tomato in bright sunlight has a distinctive qualitative character. We can designate these qualities by mentioning their causes: experiential qualities of the sort attendant on looking at brightly illuminated ripe tomatoes. But we must not confuse qualities of the cause with qualities of the effect. An *experience* of a red tomato what we might call a 'red experience' need not be red. In fact, an experience, unlike a ripe tomato, is not the sort of thing that could be red. When you hallucinate a red tomato, or, for that matter, experience a vivid reddish after-image, you undergo an experience something like the experience you undergo when you see a red tomato in bright sunlight. And again, although your experience is *of* a reddish, round object, your experience is not itself round or reddish.

The point of all this is to suggest that Searle's contention that when it comes to the mind, appearance *is* reality, is scarcely a straightforward doctrine. If Searle means that when you undergo a reddish after-image, when something appears reddish to you, then something *is* reddish if not something outside you, then a mental something the contention looks unwarranted. If, however, we interpret Searle as saying something weaker, namely that when you experience something, your experience has a distinctive character, then it is not clear how deeply it cuts against Dennett.

Suppose we interpret Dennett charitably as denying that experiences have the qualities of experienced objects. A vivid visual experience of a brightly illuminated red tomato need not itself be red. Then Searle's complaint that Dennett cannot account for the appearances is misguided.

Searle's attack is on the right track in one respect, however. If we distinguish carefully the qualities of objects (hallucinatory or otherwise) from the qualities of our experiences of those objects, then there is no particular incentive to introduce higher-order states of mind beliefs about one's pains, for instance to account for the qualities of conscious experience. If your having a conscious experience is a matter of your being in a particular state with particular qualities, then no fancy philosophical footwork is required to accommodate conscious qualities.

In any case, the move to higher-order states to account for conscious experiences ought immediately to arouse suspicion. Suppose you believe that France is hexagonal. Your having this belief, on most views, Dennett's included, need not be a matter of your undergoing a conscious experience. Now imagine that you come to believe that you believe that

France is hexagonal. Your having this belief is a matter of your being in a particular second-order state, your having a belief about a belief. But if your first-order belief is not conscious, why should the addition of a second-order belief-about-a-belief constitute a conscious state? It is not to the point to note that self-reflective thoughts are often conscious. The question is whether consciousness is constituted by second-order thought. Surely you are conscious of many things your surroundings, for instance, or the disposition of your limbs without being aware that you are aware of these things. Second-order states of mind, although undoubtedly important, seem ill-suited to marking off the boundary between 'conscious' and 'non-conscious'.

Dennett has remarked in several places (such as "Self-portrait", in Brainchildren) that his overall philosophical project has remained largely the same since his time at Oxford. He is primarily concerned with providing a philosophy of mind that is grounded in empirical research. In his original dissertation, Content and Consciousness, he broke up the problem of explaining the mind into the need for a theory of content and for a theory of consciousness. His approach to this project has also stayed true to this distinction. Just as Content and Consciousness has a bipartite structure, he similarly divided Brainstorms into two sections. He would later collect several essays on content in The Intentional Stance and synthesize his views on consciousness into a unified theory in Consciousness Explained. These volumes respectively form the most extensive development of his views.

In Consciousness Explained, Dennett's interest in the ability of evolution to explain some of the content-producing features of consciousness is already apparent, and this has since become an integral part of his program. He defends a theory known by some as Neural Darwinism. He also presents an argument against qualia; he argues that the concept is so confused that it cannot be put to any use or understood in any non-contradictory way, and therefore does not constitute a valid refutation of physicalism. Much of Dennett's work since the 1990s has been concerned with fleshing out his previous ideas by addressing the same topics from an evolutionary standpoint, from what distinguishes human minds from animal minds (Kinds of Minds), to how free will is compatible with a naturalist view of the world.

10

Radical Interpretation and its Philosophy

Introduction

It might seem incredible that anyone could be tempted to suppose that minds resemble coordinate systems. After all, we seem intimately acquainted with our own minds, and this acquaintance appears not to be a matter of our imposing any coordinate-like system on ourselves. Further, and perhaps more to the point, it is hard to see how any such theory could possibly succeed. Pretend for a moment that ascribing states of mind resembles the application of a coordinate system on a region of space. This application of a coordinate system is something we do, something that evidently depends on our having thoughts, intentions, and a broad range of distinct states of mind. This suggests that if minds are like coordinate systems, every mind would depend for its existence on a pre-existing mind! If being a mind depends on the imposition of a coordinate-like system, then this preexisting mind, too, must depend for its existence on some further mind. We are thus led to a regress of minds, each depending on the prior existence of some distinct mind.

Let us bracket this regress worry for the moment, and look in more detail at attempts to make out what I shall label 'interpretive' accounts of the mind. Once we are clear on what such accounts amount to, we shall be in a position to evaluate the seriousness of the envisaged regress. We shall see that the issues are less straightforward than my sketch of the regress problem above might suggest.

Davidson and the Propositional Attitudes

Davidson's focus is exclusively on what philosophers call the 'propositional attitudes': beliefs, desires, hopes, fears, intentions, and the like, insofar as these are taken to have 'propositional content'. Davidson is silent on the nature of sensation and imagery, for instance. Because Davidson's work has done much to set the agenda in the philosophy of mind, some philosophers have embraced the view that minds are to be understood *solely* as congeries of propositional attitudes. Other facets of our mentality are taken to be reducible to the propositional attitudes, or ignored. None of this is part of Davidson's program, however. Indeed, as I shall try to show, that program is unthinkable in the absence of a host of 'non-propositional' states of mind.

As a first step, consider the traditional conception of a propositional attitude. Your having a belief the belief that it will rain, for instance is a matter of your taking up a particular sort of attitude an attitude of belief or acceptance toward a particular proposition the proposition that it will rain. You might harbor the same attitude toward a distinct proposition, in which case you have a different belief; or you might evince some other attitude toward the same proposition: you might believe, desire, hope, fear, or, if you are a rainmaker, intend that it will rain.

Attitudes are familiar states of mind. What of propositions? Although philosophers are fond of invoking propositions in discussing states of mind, I know of no simple account of what propositions are meant to be. At an intuitive level, you might distinguish *propositions* from *sentences*. The following sentences could be said to *express* the same proposition:

(a) It's raining.

(b) Il pleut.

(c) Es regnet.

So considered, propositions are 'abstract entities'. In this regard they resemble numbers – *numbers*, as distinct from *numerals*, labels we use ('five', 'cinq', '5' and 'V' for instance) to *designate* numbers. Sentences are to propositions as numerals are to numbers. Philosophers have also identified propositions with a variety of other exotica, including sets of 'possible worlds' and states of affairs. Some philosophers who speak of the propositional attitudes, including Davidson, contend that talk about propositions can be rephrased and replaced by talk of something else. For purposes of discussion here, the notion of a proposition can be left at an intuitive level: a proposition is what a sentence expresses. Whatever else a proposition is, it must be representational and capable of being true or false.

Semantic Opacity

One notable feature of the propositional attitudes is their fine-grainedness or definiteness. Your believing that Socrates is wise differs from your believing that the husband of Xanthippi is wise, even though Socrates *is* the husband of Xanthippi. Beliefs inherit this feature 'intensionality' (spelled with an 's') from the propositions: the proposition that Socrates is wise differs from the proposition that the husband of Xanthippi is wise. You may believe that Socrates is wise, but, never having heard of Xanthippi, fail to believe that the husband of Xanthippi is wise or even that the husband of Xanthippi is not wise. The (somewhat technical) point here is that belief and the other propositional attitudes possess 'semantic opacity'. A capacity for belief includes a capacity for thoughts that differ not merely in *what* they represent, but also in *how* they represent.

Davidson contends that any account of belief must honor semantic opacity. This means that it could make sense to ascribe beliefs to a creature only when it makes sense to suppose that the creature in question has a capacity to represent states of affairs in different ways. Does the neighbor's dog, Spot, have such a capacity? Can we sensibly suppose that Spot can, as we can, represent his master or his food dish in different ways? Or are representations we are inclined to ascribe to Spot 'semantically transparent'; are they merely simple devices for pointing at the world?

Such questions raise a host of issues that we shall have to set aside for the moment. Looking ahead, I might simply note that on Davidson's view, there is an intimate connection between the capacity to use a fully fledged language and a capacity for what I have called representing the world in different ways. If Davidson is right, then only creatures capable of language are capable of thought. You may find this consequence unpalatable. Surely Spot has beliefs! Surely prelinguistic infant human beings think! If this is your response, then you should carefully evaluate Davidson's approach to the topic and consider where you think he goes wrong.

Radical Interpretation

According to Davidson, an understanding of the nature of beliefs, desires, intentions, or any other propositional attitude must include a grasp of what is required for the interpretation of speech. Think of what might be involved in your understanding what I say when I utter some sentence. If you and I share a language, then you interpret my utterance unthinkingly and automatically. Nevertheless, your capacity to understand what I say, as opposed merely to hearing my utterances as patterns of sounds, as an infant or non-English-speaker might, includes a complex ability, one not shared by those unfamiliar with our language. We could think of this ability as the possession of a technique, a collection of principles that enable you to associate a meaning with each of my utterances.

Before venturing further, I should note that in speaking of 'meaning' here, I am speaking of what, for lack of a better term, might be called 'literal meaning'. We can distinguish literal meaning from 'speaker meaning'. The distinction is illustrated by a case in which I utter 'The floor needs mopping', meaning that I want you to mop the floor. The literal meaning of my utterance is that the floor needs mopping. In uttering this sentence, however, I mean for you by way of your understanding of the sentence's literal meaning to recognize that I want you to mop the floor. You understand the literal meaning of my utterances when you understand the sentences I utter. Whether you understand what I might hope to accomplish in uttering those sentences, what I might be driving at, or whether you have a grasp of the 'deeper' meaning, if any, I might have in mind is a different matter.

Let us focus for a moment on simple declarative sentences. Declarative sentences ('The floor needs mopping') are to be distinguished from interrogative sentences ('Does the floor need mopping?'), imperative sentences ('Mop the floor!'), and the like. A long tradition has it that declarative sentences are fundamental, at least in the sense that our understanding of any sentence depends on our understanding of its declarative root. Now consider what it is to understand a declarative sentence, to understand what such a sentence says. One possibility is that you understand what a sentence says when you understand its 'truth-conditions': what is the case if the sentence is true (and what is the case if it is not true). The notion of a truth-condition is intended to correspond to what I earlier called 'literal meaning'.

How does any of this help? Well, we are looking for an accounting of what is involved in your understanding my utterances. At the very least this would seem to include your being able to associate a truth-condition with each sentence I produce. According to Davidson, this ability is constituted by your possession of a 'theory of truth' what I shall call a '*T*-theory' for those utterances. A *T*-theory, a theory of truth, is not, despite its name, a theory about the nature of truth. *T*-theories assign truth-conditions to sentences a speaker utters or might utter. Far from explicating truth, such theories presuppose a prior grasp of the concept of truth. You are in a position to deploy a *T*-theory only if you already understand what it is for sentences to be true (or fail to be true).

T-theories are modeled on theories of truth devised by Alfred Tarski for 'formal languages' of the sort deployed by logicians. If you have studied logic or computer programming, you have encountered examples of formal languages. A *T*-theory generates, by means of finite sets of rules, a '*T*-sentence' for every sentence in the language. *T*-sentences have the form

(*T*): *S* is true if and only if *p*,

where *S* is a description of a sentence uttered (or one that might be uttered), and *p* expresses that sentence's truth-conditions.

You might think that such a procedure would be hopelessly crude. Consider sentences (a) and (b) below:

(a) Jocasta is running.

(b) Oedipus's mother is running.

'Jocasta' and 'Oedipus's mother' are co-referring, so these sentences have the same truth-conditions. They do not, however, have the same meaning. How then could we hope to use a theory that focuses on truth-conditions to make clear what we do when we interpret that is, understand the meanings of utterances?

The gap between what we ordinarily regard as a sentence's meaning and the conditions under which it is true is narrowed, however, when we recognize that a theory of truth yields truth-conditions systematically for every sentence in a language. Natural languages encompass an infinite number of sentences, and theories of truth are finite. As a result, a theory of truth must make use of the compositional structure of language. Sentences can be divided into elements words that appear in other sentences. The truth-conditions (or meanings) of sentences depend on these elements and their arrangement. If it is possible to give a Tarski-style truth theory for a natural language (a big if), *T*-sentences implied by that theory should mirror, or at least approximate, native speakers' judgments about meaning.

These cryptic remarks will become clearer when we look at examples of *T*-sentences. We shall discover that the *T*-sentences that specify the truth-conditions for 'Jocasta is running' and for 'Oedipus's mother is running' are different. The moral: a *T*-theory does more than merely associate sentences and truth-conditions; it does so in a way that distinguishes sentences that differ in meaning yet are true or untrue under the same circumstances. This result is assured by the requirement that *T*-theories incorporate finite sets of rules.

What is the significance of this talk of 'finite sets of rules'? The formal languages deployed by logicians, as well as natural languages such as French, Urdu, and English, include an infinity of sentences. We who use these languages, however, are finite beings. This suggests that whatever our understanding of a language comes to, it cannot merely be that we have learned to associate a particular meaning or truth-condition with every sentence. It appears, rather, that we learn the elements of our language together with a relatively small set of principles for combining these elements so as to yield meaningful sentences. Your understanding of the words 'tiger' and 'warble', together with your grasp of rules for combining these words, enables you to understand the sentence 'Tigers warble', although it is most unlikely that you have encountered this sentence before.

The rules at issue here are not rules you consciously entertain or apply. In this respect they resemble rules you learn when you learn to play a game by playing it. We learn the rules of checkers (draughts) and tic-tac-toe (noughts and crosses) this way. Although we are competent at both of these games, most of us would be hard-pressed to spell out the rules we follow when we play them. You can gain a sense of their complexity by trying to imagine programming a computing machine to play checkers or tic-tac-toe. In doing so, you would be obliged to make the rules utterly explicit, a manifestly non-trivial task.

The idea, then, is that we can provide an account of what is included in your understanding my utterances if we can make explicit a finite collection of rules that associate a meaning or a truth-condition with each sentence I might utter. One implication of a view of this sort is that understanding a sentence in a language requires understanding the whole language. If this seems implausible, consider: there is something puzzling about the notion that someone could understand the sentences 'Birds warble' and 'Tigers growl', and yet have no idea what the sentence 'Tigers warble' means.

Think of a word as analogous to a chess piece. You grasp the significance of a chess piece a rook, for instance when you understand all the moves it can and cannot make. Similarly, to understand a word is to understand its role in sentences, the contribution it makes to the meaning of sentences in which it occurs. If understanding a sentence requires understanding the words that make it up, and an understanding of those words requires understanding their role in all the sentences, then understanding the elements of a language must include understanding the whole language the language made up of those elements.

But wait. Surely someone could understand the French sentence 'Il pleut' ('It's raining') without understanding other French sentences?

The issues here are delicate, and a satisfactory resolution of them would take us far afield. The idea, however, is that you can understand an utterance of 'Il pleut' without understanding other French sentences only because you can be confident that this sentence bears a relation to a French-speaker's actual and potential utterances that mirrors the relation that the sentence 'It's raining' bears to sentences of English. Your confidence is based on collateral information you possess concerning human beings and their use of language. Note, however, that you could be wrong in this case. The person uttering 'Il pleut' might not be speaking French at all, but some other language containing a sentence that *sounds* like the French sentence but *means* something altogether different.

One way to factor out extraneous information and thus

to see what is involved in understanding utterances is to imagine that you are in the position of interpreting the utterances of a speaker whose language is entirely unfamiliar to you. All you have to go on are the speaker's utterances, the context in which they are uttered, and the speaker's non-linguistic behavior: the speaker's gestures, the direction of his or her gaze, and the like. And we could say that an account of what is included in anyone's understanding of any utterance must appeal only to resources available to such a 'radical interpreter'. To move beyond these is to assume part of what it is we are trying to explain. This, at any rate, is Davidson's idea.

T-theories

When you understand a particular utterance, according to Davidson, you associate that utterance with a truth-condition. Suppose you understand an utterance of 'Il pleut'. Your understanding amounts to your recognizing that the sentence uttered is true if it is raining, and false otherwise. And this is reflected in the '*T*-sentence'

(*T O*): 'Il pleut' is true if and only if it's raining,

which is an instance of the schema introduced earlier:

(*T*): *S* is true if and only if *p*.

Again, *S* is a description of a sentence uttered (or a possible utterance), and *p* is an expression of *S*'s truth-conditions.

Before venturing further, we need to distinguish the language in which *T*-sentences are formulated (your language) from the language you are interpreting. Philosophers call the language you set out to interpret the 'object language' and the language you, an interpreter, use, the 'metalanguage'. If you speak English and you are interpreting utterances produced by a French-speaker, then English is the metalanguage and French is the object language. If we imagine your French respondent interpreting you, then for that respondent French is the metalanguage and English the object language.

Suppose, now, that you and I are both speakers of English. I utter a sentence, 'It's raining', and you understand my utterance. In what sense do you need to interpret me? If we share a language, and if we know this, then your understanding my utterances will, on the whole, amount to your taking those utterances at face value. In this case the metalanguage and the object language coincide. When that is so, the truth-conditions of a sentence uttered can be specified by using the sentence itself. If, for instance, you advance a *T*-theory in English for utterances I, a fellow speaker of English, produce, you might express the truth-conditions for my utterance of 'Tigers are striped' by using that very sentence:

(*T 1*): 'Tigers are striped' (uttered by J. H.) is true if and only if tigers are striped.

In this case, *T*-sentences will consist of a sentence inside quotation marks, followed by 'is true if and only if' followed by the sentence itself, 'disquoted'.

Do not be put off by the apparent triviality of (*T 1*). A *T*-theory must include resources for generating every sentence of the language to which it applies. Your knowing the truth-conditions of some sentence involves your having mastered (albeit unselfconsciously) a theory that implies a theorem of the form (*T*), a *T*-sentence, for that sentence. Such a theory implies indefinitely many *T*-sentences, however. You understand my utterance of a particular sentence only if you are in a position to understand my utterance of indefinitely many sentences. On this view, your appreciating the meaning of a sentence requires not only that you appreciate the meanings of many sentences, but also that you grasp systematic relations among sentences of the sort captured by rules used to generate *T*-sentences.

From T-theories to *I-theories*

Davidson contends that to interpret my speech, you must be in a position to associate meanings truth-conditions with my actual and possible utterances, and to do so systematically. But this is achievable, he thinks, only if you are *simultaneously* in a position to decipher my propositional attitudes: my beliefs, desires, and intentions. I utter a sentence with a particular intention to inform, to deceive, to amuse, to threaten because of what I believe, what I take the sentence to mean, and what I might hope to accomplish in uttering it. A theory of interpretation, what I shall call an '*I*-theory', provides an accounting of all these attitudes at once. To understand my speech you must understand what I believe and desire; and a grasp of my beliefs and desires requires that you understand my utterances. (One consequence of such a view (foreshadowed earlier) is that only creatures capable of linguistic utterances could be subjects of propositional attitude ascriptions: thought requires talk.) How might it be possible to break into this circle?

Davidson's suggestion is that interpretation rests on our ability to identify the primitive attitude of 'holding true' applied to sentences. Without prior knowledge of my language or my beliefs and desires, you might ascertain that I hold a particular sentence true. This does not presuppose that you know what I mean in uttering this sentence, or what I believe. For this reason, your discovery that I hold some sentence true could constitute *independent* evidence for any hypothesis you might venture as to what I mean and what I believe. I will hold true the sentence 'Tigers are striped' only if I believe that tigers are striped and I take the sentence to mean (or to be true if and only if) tigers are striped. In interpreting my speech, then, you begin with guesses about what I believe and what my utterances mean, and check these guesses against sentences you take me to hold true.

Suppose, for instance, I hold true the sentence 'Pythagoras is peculiar'. I do so because of what I believe (among other things, that Pythagoras is peculiar) and what I take the sentence 'Pythagoras is peculiar' to mean (namely, that Pythagoras is peculiar).

Pace some theorists, this does not imply that if you are to interpret me, I must be truthful. You might, for instance, discover that I am an habitual liar: for any sentence, *p*, in general I hold true not-*p* when I utter *p*. In this respect, it is useful to distinguish the philosopher W. V. Quine's notion of 'assent' to sentences from the attitude of holding true; we can and do assent to what we do not hold true. So long as you have some way of teasing out what sentences I hold true, you have a way of testing hypotheses about what my utterances mean in conjunction with what I believe. (If this strikes you as an impossible task, think of puzzles in which you are required to interrogate informants, some of whom tell the truth and some of whom are chronic liars, in order to discover the answer to some question.)

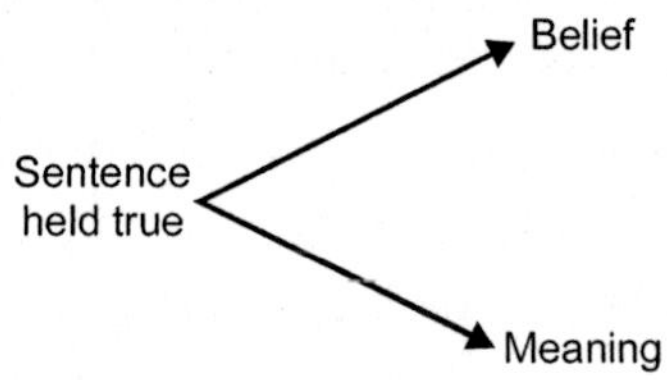

Fig. 10.1

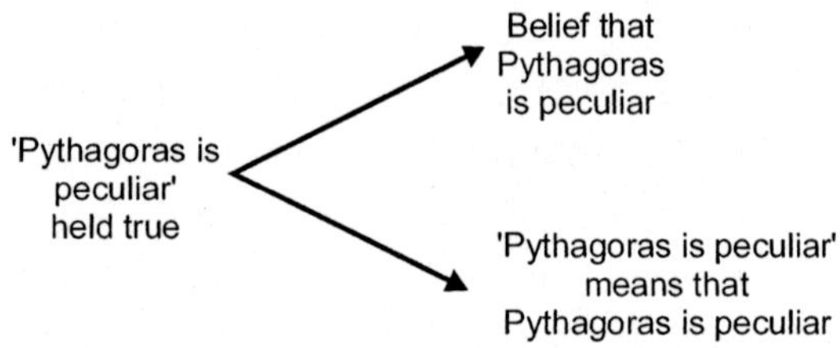

Fig. 10.2

Decision Theory

The envisaged interpretive technique is based on an insight afforded by *decision theory*. Decision theory provides a formal account of choice or preference in terms of agents' *probabilities* and *utilities*. The guiding idea is that an agent's preference for one course of action over one or more competitors depends on the relative desirability (for the agent) of the actions' outcomes and the probabilities associated (by the agent) with these outcomes.

You must choose between going to the movies or hiking. The outcomes of these choices could have different values or utilities for you, and these values or utilities might be affected by a variety of possible circumstances. You might enjoy hiking more than the movies, for instance, but not if it rains. Your overall preference is determined by the relative utility or desirability of outcomes weighted by their probability. If the chance of rain is small, you opt for the hike; otherwise you choose the movies.

Probabilities and utilities are beloved by decision theorists because they are expressible numerically. This means that decision theory can be given a precise formal characterization of rational choice. One important consequence of the theory is that given an agent's preferences for various courses of action, it is possible to derive a *unique* assignment of probabilities and utilities for that agent.

The fact that decision theory puts us in a position to make a unique assignment of probabilities and utilities beliefs and desires makes it appear that decision theory is a straightforward empirical theory: we hypothesize beliefs and desires and test our hypothesis by noting agents' preferences.

The appearance is misleading. Decision theory might be thought of as affording a framework within which we can represent important structural features of human decision-making. In this respect, applications of decision theory resembles applications of coordinate systems or familiar systems of measurement about which I shall have more to say presently. For the moment, I shall note only that on Davidson's view, a theory of interpretation, an *I*-theory, includes two components: (1) a Tarski-style theory of truth, a *T*-theory, coupled with (2) a decision theory. Evidence for a theory of interpretation consists of agents' attitudes toward sentences uttered, most particularly the attitude of holding true. Just as in the case of orthodox decision theory, agents' beliefs and desires (construed as probabilities and utilities) are taken to determine agents' preferences, on a theory of interpretation, agents' beliefs, desires, and meanings (truth-conditions associated with sentences) are taken to determine what sentences those agents hold true.

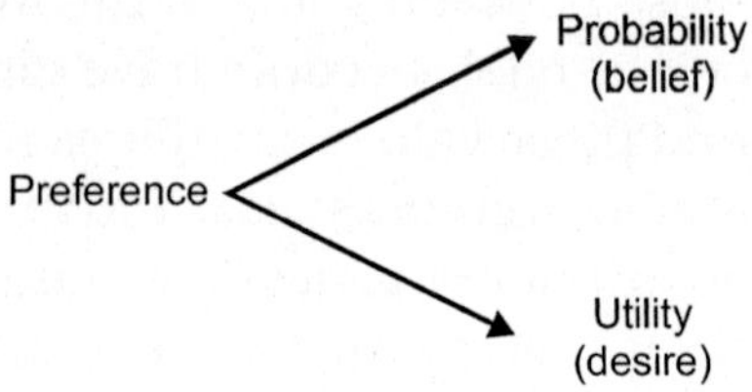

Fig. 10.3

In interpreting me, you in effect advance a theory that ascribes to me a universe of beliefs, desires, and meanings, and is constrained by sentences you take me to hold true.

Charity

In the course of interpreting me, the *I*-theory you develop assigns 'contents' simultaneously to my utterances and to my propositional attitudes. You can adjust for apparently anomalous utterances by supposing that you are wrong about what I mean, or that I have a desire to deceive you, for instance, or that I am being ironic, or by supposing that I harbor a false belief. This might suggest that an *I*-theory need answer only to a requirement of consistency: if your theory results in an implausible prediction as to what I hold true, you are free to adjust the theory by changing what you take me to believe or mean to secure a more acceptable prediction.

Imagine that we are watching a vintage episode of *The Avengers*. I remark, 'It's wonderful to see a bloke who can wear a bowling hat without appearing ridiculous.' You are momentarily baffled: *bowling hat*? Then you realize I meant that it was wonderful to see a bloke in a bowler hat a *bowler*. In so doing, you engage in a bit of radical interpretation. You have evidence that I hold true the sentence 'It's wonderful to see a bloke who can wear a *bowler* without appearing ridiculous.' What *do* I mean? Well, one possibility is that I believe we are watching a suave character sporting a bowling hat and take 'bowling hat' to denote bowling hat. Another possibility is that, at least on this occasion, I mean by 'bowling hat' what you mean by 'bowler', and that I (in effect) believe that we are watching a character wearing a bowler. Either hypothesis is consistent with your evidence. Does this mean that both hypotheses are equally satisfactory?

Davidson does not think so. According to Davidson, propositional attitude ascriptions are governed by a Principle of Charity: you must count me right in most things. If you are attempting to discover what I believe and what my utterances mean, you cannot but suppose that my beliefs are largely true. Without this grounding assumption, any consistent *I*-theory might be as good as any other. An *I*-theory must optimize the truth of my beliefs, then, while simultaneously making sense of my utterances.

In the present case, this means that you will interpret my talk of 'bowling hats' as talk of bowlers. To do otherwise to imagine, for instance, that I mean by 'bowling hat' just what you would mean by the term would oblige you to suppose that I had a host of false beliefs, including the belief that bowlers are worn for bowling. Charity requires that you adjust your *I*-theory in a way that optimizes the truth of my beliefs.

Indeterminacy

Astute readers will have guessed that, even assuming the Principle of Charity, there is no guarantee that a unique theory of interpretation will be forthcoming for any speaker. It is possible for there to be wildly divergent *I*-theories for a given speaker, each compatible with all actual and possible evidence. You and a companion, working independently, might construct *I*-theories for me. Both theories fit all the evidence either of you have or could have, both enable you to make sense of my utterances, and to converse with me on endless topics. Both make my beliefs mostly true. On comparing notes, however, you discover that the two theories systematically assign different meanings to my utterances! In the extreme case, you interpret my utterance of a particular sentence as meaning 'Tigers are striped', and your companion interprets the same utterance as meaning 'Rabbits are furry'. What has gone wrong here? Which of you is right - if either is right? And how would you decide?

We are face to face with the notorious doctrine of the 'indeterminacy of interpretation'. Quine, a forerunner of Davidson on these matters, has argued that every utterance is susceptible to endless perfectly adequate but incompatible interpretations or 'translations'. These translations can be compatible with all a speaker says, or would say. You might think this means that it would be difficult or impossible for us tell which of a pair of competing translations is right. But Quine's idea is more disquieting: *all there is* to what a speaker means is spelled out in a translation that fits everything a speaker says or would say. The possibility of competing but equally adequate translations shows only that there is no further 'fact of the matter' as to what speakers mean.

Quine distinguishes (what he calls) the 'indeterminacy of meaning' from the kind of 'underdetermination' we encounter in evaluating scientific theories. Two scientific theories can fit all the evidence, indeed all the evidence we can imagine, yet one theory can be correct, the other not. In science, theories purport to capture an independent reality. But when it comes to meanings, Quine contends, there *is* no independent reality, no reality beyond speakers' dispositions of the sort captured in systematic translations of their utterances. This is not to say that translations cannot be wrong. On the contrary, some translations could fail to mesh with actual and possible observations of agents' speech behavior. But every translation that *does* fit such observations would equally lay claim to capturing speakers' meaning.

Davidson agrees with Quine that indeterminacies of this sort are inevitable. He differs from Quine, however, in suggesting that indeterminacies that turn up in *I*-theories are entirely benign. Equally charitable *I*-theories consistent with all of an agent's preferences amount to no more than 'notational variants' of one another. The situation resembles that in which temperature is assessed in Fahrenheit or Celsius. I say that water freezes at 0°C, you contend that it freezes at 32°F. Which assessment is correct? The question assumes what is false, namely that there is some definite feature of the world concerning which the two assessments might differ. Rather, they are simply two ways of capturing the same fact. In this respect, Davidson's conception of radical interpretation is to be distinguished from Quine's conception of radical translation. Radical translation leaves open the prospect of more far-reaching substantive indeterminacies. The reasons for this are technical and need not concern us here. Our goal is to develop a feel for Davidson's special conception of mind.

The Omniscient Interpreter

I have described Charity as mandating that we ascribe beliefs to agents so as to optimize the truth of those beliefs. In practice, this means that you ascribe beliefs to me in such a way that they come out mostly true by your lights: you make my beliefs consistent with your beliefs as nearly as possible. But now we confront an apparent difficulty. There is an obvious and important difference between what *is* true and what any finite agent *believes* to be true. Suppose that many or most of *your* beliefs were false. These false beliefs would carry over into your interpretations of others.

Davidson argues that this way of thinking about the matter misses an important feature of Charity. Consider your beliefs. The beliefs you *actually have* are those that would be ascribed to you by an interpreter who knew all there was to know about you and your circumstances, an interpreter in possession of *all* the evidence, an *omniscient* interpreter. This is just to say that your beliefs *must* in fact be optimally true. If your beliefs are of necessity optimally true, then there can be no deep difference between your ascribing beliefs to me in such a way that they are optimally consistent with your beliefs and your ascribing beliefs to me in such a way that your ascription optimizes truth.

Could this possibly be right? Perhaps; so long as we take seriously Davidson's perspective on belief ascription. The object of a particular belief what that belief is a belief about is, Davidson supposes, fixed in part by its cause. Your belief about a tree concerns a particular tree because it is caused by that tree. We ascribe beliefs, then, partly by reference to their causes. We can of course be wrong about these, we can *misascribe* beliefs; but it cannot be the case that an ascriber's beliefs are mostly false. They concern their causes, quite independently of what anyone, including the believer, takes these causes to be. This is just a more prosaic way of saying that the beliefs you, as ascriber, possess are those that would be ascribed to you by an omniscient interpreter.

How plausible is it to imagine that beliefs concern their causes? It is surely possible for a bump on the head to cause me to believe that Napoleon died in battle. The cause of this belief is a bump on the head, yet my belief concerns not the bump, but Napoleon.

It is central to Davidson's view, however, that beliefs, like meanings, cannot be ascribed singly. In ascribing a particular belief to me, you implicitly ascribe a world of other beliefs those beliefs, namely, implied by the *I*-theory you invoke. It is this holistic edifice that must satisfy Charity and the demand that the objects of belief are fixed by their causes. A correct theory of interpretation can accommodate false belief against a background of largely true belief. All things considered, then, an *I*-theory that depicts me (on the basis of what I say and do) as having acquired a belief about Napoleon as a result of a bump on the head could easily turn out to be more charitable than a theory that ascribes to me a belief about a bump on the head.

Interpretation and Measurement

Consider what is involved in the explanation of a phenomenon or domain of phenomena. Explanation takes many forms. An explanation purports to make clear, or make sense of, or facilitate our grasp of something we hope to understand. One familiar sort of explanation is decompositional: we come to understand complex entities by seeing how their parts fit together and interact. You come to understand heat by recognizing that heating an object agitates its constituent molecules, and that this agitation is transmitted to adjacent molecules from the hot sand on the beach to the soles of your feet. You grasp the operation of a clock, or a machine that wraps candy bars, or a cold front, or liquidity by discovering the mechanism responsible for the behavior of clocks, candy-wrapping machines, cold fronts, and liquid substances. In these cases you come to understand the mechanism by seeing how it works, how its parts interact with one another and with their surroundings to produce a particular kind of outcome. Mechanistic explanation of this sort is common in the sciences, and in engineering, medicine, and everyday life.

Another sort of explanation, a sort much beloved in psychology and the philosophy of mind, is functional explanation. In giving a functional explanation, you 'abstract' from physical details of a mechanism and consider it exclusively in terms of the causal roles of its constituents. We can describe the operation of a steam engine, or a computing machine, or the digestive tract of a human being without concern for the 'physical implementation' or 'realization' of these things.

A very different way of understanding a domain of objects is to devise a perspicuous description of the domain's structure. This can be accomplished by overlaying the domain with another domain whose structure is antecedently well understood. We employ calibrated yardsticks, pan balances, and thermometers in describing the lengths, weights, and temperatures of objects. Similarly, we comprehend the layout of the surface of our planet by imposing a coordinate structure on it. Once in place, this system of coordinates enables us to specify areas, distances, and locations of objects and occurrences on the planet's surface. It enables us to offer certain sorts of prediction, too. If you know the velocity of an object moving across the surface of the planet and you know its location at a time, you can predict its location at some future time. If you know the location of an object and its distance and direction from another object, you can fix the location of the second object.

Coordinate systems represent a special case of measurement: the application of the domain of numbers to a domain of objects or properties. When we describe an object as 12 meters long or as weighing 110 kilograms, what features of the object correspond to these numbers? The question is misleading. Ordinary physical objects in ordinary settings exhibit a relatively enduring structure that lends itself to description via antecedently understood formal systems. The structure of these descriptive systems, the relations among their elements, is crucial; the particular elements that make them up are in one respect arbitrary. We can express weights in kilograms or pounds, length in meters or feet. What is important is that the numbers we choose, and the axioms governing their combinations, exhibit an appropriate structure.

Consider again the use of a coordinate system in mapping the surface of the earth. Your choice of a system is, in part, arbitrary. You might use a Mercator projection or a spherical projection, for instance. Notice that a geographical region appearing in a Mercator projection can look very different from the same region represented in a spherical projection. I can recall being baffled as a child by the apparent difference in the relative size of Greenland on the globe in the front of my fourth-grade classroom and on the large map on the wall above the blackboard. On the one, Greenland seemed to be only a little larger than Texas; on the other, it appeared nearly as big as the whole of North America. I wondered how large Greenland was *really*; both maps could not be right. (My teacher's explanation: the wall map was larger than the globe!) But of course *both* maps were right. My mistake was to compare objects on one map with objects on another without taking into account that the mapping systems, although 'structurally isomorphic', were different.

The example provides a nice illustration of what, according to Davidson, indeterminacy of interpretation amounts to. Distinct *I*-theories might appear to ascribe wildly different beliefs or meanings to an agent, yet each theory could be correct. It need not follow that there is no 'fact of the matter' as to what the agent believes, however, any more than it follows from differences in maps of the sort illustrated above that there is no fact to the matter as to the relative size of Greenland. The appearance of mystery comes from comparing items across representational systems without taking into account the systems in which those items are embedded.

Structure and Content

Let us say, then, that the structure and point of *I*-theories is analogous to that of coordinate systems. We know in advance that anything describable by means of such a system must have certain properties. In the case of a coordinate system, if one object, *A*, is to the northwest of *B*, and *B* is to the northwest of *C*, then *A* is to the northwest of *C*. Objects that failed to satisfy these conditions could not usefully be represented in such systems and could not be said to have straightforward locations. In the case of an *I*-theory, if an agent prefers *A* to *B* and *B* to *C*, then the agent prefers *A* to *C*. Creatures who failed to satisfy this condition not in the sense that they exhibit intransitive preferences, but in the sense that they fail to exhibit anything identifiable as an appropriately transitive repertoire of choices would not satisfy an *I*-theory and could not be said to have straightforward preferences.

If we are to avoid confusion, we must distinguish internal constraints on an *I*-theory (or a coordinate system) and descriptions of agents (or geographical regions) *in terms of* the theory (or coordinate system). In deploying a coordinate system, you make use of a well-behaved geometrical structure the features of which can be described quite independently of features of the world on which it is imposed. Similarly, in deploying an *I*-theory we make use of a framework that can be characterized abstractly and independently of its applications. In applying coordinate systems or *I*-theories, we overlay one domain of objects with a structure that makes salient the structure of the target domain. The target domain itself exists independently, as do the objects and properties that make it up. Our description of this domain reflects both those independent features and features of the coordinate system or *I*-theory in terms of which those features are described. Clearly, we must not mistake features of the one for features of the other. To do so would be like mistaking latitude and longitude lines on a map for physical features of the terrain. If Davidson is right, then imagining that talk of the propositional content of beliefs, desires, and intentions is talk about mechanistic components of agents is to make a mistake of this sort.

Consider a simple geographical truth, Adelaide's being south of Alice Springs. This truth depends on the application and orientation of a coordinate system and on system-independent features of a particular region of our planet. Imagine now that you correctly ascribe to me the belief that tigers are striped. The truth of this ascription turns on the application of an *I*-theory and on theory-independent features of me, ultimately my dispositional makeup. On Davidson's view I possess beliefs with settled propositional contents in something like the way cities possess locations. We do not imagine that locations have distinctive physical 'realizations' (or that they are 'multiply realizable'), nor are we tempted to suppose that if locations are not physical, they must be non-physical. The same holds for the propositional contents of beliefs, desires, and intentions.

We ascribe propositional attitudes to agents whose behavior (actual and potential) accords with those ascriptions. One possibility is that it so accords because the ascriptions, if correct, pick out components of a mechanism responsible for the behavior. (This is the kind of picture promoted by the Representational Theory of Mind. Beliefs and desires are sentences in the Language of Thought occupying 'belief boxes' and 'desire boxes'.) But if Davidson is right, there would be no need to suppose this. Propositional attitude ascriptions, and the *I*-theories that license such ascriptions, need not provide quasi-mechanistic explanations of behavior, any more than talk of the location of a city or the direction in which it lies from some other city provides a geologically illuminating assessment of the terrain.

If this were so, then the kind of explanation of agents' intelligent behavior we obtain in reckoning their beliefs, desires, and intentions would not be functional, mechanical, or decompositional explanation, but a kind of explanation the success of which stems from its exposing and describing in a systematic way the structure of a complex phenomenon. Such explanations have predictive force not because they uncover hidden mechanisms, but because they apply to potential utterances and deeds, as well as to actual utterances and deeds. Less mysteriously: propositional attitude explanations illuminate, and thus partly explain, the structure of certain sorts of dispositional system. These explanations work not because they pinpoint gears, levers, and springs in the underlying mechanism or because they uncover an isomorphism between interpretive elements and components of the mechanism, but because they reveal a structured system of dispositions describable by means of an antecedently well-understood domain, a domain plotted in theories of truth and decision theories.

Putting all of this together, we could say that to the extent that we can be subjects of propositional attitude ascriptions, our behavior, or rather the dispositional basis of our behavior, accords with a particular sort of theory. Its so according yields a kind of explanation of it. The explanation is not mechanical or decompositional, or functional, however; it differs in kind from such explanations. A mistake made by philosophers of mind and by some psychologists is to imagine that an *I*-theory describes a mechanism, perhaps at a functional level, components of which correspond to elements of the theory.

Mental Causation and the Propositional Attitudes

A difficulty remains. On the view I have pegged to Davidson, explanations that appeal to the propositional attitudes are non-mechanistic. Such explanations illuminate human behavior by invoking a structure defined by an appropriate *I*-theory. But if this, or something like it, is right, it would seem to be at odds with another idea of Davidson's, the idea that *reasons are causes*: beliefs, desires, and intentions explain actions only insofar as they are *causes* of those actions.

Suppose your flipping the light switch is explained by your desire to illuminate the room, together with your belief that by flipping the switch you will illuminate the room. Suppose too that the success of an explanation of this sort does not rest on the identification of an internal mechanism responsible for your flipping the switch. Although the success of the explanation undoubtedly depends on your neurological condition (and on much else besides), its success need not require that there be a simple correspondence between components of your explanation, particular propositional attitudes, and particular kinds of neural state or event. Even if the explanation is correct, then, this implies nothing about the character of the mechanisms responsible for your behavior other than that they must be such that they are capable of producing behavior of this sort.

Still, the explanation includes an important causal ingredient. It is part of the explanatory framework invoked when we appeal to beliefs, desires, and intentions that an agent can have a reason, *R*, to perform a particular action (where a reason consists of a belief-desire pair), and perform the action for a reason, but not perform the action *for* reason *R*. In this case, *R* does not account for the agent's behavior because it is not part of the agent's reason for doing what he does.

Imagine that you want to eat a healthy breakfast, and believe that you can eat a healthy breakfast by eating the steaming bowl of Brussels sprouts on the table in front of you. Suppose, in addition, that you are keen to learn self-discipline and believe that your eating a bowl of Brussels sprouts for breakfast would contribute to this end. Here you have distinct reasons for a single action. You might act for *both* reasons: you plunge your spoon into the bowl because you want to eat a healthy breakfast *and* because you want to nurture self-discipline. But it could just as easily be true that you act on one of the reasons and not the other: you eat the bowl of Brussels sprouts because you want to eat a healthy breakfast, and *not* because you want to learn self-discipline. In such cases it is hard to understand the 'because' here noncausally. Indeed, as Davidson himself has emphasized, the role of propositional attitudes in explanations of behavior appears to be through and through causal: propositional attitude explanations of actions are explanations in terms of reasons, and reasons are causes.

Suppose this is right. Its being right need not be due to belief and desire ascriptions ascriptions of reasons picking out definite pieces of the causal mechanism responsible for your doing what you do. What you do depends on the dispositional character of your body and nervous system. This dispositional character is what ultimately licenses ascriptions of beliefs and desires. As we have seen, according to Davidson, the ascription of propositional attitudes involves the application of something like a theory of interpretation, an *I*-theory. This theory provides a perspicuous description of a complex dispositional system.

How might this help reconcile Davidson's view of propositional attitude ascription with our conviction that propositional attitudes figure in causal explanations of actions? Reflect for a moment on the implications of the idea that *I*-theories hold of agents in virtue of the dispositional structure of those agents. Dispositions can exist, can come and go, without being manifested. An object can possess distinct dispositions the manifestation of which in the object's behavior would be indistinguishable. One of these dispositions could be manifested without the others being manifested. An object might possess distinct properties, *P 1* and *P 2*, each of which, in concert with the object's other properties (and properties of objects nearby), disposes the object to turn green when heated. When the object is heated and, as a result, turns green, this might be due to its possessing *P 1*, or to its possessing *P 2*, or to its possessing both *P 1* and *P 2*. We may have trouble *deciding* whether *P 1*, or *P 2*, or both *P 1* and *P 2* are responsible for the change of color, but that is a separate issue.

Now, what of action? I explain an action, your ingesting a bowl of Brussels sprouts, by citing your desire to cultivate self-discipline. In so doing (as we are supposing), I explain your behavior by imposing a framework provided by a theory of interpretation, an *I*-theory. Your behavior satisfies this theory. But note: an *I*-theory according to which you act on your desire to learn self-discipline differs from an *I*-theory according to which you act on your desire to eat a healthy breakfast. True, your behavior here and now, your eating the Brussels sprouts, accords with either theory. But this is only part of what the theories address. *I*-theories range over dispositional systems. And the dispositional makeup of an agent whose behavior accords with the first theory differs from the dispositional makeup of an agent whose behavior accords with the second theory. To be sure, there is an epistemological hurdle to be negotiated in discovering which theory is correct. But, as in the case of ordinary, nonmental dispositional systems, that is another matter.

Explanations appealing to propositional attitudes are sensitive to dispositional, hence causal, differences in agents whose behavior they endeavor to explain. This need not, if Davidson is right, depend on the presence of anything like a one-to-one correspondence between propositional attitudes and bodily components. In the ordinary case, your desire to act in a particular way explains your so acting only if you would not have acted as you did had you lacked the desire. This is because, were you such that you lacked the desire, were you such that an *I*-theory ascribing the desire to you would not be correct, your dispositional condition would have been such that you would not have behaved as you in fact behaved.

What of a case like that of your eating a bowl of Brussels sprouts in which you have *two* reasons, either of which would account for your behavior? In such cases it might well be false that had you not possessed one of the reasons, you would not have eaten the Brussels sprouts. Had you lacked the one reason, you might still have had the other; and this reason might have accounted for your behavior. The example provides a reminder that the use of counterfactual and subjunctive conditional locutions to capture dispositional characteristics of objects yields at best partial results. We must appeal to actual dispositional differences between the two cases.

Imagine a pair of agents, Wayne and Dwayne, both of

whom harbor the desires discussed earlier: the desire to eat a healthy breakfast and the desire to cultivate self-control. Both Wayne and Dwayne believe that they can satisfy these desires by eating a bowl of Brussels sprouts, so both have reasons to eat the Brussels sprouts. Imagine that Wayne and Dwayne each eat a bowl of Brussels sprouts: Wayne does so because he wants a healthy breakfast, and Dwayne does so because he wants to cultivate self-control. Although Wayne and Dwayne are both disposed to eat a bowl of Brussels sprouts, they nevertheless differ dispositionally: the dispositional basis of Wayne's action differs from the dispositional basis of Dwayne's action. And it is in virtue of these differences that Wayne and Dwayne satisfy distinct *I*-theories.

If Wayne and Dwayne have the same desires, why should we imagine that they satisfy distinct *I*-theories? Desires differ in intensity. You and I might both crave a Whopper, but your craving might outweigh mine, at least in this sense: your desire has greater motivational force within your psychological economy than my desire has within mine. We need not consider the question of whether desire strength can be compared *across* agents. All that matters here is that, *within* an agent, the relative strength of desires may vary considerably. This is built into our concept of desire. And it is reflected in decision theory by the utilities assigned to outcomes of actions, the objects of desire.

Another part of the conceptual apparatus associated with desire is the principle that when agents act deliberately, they do what they 'most want'. It is possible, then, for Wayne and Dwayne to have identical desires, but for those desires to differ in their respective levels of motivational strength for each agent. When this is so, different desires can 'call the shots': both Wayne and Dwayne eat a bowl of Brussels sprouts, but Wayne does so on the basis of his desire for a healthy breakfast, and Dwayne does so on the basis of his desire to learn self-control. Decision theory provides a way of distinguishing Wayne and Dwayne, and this is reflected in the *I*-theories we deploy in interpreting their behavior. Both are grounded in the dispositional systems that underlie Wayne's and Dwayne's actions.

An Apparent Regress

We have been examining Davidson's idea that ascriptions of propositional attitudes and the explanation of behavior by reference to propositional attitudes are a matter of superimposing a metric on a complex domain in a way that makes salient a structural component of that domain. In this respect, the ascription of beliefs and desires resembles our ascription of temperature, or length, or location. In each case we invoke a descriptive framework the structure of which is fine-grained, orderly, and antecedently well understood. In the case of temperature and length, we make use of properties of numbers organized in simple axiom systems. In the case of the propositional attitudes, we exploit semantic features of the sentential structure of our language in concert with a theory of rational choice.

Like explanations generally, explanations that appeal to the propositional attitudes are 'projective' (they extend to new, even unanticipated cases), hence predictive. If Davidson is right, this is due not to their denoting discrete components of a mechanism responsible for behavior, however, but to their applying to agents in virtue of those agents' overall dispositional structure. We are apt to be misled by our everyday practice of explaining the behavior of an agent on a particular occasion by ascribing to that agent individual beliefs, desires, and intentions. This makes it appear as though distinct components of the agent correspond to each of these. On Davidson's view, however, individual propositional attitude ascriptions are grounded in an implicit theory of interpretation. An ascription of a belief, desire, or intention is correct only in the case that it is implied by an *I*-theory satisfied by the agent. This suggests a parallel with measurement and our use of coordinate systems. In measuring the lengths of particular objects, we import a system of numbers; in locating objects in space, we impose a system of coordinates. We can make nothing of lengths or locations independently of such systems.

The practice of explaining behavior by reference to the propositional attitudes is sometimes labeled 'folk psychology'.

Folk psychology, like folk medicine, is useful, even indispensable. Neither folk practice, however, aims to reveal details of the underlying mechanism. Nor does the apparent success of either practice depend on its revealing such details. This need not mean that folk psychology is ripe for replacement (or elimination) by neuroscience. Folk psychology and neuroscience are not competitors, any more than cartography and geology are competitors.

Is this the end of the story? Have we provided a total theory of mind? Surely not. Davidson's theory is silent about the sensory aspect of our conscious lives. Even if we focus exclusively on our intentional characteristics – our thoughts, for instance it is clear that Davidson's story cannot be the whole story. Indeed, this is implicit in the story itself. On Davidson's view, an agent's harboring propositional attitudes (beliefs, desires, reasons for action) depends on that agent's being interpreted. Just as a coordinate system is something we impose on a region of space, so an agent's possession of beliefs and desires is tied to the imposition of an *I*-theory on that agent. The activity of interpretation itself, however, evidently involves interpreters' possessing propositional attitudes themselves. This points toward a regress of the kind foreshadowed at the outset of the chapter: my propositional attitudes depend on your interpreting me; your propositional attitudes depend on someone interpreting you; that someone's propositional attitudes depend on some further someone; and so on. How could such a process get off the ground?

Two responses to this worry are worth mention. First, Davidson's idea is that the practice of deploying *I*-theories and ascribing propositional attitudes requires a *community* of interpreters. Consider a two-person community consisting of you and me. The idea is not that I have propositional attitudes courtesy of your invoking an *I*-theory to account for what I do, and that you possess your propositional attitudes from some third source. Rather, we interpret one another. We engage in practices that, once they reach an appropriate level of sophistication, constitute the application of *I*-theories.

Although agents' possession of propositional attitudes depends on their being interpreted, the sense of dependence in play here is not the causal sense. The relationship between your deployment of an *I*-theory for me and my possession of propositional attitudes is not a causal relation. It is not causal any more than the application of a coordinate system to the earth's surface is a matter of causing the earth to possess new features.

If it sounds excessive to insist, as Davidson does, that your possession of propositional attitudes depends on your place in a community of interpreters, consider an analogy. Imagine a world that includes no conscious agents. In that world is anything 1 meter long? 'Well,' you might be tempted to say, 'in one sense, yes, and in another sense, no.' A world lacking conscious agents could contain objects that would, if placed beside meter sticks in our world, align perfectly. Still, something's being 1 meter long apparently depends on the presence of a measuring convention, and this presupposes intelligent agents. Suppose the system of meters and centimeters we now use had never been invented. Is it so clear that objects that we now describe as 1 meter long would have been 1 meter long? And is it so clear that a molecule-for-molecule duplicate of you languishing in a world lacking other similar agents could possess just the propositional attitudes that you possess?

A second response to the regress worry pushes us beyond Davidson. Pretty clearly, there is more to thought than the having of propositional attitudes in the strict Davidsonian sense. Davidson may be right about the propositional attitudes, but it may also be true that the kinds of capacity required to have beliefs, desires, and reasons for action include a host of important *non-propositional* mental capacities. Although much of our thinking has a linguistic flavor, much of it does not. A carpenter building a cabinet makes use of *spatial imagery* to see how parts will fit together. This imagery is evidently non-propositional and nonverbal. It resembles qualitatively a range of visual and tactile experiences familiar to the carpenter.

My suggestion is that 'non-propositional' thought of this sort undergirds intelligent action generally, and, more particularly, the kinds of linguistic practice on which Davidson focuses. It is easy to lose sight of such things when we set out to write about or discuss such topics. You use language what else? to tell me what you are thinking and to describe my thoughts. It need not follow, however, that your actual thoughts, or mine, are linguistic or 'propositional' in character. Even when our thoughts are explicitly linguistic when we talk to ourselves this is arguably at bottom a form of imagery: *verbal* imagery.

I shall have more to say about imagery and 'non-propositional' thought in the subsequent chapters. The point here is merely to suggest that the inter-pretational practices Davidson discusses float on the surface of a sea of mentality about which Davidson's theory is silent. We should err were we to interpret this silence as denial. Davidson restricts the scope of his inquiry, but we need not follow him in that regard. If we hope to acquire a grasp of the mind as a whole, we had better not follow him.

Davidson's work is well noted for its unity, as he has brought a similar approach to a wide variety of philosophical problems. Radical interpretation is a hypothetical standpoint which Davidson regards as basic to the investigation of language, mind, action, and knowledge. Radical interpretation involves imagining that you are placed into a community which speaks a language you do not understand at all. How could you come to understand the language? One suggestion is that you know a theory that generates a theorem of the form's means that p' for every sentence of the object language (i.e. the language of the community), where s is the name of a sentence in the object language, and p is that sentence, or a translation of it, in the meta language in which the theory is expressed. However, Davidson rejects this suggestion on the grounds that the sentential operator 'means that' is sensitive not only to the extensions of the terms that follow it, but also to their intensions. Hence, Davidson replaces 'means that' with a connective that is only sensitive to the extensions of sentences; since the extension of a sentence is its truth value, this is a truth functional connective. Davidson elects the biconditional if and only if – as the connective needed in a theory of meaning. This is the obvious choice because we are aiming at equivalence of meaning between s and p. But now we have a problem: 's if and only if p' is an ungrammatical sentence because the connective must link two propositions, but s is the name of a proposition, and not a proposition itself. In order to render s a proposition we need to supply it with a predicate. Which predicate is satisfied by s if and only if the sentence named by s, or a translation of it, is the case? In other words, which predicate is satisfied by "bananas are yellow" if and only if bananas are yellow? The answer is the predicate truth. Thus, Davidson is led to the conclusion that a theory of meaning must be such that for each sentence of the object language it generates a theorem of the form 's is truc if and only if p'. A theory of truth for a language can serve as a theory of meaning.

11

Representational Theory of Mind and Philosophy

Introduction

The idea here is that your forming a belief that the window is open is a matter of a symbol expressing the proposition that the window is open being deposited in your 'belief box'. In the same vein, your wanting the window to be open is your having such a symbol in your 'desire box'. Your belief box and your desire box are connected in distinctive ways to the rest of the system constituting your mind. If a symbol representing the proposition that the window is shut is in your desire box, for instance, this might in conjunction with the presence of various other symbols in your belief and desire boxes lead you to walk across the room and lower the window. The presence of the same symbol in your belief box (assuming that it is absent from your desire box) might and, again, in conjunction with the presence of other symbols in your belief and desire boxes lead to very different behavior.

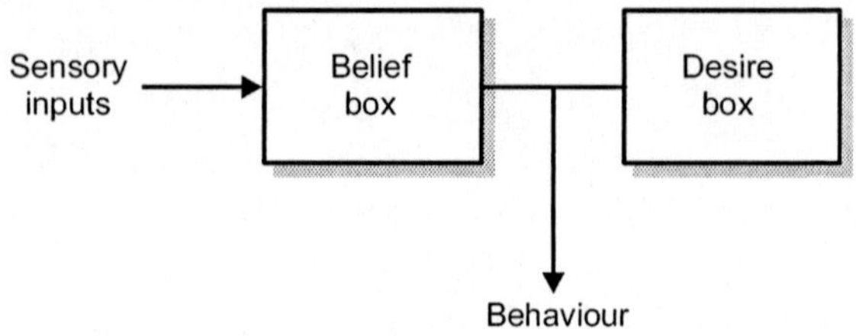

Fig. 11.1

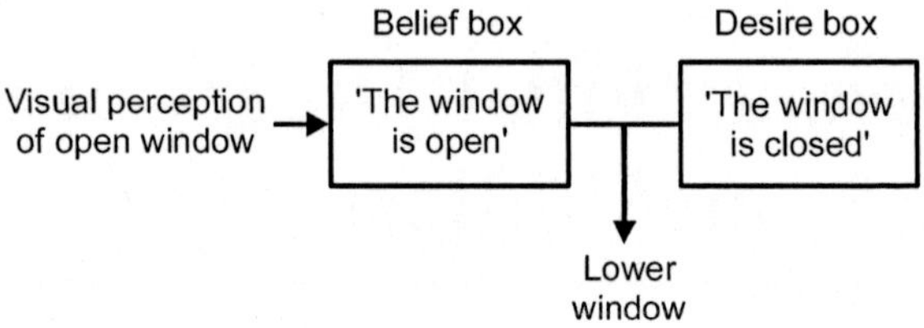

Fig. 11.2

This way of thinking of functional systems enables us to see more clearly how creatures with very different beliefs and desires might nevertheless be seen as functionally on a par. You, an infant, and I might all fit the highly simplified model in Figure 11.1. We differ, however, with respect to the symbols apt to appear in our respective belief and desire boxes.

This conception of mind, 'the Representational Theory of Mind', has long been defended by Jerry Fodor. The Representational Theory of Mind requires the postulation of a system of symbols that function as 'mental representations'. These symbols make up what Fodor calls a 'Language of Thought', a biologically fixed code analogous to the 'machine code' hard-wired into an ordinary computing machine. Your forming a belief that the window is open is a matter of a sentence in the Language of Thought corresponding to the English sentence 'The window is open', acquiring an appropriate functional role or, as we put it earlier, a matter of this sentence's slipping into your belief box.

Semantic Engines

Fodor and his allies have long insisted that the Representational Theory of Mind (and with it the Language of Thought hypothesis) is 'the only game in town'. The Representational Theory of Mind provides a way of understanding how minds, higher-level entities, could systematically affect and be affected by bodily goings-on. Until someone produces a serious competitor, the theory wins by default. Or so it is claimed.

But how is all this supposed to *work*? What could it mean to speak of sentences in a Language of Thought occupying belief and desire boxes? Notice first that the focus is on 'sentence tokens'. A sentence token a particular 'inscription' is a concrete entity, something that could exert causal influence. A sentence *token* is to be distinguished from a sentence *type*. To appreciate the distinction, consider the box shown in Figure 11.3. How many sentences does the box contain? The box contains two instances or *tokens* of a single sentence *type*.

I shall not clutter the text by explicitly signaling when I am discussing sentence tokens and when I am discussing sentence types. The context should make it obvious which is intended. When proponents of the Representational Theory of Mind speak of sentences occupying belief boxes, for instance, or sentences affecting causal processes, it is clear they are speaking of sentence tokens, not types individual entities, not kinds or types of entity.

Babar is King

Babar is King

Fig. 11.3

Functionalism and the Representational Theory of Mind afford highly abstract pictures of the mind. The significance of these can be grasped only by grounding the abstractions in concrete examples. Think of the sentences on this page. Each one is the result of an ordinary material causal process;

and each one produces ordinary material effects: it reflects light in a particular way, for instance. To see why this is significant, let us distinguish *sentences* from *propositions* they express (propositions they are *used* to express). When we encounter sentences in our native language, their meanings, the propositions they express, leap out at us. But, of course, we can encounter sentences without having any sense of what they mean. This happens whenever we confront sentences in a language we do not understand.

Now imagine a device capable of manipulating sentences without regard to their meanings, but that does so in a way that coincides with the way those sentences would be manipulated by an agent who knew their meanings. Such a device what John Haugeland dubs a 'semantic engine' would perfectly mimic the performance of a native speaker, but would do so without relying, as a native speaker would, on the meanings of the sentences it manipulated. Those sentences might express propositions (at least, they express propositions when used by ordinary speakers), but the device would care only about their shapes, their 'syntax'. (*Syntax* concerns purely *structural* or 'formal' features of sentences; *semantics* concerns their *meanings*.) The device we are imagining, a semantic engine, operates on purely syntactic principles and 'formal' relations among sentences, relations definable solely by reference to the syntactic characteristics of sentences.

Is such a device possible? Not only are semantic engines possible, they exist already, and in large numbers! An ordinary computing machine is a semantic engine. We design and program computers so that they manipulate symbols in accord with purely syntactic and formal principles. The symbols are meaningful to us but the machines that deploy them care nothing about this. They operate on *uninterpreted* symbols, but in a way that honors semantic constraints.

How is this possible? How could syntax mirror semantics? If you have ever studied logic, you have already encountered an important example of a system that makes use of purely syntactic or formal principles in the manipulation of symbols, but in a way that honors semantic relations among those symbols. Ordinary rules of inference refer only to shapes of symbols. Take the rule commonly known as *modus ponens*:

$$\frac{\begin{array}{c} p \supset q \\ \\ p \end{array}}{q}$$

(In English: Where '*p*' and '*q*' are arbitrary sentences, 'If *p* then *q*', and '*p*', implies '*q*'.)

For our purposes, what is significant about the *modus ponens* rule is that it is formulated and deployed without regard to semantics, without regard to the meanings of sentences to which it applies. Even so, applications of the rule make sense; they conform to the semantics of inference. If you accept the sentence

1. If it's raining then I'll need an umbrella, and the sentence
2. It's raining, then you are entitled to infer the sentence
3. I'll need an umbrella.

This is something any English-speaker, anyone who understands English, knows. Systems of formal logic mirror this kind of semantic knowledge by means of rules the application of which requires no semantic knowledge.

The Mind as a Semantic Engine

Well and good. But what has this to do with minds? Imagine that our aim is to explain the human mind by supposing that minds manipulate 'mental representations', and that mental representations are 'encoded' by sentences in the Language of Thought. It might seem that there is an obvious objection to this project. If minds manipulate sentences, symbolic representations, then this would appear to require a sentence *understander*, some component of the mind that *interprets* the symbols. This would mean that we are explaining the mind by positing within it another mind: an *homunculus*, a little intelligent agent whose job requires that he understand sentences in the Language of Thought and respond appropriately. An explanation of this kind is no explanation. The point is perfectly general. You and I are watching a machine that sorts and wraps candy bars. You are impressed, and ask how the machine works. 'Simple', I reply. 'There is a device inside it that controls its operations.'

Against this background it is easier to appreciate the relevance of the notion of a *semantic engine*. A semantic engine is a device that performs symbolic operations manipulates symbols in a way that reflects semantic relations holding among these symbols, but does so exclusively by means of formal and syntactic principles that is, without regard to the meanings of those symbols. We can suppose, then, that minds process mental representations, without having to suppose that minds contain components little intelligent agents, homunculi that *understand* the meanings of those representations. Ordinary computing machines are realizations of semantic engines. Perhaps brains are as well. If so, and if the brain has an appropriate functional organization, then it would seem that we have gone a long way toward explaining how minds work.

You might think that there is an obvious problem with this view. When we open up the brain, we see nothing that resembles symbols or sentences in a Language of Thought. What could it be for brains to contain sentences?

Think of an ordinary computing machine. We regard it as uncontrover sial that computing machines 'process symbols'. Yet, were you to examine the inside of a computing machine while it is engaged in 'symbol manipulations', you would see nothing resembling familiar mathematical or programming symbols. Nor, incidentally, would you see any 0s and 1s, the basic ingredients of a computing machine's symbolic repertoire. The electronic patterns that function as symbols in a computing machine need not resemble our pencil-and-paper representations of those symbols. Nor could you expect to 'read off' symbols as they are manipulated by a computing machine, any more than you could hope to read off a musical score by closely examining deflections in the groove of a phonograph record or the track of a compact disk.

If the mind is a semantic engine realized by the brain, if mental operations include the manipulation of symbols, sentences in a Language of Thought, then the embodiment of those symbols in the brain need not resemble the symbols we scribble using pencil and paper. They might involve subtle electrical or chemical states; they might be embodied in connections among neurons; they might be widely distributed in networks of neurons. In any case, there is no reason to imagine that such symbols could be 'read off' the brain in the way you read words off this page. If there is a Language of Thought, its sentences could well be invisible from the point of view of an observer examining the microstructure of a brain.

The Chinese Room

The Representational Theory of Mind depicts minds as semantic engines, devices that operate on purely formal and syntactic principles, but in a way that mirrors semantics. This means, roughly, that although mental operations are indifferent to the significance of the symbols on which they operate, these operations are indistinguishable from those that might be performed by someone who understood the symbols. When you tell your desktop computer to print a document by means of a typed or voiced command, the device does not first interpret the input, then act on the basis of its understanding of that interpretation. The mechanisms that execute your command care nothing for its meaning. The machine is programmed in such a way that its syntax reflects its semantics: it operates *just as though* it understood your command.

For proponents of the Language of Thought, this is *all there is* to understanding. *You* can be said to understand the sentences on this page. The mechanisms responsible for your understanding do not *themselves* understand. If we thought they did, we would not have explained what it is for *you* to understand the sentences. We would merely have pushed the problem back; we would now need to account for those mechanisms' understanding.

Is this all there is to understanding? John Searle has argued that it is not. Searle's much-discussed argument is based on a clever thought experiment. Imagine, Searle says, that you are seated in a cramped, windowless room. At your feet is a large basket of plastic Chinese characters. You have no idea that this is what they are: you are ignorant of Chinese, and for all you can tell the items in the basket might be plastic decorations of an abstract design: *squiggles*. Periodically, through a slot in the wall, you receive a batch of plastic squiggles. Although these mean nothing to you, you have been furnished with a manual that instructs you to pass particular sequences of squiggles out through the slot when particular sequences of squiggles are passed in. Suppose you become adept at this. When a sequence of squiggles is input, you can quickly output a sequence called for by the manual. We might even imagine that, in time, you learn the manual by heart, and so your manipulations of squiggles become virtually automatic.

Now, outside the room, and completely unknown to you, lurks a group of Chinese scientists. These scientists can read the characters that are passed into and out of the room. They regard the strings of squiggles they pass into the room as questions framed in Chinese, and the strings of squiggles you pass back out as answers to those questions. (We can ignore the fact that for the answers to make sense in light of the questions, the manual will need to be very complicated indeed.) It appears to the Chinese scientists that you understand Chinese. But, says Searle, clearly you do not. You are behaving *as though* you understand indeed, you are operating as a semantic engine yet you understand no Chinese. At best you are *simulating* a Chinese speaker.

Searle's Chinese Room thought experiment is best interpreted in light of a test proposed in 1950 by A. M. Turing (1912–1954), an influential mathe-matician whose work on the theory of computation underlies the operation of modern computing machines. Turing was interested in the question whether it might be possible to build an intelligent machine. After reviewing failed attempts to define 'intelligence' (and, for that matter 'machine'), Turing proposed to define intelligence 'operationally' and in that way bypass altogether the vexed question of what exactly constitutes genuine intelligence. An operational definition takes the form of a test for determining whether the defined term applies. Turing's test is designed to ensure that whatever passes the test qualifies as intelligent.

The Turing test is based on a game Turing dubs 'the Imitation Game'. The Imitation Game is played by three ordinary people. One, an interrogator, puts questions to two players, a man and a woman, and tries to guess which is which. One of these players must answer honestly, the other tries to mislead the interrogator. To avoid giving away the game by allowing the interrogator visual or auditory clues, the players are placed in a separate room and communicate with the interrogator by means of a teletype (an early form of 'instant messaging'). By asking clever questions, the interrogator will sometimes win the game, but will sometimes lose as well. Let us imagine that the interrogator wins that is, correctly discovers which player is which about 33 percent of the time.

Now, says Turing, suppose we replace the man or woman being interrogated with a computing machine. If the machine could fool a clever interrogator about as often as a human player could (as we are supposing, about 33 percent of the time), we should say that it passes the test: it is intelligent. (If this seems too easy, you might reflect on the fact that no existing or currently contemplated computing machine comes remotely close to exhibiting the kind of resourcefulness and wit required to fool a moderately competent interrogator.)

Searle's Chinese Room can be seen as a variant of the Turing test. We can imagine that the Chinese scientists assembled outside the room are taking the role of the interrogator in the Imitation Game, and that you (seated in the room with your manual and basket of plastic squiggles) are standing in for the computing machine. (The other player, we might imagine, is an ordinary Chinese speaker seated next to you.) Suppose you fool the inter-rogators about as often as a native Chinese speaker would. What does this show? Searle argues that it shows only that you have been provided with an ingenious prop a stunningly clever manual that enables you to play the part of a Chinese speaker. But you neither speak nor understand Chinese. Because you operate just as a computing machine would (think of the manual as your program), we should *not* say that a computing machine that passes the Turing test is genuinely intelligent or that it understands the sentences it receives as inputs or produces as outputs.

Searle hopes to draw a more general conclusion from all of this. The brand of functionalism we have been discussing, the Representational Theory of Mind, is based on the idea that the mind is a semantic engine: mental processes consist of operations over uninterpreted symbols (sentences in the Language of Thought). But, contends Searle, the Chinese Room thought experiment makes it clear that there is more to minds than this. A device a robot, perhaps whose 'brain' realized a semantic engine and thereby satisfied the requirements of the Representational Theory of Mind would no doubt fool us: we should *think* it intelligent, regard it as having a mind. But we would be wrong. At best the device would be simulating intelligence and understanding, in the way a computing machine might produce a simulated weather pattern or an instance of molecular bonding.

Some proponents of the Representational Theory of Mind have accused Searle of begging the question. Searle assumes that there is no genuine understanding in the Chinese Room. But, these theorists argue, there only appears to be no understanding because the thought experiment invites us to focus on just a single component *you*, sitting in your chair sorting through a basket of plastic squiggles rather than the *whole system* of which you are but one component. Thus, while it is true that *you* understand no Chinese, *the system* that includes you the room as a whole does.

Uncommitted bystanders to this debate may feel pulled in different directions. On the one hand, Searle is apparently onto something important. On the other hand, there is some justice in Searle's opponents' complaint that the appeal of the Chinese Room stems from its tendency to make us focus on a component of a system rather than the system as a whole. I shall, however, leave the debate here, and move to consider the question of how sentences in the Language of Thought come by their semantics. In due course I shall suggest a way of reconciling these issues. Doing so, however, obliges us to move beyond functionalism and the Representational Theory of Mind, and take a prolonged excursion into metaphysics.

From Syntax to Semantics

Central to the Representational Theory of Mind is the idea that minds manipulate mental representations in the form of uninterpreted sentences in the Language of Thought. In this context, 'uninterpreted' means that the processes whereby mental symbols are manipulated operate without regard to the meanings of those symbols. In this respect, mental processes are taken to resemble computational processes. They resemble, too, your bravura performance in the Chinese Room.

If mental symbols are uninterpreted, in what does their meaning reside? Reflect for a moment on the operation of ordinary computing machines. Suppose we program a computing machine to keep inventory in a supermarket. The program keeps track of bananas, cans of soup, and cartons of milk. We might say that the computing machine on which the program runs is storing and processing information about bananas, cans of soup, and cartons of milk. The machine performs operations over symbols that designate these items, however, without regard to what they designate. Indeed, we might imagine that the very same program could be run on a different machine, or on the same machine on a different occasion, to keep track of items in a hardware store. In this case, the device would store information about nails, glue, and ant traps. We might even imagine that the very same symbols that in the supermarket case represent bananas, cans of soup, and cartons of milk, represent, in this machine, nails, glue, and ant traps, respectively.

What, then, gives a symbol manipulated by a computing machine its meaning? What makes it designate cartons of milk rather than ant traps? And, we might ask, what gives sentences in the Language of Thought their meaning (for, although it might be controversial whether states of a computing machine are in any sense meaningful, it is surely not controversial that our thoughts have meaning)? The entire Language of Thought project is predicated on the assumption that thoughts *are* meaningful, and that this is something that calls for explanation.

Note, first, that a devotee of the Representational Theory of Mind assumes (as most philosophers nowadays assume) that the meaning of a symbol is not intrinsic to that symbol. What a symbol signifies is not built into the symbol, but depends rather on how the symbol is deployed by agents (or systems) that deploy it. The symbols processed by a computing machine owe their significance to the use to which they are put by agents who program and enter data into the machine for particular purposes. When you type 'bananas' into the machine and this inscription is converted into a pattern of magnetic deflections, this pattern of magnetic deflections, insofar as it functions as a symbol, designates bananas because this is what *you* mean by 'bananas'.

We can say that the meanings of symbols processed by an ordinary computing machine are derivative of the meanings given those symbols by agents making use of the machine and its program. But this cannot be the explanation of the meanings of symbols in the Language of Thought. Your thoughts do not mean what they do because you *assign* those meanings; your mental concepts do not designate what, if anything, they designate because you *decide* what they designate. The Language of Thought is supposed to explain how we can have meaningful thoughts. If the meanings of expressions in the Language of Thought require that we assign those expressions meaning, then we have explained nothing. The assignment of meanings is evidently an activity that presupposes meaningful thought. If we are to account for the semantics of the Language of Thought, we must do so without assuming what we hope to explain.

What, then, is the source of meaning for the Language of Thought? To what does it owe its semantics? We can exclude the possibility that expressions in the Language of Thought possess intrinsic, built-in significance. And we can exclude the possibility that meanings of those expressions depend on the interpretative activities of thinkers. What options remain?

Perhaps this: expressions in the Language of Thought owe their significance to causal relations those expressions bear to goings-on in a thinker's surroundings. Thus, a particular term in the Language of Thought might designate bananas (and so stand in for the English word 'banana') because it is evoked by the presence of bananas. Another term might designate cans of soup (standing in for the English expression 'can of soup') because instances of it are brought about by agents' causal contact with cans of soup.

This sketch is, to be sure, oversimplified. The point, however, is that it is open to a proponent of the Representational Theory of Mind to advance a broadly causal account of the semantics of the Language of Thought. Such an account would be complex, and would include noncausal elements. The so-called logical terms for instance, those corresponding to the English expressions 'all', 'some', 'and', 'or', 'not', 'if... then ...' might be explicable purely by reference to relations that sentences in the Language of Thought bear to one another. But the fundamental idea is that the semantics of thought is fixed by the context of thinkers. In this respect, too, ordinary agents resemble computing machines. The significance of symbols processed by a given computing machine depends on the context in which the machine is deployed.

Levels of Description

In explicating the Representational Theory of Mind, Fodor appeals explicitly to the computer model of the mind. Mental operations are operations performed over symbols, sentences in the Language of Thought. The science of psychology aims to work out the programs controlling our behavior. These can be represented, just as computer programs can be represented, by means of flowcharts that specify, albeit 'abstractly', the causal structure of systems they characterize. Psychology, on this model, is a 'higher-level science', one that abstracts from lower-level 'implementational' details.

One advantage of such a view is that it enables us to comprehend how minds might fit into the material world, and how minds are related to brains. Minds are related to brains in something like the way computer programs are related to the hardware in which they are implemented. Minds are not identifiable with or reducible to brains for just the reasons that programs or computational operations are not identifiable with or reducible to components of the hardware on which they run. Brains realize minds much as computing machines realize particular programs. Just as, in describing the operation of a computing machine at the program level, we are describing its causal structure in abstraction from without regard to its hardware, so in describing mental operations we are describing the causal structure of intelligent agents in abstraction from - without regard to their biological hardware.

All this serves to demystify the mind. We can understand how attempts to identify minds with material entities are bound to fail, without thereby embracing the dualist notion that minds are immaterial substances. Perhaps, however, this demystification goes too far. You might worry that a computational conception of mental processes threatens to turn us into rigidly programmed robots, beings altogether lacking in spontaneity or free will.

The functionalist idea, however, is not that we blindly follow formal routines we are powerless to alter. Intelligent behavior is principled behavior. And we can think of the principles we adopt (or cultivate, or learn, or inherit along with our biological constitution) as core ingredients in our mental program. This is perfectly consistent with most conceptions of free will.

Levels of Description and the Special Sciences

Return, for a moment, to the notion that the operations of an ordinary computing machine can be described on different *levels*. An electrical engineer or a physicist might describe the operation of a given machine at the hardware level. In so doing, the engineer or physicist employs a characteristic array of concepts. A computer programmer describing the operations of the very same machine makes use of a very different conceptual repertoire.

Fodor speaks in such cases of distinctive 'taxonomies', distinctive ways of classifying and organizing descriptions and explanations of phenomena. Lower-level and higher-level sciences 'taxonomize' phenomena very differently. Taxonomic categories that specify entities of interest at higher levels need not, and typically will not, be definable in terms of categories found at lower levels. In the computer case, we cannot define computational operations in terms of material transactions in the hardware that realize those operations. One obvious problem with attempts to do so stems from the fact that computational operations are multiply realizable: the very same operation could be realized in utterly different sorts of material system. You might think that we could define higher-level operations by means of a *dis-junction* of lower-level goings-on. Thus, the summing operation might be characterizable as *either* a particular kind of brass gear and cog operation (in a Babbage machine), *or* a particular kind of operation in a device made with vacuum tubes, *or* a particular kind of transistor-based operation, *or* ...

Functionalists like to point out that such a strategy faces an obvious and crippling difficulty. The dots at the end of the tentative disjunctive specification above indicate that we shall need to add descriptions of

> *further lower-level operations if we are to provide an exhaustive lower-level accounting of our higher-level category. It would seem, however, that there are endless lower-level ways of realizing any complex higher-level operation. The prospects of reducing higher-level categories to lower-level categories, even long disjunctions of lower-level categories, are not encouraging.*

Even if we allowed a systematic mapping of higher-level categories onto long perhaps infinitely long disjunctions of lower-level categories, however, the reductive strategy flies in the face of scientific and everyday practice. Suppose we distinguish physics (or 'basic physics'), the fundamental lower-level science, from assorted higher-level sciences. Physics provides us with an inventory of basic particles and laws governing the behavior of those particles. Higher-level sciences deploy higher-level taxonomies. While physicists speak of electrons, quarks, and fundamental forces, chemists focus on atoms and molecules, and biologists take up complex molecular structures: living organisms. At still higher levels, psychologists, sociologists, and economists ply their trades.

Each of these sciences is distinguished by the way it carves up reality. Categories definitive of a given higher-level taxonomy divide reality in ways that from the perspective of lower-level sciences would seem arbitrary. Consider a simple analogy. When you play chess, you move chess pieces in particular ways. Considered from the perspective of chemistry or physics, the range of appropriate moves (those permitted by the rules of chess) would appear entirely unprincipled. Patterns and regularities exhibited in games of chess appear only at a higher level. Biological categories, seen from the perspective of physics, must appear similarly arbitrary. Biology divides up the world in ways that, so long as we remain at the level of quarks and electrons, appear contrived.

The idea in play is that the sciences operate within a hierarchy of levels: physics is at the lowest level; chemistry and biology occupy intermediate levels; and psychology and the social sciences function at the highest levels. Each science imposes a system of categories, a taxonomy, on the world.

The categories definitive of a given science mark off boundaries that are largely invisible within sciences at lower levels. This is why there is, in general, no prospect of reducing a higher-level science to a science at some lower level. Doing so would require a systematic way of drawing higher-level distinctions using lower-level categories. And this is just what would seem to be hopeless.

You might suspect that a conception of this sort goes too far. If physics is the science of everything, then why do we need the others? If the special sciences are not reducible to physics, then why should we accord them any legitimacy at all?

The answer given by functionalists like Fodor is that it is precisely because higher-level sciences make use of categories *not* reducible to those of lower-level sciences that the higher-level sciences are vindicated. As we explore the world, we discover important regularities that are, from the perspective of physics, quite hidden. These regularities hold among objects in virtue of properties possessed by those objects that correspond in no principled way to properties of interest to the physicist. To ignore such objects and properties, however, would require that we ignore endless interesting and important regularities.

To see the point, think again of the operation of a computing machine. Suppose we describe the operation of a computing machine at the most basic hardware level, in terms of electron fluctuations inside transistors. If we limited ourselves to such descriptions, let alone descriptions framed in terms of fundamental physical categories, we should miss important generalizations that appear only when we consider the machine at the level of its program. We can, for instance, understand common features in the behavior of two machines with very different material compositions running the same program: both machines are doing sums, for instance, or sending files to a printer. At the ordinary hardware level, or at the level of physics, such commonalities disappear in the way the pattern formed by arrangements of flowers in a floral clock vanish when we look just at individual plants.

From Taxonomy to Ontology

Someone skeptical about this line of reasoning might object that it shows at most that we require higher-level sciences, and the categories they deploy, only as a matter of convenience. Higher-level sciences provide us with what from the perspective of physics or chemistry are hopelessly crude accounts of goings-on in the world around us. As it happens, these crude accounts are perfectly adequate for certain of our purposes. Moreover, finer-grained accounts would require an investment of time and energy that we could ill afford. By keeping to the program level, you can understand, explain, and manipulate the behavior of your desktop computer in a way that is perfectly adequate for most everyday purposes. Those purposes aside, however, the *real* story is to be had only by descending to the hardware level and, ultimately, to the level of micro-physics.

You might reflect here on the use of familiar rules of thumb in predicting the weather:

> *Red sky at night, sailor's delight; red sky in morning, sailor take warning.*
>
> *Ring around the sun or moon, snow or rain is coming soon.*

Rules of thumb are useful, no doubt, perhaps even practically indispensable. Even so, they merely approximate much more complex and fine-grained pronouncements whose home is in the lower-level sciences meteorology and climatology, for instance, and ultimately, of course, in physics. We might see psychology in the same light. Psychology provides us with a stock of rough-and-ready generalizations that serve our purposes when we interact with one another. But these at best approximate truths at lower levels. As we descend from psychology, through neuropsychology, to neurobiology, to chemistry, we refine these approximations until we reach bedrock: physics.

Fodor is adamant that this way of depicting the relation of higher-level to lower-level sciences is misconceived. Categories embedded in a higher-level science psychology, for instance designate perfectly genuine properties of objects. These properties are certainly not reducible to properties found in sciences at lower levels. 'Being in pain' and 'believing that it is raining' designate such higher-level properties. If these properties are not found among the properties inventoried by lower-level sciences, we should not conclude that they are in some way less-than-perfectly-real. On the contrary, this is just what we should expect if psychology is an authentic higher-level science.

What makes a property genuine? On the view we are considering, a genuine property is one that makes a *causal difference* to objects possessing it. If *being red* is a genuine property, then objects possessing this property, red objects, will behave differently than objects lacking it. Functionalists in Fodor's camp most often put this in terms of causal laws. A genuine property is a property that figures in some causal law. The special sciences are in the business of formulating causal laws governing the behavior of objects falling under those laws. Genuine properties, then, are revealed by causal laws uncovered as we investigate our world. If we discover causal laws in neurobiology, or psychology, or economics, laws that govern the behavior of higher-level objects, and if these laws range over higher-level properties, then these higher-level properties must be genuine. Of course, we could be wrong about what the laws are, hence mistaken as to the genuine properties, but that goes without saying.

Two features of this view are worth emphasizing.

First, its proponents are committed to a *layered* conception of reality. The world contains *levels* of objects and properties governed by levels of causal laws. Although objects at higher levels are typically made up of objects at lower levels, it is nevertheless true that higher-level objects and their properties have a life of their own. They are not reducible to, not 'nothing but', arrangements of objects and properties at lower levels.

(A technical aside. The 'supervenience' relation is standardly invoked to explain the relation of higher-level objects and properties to those at lower levels. The idea, roughly, is that while higher-level objects and properties 'depend on and are determined by' lower-level objects and properties, higher-level objects and properties are nevertheless distinct from lower-level objects and properties. Hearts are made up of cells, and ultimately of quarks and electrons. But hearts are not *just* assemblages of electrons and quarks, and properties of hearts are not properties of electrons and quarks or assemblages of electrons and quarks.)

Second, higher-level laws are taken to be laws that hold only *ceteris paribus*, only 'other things being equal'. In this respect they differ from the laws governing the fundamental entities studied in physics. Laws governing the fundamental entities are exceptionless. In contrast, laws governing entities at higher levels are only approximate; they apply *ceteris paribus*. Do not confuse *ceteris paribus* laws with probabilistic laws of the sort mentioned in Chapter 2. The fundamental laws might turn out to be probabilistic. Their application is nonetheless universal and exceptionless. The laws we might hope to discover in psychology, or economics, or even neurobiology, in contrast, are irreducibly 'hedged'.

I mention this second point because you might be wondering about laws of psychology, laws governing the operation of the mind. Consider a law that you might think governs beliefs and desires:

(*L ø*): If an agent, *S*, wants *x* and believes that *y* is needed to obtain *x*, then *S* wants *y*.

If you want to take the subway and believe that in order to take the subway, you must buy a token, then you will want to buy a token. Although (*L ø*) governs many instances of desire formation, it is not difficult to imagine exceptions. If you believe, for instance, that you have no money, then your belief that you must buy a token to ride the subway might lead you to cease to desire to ride the subway or to a desire to panhandle.

More significantly, you could fail to form the desire to buy a token because you are, at the instant it occurs to you that you need to buy a token, knocked unconscious by a slab of falling plaster. Note that in this case we encounter a kind of intervention that involves entities and processes that fall outside the purview of psychology. Things fail to go right at the psychological level owing to occurrences at the neurobiological level. But psychological laws are necessarily silent about such occurrences: this is what makes psychological laws *psychological* laws.

The example can be extended to the laws of every special science. Each special science carves up the world in a particular way and endeavors to discover laws governing the entities falling under its special categories. These entities are made up of lower-level entities. Goings-on affecting these lower-level entities can have higher-level consequences. Changes in the molecules of your brain, for instance, can have dramatic repercussions for your brain and for your state of mind as well. But the laws of each special science concern only entities at the level appropriate to that science. Psychological laws contain no mention of molecules, although molecular events can affect psychological processes. So long as we regard the laws of a special science such as psychology to be autonomous, so long as we take them to be irreducible to laws governing lower-level entities, we can be assured that the laws must fail to be exceptionless.

Layers of Reality

Where does all this leave us? I have taken us on a rather lengthy detour through issues in the philosophy of science in order to motivate the metaphysical conception of mind that has been most influential in functionalist circles. I do not mean to suggest that all functionalists subscribe to this picture. Nevertheless, the picture has been widely influential, both in philosophy and in allied disciplines in the cognitive sciences, so it is worth spelling out. Most importantly, it provides a rationale for the view that the world is layered, that minds are higher-level entities, and that mental properties are higher-level properties. This is a central tenet of virtually all versions of functionalism.

We are left with the following picture of the mind. Mental expressions 'being in pain', 'believing that bears are furry' designate functional properties of entities to which they are ascribed. Functional properties are ultimately realized in material systems by non-functional properties of those systems. When you possess a particular mental property, the property of *being in pain*, for instance, that property is realized in you by some material property of your brain. In another kind of creature an octopus, say, or in an Alpha Centaurian that same mental property, being in pain, might be realized by a very different material property. You, an octopus, and a Alpha Centaurian all possess the property of being in pain. In you this property is realized by a particular kind of neurological process; in an octopus it is realized by a very different sort of neurological episode; in an Alpha Centaurian it is realized by a non-neurological, silicon-based process.

Pain, like any other functional property, is multiply realizable. It is anyone's guess as to what the limits are on realizers for pain. Might a computing machine be programmed to feel pain? If a computing machine could be given the right sort of functional organization, then, according to the functionalist, it could indeed feel pain: the property of being in pain would be realized by transfers of electrons across transistors or, in the case of a Babbage machine, by some sequence of rotations of brass cogs and cylinders. Meanwhile, it is time to consider an important line of criticism of functionalism that focuses on an aspect of the mind that functionalists are often accused of ignoring: the *qualitative* aspect.

12

Status of Philosophies of Mind

Introduction

Descartes, for instance, was struck by apparent differences between properties of material objects and mental properties. That focus led him to regard the mental properties and the material properties as properties of utterly different kinds of substance. Behaviorists, in contrast, were bent on making minds scientifically respectable subjects of empirical inquiry. Given their conception of scientific respectability, this meant showing that truths about minds and their contents could be paraphrased in terms of observable bodily motions and propensities to such motions.

Although it is easy to see how each of the conceptions of mind we have examined goes wrong, you would miss something important if you did not recognize that each can be seen as at least partly successful: each provides answers to questions considered especially pressing, each offers plausible solutions to high-profile problems. Notoriously, however, each leaves unanswered and unsolved a host of distinct problems as well. This is unsurprising. Theories of mind are introduced as means of coping with particular issues that are, at the time of their introduction, regarded as central.

To the extent that a theory is successful, the problems it solves recede into the background, and those it leaves unresolved become salient.

In philosophy there is a tendency to take doctrines with which we disagree and dismiss them entirely. But a view can be wrong, even mostly wrong, without being altogether wrong. When we consider the historical development of theories in the philosophy of mind, we can see that the same difficulties cycle into focus again and again. One generation addresses the qualitative aspect of mentality, the next focuses on its scientific standing, its successor takes up the problem of mental content. The cycle then starts over, each generation rediscovering what had been invisible to its predecessor.

In this context it would be foolish to claim originality for any view. Virtually every point I make in this chapter and the one to follow has been made before by other, more inventive philosophers. Chief among these are Locke and Locke's twenty-first-century philosophical counterpart C. B. Martin. The position I advance here is a version of a position Martin has developed over a period of many years, beginning in the 1950s in Adelaide. Although Locke provides its chief inspiration, I borrow freely from Russell, and, although Locke and Martin would shudder at the thought, Descartes and Wittgenstein.

Throughout this volume I have emphasized the importance of metaphysics and, in particular, ontology our best assessment of what there is for the philosophy of mind. Certain important conclusions concerning minds and their place in nature follow from what I take to be an independently plausible ontology. I outline these in the sections that follow, although I do not try to defend them in depth (see Heil 2003a). Many of these conclusions fall outside current conceptions of mind. That, I contend, is all to the good.

Metaphysical Preliminaries

Nowadays the philosophy of mind includes a significant empirical component. Many philosophers of mind see themselves as 'cognitive scientists' and make a point of distancing their pursuits from those of a philosophical tradition that distinguishes sharply between science and philosophy. The hope is that we can replace unconstrained metaphysical speculation with hard-nosed, empirically informed theorizing. This need not be taken to imply that we are to set about providing empirical answers to long-standing philosophical questions. Rather, we should replace the questions and embark on an empirically informed investigation of the territory.

It is one thing, however, to take seriously the fruits of empirical labors, and quite another thing to imagine that the deep problems that beset the philosophy of mind will evaporate if only we formulate our concerns in a way that renders them susceptible to empirical resolution. As things now stand, even if we possessed a fully adequate empirical theory of consciousness, we should be in no position to recognize it as such. Our problem is not so much the lack of detailed information, but the lack of an adequate conceptual framework to make sense of whatever information we might obtain. We have learned much and we have much to learn about the brain. But, to take one currently prominent example, it is hard to see how any conceivable neurobiological discovery could account for the qualities of conscious experience.

My suggestion is that before we can hope to advance an empirical theory of the mind, we must have a clear conception of the underlying ontology. This will give us not an axiomatic system within which to deduce truths about the mind, but a suitable structure within which to locate empirical truths. The test of an ontology is, I believe, its power: its capacity to provide a sensible overall account of how things stand. This account should comport, at least broadly, with commonsense observation constrained by the sciences. It goes beyond the sciences, however, in providing a unifying framework within which claims issuing from the several sciences can be plotted: the sciences do not speak with a single voice.

Objects

A good place to start is at the beginning. At a first approximation, the world comprises objects bearing spatial and temporal relations to one another. Some objects are complex, having objects as parts. Some objects are simple in this sense: they are not made up of other objects. I cannot offer a proof that some objects are simple. The denial that this is so entails that every object has objects as parts. I admit this as an abstract possibility, but I cannot see how it could work. (It evokes what E. J. Lowe has described as a 'vertiginous feeling'.) Complex objects depend for their existence on their parts, the objects that make them up. If every object is made up of other objects, however, there would seem to be nothing to ground the existence of any object.

I have described the world as comprising objects. I take it to be an empirical question a question for science what the objects are and what they are like. Objects might be corpuscular, particle-like, in the mold of the atoms envisaged by the ancient Greeks. Objects might, in contrast, be fields, points in or regions of space-time, or something stranger still.

If objects are fields or regions of space-time, then properties are properties *of* not *in* fields or regions of space-time. Motion of objects would then be only apparent motion: successive regions taking on and losing properties in a particular way. If you want a model, think of the motion of a scene displayed on a television screen or a train of lights moving round an old-fashioned movie marquee. Perhaps this is how it is quite generally. A billiard ball rolling across the table is really a succession of contiguous disturbances in space-time.

I have said that if objects were non-corpuscular thickenings or disturbances in space-time, motion would be 'only apparent'. Another way to think about it, however, perhaps a better way, is that this would be the deep story about motion: what motion *really is*.

Corpuscular or not, objects are bearers of properties. When we consider an object we can consider it either as a bearer of properties, itself incapable of being borne as a property, or we can consider its properties. We can consider this red billiard ball as something red, as something spherical, as something having a particular mass. In so doing, we are reckoning the ball a 'substance', a bearer of properties, itself unborne. But we can also consider the ball's properties: its redness, its sphericity, its mass. When we do this, we turn our minds to ways the ball is. Objects, then, even simple, non-composite objects, have structure. An object's properties are not *parts* of the object, however. The redness and sphericity of the billiard ball are not parts of the ball in the way its constituent molecules are parts of it. The ball is not made up of its properties.

So: an object is a bearer of properties. Although we can distinguish objects as property bearers from properties they bear, these are separable only in thought, not in reality. Objects cannot exist apart from properties, nor properties apart from objects. An object can gain or lose properties, but this is not a matter of its properties moving elsewhere. A property is nothing more than an object's being a particular way. An object can cease to be one way and come to be some other way, but these *ways* cannot be transferred to other objects or 'float free'. Nor could an object exist, lacking properties, as a 'bare particular', being no way at all.

Universals

In describing properties of objects as I have, I mean to be distancing myself from the idea that properties are 'universals'. Some proponents of universals hold that universals are 'transcendent' entities residing outside of space and time. Particular objects 'participate in' or 'instantiate' universals. Particular spherical objects might be thought to instantiate the universal *sphericity*. This conception of universals is associated with Plato. Another conception, perhaps stemming from Aristotle, but most recently defended by D. M. Armstrong, locates universals in their instances. The universal sphericity is taken to be wholly present in each of its spatially and temporally distinct instances (and nowhere else). A universal is, in a certain sense, made up of its instances, although these instances are not its parts: the universal, remember, is *wholly present* in each of its instances.

Philosophers who regard properties as universals argue that by so doing, we can solve the 'one-over-many' problem. Consider a red billiard ball and a railroad warning flag. The billiard ball and the flag are *the same* in one respect and *different* in other respects. We may put this by saying that the ball and the flag *share a property*; that they possess *the same property*; or, if properties are ways, they are the *same way* colorwise. A proponent of universals takes seriously the italicized phrases in the preceding sentence. If the billiard ball and the flag share a property, then there is some one thing, a property, they both possess. This property, redness, is common to all red objects. Similarities among objects are thus grounded in their shared properties. These are the 'one' in the 'one-over-many'. Differences are determined by properties being possessed or 'instantiated' by distinct particulars. These are the 'many'. 'Identical twins' are *the same* in sharing properties, *different* in being distinct substances.

You may find talk of universals mysterious. The mystery might be lessened slightly if you bear in mind that universals are meant to differ in kind from particulars, concrete objects such as warning flags and billiard balls. What holds for a particular need not hold for a universal. This helps only a little, however. It remains difficult to see what could be involved in an object's instantiating a universal (on the Platonic view) or what it could mean to say (as Armstrong says) that a universal is wholly present in each of its instances. I hope to bypass such puzzles by recommending an account of properties that takes properties seriously but without a commitment to universals.

Properties as Particularized Ways

Before we look more closely at the nature of properties, it might be worth asking why exactly we should imagine that the world contains such entities. Many philosophers have denied that properties exist. Talk of properties, they contend, should be replaced by talk of objects or classes of objects. A red object is not an object that possesses the property of being red, but merely an object that resembles other objects or belongs to a particular class: the class of red objects. Objects belong to this class, perhaps, because they are similar, but this similarity is an irreducible feature of the objects. Objects are what they are, *holus-bolus*.

This is not the place to discuss such views in detail. Instead I shall merely call attention to a flat-footed worry about attempts to dispense with properties. Consider two red objects. Is the redness of the objects solely a matter of the objects' resembling one another or the objects' being members of a class of objects: the class of red objects? This seems to have the order of explanation the wrong way round. The objects are not red *because they resemble one another*, they resemble one another *because they are red*; the objects are not red *because they belong to a class*, the class of red objects; they belong to the class *because they are red*. Think of the red flag and the red billiard ball. These differ in shape, size, and mass, but are similar *in color*. This natural perspective on similarity pushes us back to *ways objects are*: the flag and the billiard ball resemble one another and fall into the class of red objects because they are similar *in some respect*. And it is hard to understand talk of 'respects' here without taking it to refer to properties of objects, ways objects are.

I do not imagine that a staunch opponent of properties will be much moved by these observations. We are in a domain of philosophy where it is unrealistic to expect knock-down arguments. The most we can hope for is an account of matters that squares with our overall assessment of how things stand. In this context, we do well to remind ourselves of a simple point. Consider the sentences below:

(a) The ball is spherical.

(b) The ball is red.

Let us suppose that these sentences hold true of a particular billiard ball. Now it would seem on the face of it that the sentences do not hold true of the object *holus-bolus*.

Rather, there is *something about* the ball in virtue of which it is true to say of it that it is spherical; and *something else about the ball* in virtue of which it is true to say of it that it is red. In speaking of 'something about the ball', we are, or surely seem to be, speaking about a way the ball is. And this is just to speak about what I have been calling a property.

I have distinguished this notion of a property a particularized way an object is from notions of properties as universals. Some philosophers have used the term 'trope' as a label for what I am calling particularized ways. I resist this designation because it has become common for proponents of tropes to regard objects as 'bundles' of tropes. This turns properties into something too much resembling parts of objects for my taste. On the view I am advancing, objects are not *made up of* properties in anything like the way a billiard ball is made up of atoms or molecules. To repeat an earlier suggestion: when we consider an object, we can consider it as an unborne bearer of properties a substance, in traditional parlance or we can consider properties it bears. On this view, then, an object is not a collection or bundle of properties; an object is a possessor of properties.

A simple object an object that does not have objects as parts is nothing more than an object possessing certain properties. Complex objects billiard balls, molecules, and (what we now call) atoms are objects in a derivative sense: objects by courtesy. In just the same way, properties of complex objects, to the extent that these are distinguishable from properties of their simple parts, are properties in a derivative sense. A complex object is made up of simple objects possessing particular properties and standing in particular relations to one another. The properties we find in complex objects are themselves 'made up of' properties possessed by the simple constituents in these arrangements. On this view, there is nothing more to a complex property than this. Complex properties do not 'emerge'; they are nothing in addition to the properties of the simple constituents duly arranged.

I might note in passing that the conception of properties I favor can accommodate at least one aspect of the motivation for positing universals. Proponents of universals appeal to 'one-over-many' considerations: distinct objects can be *the same* in various respects. I say properties are particularized ways objects are. Now consider classes of exactly resembling properties. These classes will perfectly coincide with the universals as conceived of by Armstrong.

As my colleague David Robb has pointed out, the temptation to regard properties as universals could be thought to stem from a desire to have a single entity do double duty. We think of properties as *ways objects are*, and we connect these ways with *types* of object. A universal is simultaneously a type of object and a way particular objects are. But suppose we let the properties be the ways, and the types be collections or classes of exactly similar ways. Then two objects fall under a single type (both are red) not because they share a constituent a universal redness but because they possess exactly similar properties that, owing to their similarity, fall into the same class. These classes could be thought of as ersatz universals.

On this view, objects that might be thought to share a universal share, instead, membership in a class of objects possessing exactly resembling properties. The relation of resemblance these properties bear to one another is a primitive, 'internal' relation. Objects resemble one another in virtue of their properties; properties the basis of resemblance resemble one another (when they do) *tout court*. Suppose properties á and â are exactly resembling. Then this resemblance is intrinsic, 'built into' the properties. One consequence of this is that, if property ÷ exactly resembles á, then ÷ exactly resembles â as well.

Let me say a word about a matter that might worry some readers. I have described properties as ways objects are. This gives the impression that the properties are exhausted by the ways actual, existing objects are. There are, however, ways objects could be but no object is – or, for that matter, no object ever will be. Two kinds of particle could be such that, *were* they to collide, they would yield a third kind of particle possessing unique properties. (I discuss a case of this kind below.) This could be so, even if the requisite collisions never took place. So: there are ways objects could be but no object is (or ever will be). Thus put, ways might appear mysterious, ghostly. We can avoid the mystery by noting that non-actual possible ways are prefigured in the ways actual objects are. Properties of existing objects are dispositional for (they are 'directed to' and 'selective for') manifestations themselves properties, ways objects could be that need never occur. The intrinsic 'readinesses' of actual properties ground claims concerning non-actual, possible ways.

The Dual Nature of Properties

Properties are ways objects are. I regard this view as close to the commonsense conception. We distinguish the red of a billiard ball and the red of a railroad warning flag, even though these two objects may be precisely the same shade of red. There are two 'instances' of red, one belonging to the ball, the other to the flag. Now it is time to look more closely at the nature of properties.

Every property, I contend, endows its possessor with both a particular disposition or 'causal power' *and* a particular quality. Consider the property of being spherical. In virtue of its possession of this property, a billiard ball has a particular quality, the quality we designate by the term 'sphericity'. But equally, in virtue of possessing this property the ball possesses certain dispositions or causal powers. (I shall use these terms interchangeably although, because I take causality to be explicable by reference to dispositionality, I prefer 'disposition' to causal power.) The ball is disposed to roll, for instance, when placed on an inclined surface.

In an effort to keep matters simple and in focus, I am oversimplifying here. The qualities and dispositionalities of any particular object result at least from the properties it possesses and relations these bear to one another. A ball's disposition to roll, for instance, depends both on its being spherical and on its being solid. Every property contributes in a distinctive way to the qualities and dispositionalities of objects possessing it. I am streamlining the discussion in another respect as well. Throughout the chapter I shall cite familiar features of objects as examples of properties redness and sphericity, for instance. For various reasons, I doubt that either redness or sphericity is a genuine property. These serve well enough as illustrations, however, and they have the advantage of keeping the discussion from becoming hopelessly abstract.

The idea that properties have a dual nature is to be distinguished from the notion that there are two kinds of property: dispositional properties and 'categorical' (non-dispositional, purely qualitative) properties. On the latter view, it makes no sense to suppose that a property could be both dispositional and qualitative. Every property is purely one or the other. A dispositional property, for instance the property of solubility possessed by a salt crystal, or the property of being fragile possessed by a delicate vase, is to be distinguished from categorical (that is, non-dispositional, purely qualitative) properties such as being red or being warm. In virtue of their possession of dispositional properties, objects behave in particular ways, or would behave in particular ways under the right conditions. In virtue of their possession of categorical properties, objects exhibit particular qualities.

Under the assumption that dispositions and qualities are associated with distinct kinds of property, philosophers have been moved to advance a variety of theories. For some, the two kinds of property are irreducibly distinct. Others, however, noting that a property that endowed its possessor with no causal powers or dispositions whatsoever could make no difference at all in the world, have doubted the existence of non-dispositional, categorical properties. Such properties would be, for instance, undetectable assuming that our detecting a property requires our being causally affected by it in some way. Moreover, as these philosophers point out, the usual examples of allegedly categorical properties are unconvincing. Take being red or being warm. Surely, an object's being red is what disposes it to reflect light in a particular way, and an object's being warm disposes it to affect the surrounding air differentially. When we consider properties ascribed to objects by the sciences, these seem invariably dispositional: having mass, for instance, or having negative charge, is characterized exclusively by reference to ways in which possession of these properties affects or would affect the behavior of their possessors. Considerations of this sort have convinced some philosophers that every genuine property is a dispositional property.

Another contingent of philosophers, however, appeals to the strangeness of the idea that properties could be purely dispositional. A world consisting exclusively of objects possessing dispositional properties would seem to be a world in which objects would be forever poised to act, but never act. An object's acting would be a matter of its dispositions' being manifested. But if a manifestation were itself nothing more than a pure disposition, a disposition to be manifested in a particular way under the right circumstances, then the situation would resemble one in which a bank check is backed by a check, which itself is backed by a check, and so on indefinitely. Unless a check is ultimately backed by something other than a check, it is worthless; and similarly, unless a disposition issues in something other than a pure disposition, nothing occurs.

This point might be expressed slightly differently. A disposition is itself a manifestation. If every manifestation were nothing more than a disposition for some further manifestation, the result would be an unwelcome regress. The world evidently contains actualities as well as potentialities pure dispositionalities. Imagine a row of dominoes lined up so that, were the first to fall, it would topple the second domino, which would topple the third domino, which would topple ... Now imagine that *all there is* to the dominoes is their power to topple and be toppled. It is hard to see how any toppling occurs; there are no *things* to topple or be toppled.

For devotees of possible worlds, Simon Blackburn, puts the point this way:

> *To conceive of* all *the truths about a world as dispositional is to suppose that a world is entirely described by what is true at* neighboring *worlds. And since our argument was a priori, these truths in turn vanish into truths about yet other neighboring worlds, and the result is that there is no truth anywhere.*

Aware of these difficulties, some theorists have suggested that dispositional properties must be 'grounded in' non-dispositional properties. A dispositional property, on this view, might be a 'higher-level' property, a property had by an object in virtue of its possession of some 'lower-level' non-dispositional property. Consider the dispositional property of being fragile. This is a property an object this delicate vase, for instance might have in virtue of having a particular molecular structure. Having this structure is held to be a lower-level non-dispositional property that grounds the higher-level dispositional property of being fragile; the vase is fragile, the vase possesses the dispositional property of being fragile, in virtue of possessing some non-dispositional structural property.

What are we to make of this suggestion? You might wonder what more there is to an object's possessing a given higher-level property beyond the object's possessing its lower-level grounding property. Sticking with the example above, suppose that being fragile is a higher-level property had by this vase in virtue of its having a particular lower-level property a certain structure, perhaps. In what sense exactly does the vase have two distinct properties here: a non-dispositional structural property and a dispositional property? For that matter, in what sense is the vase's *structure* non-dispositional? Surely it is its molecular structure that itself disposes the vase to reflect light in a particular way, to remain rigid at moderate temperatures, to make a particular ringing noise when tapped by a spoon, and, yes, to shatter when struck by a hard object. If having a certain structure is a property, then it would seem to be as dispositional as any other property one could imagine.

Proponents of the idea that dispositions are higher-level properties point to the fact that objects with very different molecular structures could turn out to be fragile. This, however, ought not to incline us to doubt that the property of being fragile possessed by this vase this vase's fragility is a perfectly ordinary ('lower-level') property of the vase, perhaps the very property we have been discussing: having a particular structure. That would fit nicely with the view I am advocating. Properties have a dual nature: every property is at once qualitative *and* to the dispositional, every property contributes in a distinctive way to the qualities and dispositionalities of objects possessing it. We can separate these natures only in thought just as we can mentally separate a triangle's triangularity from its trilaterality by considering the one without considering the other.

Locke dubbed this activity of mental separation 'partial consideration'. It is what enables us to consider an object's color without considering its shape, or its shape without considering its color, even if every object with a shape must be an object with a color.

What relation does the dispositionality of a property bear to its qualitative nature? These are not merely necessarily connected, like triangularity and trilaterality. They are, rather, the selfsame property, differently considered. A relationship of this sort resembles that found in ambiguous figures.

The same lines make up both figures. We can distinguish the figures in our minds by shifting our attention. But one figure cannot be present without the other. In the same way, a property's intrinsic dispositionality and qualitative nature are separable only in thought.

The ambiguous figure is designed to illustrate the thesis that a property's dispositionality and qualitativity are not 'aspects' or 'sides' of the property; they are the property itself, differently considered. A property's dispositionality *is* its qualitativity and these *are* the property itself. Properties are powerful qualities.

In any case, the idea that objects' dispositional features are grounded in their structure appears to be a non-starter. Structures themselves are evidently dispositional as well as qualitative. More significantly, if we can so much as conceive of simple objects, objects that lack parts hence lack structure in the relevant sense we must conceive of those objects as possessing dispositionalities. They are not, at any given moment, doing all they are capable of doing. If there are elementary particles, these particles are certainly capable of endless interactions beyond those in which they are actually engaged at any given time. Everything points to dispositionality's being a fundamental feature of our world.

The debate over whether properties are dispositional or categorical has had the following form. One side points out that the notion of a non-dispositional property is the notion of a property that would make no difference to its possessor. It is concluded that no genuine property is categorical in my terminology, no property is qualitative – or that the qualitative side of things is derived somehow from their dispositionalities. The opposing side focuses on the elusiveness of pure dispositionality and concludes that dispositionality must have a non-dispositional, purely qualitative, ground.

The problem is merely that inappropriate conclusions are being drawn. Suppose every property is dispositional. It does not follow that no property is qualitative. Similarly, if every property is qualitative, it does not follow that no property (or no genuine first-order property) is dispositional. Neither of these conclusions follows, because the arguments behind them are consistent with the position advanced here: every property has a dual nature, every property is *both* dispositional *and* qualitative.

Before we move on, I might point out the naturalness of this conception of properties. Consider a property such as the property of being square. This property is a good example of what have standardly been regarded as categorical properties. Let us concede that the property of being square endows its possessors with a certain quality the quality we associate with squareness. But it is equally true that being square endows objects with certain powers or dispositions. A square peg would pass through a square hole, but not a round hole (where the diameter of the hole matches the length of a side); a square peg would reflect light differently than a round peg; a square peg would feel different to the touch than a round peg. It is hard not to conclude that being square squareness is simultaneously dispositional and qualitative. In this it resembles every other property; or so I contend.

Manifestations of Dispositions

If we are to take dispositionality seriously, then we must distinguish dispositions from their manifestations. A disposition can be perfectly real, wholly present here and now, yet remain unmanifested. A vase can be fragile without ever shattering, a substance can be soluble without ever dissolving.

Dispositions typically require for their manifestation suitable *reciprocal disposition partners*. If salt is soluble in water, then the dissolving of this crystal of salt is the *mutual manifestation* of the salt's solubility and the surrounding water's being a solvent for salt. A property's dispositionality is intrinsic to it. *Manifestations* of this dispositionality typically depend on the presence of reciprocal dispositions. The reciprocity of dispositions means that a single disposition can manifest itself differently with different reciprocal partners. Litmus paper turns pink when immersed in acid, but blue when immersed in a base. The micro-structure of a metal makes it opaque and electrically conductive different kinds of manifestation with different kinds of partner: ambient light radiation in one case and electrical charge in the other.

One further element is required to complete the picture. I have said that things is derived somehow from their dispositionalities. The opposing side focuses on the elusiveness of pure dispositionality and concludes that dispositionality must have a non-dispositional, purely qualitative, ground.

I am inclined to think that both sides' arguments are right in one respect and wrong in another. The problem is merely that inappropriate conclusions are being drawn. Suppose every property is dispositional. It does not follow that no property is qualitative. Similarly, if every property is qualitative, it does not follow that no property (or no genuine first-order property) is dispositional. Neither of these conclusions follows, because the arguments behind them are consistent with the position advanced here: every property has a dual nature, every property is *both* dispositional *and* qualitative.

Before we move on, I might point out the naturalness of this conception of properties. Consider a property such as the property of being square. This property is a good example of what have standardly been regarded as categorical properties. Let us concede that the property of being square endows its possessors with a certain quality the quality we associate with squareness. But it is equally true that being square endows objects with certain powers or dispositions. A square peg would pass through a square hole, but not a round hole (where the diameter of the hole matches the length of a side); a square peg would reflect light differently than a round peg; a square peg would feel different to the touch than a round peg. It is hard not to conclude that being square squareness is simultaneously dispositional and qualitative. In this it resembles every other property; or so I contend.

Causality and Dispositionality

Causal truths are ultimately grounded in the mutual manifestations of reciprocal disposition partners. Consider a simple causal sequence, a key's opening a lock. The effect, the lock's being open, is a mutual manifestation of dispositions possessed by the lock and the key. The cause, the key's turning, is itself the mutual manifestation of reciprocal disposition partners that include the key and the hand holding the key.

The dispositional model encourages us to replace the image of linear causal sequences or chains with a conception of the world as an inclusive dispositional network, what Martin calls a 'power net'. An advantage of this picture is that it enables us to dispense with misleading talk of causes versus 'background' conditions. Consider a match igniting when it is struck. It is customary to think of the cause as the striking and the effect as the igniting. But the match would not ignite in the absence of oxygen. Is the presence of oxygen, then, a part of the cause? The presence of oxygen is not obviously part of the event the striking that we have identified as the cause. Perhaps the presence of oxygen is a 'background' condition required for the cause to have the effect it has.

This way of looking at the matter requires that we distinguish causes from background conditions in a way that appears metaphysically arbitrary. If, in contrast, we see the match's igniting as the mutual manifestation of reciprocal disposition partners that include the surface on which the match is struck, the surrounding oxygen, and the chemical makeup of the match tip, we can assign equal credit to each of these contributing factors.

Another potential source of embarrassment for the prevailing view of event causation concerns the relative timing of causes and effects. A cause must precede its effects. But, as Hume noted, if a cause precedes its effect, there would seem to be a temporal gap or boundary between the occurrence of the cause and the onset of the effect. The causing event (or event component) would be over before its effect begins. But how can a completed event influence an event occurring now? If, in contrast, the causing event and its effect are temporally simultaneous or overlapping, it would seem that the portion of the causing event that occurs after the onset of the effect could not be implicated in the occurrence of the effect. Suppose you cause your car to move by pushing it with a particular force. Do you first push the car and then the car moves? Your pushing (with a particular force) and the car's moving are apparently simultaneous. Of course you set about pushing the car prior to pushing it and prior to its moving. The car is not moved by your setting about pushing it, however, but by your pushing it.

If we replace the traditional Humean picture of event-causation with Martin's 'power net' conception, such worries recede. Events are mutual manifestatings of reciprocal disposition partners. Reciprocal disposition partners do not stand in relations of succession to one another. The model is not that of links in a chain, but of playing cards remaining upright by mutually supporting one another on a table top.

What of 'probabilistic' causation: causal relations in which causes apparently yield effects only with a certain probability? The quantum theory seems to tell us that probabilistic causation is the rule rather than the exception. Philosophers who favor accounts of causation based on causal laws explain probabilistic causation by building probabilities into the laws. What might the analog be for a disposition-based account? Here is one possibility. Every property has a perfectly definite dispositionality. This dispositionality will manifest itself in a definite way given particular kinds of reciprocal disposition partner (and in the absence of 'blockers'). How could probabilities enter the picture?

Suppose basic properties (or some of them) were *oscillatory*. Consider an apparent case of probabilistic causation. *C*'s cause *E*'s 60 percent of the time and *F*'s 40 percent of the time under comparable conditions. Now, imagine two properties, *C 1* and *C 2*, such that (1) *E* is a mutual manifestation of *C 1* and reciprocal disposition partner *P*; (2) *F* is a mutual manifestation of *C 2* and reciprocal disposition partner *P*; (3) *C 1* and *C 2* oscillate: *C 1* alternates with *C 2* in such a way that, in general, any object possessing *C 1* or *C 2* will possess *C 1* (but not *C 2*) about 60 percent of the time, and *C 2* (but not *C 1*) about 40 percent of the time; (4) it is built into *C 1* and *C 2* that they oscillate in this way.

It might seem that shifting the locus of probability from causal transactions (or disposition manifestations) to properties gains us nothing. I am not so sure. Yes, property oscillation would be a surprising phenomenon. Oscillation strikes me as less surprising, however, than the idea that the very same properties, with the very same reciprocal disposition partners, manifest themselves differently on different occasions.

It is time to move on. I do not imagine that these brief remarks provide anything approaching a decisive rebuttal of the prevailing view of event causation. I want only to indicate that the appealing simplicity of that view requires our complicating it in various unattractive ways. These complexities are nicely resolved within the dispositional model. To that extent, at least, the model appears viable.

Complex Objects

The world, I have suggested, includes a dynamic arrangement of objects. Objects can be simple or complex. A complex object has objects as parts. Simple objects have a kind of structure a simple object is an object with properties but no substantial parts.

This last statement requires amplification. Assume for a moment that simple objects are something more than space-time points. A simple object, although not made up of other objects, could nevertheless have spatial or temporal parts. A simple object might, for instance, have a top and a bottom half; these halves might have definite spatial dimensions. If a simple object persists through time, then we can speak of its temporal parts by analogy with its spatial parts. We could speak of the object-on-Tuesday, for instance, and distinguish this from the object-on-Wednesday. Spatial and temporal parts of an object are not, however, themselves objects. Although a sphere has two spatial halves, a sphere need not be made up of these two halves in the way a pencil is made up of a wooden shaft surrounding a cylinder of graphite. Unless otherwise noted, when I speak of parts of objects in what follows, I shall mean not spatial or temporal parts, but substantial parts, parts that are themselves objects.

Complex objects have objects as parts. These parts could themselves be complex, but we might hope eventually to arrive at simple objects, those not made up of distinct objects. Let us say that complex objects are constituted by their constituent objects. Every object, then, is constituted by simple objects. Is there any more to complex objects than this? Many philosophers have thought so.

Think of a statue and the particles that make it up. Is the statue just the collection of particles? It would seem not. The collection of particles could change, and the statue remain. We could repair the statue and replace a piece that has broken off. When we do so, the result is a new collection of particles, but the same statue. More dramatically, we could destroy the statue by grinding it to dust without destroying the collection of particles. The statue and the collection of particles have distinct persistence conditions: the statue could continue to exist when the collection of particles does not, and the collection of particles could survive when the statue is destroyed.

Perhaps we could say that the statue *is* the collection of particles arranged in a particular way: the statue is the particles plus their arrangement. If the statue is ground to dust, its particles remain, but their arrangement is lost. However, it looks as though we could replace particles yet the statue, but not the collection, would remain, so long as we preserved the arrangement. Or we might alter the arrangement, thus modifying, but not destroying, the statue.

Considerations along these lines have led philosophers to the view that statues, and indeed complex objects generally, are distinct from arrangements of their constituent parts. True, they are, at any given time, *made up* of a collection of parts. But this just shows that there is more to an object's identity than the objects that make it up and the relations these bear to one another. In the case of the statue, we could imagine two spatially overlapping objects: the statue (characterized by its identity conditions over time) and a collection of particles (characterized by its very different identity conditions over time).

The resulting picture is of a world consisting of 'layers' of objects and properties. A statue, we might say, is a higher-level object; the particles that make up the statue, and perhaps certain collections of these particles, are objects at a lower level. Now it seems possible to explain the role of the special sciences. Physics is the science of objects at the basic level. Each special science biology, for instance, or meteorology, or psychology deals with some domain of higher-level objects. The world comprises, then, not just objects, but a *hierarchy* of objects at distinct levels.

This layered conception of reality is widely accepted. I believe it is mistaken. Appeals to levels of reality, ontological hierarchies, lead to a distorted picture of how things stand and to a multitude of philosophical puzzles and mysteries. Let us return to the statue. We have agreed that the statue is not to be *identified* with the collection of particles that make it up, nor even with the collection of particles arranged in a particular way. In so agreeing, however, we are taking 'collection' in an especially rigid sense. In this sense, a collection is destroyed when it loses a single member, when a member is replaced by a duplicate, or when a new member is added. I propose that we consider a more relaxed notion of a collection. This relaxed notion is the notion we deploy when we think of a stamp collection, or a collection of baseball cards or paintings. In this relaxed sense, a collection can gain or lose members, and yet remain the same collection. How many members can a collection gain or lose, how much can a collection change and still remain the same collection? This may be partly a matter of decision.

When we consider the statue as a collection of particles in this relaxed sense, it is rather more plausible to say that the statue is 'nothing over and above', 'nothing other than', *is just* this collection of particles appropriately arranged. Still this may not be not quite right. Arguably, statues are artifacts, produced by intelligent creatures with particular ends in mind. An appropriately arranged collection of particles that 'fell from the sky' or was produced by the random action of waves on a rocky outcropping would not be a statue although of course you might mistake it for one. A statue, then, is not merely an appropriately shaped collection of particles. In order to constitute a statue, a collection of particles must have the right kind of causal history. This history must include intelligent creatures and their states of mind.

Now suppose we build all this into our picture. That is, we take the collection of particles (in the relaxed sense of collection) and add to it not merely relations these particles bear to one another, but also relations they bear to other particles, themselves members of collections of particles. The relations will be complex indeed; they will very likely exceed anything encompassable by a finite human mind. Moreover, owing to our electing to deploy 'collection' and 'appropriate arrangement' in a relaxed sense, the possibilities for variation will be endless.

This is merely to say that there is no prospect of providing a definition of a statue, or even a finite set of necessary and sufficient conditions for something's being a statue, by appealing only the vocabulary of particles and relations among these. To regard this as an impediment to ontological reduction, however, is to miss the point. My contention is not that talk of statues is translatable into, or analyzable in terms of, talk of particles and their relations. The idea, rather, is that this is all statues are; statues are nothing other than, distinct from, or over and above collections of particles, where 'collection' is taken in the relaxed sense to include relations these particles bear to one another and to other collections.

Imagine that God sets out to create a world containing statues. God can do so by creating simple objects and ensuring that they bear the right relations to one another. The creation of a single statue could well require the creation of a dynamic arrangement of micro-objects extending over time and taking in an impressive spatial region. If a statue requires the existence of intelligent creatures with particular thoughts, then other collections of simple objects with similarly dynamic and extended spatial and temporal relations will need to be included as well.

Again, the thesis is not that 'statue' can be defined or analyzed in terms of atoms or molecules and their relations. There is no hope of spelling out detailed conditions of individuation or persistence in terms of constituent objects and their relations. Rather, the *truth-makers* for claims about statues are ultimately arrangements of simple objects:

something is a statue in virtue of its being a collection (in the relaxed sense) of simple objects bearing appropriate relations to one another and to other collections of simple objects. There is no question of specifying these collections independently of our statue concept, nor is this required. The suggestion is not that we might reduce talk of statues to talk of electrons and quarks. The picture I am offering is an ontological picture, not a reductive account of the meanings of words.

Many philosophers find this picture hopelessly austere. It appears to them to deny reality to anything but the simple objects and relations these bear to one another. In the words of the ancient Greek atomist Democritus, only the atoms and the void are real. But this is to caricature the view recommended here. Statues exist, all right; it is just that they are nothing in addition to arrangements of simpler objects. Statues are not higher-level entities except in the ontologically innocuous sense that they are complex entities made up of simpler constituents in complex arrangements. And this is so, as well, for every putatively higher-level entity, including ourselves, our social institutions, and the products of these.

A final point bears mention. The example of a statue and particles that make it up encourages the idea that the universe is grainy: complex objects are assemblages of simple objects that are themselves corpuscular. Although I admit this as a possibility, it is not the only possibility and, if physics is to be believed, it is not even an especially likely possibility. Imagine, for a moment, that simple objects are regions of space-time or the quantum field that themselves possess certain properties. Such objects are not particle-like, although we could well experience them as particle-like.

I do not think any of this would affect anything I have said here. I have, to be sure, spoken of statues and their constituent particles, but this could be regarded as nothing more than a way of speaking about frighteningly complicated arrangements of disturbances in space-time. As it happens, the world is such that these disturbances are rarely isolated affairs. They 'clump together' in particular ways. This 'clumping' gives rise to what we describe (to my mind, quite correctly) as statues and the particles making them up. Their 'clumping' is explained by the dispositionalities of the fundamental entities (or, in the case that there is but one of them, the fundamental entity).

Although I remain officially agnostic on the question whether objects are ultimately particles, or fields, or something else this is not, after all, a question for a philosopher to decide I shall continue to treat objects as 'continuants', moving about in space and persisting over time. This is purely a matter of linguistic convenience. I am supposing that the truth-makers for claims about objects could turn out to be something that does not match our ordinary conception of objects as persisting, mobile, self-contained entities.

Emergence

This compositional picture is meant to apply to properties as well as objects. Complex properties are properties of complex objects. A complex property is nothing over and above the properties of a complex object's constituent objects arranged as they are.

This conception stands in marked contrast to the view that properties of wholes are 'emergent'. The world consists of simple objects. Properties of these simple objects are simple properties. (It could turn out, and indeed it appears altogether likely, that there are, in fact, very few simple properties or kinds of simple property.) Every combinatorial possibility is written into the simple properties. These include possibilities that have never been and will never come to be. New combinations of properties are just that: new combinations, not new properties.

Does this mean that emergence genuine emergence, the emergence of genuinely new properties (as distinct from new arrangements of old properties) is impossible? Not at all. If emergence occurs and we have no reason to doubt that it does it occurs at the basic level. At the basic level what is emergent cannot be reduced to anything more basic. Imagine, for instance, that the universe contained just two kinds of elementary particle, *á*-particles and *â*-particles. Prior to some particular time, these particles never interact owing, perhaps, to their occupying non-overlapping spatial regions. Eventually, however, an *á*-particle and a *â*-particle collide. The result is the emergence of a new kind of elementary particle, a gamma particle. Something like this might have occurred during, or immediately after, the Big Bang. It might occur nowadays in particle accelerators.

The compositional picture obliges us to distinguish complex properties that are nothing more than (possibly novel) combinations of simple properties, from genuinely emergent basic properties. The possibility of basic emergent properties is written into (that is, is intrinsic to) the properties that serve as the vehicles of their emergence. In this regard, all the possibilities flow from the simple properties. These possibilities include the possibility of complex, nonemergent properties and the possibility of simple, noncomplex emergents.

Levels of Being

Does the ontology I am recommending fly in the face of everyday experience or our ordinary take on reality? It does, certainly, fly in the face of a popular philosophical refrain according to which the world is *layered*: the world incorporates *levels* of objects and properties organized hierarchically. Levels are philosophical posits introduced as ingredients of philosophical theories. Such theories are, often enough, designed to account for our everyday experience. In rejecting a philosophical posit and the theory in which it is embedded, however, I am by no means recommending that you turn your back on everyday experience. On the contrary, I am offering a competing account of the basis of that experience, one that, with luck, also meshes with what the sciences tell us about our world.

At this point, someone could dig in. The layered view of the world, it might be argued, comes not from everyday experience, but from *science*. The special sciences concern objects and properties occupying distinct ontological strata. Each level is autonomous with respect to those below it, in the sense that it cannot be reduced to lower levels. Laws governing higher-level objects are not replaceable by or derivable from lower-level laws. Nevertheless, objects and properties at higher levels are in some way grounded in objects and properties occupying lower levels. The favored account of this grounding relation is thought to be captured by the notion of 'supervenience': higher-level items 'supervene' on those at lower levels. This means, roughly, that higher-level differences require differences at lower levels; lower-level objects and properties suffice for higher-level objects and properties, but that the higher-level supervening objects and properties are distinct from their lower-level grounds. The distinctness of higher-level items is reflected in (or perhaps is constituted by) their being governed by distinct laws of nature.

Predicates and properties

Properties, as I have characterized them, are concrete features of the world: particularized ways objects are. Such features are to be distinguished from our representations of them. We can distinguish the *property* of sphericity being spherical from the *predicate* 'is spherical', a linguistic expression the role of which is to name or designate a property. Does every property have a linguistic designation? That seems unlikely. As we learn more about our world, we uncover new, as yet unnamed, properties. Laboratories and particle accelerators are designed to facilitate the creation of new properties, properties not previously encountered. When this happens, we are obliged to invent a new name or devise a descriptive predicate.

This much seems obvious. What is less obvious, however, is whether every predicate designates a property. To be sure, some predicates apparently designate nothing at all: 'is a square circle', for instance. The predicate 'is a cure for the common cold', although perfectly meaningful, apparently fails to designate any property of any object. We could, of course, discover that it does, or, more likely, learn how to manufacture objects possessing properties in virtue of which they answer to the predicate.

Other predicates present different challenges. Consider the predicate 'is good'. It is a matter of some controversy whether this predicate designates a property of objects, or whether it serves merely to signal a speaker's approval of objects or events. When you tell me that Brussels sprouts are good, are you saying that Brussels sprouts, in addition to being leafy, green, and pungent, possess the property of being good? Or are you rather *commending* Brussels sprouts (perhaps *because* they are leafy, green, and pungent)? We need not try to answer this question here. It is enough to recognize that it is at least a matter of dispute whether 'is good' designates a genuine property.

What of a predicate like 'is a stone'? Does this predicate designate a property possessed by objects, those qualifying as stones? There are stones, undeniably. But is there *a* property, *the property of being a stone*, possessed by every stone and in virtue of which it is true that it is a stone? This may strike you as an odd question, but bear with me. Perhaps we can see our way through at least one philosophical thicket, and begin to pull some of the lessons of this chapter together.

Properties, Realism and Antirealism

Philosophers sometimes argue as follows:

(A): Take a predicate, "Either" designates a property or it does not. If "designates a property, then to say that something, á, is is to say something true (if á has) or false (if á lacks). We are realists about's insofar as we take" to express a property. Otherwise we are antirealists about's.

Antirealists about a given domain hold that entities in the domain are either non-existent or in some way language or mind dependent. Most of us are antirealists in the first sense about ghosts and unicorns. We deny that such things exist. To put this into the philosophers' linguistic mode: we believe that the predicate 'is a ghost' and the predicate 'is a unicorn' designate nothing at all. (One qualification: any consistent predicate can hold true of agents' beliefs. It might be true of you that you *believe* there are ghosts or unicorns.) Relative to believers in such things, we could be described as 'eliminativists' about ghosts and unicorns.

Other antirealists are more subtle or devious. They hold that sentences apparently ascribing's to objects need to be understood not as straightforward *ascriptions* of, but as something else. 'Expressivist' views in ethics are a familiar example. To say that á is good, for instance, is taken not to ascribe a property, goodness, to á, but to express the speaker's approval of á.

All this is good fun, but what are we to say about thesis (A)? My suggestion is that (A) mischaracterizes realism. One source of this mischaracterization is a failure to take seriously the distinction between predicates and properties. And one result of a tacit allegiance to (A), or something like (A), is that the kind of ontology introduced in this chapter is unjustifiably cast in an especially unflattering light.

To see what is wrong with (A), consider how a predicate might be thought to hold true of an object. The predicate 'is spherical', we might say, holds true of a billiard ball in virtue of the ball's possessing the property of being spherical. Now consider the predicate 'is a stone'. Most of us would agree that this predicate holds true of many objects: many objects are stones. Does 'is a stone' name or designate a property of objects, a property (a) shared by all stones, and (b) in virtue of which those objects answer to the predicate 'is a stone'?

Philosophy of mind is a branch of modern analytic philosophy that studies the nature of the mind, mental events, mental functions, mental properties, consciousness and their relationship to the physical body, particularly the brain. The mind-body problem, i.e. the relationship of the mind to the body, is commonly seen as the central issue in philosophy of mind, although there are other issues concerning the nature of the mind that do not involve its relation to the physical body.

Dualism and monism are the two major schools of thought that attempt to resolve the mind-body problem. Dualism can be traced back to Plato, Aristotle and the Sankhya and Yoga schools of Hindu philosophy, but it was most precisely formulated by René Descartes in the 17th century. Substance Dualists argue that the mind is an independently existing substance, whereas Property Dualists maintain that the mind is a group of independent properties that emerge from and cannot be reduced to the brain, but that it is not a distinct substance.

13

Voluntarism in the Nineteenth Century

Introduction

The Critique of Judgment, to give it its usual English title, has often and correctly been thought of as filling the gap created by its two predecessors. The gap was not merely that of beauty, whereas both truth and goodness had already been given their niches, but that between the scientific and the moral order. In both scientific laws and moral judgments there was a fusion of the universal and particular, in that in the former case a universal assertion was found to hold true of a particular event and in the latter particular acts were to be corrected by universal commandments. But in the case of a picture or a poem or any other object, whether natural or artificial, which we feel to be beautiful, we recognize its stubborn individuality and we are impelled to do nothing whatsoever but look at it. Since it is, let us say, a material object, it belongs to the phenomenal world; and since it belongs to that world we can describe it as we would any other item in the vast inventory of that world. But the feeling of beauty is clearly not scientific classification. Again, a picture or a poem or a landscape may "say" something and thus gain moral relevance, as when critics point out the great moral lesson of Michelangelo *Last Judgment* or explicate a sermon in stones. But to translate a picture into an essay is not to be touched by its beauty and, in fact, it has often been believed that the more closely a work of art approaches an imperative the more it loses its aesthetic character. Kant is no more trying to write history in the *Critique of Judgment* than he is in the *Critique of Practical Reason.* He assumes that aesthetic judgments can be true and false; that they arise out of a kind of feeling—or sense of beauty; that this feeling is not an impulse to take practical action; and he then attempts to discover how all this is logically possible. He knows that some works of art have had a moral purpose, but he insists that this purpose is irrelevant to their aesthetic value. The object, then, when viewed aesthetically is a more complete analogue to the universe itself than either a scientific object or a moral act. Keats's famous verse on the silent form which teases us out of thoughts as does eternity would be a perfect brief summation of the whole idea.

In Kant's more prosaic language the faculty of appraisal always judges the fitness of means to end. But, however prosaic the language, the problem which confronts the man who contemplates a work of art is charged with paradox. For no one can announce by inspection the end for which a work of art has been produced, to say nothing of that for which a beautiful natural object has been created. The teleology inherent in the formula is not that of the Bridgewater Treatises, for Kant insists that beauty is useless. Here the analogy with the macrocosm gains significance. Every beautiful object exists for its own sake and need be related to nothing beyond itself. The fitness which is involved is the congruence between the work of art and our own minds. The first *Critique* had demonstrated this congruence as far as science is concerned; the second as far as ethics enters the picture. But the third presents the human mind face to face with that which is its object, not reasoning about it, not attempting to utilize it, but simply and clearly looking at it. But what it sees is the congruence in question conveyed through the physical object but not identical with it. The aesthetic experience for him is immediate apprehension usually employed in the perception of sensory qualities, of universal principles usually discovered through rational analysis. That the work of art embodied universal traits had been said as early as the third century by Plotinus, and the whole Neo-Platonic school had repeated that beauty was a sensuous manifestation of the ideal. But the ideal in that case was simply the generic characters of the class of beings to which the object naturally belonged. Thus a painting of apples revealed sensuously the essence of apple-hood and a painting of Venus the essence of female beauty. By what magical power this was possible had never been made clear, and the principle remained one of those rhetorical flourishes highly charged with emotion which seemed to satisfy men who would like works of art to have supernatural traits. But what was universal in Kant's theory was not the Platonic essence at all; it was the kind of order which the universe is known to have through science. One might say that when Newton saw the apple fall, he saw not merely that specific event but the law of gravitation in action. If the moon falls on the earth and the planets on the sun as the apple falls to the ground, then the fall of the apple becomes more than a single historical event. It becomes evidence for and an example of a universal event. But the point of Kant's argument is that we are able to apprehend this universality by feeling, without reflective thought.

There are several reasons to support this theory. First, all beauty was supposed to be sensory. The very name *aesthetics* was invented by Baumgarten because he believed that beauty lay in the sensory field. It was of course not only a badly chosen name, since aside from a few ordinary sensory experiences, like the color of the sky, the sound of a bird, or the taste of something agreeable, no aesthetic experience ever was confined to sensory apprehensions. It is perhaps through sensory apprehensions that we grasp the meaning of a beautiful poem or an ugly one for that matter but the meaning of the words and phrases is not bounded by their sound. But whether badly chosen or not, the tradition that beauty was an affair of the senses was too strongly founded to be questioned. Second, it was always assumed, as it is still today, that differences in taste were unimportant and that the "laws" of beauty were binding on all men alike. Hence, regardless of whether beauty is apprehended by our sense organs or not, it must be something which transcends the limits of any individual's experience. Third, it must be subject to rational discourse while not attainable by the reason. That is, we must be able to argue about the relative beauty of two objects while admitting that feeling the beauty is not identical with knowing that an object is beautiful. This may well have arisen from the one experience of beauty which all men must have had at some time or other in their lives, that is, in sexual attraction. No one ever fell in love and I am speaking of straightforward physical love with a woman because he first measured her and found that she had the same measurements as the Venus de Milo. It is true that most books in aesthetics seem to have been written by eunuchs, but that need not concern us here. My one point is that there is at least one occasion on which a man feels the attraction of something beautiful without knowing (or caring) why it is beautiful. Finally, we repeat that the aesthetic object is always an individual object, *this* poem, *that* picture, *this* person, not *a* poem, *a* picture, *a* person. The beautiful object thus combines, or seems to combine, the conflicting properties of the universal and the individual. To make it so abstract as to become really universal is to rob it of its aesthetic properties. To make it completely sensory is to make it unintelligible.

The paradoxical nature of the beautiful object was to become a paradigm for the Post-Kantian philosophers. But even in non-philosophical German literature paradox was to become a stock-intrade of the Romanticists. Friedrich Schlegel famous *Lucinde* is a case in point. There we find the hero writing to his beloved, "Through all stages of humanity do you accompany me from the most exuberant sensuality to the most spiritual spirituality and only in you did I see true pride and true feminine humility." The very fact that two lovers are bound together in unity, "not merely for what we call this or that world, but for the one true, indivisible, nameless, infinite world, for our whole eternal being and life", is supposed to add value to a love which would have been inferior if the two had retained their duality. Yet without the duality there could be no union and without union no fulfillment of love. But the ultimate paradox of the story occurs in the section called *Longing and Repose* where Lucinde asks her lover Julius why she always feels the most serene repose in deep longing. "Only in longing," answered Julius, "do we find repose. Yes, repose comes only when our spirit is disturbed by nothing in its longing and search for that wherein it can find nothing higher than longing itself." Longing which might be satisfied would be longing defeated. Man's spirit must strive after goals which it can never hope to reach. So Lessing in his famous epigram on the search for truth, so Goethe in his repeated theme of the eternal feminine. Don Juan who passes from woman to woman becomes the hero of the school, for his very infidelity is really a search for the ever retreating ideal. Don Quixote by the very absurdity of his quest is the symbol not merely of the pathos of human ambition but of the one reality which man can grasp. The blue flower of Novalis, never to be found, but the more precious for that, might be set up as the emblem of the same group. And even Schubert wrote two songs entitled Sehnsucht.

Fichte

To see man caught in a current of restless striving for ideals which he can never attain might have become the center of a pessimism as deep as that of Schopenhauer. But the first post-Kantians did not go that far. In Fichte, for instance, what was longing in *Lucinde* turns into a cosmic process. The things-in-themselves, which were unknowable in Kant, were tossed out of the philosophic baggage as nonsense. If they are really unknowable, we may just as well forget all about them for whatever we say of them is bound to be false. Their mere existence cannot be asserted, for to assert that something exists is to know something about it. The one thing we can know is our spiritual life and that life is to be discovered not in the calm of contemplation but in striving.

The reason which in Kant had its theoretical possibilities was turned into the will-in short into Kant's practical reason—and whereas in Kant its demands could establish certain moral postulates, in Fichte it could create the world itself. The will must have something to achieve, something to act upon, something to overcome. But since there is no evidence of any existing thing to be derived from volition itself, the existence of a world must be found in the nature of volition. Fichte's will was not mere longing. It was striving for ideals. But Fichte, dramatizing the national situation of his country, saw that the achievement of the ideal could only come about through the conquest of the real. One cannot fight the good fight without an adversary, but where was the adversary to be found?

In the technical jargon of philosophy the Ego posits the Non-Ego to become more of an Ego. But in the language of common sense we set up our own adversary to overcome it. It never will be overcome, and if it were to be we should be aimless souls with nothing to do.

Now this boils down to the fact that philosophy must reorient itself away from science and toward morality. The hard objects of the material world must be given ethical significance, must not be interpreted in the quantitative terms of physics but in terms of their relation to our moral life. The only ethical meaning which we can give to them is that of opposing the human will. That is why they exist. That alone makes their existence intelligible. That does not entail the belief that science has no value; but it has limited value since it can never reach reality itself. Once it is proved that reality has no moral color, nor intellectual, then all things must be reinterpreted in relation to the good. The Ego's positing of the Non-Ego is such an ethical reinterpretation. When the theoretical "plain man" asks what is the meaning of things, he is asking a question similar to that of Fichte. The answer could have been aesthetic as well as ethical. Man's sense of beauty could have been set down as his fundamental trait and all reality interpreted as elements in a cosmic work of art in which beauty would have taken the place of truth. But Fichte was a hard working man himself, a great patriot who will always be remembered in Germany for his stirring speeches to what he called somewhat optimistically the German Nation, and man's striving after perfection was to his way of thinking the secret of all life. He could also have assumed that the moral will, through no desire of its own, was set down by God or Chance in a hostile universe which he was determined to overcome. But his reading of Kant convinced him that the world of fact could never be the world of value except insofar as human beings were involved in it. What reality it has is discovered in its opposition to us, not in its simple resistance to pressure, as in Destutt de Tracy, but in the possibility of its frustrating our desires. What gives Fichte's philosophy a novel twist is his belief that we need and want such a world to oppose us.

But in his own exposition the matter was set forth in purely dialectical fashion. Looking for a method which would give him absolute certainty, he was forced to avoid any empirical judgments which might be true but would be only relatively true. Just as Descartes had concluded that the one incontrovertible truth was self-identity, so Fichte concluded that the one incontrovertible truth was the Law of Identity, A is A. The symbol A in this expression may stand for either a thing, or a concept, or a sentence; its reference is immaterial to Fichte's argument. It may be interpreted as meaning that a term must not change its significance in a chain of reasoning, that a given thing does not change its "nature," or that tautologies are always true or consistent. But what is important for Fichte is that the Law of Identity is asserted by someone; it is a judgment and the only judge is the Ego, the judging mind. Identity then must be found primitively in the self-identity of the Ego, for there is nothing else, of which one has any certainty, to find it in. Further than all this there is a necessary and not merely empirical identity between the two *A*'s. We can give no reason beyond the judgment itself for the necessary identity and yet we believe that it is self-evidently so. This to Fichte's mind is proof that the necessity of the identity is to be found in the being who asserts it, and thus the first certain principle of his metaphysics is the Ego's assertion of its own being. The problem now is to get beyond one's selfawareness. Are we self-enclosed like Leibniz' monads, windowless, incapable of knowing anything external to us, incapable of knowing that there is anything external to us? The belief which we have in the existence of other minds, as well as in a world external to our consciousness, the belief that there is a legitimate distinction to be made between dreams and waking life, hallucinations and veridical perceptions—are such beliefs illusory? Are the distinctions preserved in common language between what we think and what actually is unnecessary distinctions? One might imagine that if we can be certain only of our own being, we should stop at this point unless we are to supplement certainty with probability.

But like most philosophers Fichte wants to substantiate the beliefs of common sense insofar as those beliefs will give him the kind of system which he wants. His wants, which clearly existed before he began to philosophize, were in part determined by the philosophical conclusions of his predecessors, especially Kant, and in part by the kinds of questions which he was putting to philosophy as a discipline. When, for instance, a philosopher wants to prove the existence of God, he usually stops when he has done so. When he wants to give some ground for believing in universal values or the immortality of the soul, for the infinite divisibility of space or the non existence of mind as distinguished from matter, he is usually satisfied when he has accomplished his purpose. The legitimacy of a problem seldom seems to be itself a problem. Few philosophers have ever raised the question of the orientation of philosophic meditations. This is to be sure a psychological, not a logical, problem and that may be the reason why it has aroused so little interest. In any event it remains one of the darkest corners of the history of philosophy, and all one can say about it is that individual philosophers put different questions to both the universe and the reason and are satisfied with different answers to them. Why Fichte wanted to escape from the cramping circle of solipsism may have been merely because he accepted the existence of an external world on the grounds of tradition or common sense and then tried to justify his attitude.

There was a simple way out of the difficulty furnished by the old principle: All determination is negation. That is, if the word *I* is to have meaning, it must select out of all possible beings one or one set of beings. Such selection is equivalent to negating all the others, the *not—I's*. To assert the existence of the Ego is then equivalent to asserting that it is not the non-Ego. And one sees that one has already made an implicit judgment to the effect that there is something which is not the Ego and with which it may be contrasted. Fichte does not overtly argue from this principle but seems to assume that we have an idea of negation which permits us to assert the identity of B and not A. No one indeed would deny this, but he might deny that if in fact we are aware only of our own existence, we could appeal to any logical formulas to express anything other than our own existence. The minute we also accept the traditional rules of logic, at a minimum the three Laws of Thought, we have procedural rules for transforming the initial assertion into a variety of other assertions. But Fichte limits himself to the Law of Contradiction and points out that the very assertion of the existence of the I implies the existence of the non I, thus giving it the same certainty as that of the initial proposition. He does not, it should be emphasized, infer existence from essence; on the contrary the existence of the I is found in the necessity of there being a subject to assert or judge. And so far all the distinctions are within the consciousness of the Ego. Within that consciousness there is an obvious conflict, the assertions of two contradictory beings, the Ego and the not Ego, neither of which means anything without the other. Strictly speaking, it is not so much contradiction which is involved here as difference. But in view of Fichte's apparent acceptance of the Laws of Thought as inherent to the operations of the judging subject, the only way in which the difference can be expressed is through the Law of Contradiction. And that to his way of thinking gives him the right to lay down a Category of Negation as implicit within the Category of Assertion. Each category is essential if definite meaning is given. to what is known. The Ego becomes a universal term meaning nothing in particular until it is limited by something other than itself, the Non-

Ego, and the Non-Ego would have no meaning if it were not limited by its contradictory, the Ego. That all this is rooted in the nature of thought itself does not make it subjective in a bad sense, since we have no certainty of anything other than thinking. To call it "merely" subjective would mean that we have an idea of something nonsubjective, and the fact of the matter is that we have no such idea as yet. We have simply certainty of the interplay between two contrary ideas which are reciprocally interdependent.

But there is one feature of the I which distinguishes it concretely from the *not*—I. That is its activity in assertion. The difference between the Ego and its opposite does not swim up to the surface of consciousness of its own accord; judgment is essential to the recognition of an object about which the judgment is made and judgment is action. But if the judging subject is active, the object which is judged must be called passive. And this gives us a picture of the mind which is the very opposite of that drawn by the empirical tradition. According to that tradition, the subject received influences from a nonsubjective world impressions, primary ideas, sensible species, the eidola of Democritus. The human being has a mind which is, to use Locke's phrase, white paper at birth, and whatever contents there may be in the mind are put into it from external sources. In Fichte it is the mind itself which is active and knowledge has to be interpreted as something which the subject does to the object. The power which the mind exercises over the object is called by Fichte in the *Grundlage* Imagination. This is neither idle daydreaming nor uncontrolled fantasy. It is the activity of a mind constructing and organizing things to its own ends. But though its ends are its own, they are determined by its essential nature and that nature, as we have said above, is that of the Practical Reason. In other words, the world of knowledge cannot be produced by a non-mental agent, for there is none. It cannot spontaneously occur, for such words would explain nothing. It is not discovered by simple inspection, for we do not all seem to have the same scientific knowledge either at birth or at maturity. Organization must be made for a purpose which would be relevant to the needs of the Practical Reason and those needs are moral. The world then must be interpreted in ethical terms, and the whole of Fichte's ethics is an attempt to show that every feature of the universe has relevance to our moral needs. That these needs will never be completely met in this world is of no importance. For, as we have said, the Romantic thinkers thought none the less of aspirations because they could never reach a conclusion.Perhaps the most famous of Fichte's systematic statements of his whole theory occurs in the *Vocation of Man*. This work is divided into three parts, significantly called *Doubt, Knowledge, and Faith.* It is worth observing that the doubts of the hero rest, as those of the Savoyard Vicar did, on natural science and its supposed implications. Since the description of science became typical of thoughts on that subject up to our own time, I outline them briefly here.

1. Science gives us a world in which everything is determined; "it is what it is and nothing else". All existence is determined by inexorable law and there is no possibility of any break in the causal series. Causal necessity explains all that happens and consequently whatever is a part of the natural order is as it is because of antecedent events.
2. Though causal efficacy is an expression of a power inherent in whatever is causal, yet the expression of that power is itself limited and determined. Each cause does but one kind of thing: each seed develops under the proper conditions into but one kind of plant, each chemical substance unites with others according to specific laws. Because of this generalizations can be made and natural science forms a deductive system.
3. But the whole cosmos is interconnected so that whatever happens in any part of it has its effect upon the whole and is caused by the organic structure of the whole. "In every moment of her duration Nature is one connected whole; in every moment each individual part must be what it is, because all the others are what they are; and you could not remove a single grain of sand from its place, without thereby,

although perhaps imperceptibly to you, changing something throughout all parts of the immeasurable whole". Fichte does not explain how any change could take place in such an interconnected system and indeed does not raise the question. It would seem, however, that if the universe is such a whole with all parts dependent on all others, any change would be impossible, except perhaps a shift in the spatial position of some of the parts. That too would be questionable, for what would cause them to change? This particular doubt, however, did not trouble many people who believed in the organic structure of the cosmos, and it has been a metaphor employed from the days of the Stoics to those of the later Marxists. As far as the German philosophers were concerned the metaphor probably owed its power to their liking for plants as typical of natural processes, a liking which we have already seen in Herder.

4. If Nature is thus a strictly determined system, human beings insofar as they belong to Nature are also strictly determined in everything which they seem to do. When I think, it is because of natural laws, the same laws as operate in the growth of a plant or the movements of an animal. Because of the interconnection of natural beings, I am what I am, and it is absolutely necessary that I should be so.

5. My feeling of freedom is justified only to the extent to which I contribute something to the everlasting series of natural events. But so a tree, if it were conscious, would have a feeling of being free as it achieved its destiny as a tree. Whenever some other being, the woodsman for instance, intervened in its history, it would feel the blows of necessity, and similarly, when we are not aware of the external causes which act upon us, we too have the sentiment of freedom. "In immediate consciousness, I appear to myself as free; by reflection on the whole of Nature, I discover that freedom is absolutely impossible; the former must be

> subordinate to the latter, for it can be explained only by means of it". For this reason my feeling of activity is an illusion. "I do not truly act at all, but Nature acts in me".

These five principles are set down as absolutely true and as the cause of despair. They seem to overthrow the whole structure of morality and to deprive the world of moral value. Why should a man strive for anything, if his striving itself is the effect of causes over which he has no control? Why not relax and let Nature operate as she will? But relaxation itself is beyond one's reach unless one is so disposed by the cosmic order. If this be so, then there is no sense whatsoever in an individual's attempting to be either moral or immoral. He will be whatever the natural order forces him to be. What is wanted is justification for seeking the good with perfect freedom and responsibility. "There shall be a Supreme Good in the spiritual world; I shall have the power to seek this with freedom until I find it, to acknowledge it as such when found, and it shall be my fault if I do not find it". Such is man's aspiration. How can he justify it?

Presumably on the principle *ex nihilo nihil* Fichte points out that if he is to be free, he must already contain some free element in his make-up. An examination of his consciousness shows him that when he makes choices he has knowledge of various courses of action. He acts upon one rather than the others. These alternatives are all contained within his thought so that acting upon one of them is the fulfillment of something already present *in potentia*. And action thus becomes an expression of a potency contained within the thought of an individual. But nothing like this seems to occur in the nonhuman world. There everything takes place because of forces external to the being which is changing, nothing changing literally *of its own accord*. My nature is twofold, one part being submissive to natural law, the other to thought. "Thought is no longer the mere faculty of observation; it is the source of action itself". This is the key-sentence to the rest of Fichte's philosophy unless I have misread him. Out of it can be derived the whole voluntaristic tradition of our time, a tradition which manifested great variety in its forms but which as a whole fused man's reason with his will.

The second part of the *Vocation of Man* is a justification of this idea. The sensible world is first reduced to a set of Berkeleyan ideas. The notion of an independent substratum is easily disposed of as an *X* of which we can have no knowledge. All knowledge then is seen to be self-knowledge, for even when we are not aware of mental activity and it is important to note that there is some of which we are not aware it is still mental, spontaneously occurring as an expression of our unconscious thinking. Even the appearance of an external world turns into a projection of the subjective world. "There is no outward sense, for there is no outward perception. There is, however, an outward intuition; not of things, but this outward intuition this knowledge apparently external to the subjective being, and hovering before it is itself the thing, and there is no other". In other words the feeling that the world of perception is external to us is no more than a feeling. We see some of our conscious states as if they were not ours, just as in dreams we are unaware of their internality. The reason why this is true is that space is on Kantian principles a form of intuition and when we intuit we see things in space. One's consciousness is thus dual: it may be directed toward sensations, feelings, dreams, aspirations, or may project in spatial form the contents of those states of mind. In this way we create an external world which stands in opposition to the internal. The distinction between the Ego and the Non-Ego lies within consciousness itself. "What I call *I*, is therefore absolutely nothing more than a certain modification of consciousness".

But this too is disappointing, since the world dissolves into a dream. The dream frees man from the nightmare of a strictly determined cosmos, but it does no more. For the acquisition of a more satisfying universe, man must turn to Faith. Man is aware of something beyond knowledge, but since it is beyond knowledge he must find it by some other means. "The innermost depths of the soul" tell him that his vocation is not "for idle contemplation" of the self nor "for brooding over devout sensations"; "thine action and thine action alone, determines thy worth". Just what the innermost depths of the soul are, just what the importance of their message is, why man should listen to it, are left unclarified. But one suspects that the innermost depths of the soul are Pascal's heart, Rousseau *sentiment*, and the innate ideas of the English Platonists. They are whatever the faculty is which tells us that an answer to a question is unsatisfactory, however logical it may be. That faculty perhaps is that which gives us real as opposed to notional assent, in Newman's terms. It is the compulsion to disbelieve as well as to believe, the urge to commit oneself to a course of action. If I string out these possible synonyms for Fichte's innermost depths of the soul, it is to suggest that Fichte was not isolated in positing some such power. Just as Kant knew that he was a moral being and that therefore the world must make it possible for him to be moral, so Fichte is as certain that he is an active being. "There is within me an impulse to absolute, independent self-activity. This impulse I feel along with the perception of my own existence, it is inseparably united to my consciousness of myself". Its trustworthiness as a guide cannot be substantiated by knowledge, for knowledge always requires further substantiation. That substantiation in the last resort is always "a voluntary acquiescence," "a resolution of the will to admit the validity of knowledge", and hence a man has the right in this ultimate situation to will to believe in his vocation.

The voice from the innermost depths of the soul, or conscience, first tells man that other people are also self-existent, free, substantive beings independent of him. They have their own purposes and freedom to accomplish them, and we must recognize their freedom and independence. This is of course Kant's categorical imperative in the form of commanding men to treat their fellows always as ends, not means. Second, it convinces me that if I act, my action will have an end and that the end must always be better than what I possess or am at present. I must strive for the betterment of the human race. I must work for the conquest of Nature "until, at length, no farther expenditure of mechanical labor shall be necessary than what the human body requires for its development, cultivation, and health; and this labor shall cease to be a burden". I must work to reform the cruelty of man to man which in the long run is man's desire for power over others. I must therefore strive for the furtherance of obedience to the categorical imperative. But Fichte is too realistic to think that any one man's effort can achieve these noble goals. And his most pathetic confession appears when he says, "It cannot be intended that those savage tribes should always remain savage". For where does his information of the intentions come from and whose intentions are they? They are, as might be expected, the intentions of God, and from here on Fichte writes many an eloquent page on his vision of the future of humanity. It is a vision which few would care to reject, but unfortunately it could be justified on grounds quite different from Fichte's. In fact, he spends less time justifying it than in describing it. Briefly, it rests upon the assumption of the freedom of all men seen as active wills, united and fused into the Absolute Will. Man's vocation then becomes that of living as an integral part of God's Will, which is what man ultimately is. Fichte knows only too well that it will require eternity to fulfill this vocation, but that to him is simply proof that our souls are and must be immortal.

Schelling

In an early work *On the Ego as the Basis of Philosophy*, Schelling says that he believes "that man was born for action not for speculation." This innocent sentence contains within it the kernel of a voluntarism which did not stop until the whole cosmos was interpreted as an active being. The will of man which had been so essential to the philosophy of Schelling's teacher, Fichte, was now extended into a metaphysical principle whose domination was much greater than the moral life. Before Schelling concluded his speculations, the whole of Nature became active in precisely the same way in which man was active, with the same goals and the same problems in the achieving of them.

If man is born for action, he must be free to act and, consequently, one of Schelling's first tasks was to provide for human freedom. This was accomplished, or at least its author thought it was accomplished, in his treatise called *Philosophical Investigations into the Essence of Human Freedom.* But even earlier, in his treatise on the Ego, he had laid it down as an incontrovertible principle that only in the self-identity of the human Ego could any sound basis for a philosophy be discovered. The basis for the assertion of the self is that of Fichte: it is the one thing that is known with certainty, and the knowledge which one has of it emerges out of action. For self-knowledge in the sense of reflection upon the contents of consciousness can never give us anything but the flux of perception. But we are not asking for appearances; we are seeking reality. And the only reality of which we have primordial knowledge is the subject's self-assertion which is an act. This act is absolutely free, since it is conditioned neither by experience, being rather constitutive of experience, nor by unknowable things-in-themselves. It simply *is*. This would amount to little more than nonsense were it not that Schelling has rejected the conception of the human mind as a contemplative being mirroring in some way things and events in a world external to it. He has accepted as irrefutable the subjectivism of perceptual data and also the Kantian thesis that the world owes its organization, its form, to the activity of the mind. The question remains of how and why the mind acts as it does. In Fichte the answer was ethical. The Ego needed an adversary in order to become more of an Ego. The creative act was committed lest the Ego fade into nonentity. Similarly in the early Schelling, the Ego first of all asserts its own identity, and it is an identity which persists through time.

But in order to maintain its identity the Ego must be absolutely free. *Das Wesen des Ichs ist Freiheit*; the essence of the Ego is freedom. The moment it is conditioned or determined or modified by something not itself, it ceases to be itself; it becomes the plaything of whatever external forces act upon it. How then can we know that which is not an object of knowledge? By what Schelling calls an intellectual intuition, which requires no distinction between subject and object. This is the kind of intuition which is usually attributed to the beatific vision of the mystics, in which both the mystic and his object are fused into a union which is cognitive without being rational. The Ego remains itself while intuiting itself; it catches itself, so to speak, on the wing. When known in this way it is not objectified. Schelling's anxiety to preserve it from objectification rests upon his assumption, taken over from Kant, that objectification would turn the Ego into an empirical thing like the ordinary objects of perceptual experience. It must be and remain an active subject whose activity must never be diminished. That is why also it must be completely one; its unity must be absolute and permanent. It is in the situation of Plotinus's One who, though all creation emanated from him, had nevertheless to maintain his unity, lest he be submissive to some divisive force from without. And there was nothing without.

In short, Schelling's basic attitude toward the Ego is that of a romantic critic toward a work of art. The work of art must never be analyzed into its component parts, for fear of breaking down that unity which is supposed to confer a higher value upon it. The pathos of unity is very impressive to a man of this temperament. Collections of disparate elements, even formal constructions of parts which retain their separateness to the observer's eye, seem less valuable to such men than beings whose unity is undifferentiated. There is no point in arguing here the relative merits of unity and variety or even of variety within unity, but there decidedly is point in indicating how our philosophers felt about it. We are supposed then to appreciate a work of art as a whole, not as an assemblage of parts, and it has often been proclaimed that the parts are what they are only in respect to the whole. If this is so, then it could be maintained reasonably enough that whatever multiplicity exists in a picture is determined by the picture as a unified whole; if the finished product were different, then its parts would be different. The analogy between a work of art and the Ego is far from being complete since we know that a picture or poem or piece of sculpture is made bit by bit during a passage of time, whereas the philosopher's Ego is already there when he intuits it, already whole and complete. All differentiation occurs within it. But even when the Ego is thought of as progressing in time, fulfilling its function, achieving its ideals, the functions and ideals are *its* functions and ideals and cannot be explained as things imposed upon it from without. The Ego of the Post-Kantians is the grandchild of the Leibnizian monad which was also self-enclosed, a unit, and an active unit. The monad's history, too, could not be explained by scientific procedures, that is, by any causal relations which it might be supposed to sustain. The only metaphor which may serve to explain what it does is that of exfoliation. Leibniz's God might have His reasons, but the monads behaved according to their own inner natures, and the only difference between the inner nature of one and that of another lay in the degree of activity which they manifested. They too were free in that once created they were determined only by themselves.

Unfortunately for the simplicity of Schelling's theory, tradition demanded that some recognition be made of God, the Supreme Will. One can discount man's dependence on the physical world by pointing out that in the long run it is a creation of the mind. But one cannot so easily discount man's dependence on God, if one believes in God. The human will at first sight then seems to be suspended between a physical world, strictly determined by mechanical law, and the Divine Will. If man's will is somehow dependent upon God's, then in what does man's freedom consist? It turns out to consist in the very nature of God: "God is not a God of the dead but of the living". An all-perfect Being could not have wanted a purely mechanical cosmos as His child. Whatever else creation may be, it must reflect the freedom of its Creator; it must be God's self-revelation. But if the creatures reflect the being of their Creator, they too must be free and selfactivating. It is a long cry from this view of the cosmos to that of the seventeenth century philosophers who could think of no higher praise of God than that He was a perfect clockmaker. We are now in the age and region where the biological metaphors have become dominant. And consequently Schelling's conception of God is that of a center of infinite power which flows out of

Him and becomes individuated in the process. The individuation of His creatures makes it possible for human wills to be individual wills, though Schelling does not explain how the infinite and divine power does individuate itself. He is basing this theory if it can be called a theory on his interpretation of Spinoza's *Ethics*, rather than on Plotinus. In Spinoza too the individual minds exist as manifestations of one of God's attributes, but the problem of individuation did not arise for him. It did not arise, one imagines, since he thought of the mind as essentially rational, not volitional, and reason was of such a nature that two reasons would always operate in precisely the same way. But wills, however harmonious they may be in fact, need not be harmonious. And since man was made to act and not to speculate, he must be thought of as a center of action uncontrolled by the necessities of logic. Such volition is indeed "groundless, eternal, and self-affirmative". And insofaras the human will exists independently of reason or corporeal determinants, it is precisely like the Divine Will.

But now another paradox arises. It is all very well to strive, to long, to aspire, to act, but all such verbs demand objects. There must clearly be some end in sight toward which one is striving, even if, as in Fichte, the end will never be attained. As we see the Primal Will, it manifests itself in the order of Nature. Volition itself is unordered and undisciplined, but when it strives to realize a goal, it has to bring order into its acts. In Schelling's more rhapsodical language, "All birth is a birth out of darkness into light: the seed must be buried in the earth and die in darkness in order that the lovelier creature of light should rise and unfold itself in the rays of the sun". Similarly reason emerges out of tile darkness of unreason, and we must envision the progress of the will as the emergence of longing into the clarity of reason. This process to Schelling is typical of all cosmic processes, and the idea which developed into it became the kernel of his philosophy of nature. For as each level of being is unfolded out of lower levels, the cosmic will, still striving and individuating itself, forms new kinds of being. Each of these levels has its own polarity. There is no need to overload these pages with the details of the system, since they no longer could be taken seriously. What is important is that Schelling refuses to relegate the natural order to a realm of unreality, but sees man's fate as integrated into that of the cosmos. The activity of Nature, he insists, is exactly similar to that of man. Whether life differentiates itself into male and female or matter into light and gravity is not of fundamental significance, and in fact it would be next to impossible to dispute questions such as these unless they were made clearer than Schelling left them. But in viewing the cosmos as an interplay between freedom and determinism, with man's will self-determined to seek definite goals, he undoubtedly laid the foundations for later philosophies of nature, such as Bergson's, in accordance with which evolution is neither strictly determined nor strictly teleological. The process can best be named lyrical in the sense that a child's spontaneous singing might be called lyrical. The child does not plan the song ahead of time; he creates it as he sings. We shall, I hope, see how the self-expressive process becomes the evolution of the Idea in Hegel, how by what was called the logic of the situation an act of will leads over to its contradictory. For even if we will to achieve the simplest of ends, that end is the cessation of volition, a denial of the source from which it arose. But since one cannot stifle activity without annihilating the whole universe the end itself can never be a "mere thing," but must be also a process striving toward other ends.

Nature then became for Schelling as he advanced in years a stage on which there was constant interplay between two opposing forces, resisting and striving. But the forces of striving and resisting were not ultimately centered in two different *things*; they were both manifestations of the one ultimate being and that being he could only call Nature. Now the one common example of a being which manifests tension and inner conflict—other than the human being himself—is the work of art. Few critics of the eighteenth century would have thought of a picture or poem as anything other than a vision of purest unity, coherence, and clarity. Their minds were still dominated by what might be called the Cartesian ideal. But as the Romantic Movement got under way, the work of art was seen to be a balance of opposites, the grotesque and the sublime, unity and multiplicity, form and color, in fact, any pair of contradictories which the critic or philosopher happened to be interested in. The conclusion to Schelling *System of Transcendental Idealism* deals with the work of art as a paradigm of the natural scene. The work of art, whatever else it may be, is the product of the artist's free imagination restricted by the material with which he is working. Lessing in his *Laocoön* had emphasized the differences between such an art as poetry and that of sculpture which resided in the differences between words and stone. He attempted to lay down rules which would preserve these differences, rules which forbade the artist to violate the restrictions of his material. But in Schelling one of the principal features of a work of art is the interplay between the artist's intentions and the possibility of their frustration. The ordinary experience of not being able to find words to express what one is feeling is an example of the struggle between freedom and determinism which Schelling saw in artistry. One believes that one has an idea; one discovers that the materials by means of which one can alone express it are inadequate. Yet a struggle goes on to make one's meaning clear. So the sculptor struggles to take a solid and heavy material and to use it to express what might be better expressed in words or paint or possibly even in music.

Moreover the work of art is also a duality of consciousness and unconsciousness, for both the artist and the spectator remain in the conscious world whereas the work of art itself is a material object. The artist is trying to put ideas and feelings into material form, the spectator to draw out of the material form ideas and feelings. The picture is thus more than matter, colored areas on a flat surface; it is the potentiality of feelings from the spectator's point of view and the expression of the same from the artist's. To interpret it from either of these points of view exclusively would be to falsify its nature. So the natural order may be thought of as a work of art, not that it is something created once and for all, a beautiful object which we can contemplate and admire, but as itself both spontaneity and causality. Any natural event for Schelling may be viewed as either a spontaneous force or a limiting and frustrating force. It would be just as false according to his way of thinking to interpret Nature as a sheaf of undetermined spontaneous forces or as a mosaic of atomic parts bound together into a static pattern. It is a fusion of both. The Creator's will did not operate by first reasoning out a pattern which He wished to follow in material form; the artist, too, thinks in terms of his material. The cosmos must then not be thought of as the accomplishment of a preformed idea; the idea itself included its realization. Just as it is impossible to put a poem into stone or paint, so it was impossible to put the cosmic scheme into any other form than that in which it occurs. It will be observed that such a theory of artistry eliminates any consideration of *genres* except in the most abstract manner. What is important about, let us say, *King Lear*, is not its exemplification of the class "tragedy," but its own individuality, its own peculiar and unique manifestation of Shakespeare's creative impulse and the possibility of satisfying that impulse through words. We shall see a similar theory when we come to Croce.

There is still another feature of art which was all-important for Schelling. That is that he supposed the spectator to grasp the work of art as a whole in a single glance. The immediacy of comprehension made aesthetic knowledge different from rational knowledge or sensory intuition, for unlike rational knowledge it was not discursive, proceeding step by step from premises to conclusion, and unlike sensory intuition it "said" something. One may wonder why immediate knowledge is any better than any other kind, but tradition even today maintains that it is better to know than to knowabout, and I suppose that no one would deny that the kind of knowledge one gets from looking at a picture is better than the kind one gets from reading books about it. At any rate it is different, though why it should be called "knowledge" is less certain. But if it is actually possible to grasp the entire meaning of a picture or poem in an immediate act of comprehension, then it must be admitted that something unique has been discovered in the field of cognition. That Schelling gave such importance to art is worth recording since he was one of the earliest philosophers to do so. When he calls art the "organ of philosophy," he is giving to the artist a rank which he had never had before. Aesthetic intuition rises above both science and ethics and the highest value becomes, not truth or goodness, but beauty. Beauty, however, like all other distinctions, evaporates into the absolute identity of the conscious-unconscious whole, so that in the long run it becomes impossible to make any clear and distinct assertion about any one feature of the universe.

Schopenhauer

Intellectual intuition according to Schelling was the most perfect form of knowledge, for it combined within itself the advantages of direct inspection and those of intelligence. Since we grasped the significance of works of art by its means, and art was the principal "organ of philosophy," an intellectual intuition of the natural world would be presumably the goal of all philosophers. But an intellectual intuition gives one a symbol of the universe, a sort of emblem, which synthesizes all contraries in one grandiose image. Post-Kantian German philosophy proceeded by the erection of basic metaphors which became cosmic myths, or what the late Professor W. P. Montague called "great visions." Instead of advancing step by step in logical sequence after a preliminary analysis of a single problem, in the fashion of both the English Empiricists and the descendants of Descartes, the Post-Kantian idealist first formed a vision in terms of which he believed himself able to reinterpret not only the basic elements of human life but also those of the universe itself. He was seeking a single all-inclusive formula, such as the Principle of Identity, out of which all else could be derived by dialectical means. We have seen this operation in Fichte and Schelling. We have seen Kant's Practical Reason turn into the active will of Fichte and Schelling. In Schopenhauer (1788–1860) this will is retained as the central fact in the universe, and its nature is used to solve problems arising not only out of the human situation but even those supposedly involved in the nature of the universe as a whole. From his doctoral thesis *The Fourfold Root of the Principle of Sufficient Reason* to his later essays his voluntarism grew until it was extended into every corner of the world. But it was voluntarism with a difference, and indeed Schopenhauer's philosophy as a whole is unique in modern philosophy, both in its structure and in its consequences.

The Fourfold Root is, as its title suggests, a detailed study of the Principle of Sufficient Reason. This principle, which was a particular favorite of Leibniz, was usually stated baldly as the rule that nothing occurs without a sufficient reason why it should be as it is and not otherwise. Sometimes the reason in Leibniz is causal and sometimes purposive, and one of Schopenhauer's tasks was to show how the two kinds of reason differed. For him a cause could only be the cause of a change and changes could occur only in the states of things, their attributes or qualities or position in space, never in their substance. The substance or matter of anything was immutable, for the simple reason that there must be something which supports or undergoes the change but which does not itself change. This idea was necessitated by the traditional idea of substance as well as by the theory which Schopenhauer accepted from Kant that the qualities of things are contributed to them by the mind. But if substance itself is immutable, then it cannot be a cause of any change and we must look for causation only on the level of the perceptual screen. Thus far he agrees with Hume but proceeds to correct Hume by demonstrating that the necessity which we find in the causal relation is not the effect of habit but is due to the operations of our own mind. The Principle of Sufficient Reason then will not be proved since it cannot be proved. It cannot be proved since it is that on which all proof rests, and when we attempt to prove it we argue in a circle. Causation is its application to series of changes in the world of observation; reason has nothing to do with this world but is confined to inference which Schopenhauer maintains has nothing to do with existence. Reason will be found in logic; causation in natural science. Reason emerges out of the implications of our ideas; causal laws out of observed series of changes. But both are an expression of our ways of thinking.

But along with logical necessity and physical necessity are two other types of necessity: mathematical and moral. The distinction between logical and mathematical necessity would be rejected nowadays as illegitimate since mathematics has been derived from logic. To Schopenhauer logic was still the "art of thinking" and its rules, since they applied to all thinking regardless of whether its subject matter was mathematical or not. Moral necessity is the compulsion we all, animals as well as men, experience when we are presented with a motive to do that which is in accordance with our innate and unchangeable nature. Moral necessity is not always recognized since we are too ignorant of the minute and numerous elements of animal life. The living will is not free in the sense of being able to do anything whatsoever. It appears free only because we are ignorant of that which impels it to do what it does. Absolutely free will in the sense of the will's being able to act without motivation and in either of two contradictory manners seems nonsensical to Schopenhauer. The will acts to satisfy itself, and the kinds of satisfaction which it chooses are determined strictly by the kind of will it happens to be. The will of one kind of beast seeks one kind of life and that of another, another. If human beings differ in their aspirations, it is simply because they are more individuated than other animals. But given any man, he will be found to act with consistency insofar as his fundamental nature is known. The only trouble with this theory would seem to be that one knows a man's nature by what he wills.

The Principle of Sufficient Reason then becomes for Schopenhauer the principle of all explanation and is differentiated according to the subject-matter which is under discussion. One should not attempt to answer physical questions with moral answers or logical questions with physical answers. The Principle is a synthetic expression of four specific types of explanation. Since these types of explanation apply to four types of being, none of them can be applied to the universe as a whole, in so far as the whole is conceived as a synthesis of its four parts. Moreover, the parts all belong to the phenomenal world in which alone will be found time and change. The universe as a whole can be assigned no cause, no purpose, no motive, no sufficient reason, and Schopenhauer's claim to be a true disciple of Kant is justified in that he also believes no metaphysics to be possible if metaphysics is to be expressed by the Pure Reason. There is no reason for the Principle; it is the reason itself. A metaphysics must be therefore constructed in some other fashion and by some other tool.

That tool turns out to be the will itself. But since nothing universal can be explained, Schopenhauer concludes that the will must be self-substantiated. It is simply the will-to-live and living is its goal. The development of this thesis is found in Schopenhauer major work, *The World as Will and Idea*. The word "idea" in this title is in German *Vorstellung*, sometimes translated "representation." It denotes the Lockean rather than the Platonic idea and thus represents an object which cannot be directly perceived. Thus a sound would be a *Vorstellung* representing the appropriate airwaves which themselves are not perceived except as sounds.

In the *Fourfold Root* Schopenhauer had given a detailed account of how the mind manufactures ideas. This work, according to its author, serves as an introduction to the larger one. It introduces it in the sense of laying down arguments which will fortify the theory that the world as we perceive it, its qualities and its organization, is a product of the mind. The subjectivity of the qualities had been proved by Berkeley and Hume, of the organization by Kant. Schopenhauer emphasizes this, extends it to the past and future, in order to show later that the fabrication of an objective world exists for the satisfaction of the needs of the will. Deeply learned in the biological and psychological theories of his day–the first edition of *The World as Will and Idea* appeared in 1818–he attempted a demonstration of the utility of a world of ideas. But since ideas are always the ideas of a mind, the one reality which we can intuit directly, the problem is transmuted into that of explaining in what the mind consists. It cannot be a thing, in the sense that a material object is a thing, a spiritual substance which reflects as a mirror the external world, for that kind of mind had been destroyed once and for all by Kant in his first *Critique*. Whatever Schopenhauer may have thought of his post-Kantian colleagues, those professors with whom he was exasperated, he was developing a notion which both Fichte and Schelling had already adumbrated, that the mind was essentially a kind of activity. But, shrewder than they and less addicted to proving traditional religious tenets, he was able to follow what he believed to be the implications of his premises to their logical end. In this respect, and in this only, he resembled Spinoza. For Spinoza also accepted a method and certain assumptions about the universe and by a rigid logical procedure drew out of them an entire philosophy which went so far beyond the philosophy of his predecessors that it became a complete repudiation of them. The comparison is of peculiar interest to historians of ideas since both men illustrate what happens when a philosopher is free to pursue his studies with a minimum of preconceptions.

The world of external objects is known to the mind, whether animal or human, through the immediate feeling of bodily changes, changes in vision, hearing, olfaction, and so on. But as soon as a change is felt, a cause is assigned to it. The assignment of a cause is not the result of reflection, of abstract thinking, but is as immediate and intuitive as the feeling of the bodily change itself. Because of it there arises the perception of external objects. Thus when our brains are influenced by light rays through the optical apparatus of our eyes and optic nerves, it is our bodies which are modified; but we see the visual object as something external to our bodies. We do not feel the color as a bodily change, though it really is one, but immediately project it into a world external to both our bodies and minds. If we did not do this spontaneously and immediately, we should have but the dimmest consciousness, as in the moment of awakening from sleep. But the change from dull sensation or feeling to clear perception could not come about if nothing were involved but the sensory nervous system. If that were the unique source of perceptual knowledge, we ought to see two objects since we have two eyes, objects upside-down since the image on the retina is inverted, and so on. Since somehow or other we succeed in fusing the two images into one, in inverting their vertical axes, some other power must be involved by means of which we interpret what we see. That power Schopenhauer calls the understanding which operates unconsciously through the causal law.

It would seem to follow that the external world is somehow unreal. Few terms are more ambiguous than "real" and "unreal," but Schopenhauer warns his readers that he is not maintaining the relation between subject and object to be causal. There can be no causal relationship, he maintains, except among objects. The relationship between subject and object is prior to all knowledge and the Principle of Sufficient Reason does not apply to the subject whose instrument it is. The subject and object form a realm apart, division within which is made simply for purposes of discussion. The objective world as a set of ideas is organized through the causal law. It is quite as real as anything else and is neither the effect of the subject, to which causality cannot be applied, nor its cause. It is not independent of the subject since it is a set of ideas and ideas which are organized by the understanding. Schopenhauer here is fighting the theory of a blank mind on which an alien and external world of a nature entirely different makes its impressions as well as that of a mind which pours out of itself a collection of sensory qualities. He is taking seriously the Kantian theory that causality is a category of the understanding and that it must be limited to that domain in which it properly applies. We have already seen the difficulties which arise out of the theory that two entirely different kinds of things can sustain a causal relation. Leibniz' famous figure of the mill in which wheels and belts go moving around was elaborated to show how impossible it was to derive mental beings from a purely material source. Somewhere in the series of events a surd would arise, in this case the emergence of the idea. It is likely that in the back of Schopenhauer's mind lay the traditional notion that causation demanded an identity of substance lest the *dictum ex nihilo nihil* be violated. Hume's protest against the reading of necessity into regularly repeated series of events led some philosophers to reinterpret causation and to maintain that if we could establish such regular series, we had explanation enough. But since one could not infer from the proposition "B always follows A" the proposition "B necessarily follows A," the traditional view of causation persisted.

If the power of forming objects through the immediate intuition of space is common to all life, then the animals as well as human beings must share it. No reasoning is involved: the dog snaps at a piece of meat which is thrown to him as if he already had judged the spatial distance between his mouth and the meat, just as a man leaps over a barrier without first calculating its height with a measuring rod. Reason is a transformation of the immediately perceived relations between things into permanent abstract thoughts. It has nothing to do with immediate knowledge. We all begin with the immediate objects of the understanding, whether we are scientists or animals, and the only difference between minds is the degree to which they are able to make these abstractions. The discovery of a great scientific law, like that of gravitation, is made first as "an immediate intuition an *apercu*, a flash of insight". Reason then justifies this flash of insight by incorporating it into a system of abstract ideas, just as it justifies our practical plans for future action. A person then may be very agile in understanding without being capable of much reasoning, and similarly animals themselves may vary greatly in grasping causal relations and none of them, as far as we know, do any abstract reasoning. In human beings understanding and reason support each other. Our abstract concepts take the place of direct experience or memory. But a good part of life can continue to go on without much in the way of reasoning. Nevertheless this power distinguishes us from our brothers, the beasts. Like them we will; unlike them we think and know.

The abstract ideas by which we think and know are distinguished from the concrete ideas of perception. They are the ideas of classes of ideas. Schopenhauer exemplifies them by such ideas as "relationship," "virtue," "investigation," "beginning." They are ideas of ideas. But though they are all-important for thinking, they are useless for practice. "We must remember that no one ever became an artist by the study of aesthetics; that a noble character was never formed by the study of ethics; that long before Rameau men composed correctly and beautifully, and that we do not need to know thorough-bass in order to detect discords: and just as little do we need to know logic in order to avoid being misled by fallacies". This is especially true in the case of logic, since logic is the formulation of the methods by which we think and have to think; it is a complete and self-contained discipline. Insofar as it throws light upon the procedures of reason, it is highly valuable. It illuminates the nature of reason, but that is all. This is not said in depreciation of the subject, but rather in the hope of showing its true place and value in life. Yet it grew out of practical needs, Schopenhauer maintains, for it arose from the practice of debating. This notion that pure theory arises out of practice was to become a cardinal point in a philosophy contemporary with that of Schopenhauer, namely, the philosophy of Auguste Comte. But theory is not a control of practice except accidentally. It is always susceptible to correction from practice. Nevertheless, it is not to be despised. For rational knowledge is universal in scope, communicable through language, and capable of preservation. Direct sensory perception is limited to the moment and place in which it is experienced and has no relevance to anything else. By substituting concepts for percepts, one may deduce accurate results which will be certain. If our reasoning is correct, the anticipated results will follow. It is thus useful as well as elegant. Its greatest value lies in its ability to be preserved and communicated, and the obvious value of this for social life needs no justification. But all this cannot take the place of direct intuitive discovery and when it is substituted for it, may lead only to irresolution. It should, in short, be kept in its proper place, and that place is not the place of the understanding. Understanding, direct perception, is the ultimate ground of all reasoning; it furnishes those absolutely true premises upon which theory is based and which serve as a test of its truth.

Now no matter how much we may know of the world about us, we shall never be able to penetrate into its inner nature. For the world of knowledge is the world as idea, and ideas are representations of things which exist beyond them. All science, however detailed and well organized, is bound to be limited to the powers of thinking, and this will give us nothing but images and names. "We are like a man who goes round a castle seeking in vain for an entrance, and sometimes sketching the facades". What makes us think that there is anything other than a façade to this castle round which we move? Only the fact that we too live in such a castle, the body, which is to us a set of ideas, and yet we immediately are aware of a force within which activates it. This force is the will. In this one case we are aware both of the outer and the inner nature of something. The body exists as an idea in perception, behaving in accordance with all the laws which govern the behavior of other bodies. But, happily for philosophy, we also are aware that to every act of will there corresponds an observable movement of the body which is its outward expression. It is not the effect of the act of will but the act itself viewed from without. Thus we can say that the body is the act of will objectified. Schopenhauer is careful to distinguish between resolutions regarding future action and genuine acts which are occurring now. The former are simply rational deliberations from which no act may eventuate. The relationship between the will and bodily action is so intimate that it is possible to say that just as every act of volition is also a bodily act, so is every impression made upon the body an impression made upon the will. "As such it is called pain when it is opposed to the will; gratification or pleasure when it is in accordance with it". Only those impressions which result in sensory data are irrelevant to the will. They are the source of ideas. Yet when they are abnormally strong as in blinding light or deafening noise they will affect the will as pain. The identity of will and body cannot be demonstrated, since there are no ideas corresponding to it. It is a philosophical truth from which all logical, empirical, metaphysical, and metalogical truths follow. To paraphrase Schopenhauer's argument one might say that self-consciousness cannot be proved; it has to be experienced. The trouble arose when he came to interpret involuntary movements, respiration and the pulse, for instance, as voluntary. In such cases, as in the case of admittedly material motions, he had recourse to unconscious volition. His treatise on *The Will in Nature* is an illustration of how he worked out this type of interpretation.

The pessimism for which Schopenhauer is most famous followed directly from the theory of the will's nature. If the will is the willto-live, all its doing must be thought of as ancillary to its own satisfaction. To say that life is either good or bad becomes nonsense, since those two adjectives are supposed to denote ends which can be justified intellectually. In his own language the will is groundless and it is only its manifestations in the world of the understanding which can be explained. Since explanation always proceeds according to the Principle of Sufficient Reason and that principle has no relevance to the will itself, all the motives in the world will be ineffectual in modifying its conduct. It simply hungers after life and whatever will satisfy that hunger will be of value to it. We are back again at Duns Scotus's God, at Machiavelli's

Prince, at Hobbes's sovereign, at Rousseau's common will, at Kant's Practical Reason. To use the traditional slogan, a thing is good because we want it; it is not wanted because it is good. Because the brain is an organ needed by the will like all other organs for its own purposes, thinking must be revalued in terms of the will, and presumably even truth will be determined by the vital need which it justifies. Strictly speaking, the world is no more bad than good but, for some reason or other, Schopenhauer seemed to feel that failure to attain an end which was good in itself was an evil. Here he had more common sense but less consistency than his pet antagonists, Schelling and Hegel. To continue striving for unrealizable ends seemed foolish to him, an example of how the will cheats us. But who is being cheated? If we are the will, not something which possesses a will, there is no way for the will to cheat anyone other than itself. The reason may indeed be an instrument devised for vital ends, but in that case one might be expected to declare those ends self-justified and to construct a scheme of values in which the good would be all that furthers living and evil all that hinders it. It was this step which Nietzsche was to take.

To those of us who live in the post-Freudian period it will seem as if this theory of thinking was Freud's theory of rationalization. Freud had read Schopenhauer, according to his official biographer, and it is at least plausible that his belief in the subordination of reason to the will was suggested to him by Schopenhauer. The theories are far from being identical except in this one point, and furthermore Freud provides a victim for the intellect in the social group which makes demands upon the individual that he cannot honestly fulfill. Why these demands should be made is no more explained than why Schopenhauer's will should fabricate reasons whose ostensible purpose is different from their real purpose. If the Freudian will is sexuality and if it is homogeneous, the same in all men at birth, it is strange that groups of men do not recognize its true nature and that society is not so organized as to satisfy it. If each man's will is individual and may vary congenitally, let us say, from heterosexuality to homosexuality, then the clash in ends could and probably would create social conflict. But that is not his theory. So in Schopenhauer the will is homogeneous in the human race, striving after the same satisfactions and yet unwilling to exhibit itself in its true nature. Schopenhauer's pessimism is a reversion to an intellectualistic scheme of values which seems hardly congruent with his metaphysics. If knowledge "proceeds originally from the will itself a means of supporting the individual and the species, just like any organ of the body", then one would imagine that we should proclaim anything which gave that support good and anything which impeded it, bad. So we usually do, says Schopenhauer, but we ought not to.

Our problem, then, is that of defeating the will-to-live. This can be done in only two ways: by contemplation of the Platonic Ideas in works of art and by identifying ourselves with others through charity. The former way defeats the will since, following Kant, a work of art has no practical claims. There is nothing that we can do to prevent Macbeth from committing murder or King Lear from being a senile fool. We do not eat the food and drink the wine in a Dutch still-life nor like Pygmalion fall in love with our statues. A work of art freezes life, and when we enter into it we are in a timeless and spaceless world in which the will is powerless. Similarly when we look upon the insane striving after life on the part of our fellow beings, pity for their insanity may lead us to deny our own will and through resignation to achieve a state of holiness. Quoting Calderon, Schopenhauer maintains that the greatest sin of man is being born, for his differentiation and separation from the Primal Will which pervades all creation is the occasion of all his suffering and eventual death. The true solution of our difficulties is that preached by the Buddhists, emancipation from all desire and hence from all individuality. One who shrinks from so profound a denial of life had best first read the concluding chapters of *The World As Will and Idea* and then turn his eyes to the spectacle of world conflict, programmatic deceit on the part of groups as well as of individuals, organized hypocrisy, and cruelty on a scale never before equaled in human history. If ever there was a period in which the theory of the primacy of the will seemed exemplified, this is it. It cannot be denied that the twentieth century has seen greater scientific and technological success than any of its predecessors except that between 1450 and 1550. But in both instances our knowledge was put to the service of our desires and those desires were held to be self-justified. Despite almost universal intellectual education, our moral education is as rudimentary as ever, and though organized religion makes feeble protests, the faithful are as non-chalant about applying the ethical standards which they profess to believe as the infidels. It is with a kind of relief that one turns to a man who was willing to take the consequences of voluntarism and preach a reversal of all values, Friedrich Nietzsche.

Nietzsche

An obstinate duality eventuating in conflict is found in all the post-Kantian philosophers, and most of them attempted either to explain it away or to absorb it into a synthesis of which the two conflicting elements would be necessary parts or aspects. In Kant himself the conflict arose between the understanding and the reason, the Pure and the Practical Reason, the world of phenomena and that of noumena, fact and value, and was "reconciled" in the work of art and the faculty of judgment. In Fichte the conflict appeared in the opposition between Ego and non-Ego, the ideal and the real, the striving and the goal, and was reconciled in the absolute identity of the Ego or God. In Schelling the conflict arose out of the absolute identity of the Ego which obtained meaning through differentiation, between spontaneity and determinism, between all the polarities which the cosmos exhibits, and again was reconciled in the Absolute known through intellectual intuition and symbolized in the work of art. In Schopenhauer the conflict was to be found pretty nearly everywhere: between sensory intuition and reason, reason and will, the affirmation of the will to live and its denial, and the reconciliation again was effected through art and renunciation. When one comes to Nietzsche (1844–1900) the conflict appears between two kinds of will, two temperaments, and at times within the individual himself. But the reconciliation is never attempted for the simple reason that he saw the inevitability of conflict as essential to life itself.

Though he was strongly attracted to Schopenhauer as a youth, Nietzsche soon saw that the denial of the will to live was not a program. Perhaps influenced by popular interpretations of Darwinism, he maintained that living itself could not go on without conquest. One cannot just live. One is situated in an environment which must be mastered lest it master one, surrounded by competitors who also wish to live. Natural selection pursued its course not merely by the environment's eliminating those individuals who were unfit to survive in it, but also by the other individuals who fought for their own lives and for the perpetuation of the race. Darwin had learned from Malthus that many individuals must die out from lack of food and that some were more able to get food than others. He also knew, as we all do, that natural selection is supplemented by sexual selection and the struggle for food is supplemented by the struggle for mates. Whatever may have been Darwin's own philosophy of life, his readers were often impressed by the element of struggle, and many of them maintained that if only those fit for survival survive, we should let the weak go to the wall. Hospitals, insane asylums, schools for the mentally retarded, in short brotherly love, mutual aid, and cooperation were stupid follies fostered by the weak to further their own ends. Such things were a vain protest against Nature's laws. Men should accept the struggle for life in its simplest form, favor the strong and let the weak perish.

It was in vain that writers like Kropotkin pointed to the

social organization of many animals, not merely that of men, which demanded mutual aid if the individuals were to survive. To such men the struggle for life was a concern of the group, not of the individual. In fact, there had been a long tradition that emphasized the kindliness of the lower animals toward their fellows and the singularity of internecine war among the human beasts. Such protests seemed to have less charm for their readers than the Neo-Darwinian war chants. Human warfare had seemed to be one of the differentiae of men, and in an age of conquest it may have appeared to be an expression of humanity less to be deplored than praised. Protests against war which have reappeared in the twentieth century may be, or probably are, due to our growing realization of its futility, rather than to any revulsion against its cruelty. So long as ways paid off by territorial expansion into the lands of inferior peoples, few worried about them. Those few seemed to the more bellicose to be sentimental fools incapable of meeting the hard challenge of our animality. Even now after two most horrible and devastating wars which involved almost the whole world, the main argument against war is that no one wins.

Nietzsche was not a Neo-Darwinian, though his philosophy could be assimilated to that vague and lyrical creed. His philosophy flowed out of that of Schopenhauer as Schopenhauer's flowed out of Kant's. To him the will was self-substantiated, just as it was for his master, and the principal change which he made in the basic premises was that of giving a target to the will, power. Nietzsche's will-to-power had no further aim. To ask what the power was for was senseless. Power was a good-in-itself, the one terminal value which could never be denied.

But the will-to-power might be manifested in two forms, that of the slave and that of the master. The slave gains power over others by submission, meekness, turning the other cheek. His obedience lulls the master to sleep and thus permits the slave to gain the upper hand. This, Nietzsche maintains, is the explanation of the rise of Christianity.

Christianity is the religion of slaves; it glorifies all that make men good slaves: chastity, poverty, obedience. It is a denial of life. That Christianity denies this life for another is true, and that it first arose among the oppressed is also true. That it arose to be the dominant religion in Europe is obvious. But that it arose to such dominance by enforcing a slave-morality using the term in Nietzsche's sense is far from being even plausible. Neither Constantine nor Gregory the Great were meek and submissive. And when the Protestant Reformation succeeded, it was scarcely because of the meekness of either Luther or Henry VIII. Be that as it may, the ethics which it preached was on the whole an ethics of resignation, not of rebellion. The main question which arose in the minds of Christian moralists was how far resignation should go. For on the one extreme was the quietism of Molinus and on the other the burning zeal of the great reformers. There has been to the best of my knowledge no measuring instrument devised to inform a good Christian of the limits of either affirmation or negation.

The ideal master to Nietzsche's way of thinking was Machiavelli's Prince, Cesare Borgia, who was also the hero of Gobineau *La Renaissance*. Such men were pictured as knowing what they wanted and as defining the good as the satisfaction of their wishes. There was no one to tell them what they should want and, had there been, they had no reason to listen to them. Goodness was that which was pleasing to their will and the only ethics which they needed was a book of recipes for getting it. Power, then, is that which procures satisfaction, and there is no distinguishing between a good and bad use of power except in the instrumental sense of those two adjectives. Any use of power which achieves the desired results is good; any that fails is bad. Consequently bravery is the greatest of virtues. *Was ist gut? Tapfersein ist gut.* For bravery is the very essence of the strong will. Bravery will overcome all obstacles. Bravery and its accompanying virtues are to take the place of the older virtues. They result from a revaluation of all values or, to put it more literally, from a devaluation of all values. The bravery which consists in obeying the orders of conscience regardless of personal suffering, the bravery of martyrdom, was never given its due by this thinker. But in all justice to him it must be pointed out that the second half of the nineteenth century was scarcely one in which frank and honest sincerity was the most noticeable virtue. Whatever one may think of the philosophy of Karl Marx, and we shall have something to say of it later on in this book, his aphorism that religion was the opium of the people was pretty well justified as of that period. For most organized religions, in distinction to such faiths as that of the Friends, did preach resignation to poverty and its attendant evils. The various churches did little if anything to root out the causes of human misery, and the charity which was extended to the poor in the form of alms was but a microscopic alleviation of the troubles of society. Alms-giving may have done good to the giver, but it was at best only a palliative to the recipient. Nietzsche was not alone in castigating the hypocrisy of the religious leaders of his time.

If the will-to-power is self-substantiated, then we have passed beyond good and evil. Just as in Schopenhauer the will-to-live is neither good nor bad but creates both, so in Nietzsche all values are to be redefined in terms of his will. Each is made by the situation in which the hero acts. Thus there is no pasting of value-labels on acts as such. No act in itself is anything more than an expression of the will. Arts like music and dancing which are dynamic become more fitting for the master than arts like painting and sculpture. Wagner, especially the Wagner of *Parsifal*, is to be supplanted by the Bizet of *Carmen*. The bullfight which is a test of courage expended in a spectacle would seem to be the most perfect dance. The bullfight is a struggle between wills to no end. The bull is not eaten by the matador; the matador is not, like Bellerophon or Perseus or Saint Michael, exterminating a pest. The bull is bred for one purpose alone, to fight. It is the very senselessness of the combat which gives it sense. It is a perfect example of what Theodore Roosevelt called the strenuous life, more perfect than mountain climbing, senseless as that is too, since the bull is at least alive and the struggle is between two individuals. Its glorification in our own day by such writers as Ernest Hemingway is an indication of the spread of Nietzsche's ideal. But the revaluation of all values goes beyond ethics and spreads into logic. Truth too for Nietzsche must be superseded and in its place will be put belief. What the strong man needs to believe becomes true. "There is no God," says Nietzsche, "for if there were, I could not bear not to be He." Here is an excellent demonstration of how an apparently innocent theory can be developed into unpredicted forms. When Kant announced that the Practical Reason could affirm as true those propositions which it needed for its task, he could little have foreseen how the same principle would have been applied by his fellows. But if the brain is an organ developed for its utility in survival, then its functions must be valued for what they can do for survival. And if survival is supplanted by mastery, then thinking must be oriented toward mastery. The value of thought will then be determined pragmatically and truth is fixed by an act of will. Yet, as far as I know, Nietzsche never maintained that he accepted the idea of the primacy of the will-to-power simply because it gave him the results which he wanted, though in fact he may have done so. The primacy of that will was true in the old-fashioned sense of the term; it was a fact that one was forced to accept for the same reasons that one accepts any other factual truth, the rotundity of the earth or the procession of the seasons. One cannot by an act of will determine the consistency of geometrical theorems, or the appearance of the seven spectral colors. When one comes to the choice of one's premises, since they cannot be proved logically, they must indeed be accepted by fiat. Similarly the choice of problems, what one will attempt to prove, the *demonstrandum*, is chosen freely. In the third place the method of research and demonstration is only partly determined by the problem. But this is far from saying that truth as a whole is based on free choice, to say nothing of the choice of masters.

The notion of who the master was preoccupied Nietzsche during a good part of his life. In his most famous work, *Thus Spake Zarathustra*, he is symbolized by the man alone on the mountaintop with the eagle and the serpent. "Above the bull's neck, I see the eagle's eyes," he says. And the eagle by tradition was alone able to look the sun in the face without blinking or becoming blinded. This is indeed a lofty figure of speech, and if ever a man was to cure Europe's sickness he would have to alienate himself from the crowd and have the vision of the eagle and the guile of the serpent. But by this time Nietzsche cared little for curing Europe. His task in that book, assuming that he had a task, was to cure the individual. The great mass of mankind was hopeless. But out of it might emerge a few chosen individuals who had the strength to live on their own resources. These wills, who were to be as far above mankind as man is above the apes, were not the product of evolution but were to create themselves by self-mastery. It was perhaps this program, more than his hope in the evolutionary process or even eugenics, which proved to be the greatest stimulus to the youth of his time. For as industrialism and its attendant standardization of minds increased, thinkers were more aware of the dangers of individuals becoming nothing more than social atoms. The generation of Bernard Shaw, Havelock Ellis, and Georg Brandes found in *Zarathustra* a way out of the labyrinth by leaping over its walls into freedom. The individual need not conform; he was free to rebel. The poet and the artist in general could cut themselves off from social entanglements and even if they ruled only in Bohemia, they at least could rule. Their empire was no broader than the frontiers of their own souls, but the mountain peak of Zarathustra was no broader. The proclamation of art for art's sake, of creating for oneself alone for the two slogans were in reality one was a protest against the claims of the social order. It meant the death of schools of art and the birth of the completely independent artist. If one had to choose the typical spokesmen of this movement, one would add to the name of

Nietzsche those of Whitman and Romain Rolland.

But one could also interpret Nietzsche as the proto-Nazi, though his contempt for his fellow Germans was as great as Schopenhauer's. Socialism whether national or international was scarcely to his taste. But the idea of mastery as a good-in-itself, especially when it was embodied in the person of a *Fuehrer* whom the groveling masses would obey without question, might not have displeased him. The ruthlessness of the Nazi leaders in obtaining their ends, their myth of racial superiority, their treatment of their supposed inferiors could all be justified by certain passages of his works. Moreover, there is so little system in his thinking that it is downright impossible to say what is the real Nietzsche and what the unreal. When one is confronted by a collection of aphorisms one is bound to find inconsistency. For the usual logical transitions from thought to thought are by the very nature of the case missing. One might as well try to bring order out of the mass of popular proverbs as to find a system in this writer. His thoughts exploded in disconnected epigrams whose arrangement on the printed page gave an illusion of order, but an illusion only. In a milder way one sees the same thing in Emerson, who was just as incapable of developing an idea in well-organized essays. But it is often such men who have the greatest influence.

The voluntarism/intellectualism distinction was intimately tied to medieval and modern theories of natural law; if we grant that moral or physical laws issue from God, it next needs to answered whether they issue from God's will or God's reason. In medieval philosophy, voluntarism was championed by Avicebron, Duns Scotus, and William of Ockham. Intellectualism, on the other hand, is found in Averroes, Aquinas, and Eckhart. The opposing theories were applied to the human psychology, the nature of God, ethics, and the heaven. According to intellectualism, choices of the will result from that which the intellect recognizes as good; the will itself is determined. For voluntarism, by contrast, it is the will which determines which objects are good, and the will itself is in determined. Concerning the nature of heaven, intellectualists followed Aristotle's lead by seeing the final state of happiness as a state of contemplation. Voluntarism, by contrast, maintains that final happiness is an activity, specifically that of love. The conceptions of theology itself were polarized between these two views. According to intellectualism, theology should be an essential speculative science; according to voluntarism, it is a practical science aimed at controlling life, but not necessarily aimed at comprehending philosophic truth. In the modern period Spinoza advocates intellectualism insofar as desire is an indication of imperfection, and the passions are a source of human bondage. When all things are seen purely in rational relations, desire is stilled, the mind is freed from the passions and we experience the intellectual love of God, which is the ideal happiness. According to Leibniz, Spinoza's interpretation of the world as rational and logical left no place for the individual, or for the conception of ends or purposes as a determining factor in reality. Voluntarism is seen in Leibniz's view of the laws which govern monads (individual units of which all reality is composed) in so far as they are the laws of the conscious realization of ends.

14

Three Philosophies of Action and its Results

Introduction

Pragmatism was given a name by William James and was, as he says, a doctrine of meaning first propounded by Charles Peirce in 1878. Since it was James's version of Peirce's theory which started the ball rolling, we shall deal with James. There are differences between his version of the doctrine and those of its founder; there are still greater differences between the inferences which James drew from it and those which Peirce drew. But these items of historical affiliation must wait for more detailed treatment than can be given them in a sketch of this type.

Beliefs, according to James's version of Peirce, are "really rules for action." The meaning of a belief or idea is the "conduct it is fitted to produce." We have here two different doctrines both of which need not be held by the same person. That the word "idea" has been used to mean a plan of action even in ordinary speech is indubitable. It is illustrated by the talk of a boy who says, "I've got a good idea let's do so and so." An inventor's idea of a possible machine, an artist's preliminary idea of a statue or picture or story, a scientist's idea of an experiment, would all be reasonable examples of this usage. But, unfortunately, even readers of this outline of a few modern philosophies will have recognized that a plan of action is not the only meaning of that elusive word and, in fact, any dictionary will provide plenty of others to confuse the issue. But once the pragmatist was committed to the doctrine that all ideas were rules for action, it was his duty to show that beliefs about the past, about remote regions of space, about other people's minds, about fictitious events, were all really prescriptions for doing something. It will be noticed that all plans for action by their very nature can be carried out only in the future. Consequently whatever a belief may sound like, it must be translatable into terms which can be illustrated only in future time.

The second tenet in this kind of pragmatism is that the meaning of a plan of action or idea or belief is itself the conduct it is fitted to produce. This again sounds simple enough. James cites a man looking for the right way home who discovers which one he should take by experimentation. The one which actually leads him home is the right one. Here again the futuristic element is essential to the theory. Before taking either path, the man cannot tell which one is right. He has two possible plans of action and at that moment it is incorrect to say that either is true or false. Yet common sense would say that whether the man has tried one of the paths or not, one is right and the other wrong. Similarly, common sense would say that the proposition, "Columbus discovered America in 1492," is either correct or incorrect whether anyone attempts to verify it or not. Again, we know that the sum of two finite numbers will be greater than either of the numbers without proving it by taking two or more numbers and seeing whether it is so or not.

This objection may not be as sound as it looks. An idea which has already been tested is true until it turns out to be false. One can always take a generally accepted idea and test it for oneself if one wishes. And the pragmatist would say that such ideas are dead plans of action. He is more interested in the man who is confronted by a problem which he wishes to solve. In that case he has to frame an hypothesis and the hypothesis will have to provide some means of verification. For an idea which precludes all means of verification is hardly worth consideration. This is the sort of hypothesis which James quotes the chemist Ostwald as suggesting, of trying to determine whether a brownie or an elf causes dough to rise when mixed with yeast. To solve that problem one would first have to know how to distinguish between brownies and elves, then to state clearly how either could make the yeast operate, and finally how the intervention of the one could be distinguished from that of the other. But none of this is possible. Here, common sense would say that the problem is futile; pragmatism says that it is meaningless. And obviously if the meaning of an idea is the practical consequences of the plan of action which is equivalent to the idea, then a plan of action which has no practical consequences has no meaning.

Unfortunately there is as great difficulty in telling whether an idea is meaningless as in discovering its meaning. Unless we knew the meaning of the terms "brownie" and "elf" in Ostwald's example, we could not discover that sentences including them were pragmatically meaningless. The same situation is faced today by a group of philosophers called logical positivists who hold a similar doctrine of meaning. Thus Professor Carl Hempel in an article on *The Logical Analysis of Psychology* points out that the existence or non-existence of minds, feelings, inferiority complexes, and the like, is a pseudo-problem, since the only "legitimate use" of them is as abbreviations for physicalistic statements. The physicalistic statements are of course the description of the laboratory technique which would be used to determine whether or not someone has a mind or an inferiority complex or feelings. Until such psychological terms can be translated into physicalistic terms, they are meaningless. But again, how would one know what laboratory experiments to set up unless one previously had some idea or notion or belief or definition of something whose existence was to be tested by that technique? Let me give a simpler example of this problem. I am convinced that I had a father. I have good reason to believe that he died in 1898, too long ago for me to remember him. I know of no one alive today who ever saw him. Does the statement, "I had a father," mean the manner in which I would discover that I had father? The reason why I believe it is that I believe all human beings have fathers and that I am a human being. That is a universal proposition the proof of which cannot be empirical. As a generalization it is, of course, inductive. But in my own little cosmos, it is an *a priori* certainty. It is only by my willingness to identify myself with other human beings that I can conclude to my having had a father, but that is not involved. As a matter of fact, even if my father were alive, there would be no certain way of discovering whether he was or was not my father. And yet no one would maintain that the meaning of the statement, "I had a father," is identical with the complex of statements describing the methods used to determine who that person was. One can believe that one had a father and yet have no idea who he was, and indeed there must be thousands of people in the world at any time in that situation.

My belief that I had a father may influence my conduct in ways different from those which would ensue from the belief that I do not know who my father was. If I thought that I was an illegitimate child, I might be either depressed or elated at the idea. The depression need not be explained; the reasons for it are too obvious. The elation might easily come about when I should consider my escape from many of the troubles of an Oedipus complex, the need for supporting the man in his old age, my dependence upon him during childhood and youth, his possibly unpleasant character, and so on. I have presented two possible effects upon the conduct of a person who is illegitimate in the sense of not knowing who his father was. Does not-knowing-who-one's-father-was mean that one will be either depressed or elated by the discovery of one's ignorance? If so, it is a self-contradictory idea. Yet the statement, "I do not know who my father was," is formally correct and becomes self-contradictory only when its meaning is identified with its effect on the conduct of two or more people.

But that is precisely what is wanted of a theory of meaning: a theory which will give interpersonal meanings to terms and ideas, not private meanings. And this might have been one of the most important results of James's work if it had been thoroughly done. James had in mind the technique of the laboratory scientist, and it is undeniable that experimental science has proved more fruitful than purely dialectical science. Furthermore, one of the common meanings of "meaning" is the effect upon conduct of a plan of action. This appears when someone says, "If you do this or that, you know what it means." The consequences of virtue and vice, of passion, of loyalty, are often spoken of as their meaning. James was close enough to popular usage to appear convincing to many readers and, as appeared later when the works of the Viennese Circle became better known, to get rid of puzzles by saying that they were nonsense was a godsend. It meant, of course, the death of all speculative philosophy.

From the theory of meaning there followed a theory of truth. Since truth was an idea, its meaning must be defined by the consequences of holding it. Ideas, according to James, are not true; they become true. "Ideas," he says, "become true just in so far as they help us to get into satisfactory relation with other parts of our experience." Assuming that one knows what satisfactory relations are, this is a clear statement of the process of verification. It turns out that lying behind or underneath this theory is the belief that a great part of our beliefs form a system which, I suppose, is a logical system. The test of truth then becomes consistency with ideas already tested. But now what happens when one comes upon an idea which is radically new and contradicts the main principles in which one has believed to date? Until the development of rapid transportation, there was very little need to believe in a round earth. Few of us ever circumnavigated the globe, and a belief in a relatively flat earth would "get us into satisfactory relations with other parts of our experience." Why then do we accept the ideas of the geographers who in the case of most of us are primary school teachers and believe in a round earth? Part of our experience is the scholastic environment and it is indeed more satisfactory to agree with one's teachers than to disagree with them. But it is doubtful whether men who were propounding a thesis with which the majority of their fellows disagreed were thinking of satisfactoriness in terms of pleasant social relations. Such ideas as the commonplaces of science were to James "the dead heart of the living tree"and these pejorative phrases were enough to turn him away from it. But unfortunately for those who like life, we cannot verify every idea for ourselves but must accept the overwhelming number of our ideas from others. They must have a kind of truth which is not consequences for the action of the individual. And of course James admitted that they did have this kind of truth. It resided in their consistency with the generally accepted body of knowledge. Our conduct, then, is limited in some way by this set of ideas.

Satisfaction in that case requires reinterpretation and James fell far short of providing it. When he came to certain metaphysical problems, such as the existence of God, he admitted that the debate between materialists and theists was "quite idle and insignificant" since matter and God mean exactly the same thing as far as the "actually experienced world" is concerned. To give the debate meaning, James turns to the unfinished world of the future, asks us to view the world prospectively rather than retrospectively. Materialism gives us a future without hope, and here James quotes Balfour's gloomy description of cosmic death. The theistic doctrine, "however inferior it may be in clearness to those mathematical notions so current in mechanical philosophy", guarantees us an ideal order. We need an eternal moral order and therefore we have a right to believe in it. No one will fail to hear in this an echo of Kant's postulates of the practical reason. Here there is no longer any question of the meaning of God's existence as distinguished from that of His non-existence. It is solely a question of what good it will do to believe in God. But what are we to believe in? If the meaning of an idea is its practical consequences, then the very word "God" means an eternal ideal order. But are the two phrases (1) "an eternal ideal order," and (2) "the existence of an eternal ideal order" identical? If so, then how could one distinguish between any idea which might be entertained and belief in the reality or exemplification of that idea? And if one can distinguish between an idea and belief in it, one has to set up two realms of being at least, one of which was traditionally called mental or subjective or ideal or something of that sort and the other real.

The logical positivist avoided that trap because he was much more precise than James was. The conditions for verification could be distinguished from that which was being verified; the rules which oriented verification could be distinguished as prescriptions from the terminus of verification; *a priori* principles and postulates of logical systems were not given truth in the same sense as statements expressive of fact were given. In short, the logical positivist was more careful in his analyses. Thus Feigl in his paper *Logical Empiricism*, one of the clearest expressions of the whole discipline which I have come upon, points out among other things that there are both cognitive meanings in language and non-cognitive. The former have to do exclusively with information and may be divided into the purely formal, the logico-arithmetical, and the factual or empirical. The non-cognitive concern pictorial (imaginative), emotional or affective, and directive "meanings." Omitting the details of this discussion for the paper is easily available only formal and factual statements can be true or false, and the kind of truth which a factual statement has is not that which a formal statement has. Thus the truth of pure geometry can never be tested by experiment upon physical objects and the truth of an empirical statement will be determined by one's methods of induction. In this situation the theory of meaning is shown to be necessarily more complicated than James or Peirce saw it as being and, in fact, the "realms of being" about which statements seem to be made are multiplied rather than reduced in number. For once more, when the question arises of what a set of words means, we cannot see their significance or insignificance by staring at the words. We must in the last resort ask the person who expresses them what he intended them to mean. But in that event we are back where we started from, at the interrelations between intentions and facts. Otherwise we ought to conclude that only the language which we ourselves happen to be familiar with has any meaning.

John Dewey

As James recognized early in his career as a pragmatist, a theory similar to his own was being developed in Chicago by John Dewey, as it was in Oxford by F. C. S. Schiller. Since Dewey had more followers than Schiller and since his school still has many adherents, we shall confine our remarks to him.

All epistemologists must decide at the outset of their studies whether they will analyze knowledge after it has been acquired, "the dead heart of the living tree," or whether they will study the process of acquiring knowledge. Both James and Dewey chose the latter alternative and there will be no appreciative understanding of their theories unless one sees this. Dewey says, "Genuine intellectual integrity is found in experimental knowing. Until this lesson is fully learned, it is not safe to dissociate knowledge from experiment nor experiment from experience." He is talking about how we learn, not what we know. He realizes that no one starts with an empty mind, that past knowledge or experience guides us in more ways than we are aware of, and that if one wishes, one can confine one's studies to the inner formal relations of what one already knows. But like James he is prospective for the most part. Knowledge to him is not the contemplation of what is already in the books, but is the conquest of ignorance. When he speaks of knowledge as problem-solving, he means of course that the kind of knowledge which interests him is problem-solving, not that no problems have been solved. This is the final rejection of authoritarianism. Presumably anyone could solve for himself all the old problems, and when Dewey writes about pedagogy it looks as if that were to be part of the program. But the mature man is envisioned as one who is struck with curiosity at all sorts of things, sees problems which no one saw before, and sets out to solve them. Ideas become the instruments by which this is done.

The notion of an idea as a plan of action is before us again. Our lives are primarily concerned not with looking but with action. "We think about anything and everything," he says, "snow on the ground; the alternating clanks and thuds that rise from below; the relation of the Monroe Doctrine to the embroglio in Venezuela; the relation of art to industry; the poetic quality of a painting by Botticelli; the battle of Marathon; the economic interpretation of history; the proper definition of cause; the best method of reducing expenses; whether and how to renew the ties of a broken friendship; the interpretation of an equation in hydrodynamics, etc." But who is the "we" in this long sentence? The only answer is Dewey himself. He undoubtedly thought about such things and, identifying himself with the whole human race as most philosophers do, he forgot about the millions of people who give a minimum of thought to any problem and solve it by following ritual. It is the ritual which, he would say, is usually thought of as knowledge; and nothing is easier than to describe a ritual, how the ritual grows, and why it has the peculiar character that it has taken on are very different problems. Traditional epistemology resembles a geometrical system in that every step is where logic says it ought to be. Dewey's epistemology is rather like a psychological description of how the student of geometry sees and solves his problems.

Thinking then as a process, not as a completed act, was Dewey's concern, and it was for that reason that what he called logic was not recognized as such by logicians. No final definition of truth could be given by him since he knew that whatever satisfied the inquirer would have to be given that name. Since thought always arises, he says, in specific situations, it retires from the scene as soon as that situation is handled "successfully." But obviously what is success in the case of the battle of Marathon is not success in the case of a painting by Botticelli, and definitions of "success" would be too abstract to do much good to the philosopher. Each individual is the best judge of when he has solved his problems and need only question his solution that is, make it a problem in its turn when someone else confronts him with doubts which upset him, or when he himself discovers that his solution no longer works. The two terms of these conditions are important: (1) that the correction of ideas may be a social matter, (2) that solutions to problems are dated and may have to be corrected. The former shows that the experience of all members of the human race is not identical, so that ideas which are held in common are likely to be a compromise between a variety of experiences; the latter, that a given person's experience never exactly repeats itself. Both these items might have suggested to Dewey that the only formal logic applicable to experience is the rules of statistics, but he preferred to attack formal logic as a whole rather than find a substitute for it.

When one arrives at this point it is likely that the question will arise of what part objective fact has to play in knowledge. It was traditional to consider knowledge as a reflection of the outside world. Sometimes it was believed, and the belief was called naive realism, that one had only to look and see the world as it really is, our ideas of it being perfect replicas of it. On the other extreme was the view that we could never know the world as it is but only as the human mind distorts it. In between was the theory derivative from Locke, known as critical realism, believers in which unfortunately differed widely among themselves. But all epistemologists have to admit that some statements are false and that their falsity is proved by what is called an appeal to the facts. If I want to know what the weather is like, I simply look and see. The facts are that the sun is shining or that the sky is cloudy or that it is raining or snowing or something of that sort. Why complicate the issue by dragging in hypotheses and problems and satisfaction and activity and interpretation? Dewey was well aware of the challenge which ordinary common sense presented and attempted to meet it in an essay called "*The Control of Ideas by Facts.*" After stating how the problem is handled by traditional epistemologies, Dewey proceeds to answer it in the instrumentalist manner. If we want to find out what the weather is like, we have to devise a plan for discovering it. If we are already looking out the window, we should never raise the question, for we would know the answer. Therefore, we must imagine ourselves to be in genuine doubt, and in that case we have to take steps to see what it is like. These steps have already been learned, and as adults we do not have to ponder over the right way of answering our question. We are applying a technique or carrying out an idea which we have already tested and found satisfactory. The control of the idea by the facts does not lie in a similarity between, let us say, good weather and an image of the sun shining; the sunshine is the good weather. Unless I misunderstand Dewey, the question, *What is the weather like?* should be translated into the question, *Is the sun shining?* or something similar. In that event no distinction has to be made between the weather and the sunshine (or the sensation or image of sunshine) but, rather, the sunshine is the answer to the question previously raised and its so called ontological status is irrelevant.

The trouble historically was that Dewey and his opponents were discussing two different questions. The traditional epistemologist was troubled by a situation which arose in physics out of the theories of the transmission of light and sound. Colors and sounds are (a) observed at a date later than that at which the light rays or air-waves left their sources, and (b) have properties which are not those which can be found at their sources. If we now see stars which went out of existence millions of years ago, then what we see is not the physical star, for that is no longer there to be seen. The physical star is both a mass of incandescent gases plus the light rays which extend through space-time however long and widely they travel. And if what I see or hear has properties which light rays and airwaves do not have, then what I see and hear cannot be the light rays and air-waves or else the latter must have inconsistent properties. Such a theory considers knowledge to be symbolized not merely by such sentences as, "This is a red rose," but also by such terms as "red," which say nothing about anything. The epistemologist who discusses the objectivity of colors can or cannot be in harmony with the epistemologist who is interested only in judgments. The subjectivity of a color or sound is irrelevant to the problem of what constitutes the verification of a complete sentence. But neither Dewey nor his opponents seemed to see that. The problem as phrased in the *Revolt against Dualism* can only be met by tackling the more fundamental problems of what is meant by a physical object, how we can constitute its objective frontiers that is, where does it end?—and what precisely is the difference between a physical or any other kind of object and its effect? In Dewey's thought there seemed to be no sharp break between one object and another, all things flowing into and out of one another. The gaps between the various kinds of beings were of little importance to him and the world seemed like a great continuum in which the various areas had "significant" relations to other areas. Like James, the James of *Pragmatism*, he seemed to conceive of man as wandering about in this continuum trying to get from place to place with no map but his past experience to guidc him. And unfortunately his past experience never could be counted upon to be a certain prevision of what the future held in store for him. He would not have denied, I imagine, that by limiting one's adventures to a circumscribed area, one could pretty well set up a pattern of behavior which would stabilize knowledge. And that seemed to him to be about what philosophers of the rationalistic tradition had done. And indeed when one reads the articles and books which continue to appear on sensory data, one begins to believe that Dewey was right.

Josiah Royce

Royce like Dewey had studied at the Johns Hopkins University where they had been under the influence of Charles Peirce. But Royce's interests led him toward metaphysics and religion, rather than confining him within the fields of epistemology, logic, and ethics, with the result that he is best remembered for the obsolete portions of his works. He was, as a matter of fact, much more involved in "practical problems" than his colleague James. He wrote books and articles on such questions as race relations and the elimination of war, and in fact there were few fields of inquiry into which he did not venture. His work in logical theory and the applicaton of statistics to scientific problems, though it was influenced by Peirce, nevertheless contained much that was original with him. His historical essays in *The Spirit of Modern Philosophy* are among the best productions in that field which Americans have made. Though his style has proved unattractive to the taste of our contemporaries, they would do well to overlook its Germanic ponderousness and uncover what it sometimes conceals. It was one of his tricks to use old words with new meanings and unfortunately it was a trick which worked too well.

Royce had learned from Hegel that the only way to understand a philosophy was to act as if one believed it and thus work it out "from within." For a philosophy, like any other doctrine, is as much an attitude toward the universe and human experience as it is a set of theorems. The *Phenomenology* was an experiment in thinking in this manner and, for its author, such terms as "empiricism," "materialism," "idealism," and other doctrinal labels were programs for life as a whole. They could be formulated in a system of propositions, but the propositions had implications which were as much directives as generalized descriptions of the world. A materialist, for instance, assuming him to be consistent, would be a materialist in his aesthetic appreciations, religious ideas, treatment of his friends and family, attitude toward the state, as well as simply saying that he believes everything in the universe to be describable in terms of physics and chemistry. There are no such people. But Hegel is making "thought-experiments" and the experiment would be senseless unless one believed reason capable of guiding a man's whole life. It should be remembered that reason for Hegel was the child of Kant's practical reason, and reason for Royce was the child of Hegel's reason.

His justification of this point of view is seen in all his works to which such discussions are relevant but emerges with special clearness in *The World and the Individual.* There he distinguishes between the inner and the outer meanings of ideas, and ideas, he says, are the embodiment of purposes.

They are plans of action in that the volitional and intellectual aspects of them are never separated in existence. As a purpose an idea is an act of will which demands fulfillment but is neither the mere purpose nor the mere fulfillment of the purpose. He refuses to call a color or a noise an idea, in spite of the empirical tradition, for neither is in itself a purpose nor do they evoke necessarily any action. But they may both enter into ideas when (the example is not Royce's) the red becomes the symbol of a nation or a school or the sound a command to act or desist from acting.

But a purpose which is not carried out remains a dream at most. And every plan of action is correlative to sets of circumstances which make its fulfillment possible and which will constitute its fulfillment. Thus if my purpose is to write a fugue in a certain key, the rules for fugal composition and at times the instrument or instruments for which it is being composed will determine to some extent what it will turn out to be. Again, one may have, as Royce himself did, an idea for keeping international peace. In his case the idea was set forth in his book, *War and Insurance*. His plan was never tried and the purpose remained embodied in the book which expounded it. If it had been put into practice, then the whole machinery for insuring peace when operating would have been the external meaning or the embodiment of his idea. The idea is thus not an image of objects of one kind or another. But nevertheless each idea is correlative to a single embodiment or fulfillment when precise or to a set of such embodiments when vague or general. As Royce clearly saw, this conception modifies the whole problem of the relation between ideas and being.

Now the objectors to this theory will point out that the real material world of fact stands out there stubbornly limiting our purposes and sometimes defeating them. Hence, Royce is determined to show that every brute fact is itself somehow related to the purposes of the man who is struggling to understand it. The fact, he maintains, gains cognitive relevance only by an act of the knowing subject. The meaning of the word "fact" might be equated with "that which verifies an idea." But if that is so, then the idea itself determines what facts will verify it and what will not. Before looking at the facts at all, we know that some are irrelevant. If we are measuring a room, we know ahead of time that the color of the walls is irrelevant. But how do we know this? Clearly, through our conception of what measurement is. That conception is going to determine the limits of permissible error, the instrument which we shall use to make the measurement, and the metric system in terms of which we shall make our calculations. But all this is decided upon before we begin our actual work. And all these details and others like them are conventions established by us, not by the room. When the room is being measured these conventions eliminate certain considerations as either trivial or, as said above, irrelevant. The idea or purpose which we have in mind translates the room and all its attributes into factors of cognitive significance and, however objective a being may be, as long as it is external to knowledge, it says nothing. To make it say something, we must first give it meaning within a set of ideas.

The situation, as Royce saw in one of his later books, *The Problem of Christianity*, is that of signs and their meaning. Language, for instance, is simply a conglomerate mass of sounds when considered "objectively." We have established meanings which these sounds express and these meanings can be equally well expressed, except in a few cases, in any one of a large number of sets of sounds, wherein each set is called a language. But sounds acquire meaning and do not have any in themselves. No two sounds could be much more different than *maison* and *house* and yet they mean the same thing. Consequently the meaning cannot reside in the sound as sound. The sound has become a sign of something else; it has become, to use the terminology of Professor Charles Morris, the vehicle of the meaning. So perceived objects and sets of objects turn into facts, according to Royce. If there were no human beings about, they would either have no meaning whatsoever or meaning simply for whatever animal minds might exist. An object which to us might be the fulfillment of an economic purpose, such as a fast-flowing river, to the beast might be simply a place from which to drink. And it is equally true that the same object might have a variety of meanings, the variation dependent upon the human interest which was fulfilled—or objectified—in it. Thus our river is not only a source of power, but also a supply of water, an aesthetic item in a landscape, a place for recreation. What it means depends on what purpose is being achieved, and it is only historical accident which gives it one name rather than another. For instance, rivers were called a source of motive power after they were called rivers, for the simple reason that the invention of the water wheel obviously came later than the discovery of rivers. But, similarly, in the Occident a man retains his given name throughout his life and does not change it when he enters school, leaves the university, becomes involved in a business or profession, or retires, though there are societies where similar things are done and we, too, sometimes modify our names slightly from time to time.

An idea, then, while being a plan of action, may be envisioned from either the internal or the external point of view. But if Royce had left things in that condition, there would clearly have been no one set of ideas that was eternally true, and in the long run everyone would have been able to pronounce his ideas just as true as anyone else's. This was repugnant to Royce. He advanced beyond this type of personal relativism by pointing out that no single plan of action was ever going to be completely fulfilled in a single act or by a single object. Both he and Dewey had been thoroughly drilled in Hegel's philosophy and, though Dewey rejected whatever remained of it in his system, Royce retained the notion that all ideas are interrelated and form a universal network in which every detail is dependent on every other. No individual purpose is ever to be fulfilled completely in any individual's life separated from the lives and purposes of his fellows. Students at least know that the information they acquire as they go through school and university comes from so many sources that it would be next to impossible to count them. One looks up a word in the dictionary and finds a definition. But that definition itself, though usually stated anonymously, is, as we all know, the work of dozens of brains. Learning, which seems like an individual's enterprise, is in reality a social enterprise. We speak sentimentally about the combined work of many hands, and the sickliness of the expression makes us overlook its truth. The value of what we have learned turns upon the value of the work done, and if we are misled by false ideas, the blame rests as often as not on some undiscoverable author. If we were to be precise in our statements, we should say, for instance, "This word means *xyz,* if twelve or thirteen lexicographers have made no mistake in their researches, and the trustworthiness of what they report depends on the trustworthiness of the reports of twelve or thirteen previous lexicographers, and so on." That of course is not the way we learn a language except when it is a dead language or an exotic language. But the point of the illustration is simply an indication of the complexity of terminating a purposive process.

Both Royce and Dewey shared the belief that one thing leads to another and that therefore the world must not be thought of as a collection of atomic *things* lying side by side but having no relations of dependence to one another. The minute something becomes a subject of discourse and thus acquires relevance, its interrelations may take on unforeseen importance. Royce differed from Dewey temperamentally in arguing to the infinity of external meanings which any idea would have once its internal meaning was completely fulfilled. Hence for him it made sense to say that "To be means simply to express, to embody the complete internal meaning of a certain absolute system of ideas, a system, moreover, which is genuinely implied in the true internal meaning or purpose of every finite idea, however fragmentary." There was no dialectical reason why Dewey should not have continued to this point; I suspect that the reason was purely psychological. He had no love for absolutes.

Once Royce had laid down his foundations in this theory of the nature of ideas, he proceeded to show that by emphasizing one aspect or another of the situation and neglecting the others one could construct any of the major metaphysical positions of the past. Thus by emphasizing the objects which fulfill our purposes, the facts, we have realism; by emphasizing the internal meanings and forgetting their embodiments, we have mysticism. In the former case we recognize the control which the external world has over our thoughts and forget that thinking determines what control it will have. In the latter we recognize the necessity of being immediately aware of whatever it is that we believe, that the purposes must be our purposes, and that therefore we must identify ourselves as a knowing subject possessing its objects. Immediacy when pushed to its limits denies any distinction between subject and object, and even in those epistemologies which seem farthest from the mystic limits, such as sensationalism, the distinction between subject and object disappears when one is confronted with a sensory datum. A third type of theory, called by Royce Critical Rationalism, admits the existence of both idea and object and defines the real as the "empirically verifiable truth". Reality according to this theory is whatever experience shows it to be; but first, experience includes the experience of nonphysical objects, such as moral values and mathematical beings, and second, it is always interpreted and corrected by the reason. The fourth point of view, that of Royce himself, he calls the Synthetic, for while recognizing the claims of the three preceding theories, it fuses them all into one. By assuming the "histrionic point of view," Royce is able to give a sympathetic account of realism, mysticism, and critical rationalism, and he is enabled to take this point of view because he believes philosophies to be "ways of life," and not simply sets of sentences with which the philosopher plays.

If reality is neither the internal nor the external meaning of an idea in isolation, it must be a synthesis of the two, for there is no other possibility. On the one hand stands a plan of action unachieved, on the other the possibility of achieving it. The will which aspires after the unattainable, longing for longing's sake, striving for frustration none of these acts seems acceptable to Royce. The simple fact that most of our purposes are, in fact, unfulfilled leads him merely to posit an immortal life in which they will be fulfilled. The simple fact that no human being has that perfect union of purpose and fulfillment which would make him a real individual in Royce's eyes leads him to assert that only the Absolute is a real individual. "An individual being is not a fact independent of any experience, nor yet a merely valid truth, nor yet a merely immediate datum that quenches ideas. On the contrary an individual being is a Life of Experience fulfilling Ideas, in an absolutely final form". This point of view accepts the authority of the facts (Realism), the union of reality and ideal meaning (Mysticism), and demands validity (Critical Rationalism). To adopt the Synthetic metaphysics, however, is to reject whatever seems to be fragmentary and to assert as an axiom that whatever is, is one. It was apparently inconceivable to Royce that the universe might be disconnected, a plurality of things whose relations were fortuitous, stubbornly resisting any attempt to rationalize them.

There was a streak of hard common sense in this doctrine which seldom shines through the rhetoric. To say that a man's purposes are never achieved this side of the Absolute, that the self is an achievement, not a datum, and that ultimate truth is an aspiration, not an attainment, is to say things which most of us have suspected but few have utilized as the basis of a philosophy. Royce early in his career saw that the existence of error was a clue to the nature of truth. For how can a man be mistaken unless there is sonic absolute standard of correctness or validity? It was through his ready acceptance of a man's imperfections that he developed his ideal of perfection and, however religious his language may have been, he never denied that our terrestrial life was an inquiry and not an answer. When he called himself an Absolute Pragmatist, he was emphasizing the conditions under which practice could alone be completed. Those conditions are never limited by any person's experience, for they are ideal conditions. The bewildering thing about this is that he apparently never suspected that the ideals did not form a consistent and harmonious system but quietly assumed that they must form such a system, just as Kant, certainly not the most uncritical modern thinker, assumed that the world must be so constructed that men could live morally within it.

When one asks just what the absolute set of conditions is, the answer is that it is that which makes communication possible. In the *Problem of Christianity* there is a series of chapters setting forth Royce's theory of signs and interpretation. There one will find the most concrete description of the nature of the Absolute, identified by Royce with St. Paul's Beloved Community. Interpretation becomes necessary since the data with which knowledge is concerned are not self-revelatory. They do not shout their meaning at whoever looks at them. Questions are put to them and their answers become significant only in the total context of one's purpose. That is why the same datum may have many meanings. A rainbow will mean one thing to the physicist, another to the child, a third to the man steeped in Biblical legend, a fourth to the farmer. These meanings arise in response to the problems of the individuals concerned. The simple datum, the bow of seven colors, in itself and cut off from human interests is meaningless.

The act of interpretation, out of which both philosophy and science arise, and indeed in Royce's opinion any intellectual discipline, is a third process in cognition, of which the other two are perception and conception. Philosophies of the past, says Royce, have overlooked the role of interpretation and have seen the cognitive problem as the choice between percepts and concepts. Yet no pure percept or concept was ever enjoyed by a mortal, and in actual knowledge all of us use a fusion of the two; and that fusion is interpretation. If we differentiate the types of knowledge by their characteristic objects, perception becomes the knowledge of sensory data, conception the apprehension of universals, and interpretation the knowledge of "either something of the nature of a mind, or else is a process which goes on in a mind, or, finally, is a sign or expression whereby some mind manifests its existence and its processes". That this type of cognition is not like the other two is evident when one translates a sentence from one language into another. Most of us started our classical education by reading the sentence, *Gallia est omnis divisa in partes tres.* To bring into consciousness the English meaning of that sentence demands, to be sure, a visual or auditory perception of it. The common noun in the sentence, *partes*, the adjectives, *omnis* and *tres*, and the verb, *divisa est* are universals or conceptions. But though one see or hear the sentence and know the English equivalents for the universals, one cannot on that basis alone translate. One has to have a set of rules in mind which in this case are syntactical and grammatical. Interpretation consists in applying the rules of interpretation to percepts and concepts. By the time we are fed this sentence, we have absorbed these rules and translate it at once without even being conscious of how we are doing it. If this sort of activity is not knowledge, then of course the discussion is beside the point. But the results of it resemble knowledge so closely as to be indistinguishable from it. What is the difference between looking at a rainbow and saying, "That is a rainbow," and looking at Caesar's sentence and saying, "That means, 'All Gaul is divided into three parts'"? In both cases a judgment is made which may be true or false. The only difference between them is their ostensible objects, in the case of the rainbow the object being a set of colored bands, in the case of the sentence a complex of verbal signs.

Royce points out that the process of interpretation is of varying degrees of complexity. To continue with our own example, the second sentence of Caesar's Commentary is *Hi omnes* [the inhabitants of Gaul] *linga, institutis, legibus inter se differunt.* The glossary of the textbook edition from which I am quoting apparently was made up by a man who foresaw difficulties with the word *institutis*. Consequently it is translated, "design, intention, mode of life, habit, custom." Which of these it is to be is left to the student. But how does the student know which of these renderings to make? We usually get out of the difficulty by saying that the context tells us. But that context will involve in all probability a little disquisition on the part of the Latin teacher, for unless students have changed entirely from what they were fifty years ago, the boy will have translated the word *institutions* and the teacher will have asked him what an institution is. A social situation is immediately created, and the kind of knowledge wanted will emerge only out of the common activity of the student and teacher and author of textbook, determined in part but only in part by the percepts and concepts involved.

This is a very elementary example of interpretation as distinguished from perception and conception. But it contains all the factors which made Royce insist upon its importance for any thorough epistemology. Whether we are dealing with a simple problem of meaning such as that cited or the more dramatic problems of understanding other people and ourselves, we shall come up against the same difficulties. Interpretation is always a triadic relation of which the terms are the interpreter, the sign to be interpreted, and the person for whom the interpretation is made. Now frequently the person for whom the interpretation is made is oneself, and one appears to be both interpreter and person addressed. For the self seen from this angle is stretched out in time, and the present self may be interpreting the motives and acts of the past self to the future self. Interpretation is always a conversation, a social enterprise. And though it begins as the interpretation of a given sign, the interpretation itself becomes a new sign requiring interpretation. It is an endless process which "can be terminated only by an external and arbitrary interruption, such as death or social separation". As a matter of cold fact it is usually terminated by fatigue or the force of authority, but Royce was never sensitive to the power of either.

Out of this simple *aperçu* Royce derives a metaphysics in which the greatest reality is the community of interpreters, the selves who strive for self-enlightenment through communion with others. It is a world in which the central element is the problem of meaning and the central activity the discovery of meaning. To Royce only minds could possess or confer meaning and, consequently, interpretation for him was proof of the ideal nature of reality. They stand against these men who "in desire hasten to enjoyment, and in enjoyment pine to feel desire". Since each of us at some moment or other becomes an interpreter and is dominated by the will to interpret, so each of us becomes a self and integrates his purposes into an inner community of purposes. But since no one's purposes can be fulfilled by himself alone, society, too, becomes or can become a larger self which in the long run includes the dead and those unborn as well as the living. For not only our problems, but also the tools for solving them, are in part bequeathed to us and we shall bequeath others to our children. Inasmuch as Royce firmly believes that truth in an overindividual sense must exist, he also believes in the existence of an eternal self in whom we live and move and have our being.

Dewey never went so far and was content to recognize the obstacles to complete knowledge as final. He was more willing to accept each individual as definitely shut off from entire communication with his fellows. Were one to indulge in psychological speculation, one might see in Dewey the Vermont farmer brought up in the atmosphere of the town meeting in which each man has his say and the consensus is majority rule; Royce as the Californian pioneer to whom the frontier is open and the creation of a community the major problem of life. But we shall leave such interpretations to wiser men. However, it must also be said that Dewey throughout his career was haunted by the specter of German idealism which he wished to escape from at any cost; Royce was glad to embrace it and develop it to what he believed to be its immanent implications.

Besides these more general theoretical and methodological problems, a number of empirical issues should be clarified. Although our natural language contains a set of words like narrative, narrate, story, plot, tell, etc., referring to specific speech acts and their products, it is not self-evident that the intuitive meaning of such words identifies a clearly definable set of empirical objects. Is there an effective method for distinguishing the set of narrative discourses from the set of non-narrative discourses, and can we determine for each discourse whether it is narrative or not? In case it should turn out to be impossible to decide on syntactic and semantic grounds alone whether a discourse is a narrative (in isolation), is it possible to specify the pragmatic conditions under which each discourse with some specific syntactic and semantic properties can be qualified as a narrative or not?

Furthermore, do such decisions of an observer about empirical objects correspond to intuitive procedures of speakers of natural language: do they have the ability to unambiguously distinguish, identify and compare narrative discourses; are they able to assign degrees of narrativity to a discourse; what is the nature of this ability: is it based on a fixed pattern or on a set of rules comparable with the rules of grammar?

15

Rise of Existentialism in Philosophy

Introduction

We have seen physics become mathematics, chemistry become physics, biology become biochemistry, and psychology turn into biology. The dream of Comte to develop a science of sociology has almost been accomplished through the skillful use of statistics and though most of our scientific knowledge has been put to the destruction of large numbers of our fellow men, that was certainly not the fault of science. Yet ever since the beginning of the twentieth century there has been growing dissatisfaction with rationalism. It is always difficult, if possible, to attribute to any one cause shifts in intellectual history, but surely a large part of the credit or blame for our turning away from purely rational techniques may be given to the following: the various forms of psychoanalysis which showed the influence of non-rational factors in reason; the growing influence of Marxianism which emphasized the contributions of economic interests to reason; the development of non-Euclidean geometries which destroyed men's faith in self-evident premises; the investigations into many-valued logics; conclusions reached by certain logicians that formal logic deals only with tautologies; the popularity of the various forms of anti-intellectualism which were based on religious yearnings; and the spectacle of the whole world turning to international civil war as a solution for problems the meaning of which was so obscure that each nation seemed to believe sincerely that it was fighting in self-defense.

If we omit the psychological, economic, and religious factors–and we do so at the peril of making our comment trivial we can see that there remains a logical basis for dissatisfaction with rationalism as a solution to all human problems. The most important logical element in the revolt against reason is the impossibility of equating the prior and the posterior. If time did not have a direction, this would not be so bad, but the direction is there and though many ingenious attempts have been made to explain it away, so far none has been gencrally accepted. Wherever there is a direction, there is always the possibility of prediction and also of control, and there is nothing irrational in the situation except that no equation can be set up in which the later event will be the exact equal of the earlier. Vectorial analysis may be expressed as an equation, just as chemical analysis is. But that does not mean that what is on the right hand side of the equation is entirely present somehow or other on the left.

In the second place, perhaps because of the influence of statistics, deviations within a statistical group are more noticeable than they used to be. The variations within a biological species were utilized as early as Lamarck and, as we have said previously, formed one of the important bits of evidence in Darwin's argument toward natural selection. In any event attention began to be paid to the individual thing within a class rather than to the class itself. The animal who, for instance, varied from the norm in a favorable manner had a better chance of surviving than the animal who varied in an unfavorable manner. The genius, the idiot, the man of average intelligence all began to attract attention and to induce scepticism about classifications as keys to complete understanding. This appeared early in the arts when, thanks to certain "romantic" artists and theorists, each work of art, each artist, and presumably each critic was to be appraised as an individual thing. But individuals cannot be handled through pure logic, except when they are members of unit classes. Their *haecceitas* could be manipulated perhaps as a class-concept, but since the class had but one member, one might as well stop fiddling with logic and observe. Individual things must be looked at, intuited, apprehended through observation and can be talked of only in terms which approximate their uniqueness, that is, only in terms which express those details in which they resemble other things. But they resemble nothing in their individuality by definition. Hence they are logical surds. It is worth pointing out that there was an element in the Hebraic Christian religion which brought men face to face with the same problem. I refer to individual responsibility for one's acts. If each soul is not merely existentially one but to some degree qualitatively one also, then at least two consequences seem to follow. (1) The responsibility as well as the freedom of the individual is a surd, if it depends upon the uniqueness of the individual, and there is no general law which will tell us what John Doe will do in a given situation. (2) No rationally grounded commandments can be applied to all men individually. A law, either descriptive or regulative, becomes reasonable insofar as the persons involved are alike. No one ever pretended that cretins could be expected either to obey the Ten Commandments or to exhibit those traits which descriptions of normal men and women exhibit. One may say, To the extent that John Doe is a man, he should act in such and such a manner. But after all, insofar as John Doe is John Doe, he is more or less than a man, and it is precisely that fringe of difference which will make a strict application of the law impossible.

A. Not only is an individual logical, but so too is existence. This had been known for centuries, but it had also been believed that logical orders were a reflection of existential orders. The laws of thought were supposed to be somehow or other laws of things and the distinction between logic and ontology was pretty faint. But men were apparently so impressed with the beauty and purity of logic that they seemed to feel a preference for logic rather than existence. If the world did not obey what logic said to it, that was the world's fault. And with that passion for praising and blaming the universe which all philosophers show on the slightest provocation, they were more likely to turn away from fact to theory as required by the exigencies of their thinking. Yet when the time came that experimental science convinced men that the world was going to proceed on its own course regardless of the strictures of theory, they began to accept existence as inevitable. But like the individual, existence is a surd. Nothing ought to exist, but many things do. This obvious statement contains grounds for despair or rejoicing according to temperament. There is a grain of comedy in a situation in which the real eludes the grasp of the philosopher who continues to reach for it. Philosophy is a child striving to hold water in its fist.

B. If the existent individual living in time cannot be grasped by the reason, the philosopher can flee from time and existence or can look for some other way of apprehending the real. Instead of speaking of knowing the existent, he will wake up to the fact that he is confronted with it. It is there before he can say anything whatsoever about it and it remains there to plague him even after he writes *Finis* to his book about it. This confrontation with existence, with all its terrors, its mystery, its refusal to be understood, its challenge to action, becomes the primitive fact of experience. The traditional way of envisioning man and the world had been that of contemplation, with the data of experience simply sensory components of declarative judgments. But if the world is a collection of individual things and events, the simple declarative judgment must be abandoned since one never knows what is before one. It is no more a matter of identification (*This is an apple*) than it is a matter of doubt (*What is this?*). It may be a cause of fright (*What will happen if I eat this?*) or a symbol of man's fall from grace. The individual is in a state of emotion as well as of sensation, of curiosity, bewilderment, hope, despair, joy, and so on, and all these elements of experience must be considered when reality is considered. The datum of experience becomes invested with an aura of emotional relevance which neither the Lockean nor the Cartesian tradition was willing to recognize.

1. Kierkegaard

It was something of this sort which was the starting point of a philosopher who only recently has become influential, S. A. Kierkegaard (1813–55). He saw early in his career as a theological student that sooner or later even the most stubborn rationalist makes a choice and that his choice is itself non-rational. It is made on the basis of what Professor Paul Tillich has called his ultimate concern. But who can foretell the ultimate concern of others? Where Descartes knew for a certainty that he was a thinking being, Kierkegaard knew for a certainty that the solution of conflicting claims could not be reached by the geometrical method. He was in Pascal's position, suspended between reason and faith. The only way out of the situation was to jump to a conclusion and to jump to that conclusion which was the most perfect expression of one's own needs.

But it is not only faith and reason that are in conflict. Similar conflicts exist between the ethical and the aesthetic, the good and the beautiful; between the human and the divine, man's desires and conformity to God's will; the individual and the universal, that which exists and that which is possible. Reason alone is incapable of settling such problems since they arise because of the attempt to apply the reason to the existent. One might just as well attempt to harmonize the claims of Kant's Pure Reason and his Practical Reason as to attempt to harmonize fact and value, what is and what ought to be. Reason demands universals; experience gives us only particulars. Reason demands a metaphysical God; faith gives us a religious God. One could of course choose reason as against experience, but that would mean lopping off a major part of our lives. Kierkegaard was one to insist that the whole person, the rational, the emotional, the sensitive, the volitional, be treated as a unit and that if this meant, as it did, irrationality, then irrationality was to be accepted. The acceptance of irrationality is the acceptance of the absurd. And in the field of the absurd will be found all that is individual, human, and aesthetic. The incarnation is absurd, but, like Tertullian, Kierkegaard sees no need for denying it. Love is absurd, but the whole human race yields to it. "The movement of faith must always be performed by virtue of the absurd, and this is important in such a way that the things of the world are not lost but entirely regained." Faith is not needed when reason points the way and reason stops short this side of existence.

But the Christianity of Kierkegaard demands a second type of absurdity, the absurdity of mysteries. Just as we sacrifice our reason to existence, so we sacrifice it to the supernatural and for the satisfaction of precisely the same needs. The rejection of the particular in order to find the universal is a scientific gesture demanded by the nature of science. This gesture is necessary if we are going to understand the world; but it is an abandonment of the real for the sake of the possible. So in religion we sacrifice to the universal. The story of Abraham and the Sacrifice of Isaac illustrates this. To Kierkegaard the sacrifice of Isaac is the sacrifice of that which is dearest in life for the sake of obedience to the eternal. That God the father of all mankind should demand the sacrifice of a man is rationally incomprehensible, though traditionally it is held to have prefigured the Crucifixion. But Kierkegaard is careful to point out that the greatness of the story is not Abraham's willingness to sacrifice his dearest possession. What is usually left out of the Story, he says, is dread. Dread arises out of the conflict between "the ethical expression of Abraham's action," his desire to murder Isaac, and "the religious expression," that he wished to sacrifice him. Murder and sacrifice cannot be reconciled or synthesized; outwardly a single act may be one or the other, inwardly they are always discordant. This is the central paradox of the situation. When confronted with that paradox the man of faith "plunges into the absurd," and it is that plunge which Sartre in our own time was to call commitment. Whether one has the religious interests of Kierkegaard or not, the moment is bound to come at which the plunge will have to be made. For whenever action is required, we are confronted with the absurd. In the case of

Abraham, "there could be no question of human calculation, and the absurdity lay precisely in the fact that God demanded it of him one moment and recalled the demand the next".

In his *Problemata*, which follow the *Preliminary Expectoration*, Abraham is contrasted with the typical tragic hero, in that the latter acts within the domain of morality. Agamemnon, Jephthah, Brutus the Elder, all are called upon to sacrifice their children, and they answer the call. In Abraham's case the end is beyond ethics. The tragic hero can be integrated into an ethical scheme; one can point to universal moral laws of which their acts are an exemplification. But Abraham went beyond the universal law. "There was no question of saving a nation, or of defending the idea of the state, or of appeasing the anger of the gods". His act was a purely personal act, a private undertaking. There can be no universal law which dictates private undertakings. Therefore what Abraham did is unintelligible in rational terms. He cannot express even to himself the sense of his act. He is therefore in a situation which is terrifying. For he might be mistaken and yet he continues on his way. The fundamental horror arises over the absurdity of the problem and of the solution. This is what Kierkegaard meant by the "suspension of teleology."

The suspension of teleology is the acknowledgment that a man is confronted by existence which is in itself meaningless, that he must act as if he understood what is required of him and yet there is no way of making the requirement intelligible. This is a revivification of an element in Christianity which has often been overlooked but which has never been entirely abandoned. It makes its appearance in the doctrine of the Incarnation, as Tertullian saw, of Vicarious Atonement and of Inherited Guilt. It appears again in the search for martyrdom and in the monastic vows of Chastity, Obedience, and Poverty. No clearer expression of it could be discovered than St. Francis's definition of perfect joy, seeking and finding unmerited punishment. The Christian philosophers of the Middle Ages as well as those of modern times attempted to interpret such things rationally but, after Pascal, Kierkegaard is the first philosopher to accept existence and the problems it poses. If he went unrecognized for so many years, it was perhaps attributable to the desire of Christians to reconcile their beliefs with science. Kierkegaard turned against science.

2. Jaspers

In 1913 Erich Frank, a young instructor in the gymnasium at Heidelberg, came upon the writings of Kierkegaard. The impression the Danish philosopher made upon him was profound. He introduced him to his friend Karl Jaspers, and in notes to a lecture on existentialism, as yet unpublished, he wrote, "Jaspers caught fire at once. It was in this discussion that the movement of existentialism was started."

The outcome of Jasper's meditations is to be found in a short book which he wrote called *The Way to Wisdom*. The task of philosophy in that work is differentiated from that of science as intuitive wisdom is differentiated from rational investigation. Certain problems inevitably arise in the mind of man, and though he never comes upon a final answer to them, he persistently raises them at all stages of his life and in all levels of culture. For man by nature longs to "find reality in the primal source," to apprehend it in his inner acts, "to open man to the Comprehensive in all its scope," to communicate what has been found to his fellows, and to "sustain the vigilance of reason in the presence of failure and of that which seems alien to it". Regardless of the precise meaning of such terms "the primal source of reality," "inner acts," "the Comprehensive," one feature of these phrases immediately commands attention: philosophy to Jaspers is a way of living; it is not a purely intellectual discipline. It is in fact an expression of that which is most human, for he believes all men to bc instinctively philosophical as soon as they are aware of their humanity. It is an essential part of man's nature to wonder about the natural order, its origin and destiny. No practical good will come of this, but the man without wonder is more of a beast than a man. In the second place, man is never completely satisfied by his knowledge. Satisfaction and here there is a curious similarity between Jaspers and the pragmatists-is always followed by doubt. Certainty is never enduring. Third, philosophy is self-forgetfulness. As we strive to settle our doubts, we turn away from ourselves and become "immersed in things." Wonder, doubt, self-forgetfulness become the differential of philosophizing. But the ultimate truth which this leads to is the sharp awareness of certain limits within the human situation which can never be transcended. We die, we suffer, we struggle, we are subject to chance, we become inexorably involved in guilt. These ultimates must be either accepted or evaded. They can never be explained away.

Each of these limiting situations comes from the sudden awakening to a fact. That we die would be impossible if we did not live in time. That we suffer would be impossible if we were purely material souls capable of action but incapable of being acted upon. That we are subject to chance would be impossible if the cosmos were utterly rational and hence determined. And guilt arises out of our individuality which makes it impossible for temporal man to live according to eternal principles. For similar reasons Jaspers rejects science as the clue to reality. Science, he says, can deal only with "objects in the world." By its very nature it cannot seize the whole of being Knowledge of the whole will be adumbrated in myth, poetry, and the other arts, and will seek full expression as what is implied in being human. What Jaspers is objecting to here is the attempt at giving a complete picture of the world on the basis of incomplete reports. His justification, he thinks, is found in the traditional way of considering knowledge as the absorption of truth as by a blotter, whereas human nature itself contributes something to what is observed. He is thus protesting against such philosophies as materialism or spiritualism which try to express everything in terms of some class of things, philosophies which might be called reductive. Thus Berkeley might be said to reduce the material world to a set of ideas and d'Holbach to reduce the mental world to a set of material things. The reduction is always bankrupt before it proceeds very far because neither philosopher ever saw the interplay between subject and object but forgot that "subject and object belong to each other". The tendency to philosophize in this manner Jaspers attributes to "the urge to be freed from freedom". The real human being is a person, an individual, not a specimen.

Like all existentialists Jaspers recognizes the impossibility of knowing the individual in scientific terms. But even when we cannot know something, we can know why such knowledge is impossible. The square of the circle is not a meaningless phrase, but we know that we cannot calculate it precisely and we know why. We know why we shall never discover a velocity greater than that of light. We know that if everything in the world were doubled in size, we should never be able to discover the fact and we also know why. Consequently, there is nothing fallacious in arguing rationally to the limits of rationality. Now Jaspers unfortunately calls the tool of philosophy by the sacred name of Reason. But his Reason is not the Reason of the natural scientist. It is a way of reaching complete unity, and upon examination it turns out that the only way of reaching unity is by becoming unity. But the unity which we may attain is never complete for the simple reason that we are temporal beings. We know that whatever truth we may achieve must be communicable and yet communication is never ended. It is, the words are mine not Jaspers', a continuing dialogue between finite minds seeking to comprehend the infinity of possibilities. Final truth, he says can be found only in that which transcends all becoming, that is, Being. That Being is beyond Becoming is, to be sure, no more self-evident than its obverse, namely, that Becoming is beyond Being. It is no more self-evident, for that matter, than that nothing whatsoever is beyond or above or below Becoming. Becoming may well be, as in Bergson, the ultimate, to be grasped as it and we too change, on the wing. But Jaspers would find such suggestions revolting. To him the Eleatic One, the Eternal, the Immutable, must be somehow or other the "ground" of the Heraclitean Many, Temporal, and Changing. Reason which leads us out of history to Eternity is the Reason of philosophers like Schelling who by the manipulation of dialectic were able to construct, at least to their own satisfaction, worlds which would fit their longings for security. Yet he also realizes that when we reach the ultimate unity, we are unable to say anything about it.

Though philosophy is an expression of that which is human in human beings, yet it does not occur automatically in anyone's life. Even the child who raises metaphysical questions without being aware of what he is doing, is brought up with a shock to rejecting the obvious. When he asks his parents, "Who made me?" he is suddenly confronted with the possibility that he had a beginning in time. But it is not inevitable that such a question rise to his lips. One comes up against a break in the current of existence. One makes a decision at that moment to raise a question, a free decision. "One can call it the Unnatural as opposed to the 'innocence of nature'". It is the assumption of responsibility and consequently of guilt. And therein occurs a rebirth, or at least the rise of a new personality. We leap here we have a Kierkegaardian strain out of existence into Being. And this leap will be made when a man suddenly awakes to the fact that he is more than a specimen of an abstract class, that he is a real and unique individual.

When that happens he knows that what he does is not entirely determined by the course of history, that he contributes something, if not everything, to the events in which he participates. His freedom may terrify him though one could imagine a society in which responsibility might be encouraged but in that case, as in that of Abraham, the terror is an integral part of the situation.

To pass beyond existence to Being is obviously to deny ultimate reality to the temporal. The one link between existentialists like Sartre and Jaspers, as I hope to show, is their common emphasis upon the individual man and what is involved in his individuality. But once existence is grounded in Being, it loses ultimacy and instead of being the solution of a problem, becomes a problem in itself. It may have been for this reason that Jaspers in his later years preferred to call his philosophy the Philosophy of Reason rather than Existentialism.

In his series of radio lectures, Jaspers had clarified his basic ideas when he came to expound briefly his thoughts about "the Comprehensive". The Comprehensive may be conceived in various ways: (1) as being itself, in which case it is called transcendence (God), and is contrasted with the world; (2) when thought of in terms of the subject-object relation, it may be (a) consciousness in terms of which we are all identical; (b) Dasein, presence, in terms of which we are particular individuals; (c) existence, in terms of which "we are authentically ourselves in our historicity." Existence is differentiated from presence (Dasein) in that it has a temporal dimension. When one is confronted with an object, even if that object is one's inner life, one is simply aware of something there, not of its origins or future. When we are merely conscious, we pass through a moment in which we have no consciousness of our personality, of our selves as distinct from other things. This is as neutral as awareness can be, but the moment is never self-sustaining and we soon either become aware of objects or of ourselves as existence. Yet each of these is an abstraction from the whole situation and we have no way of synthesizing them into a unity which can then be presented in communication. For communication always operates, according to Jaspers, in terms of the subject-object dichotomy, and only the mystic is able to participate in the nature of the Comprehensive. To him immersion in God's being is an awakening; "life in the body" is a sleep.

If this is the solution of our problem, then the only existence which is of any importance is Being as transcendent. And the only knowledge which is of ultimate value is the Beatific Vision. For as soon as we talk of kinds of being or of beings, we have implicitly split up the Comprehensive and have begun to talk in terms of subject and object. But Jaspers seems unaware that the very idea of Being in itself is abstracted from the copula in a subject-predicate judgment where it means no more in isolation than such a word as *above or below.* When we use the verb *to be* without a predicate, we usually mean by it nothing more than *to exist.* And in both Greek, from which the notion of Being was derived, and English the meaning of existence is common when the word to name it is *to be.* The question of whether Being or Pure Being or Being–as–Being means anything whatsoever, if it does not mean existence, cannot be decided dogmatically. But the present writer can find no meaning in it. To speak of Being, when one does not mean Existence, seems to him like speaking of fatherhood without fathers and sons, abovenesss that is above nothing, equality which subsists between no terms. One cannot plunge into pure Being until one knows wherein one is plunging, but the moment one indicates its nature, one has particularized.

Dialectically one can speak of Being as the name for everything of which we may speak. And that would seem to be the meaning of Jaspers' Comprehensive. This would include unreal as well as real things, imaginary things as well as experienced things, Non–being, I suppose, as well as Being. But to be a possible subject of conversation is not to share a property with anything else unless we are willing to assert, for instance, that inedible and edible things, visible and invisible things, possible and impossible things, and so on all have a common property. "To be" is used, as Santayana pointed out some years ago, in four different senses: (1) as identity, (2) as equivalence, (3) as definition, (4) as predication. If, then, Being is to have a homogeneous denotation, one must first prove that all four meanings contain a common meaning. If that is not done, then all talk about Being as such runs into the danger of becoming philosophical punning. To fuse the four meanings into one is analogous to fusing the meanings of homonyms into one. If we did not have writing or printing, we might confuse *meat* and *meet* since they both sound alike and insist that there must be *meathood* to be found in meethood and *meethood* to be found in meathood. This seems unprofitable. For such reasons anti-existentialists have protested against assuming that there must be a common meaning to the verb "to be."

Such protests have been unavailing however. Kierkegaard and his Christian disciples, both Catholic and Protestant, have put their finger on a weakness of traditional philosophy. They have insisted that man's place in the universe is not merely that of a perceptive animal whose mind is composed of sensory data, passively received and automatically erected into images, concepts, and all the other possessions of the soul. They have substituted for the elementary and primordial sensations of Locke and Condillac a more complete vital situation with all the shock of confronting a problem, of trying to discover significances, of wondering what to do or whether to do anything, a situation in which knowledge is only one factor. A pragmatist such as Dewey had moved in this direction when he insisted that knowledge began with the perception of a problem, but it is doubtful whether he saw the complexity of problems. Royce had a clearer view of the matter when he added to perception and conception the process of interpretation, but Royce failed to see the religious, ethical, and aesthetic motives which might introduce meanings into signs which had not been historically associated with them. Both Kierkegaard and Jaspers accentuated the ethical and religious aspects of the situation, but there was always the possibility that other impulses would intervene and did in fact intervene. These impulses were brought to the fore by both Marxianism and psychoanalysis, and the third type of existentialism, that of Sartre, played upon them.

3. Sartre

In the technical language of Jaspers, the weakness of traditional philosophy is the split which it introduces into knowledge by considering only the object or content of knowledge or by considering only the subject or the forms of thought. In reality subject and object are said to form a unit which has a comprehensive nature. Since it is neither subject nor object, and since we are limited to knowing one or the other, Jaspers gives it the name of the Comprehensive or Inclusive about which nothing more can be said than that it is. This does not in his mind mean that the Comprehensive is the sum total of all subjects and objects, but that it has a nature of its own, lies behind all subjects and objects, is in fact much like Spencer's Unknowable. Jaspers' Comprehensive, though it cannot be known in the ordinary way of perception and conception, can apparently be intuited in moments of dread, of anxiety, of guilt, for all philosophies contain intimations of its presence behind the scenes.

It would not be necessary to posit any Comprehensive if Jaspers had been willing to accept phenomena as what they are, appearances which are appearances of nothing. The suspicion will always arise in the mind of a critical reader that such reasoning as his is playing upon words. When he says that the object exists only for a subject, he seems to be arguing that since the word "object" was invented to denote that which is presented to a subject, we must continue to mean this whenever we use the word. Subjects are clearly not everything in the world and neither are objects. But neither are odd nor even numbers all the numbers that exist. Yet the odd and the even numbers all together exhaust the integers and one does not have to posit *numerality* behind or above the integers in order for some of them to be odd and some even. Jaspers is probably resorting to the honored tradition of substantialism when he reasons as he does. There must be some substance which now is subject, now object, otherwise the unity of being would be lost.

When we come to J. P. Sartre, the situation is quite different. He too accepts as his beginning the individual confronted with a world which is not himself. The individual recognizes his alienation from this world, recognizes that it is utterly different from him, that it exists out there to be apprehended and, it is hoped, understood. The opening page of his major work, *L'Etre et le Néant*, flatly denies the distinction between inner and outer natures. "The appearances of the existent are neither internal nor external; they are all on an equal footing; they all refer to other appearances and none of them is privileged." There is nothing behind them. Being and Appearance thus becomes by fiat a distinction which no longer will be accepted. All appearances together form the realm of Being and the very nature of Being is to be an appearance. But though there is nothing behind the appearances, there is something in front of them, the person to whom they appear. This person is in a state of continual change, for he exists in time. This implies an infinity of appearances and a finitude of subjects. For, as Sartre argues in this work, each subject, since it is in a state of change, may select a variety of objects seen from a variety of points of view; phenomena also reappear which would be impossible if they were limited in number. The dualism of subject and object has disappeared but, as Sartre himself points out, the dualism of finite and infinite has been substituted for it. This new dualism can be expressed as that of the appearances within any one person's experience and the totality of all possible appearances. *L'Etre et le Néant* is an attempt to discover what the appearances are.

This problem reduces to that of expelling the appearances from consciousness where they had been lodged since the time of Berkeley. Sartre maintains that no appearance is in the mind; the mind is not a receptacle. Appearances are wherever they may happen to be. The appearance of a table is in space. One's idea of the table is quite another thing. Consciousness *of* things is projected outward toward the appearances. Our distinction between ideas and that of which they are ideas can be based only on our consciousness that we are entertaining ideas. To see a table and to be aware that we are seeing a table are two different events, the latter of which is distinguished from the former only by self-consciousness. But this does not mean that there is an infinite series of awareness. On the contrary, self-consciousness is not a duality of self and consciousness of self; self-consciousness arises in the very act of being conscious. That is why Sartre puts the *de* in the phrase *conscience de soi* (awareness of self) in quotation marks. The *of* is required by French grammatical usage, but it corresponds to nothing in the realm of fact. Self-consciousness is the only manner in which there can be consciousness of anything. When we experience, for instance, pleasure, there is no consciousness of pleasure, plus pleasure; there is just pleasure which is conscious. But in the same way one can argue that our consciousness of pleasure determines pleasure. Sartre is trying to avoid a self empty of experience which is anterior to its experiences and acquires them or constitutes them. When we are conscious of pleasure, both consciousness and pleasure must be present but neither is constitutive of the other. Consciousness exists in itself and by itself as far as anyone who is being conscious knows. We emerge out of sleep in waking life and discover that we are conscious. We do not produce this consciousness, cause it, generate it, as far as we know. We simply are conscious. That fact is an ultimate.

We are now individual minds confronted with phenomena which are "out there" but represent nothing but themselves. We can thus justify all affirmative judgments, judgments that declare the existence—or being—of something, but what do we do about negative judgments? Are we to find some way of discovering "objective" non-being? For Sartre negation or nonbeing always occurs within the limits of human expectation. A man judges that he has a certain sum of money in his wallet; he opens it and finds he has three dollars less than he thought he had. Can one say that the three dollars in question exist in a realm of non-being? On the contrary, it is because we expect to find, let us say, ten dollars and find only seven, that we can say, "We have three dollars less than we thought we had." Negation arises only in the relation between man and the world. "The world reveals its non-beings only to him who first posited them as possibilities". But though the calculation of possibilities is a human act and the very idea of non-being, destruction, annihilation is human, nevertheless the world must be so constructed that we can individualize Being into beings, perceive differences between them, choose one rather than the other. We are as determined by the facts when we make negative judgments as when we make positive, as much as but no more than. The intuition of absence is discovered when one looks for something and does not find it. With the descriptive gifts which Sartre shows in his novels he pictures for us a man going into a café to meet a friend and finding that his friend is not there. What he observes exists, but it also melts into indifference as he looks about the room and its existence fades into non-existence. It is against this background of annihilation that the fact of the friend's absence appears as a positive, rather than negative, fact. It is this one man's personal absence which is seen in as striking a fashion as his presence would be if he were there. Millions of other people are also absent but their absence, or non-being, is of no importance, has no relevance to the situation involved in one's failure to find one's friend and one's success in discovering his absence. "Non-being does not occur in things through the judgment of negation; on the contrary that judgment is conditioned and supported by non-being".

What have been called negative facts, then, must confront us just as positive facts do. We have a direct apprehension of negation, of the nothing. It will scarcely escape anyone's attention that a nothing which can be perceived must be something. For to be perceptible would certainly seem to be something. If this is so, then Sartre's nonbeing, *le néant,* is to be distinguished from the traditional notion of non-being. One might imagine that being and nonbeing were simply correlative terms exhausting a universe of discourse. But it turns out that this is not the case. For Sartre points out that absence, nothingness, non-being may stimulate hatred, regret, and anguish. When a person turns out to be not what you had thought he was, when one realizes to the full the death of someone whose life was very dear, or when one fails to find that for which one was looking, one is brought up with a shock before nonbeing. It seems to reside in the bosom of that-which-is. Now it is no secret that if one starts with an affirmative, there is no way of defining a negation; but if one starts with a negative, one can reach an affirmative by simply negating the negative. The old slogan that two negatives make an affirmative is drummed into every English-speaking child from boyhood, but none of us has been shown how to erect this into a metaphysical principle. Sartre, however, recalls to his readers that every question is based upon a doubt, and since every doubt is based upon the possibility of non-being, human existence itself is colored by the idea of non-being.

If we may embroider upon this theme, we shall see that an animal whose life was conducted automatically, by unfailing instinct, would never have to put a question. Like a stone which exhibits constant behavior, behavior which is entirely predictable, such an animal would either do or die. No thinking, no problem-solving, no choice of alternatives would ever present themselves to it. But human beings are essentially animals who do question and have to choose. Negation becomes part and parcel of their nature by this fact alone. But Sartre will not accept the thesis that human nature is so estranged from nature itself that it is a world of illusion. If our conduct "implies" non-being, then non-being must be an essential element in the make-up of the cosmos. It is because of this basic negativity that we feel anguish.

Now anguish is an experience which all existentialists accentuate as somehow or other the heart of human nature. In Kierkegaard and Jaspers it is, above all, religious in its significance. But whether one is inclined to interpret it religiously or not, it arises when man is confronted by the necessity of choice, looks upon himself as free, realizes that he is a being who puts questions to the universe. This, as Sartre says, is not fear. Fear is always fear of something; anguish is anguish over nothing. It is the emotion which we feel when we realize the possibility of the void. It is thus an index to reality, a metaphysical emotion. In Kierkegaard Abraham's anguish arose as he contemplated his relation to God; in Sartre anguish arises when one contemplates reality. Who can tell whether these two phrases mean the same thing? By shifting emphasis from the denotation to the connotation of the words "God" and "Reality," one can turn an atheistic existentialism like Sartre's into a Christian or Jewish existentialism. "God" is a word which has been used to name whatever is ultimately real. Unless one can turn the meta physical God into a person as Royce did by making persons synthesized purposes it is next to impossible to understand how the two Gods can become one. The religious God may give me commands which I cannot understand and which I willingly obey; the metaphysically Real may leave me absolutely free to do or not to do and yet give me no indications about what I ought to do.

Along with the acceptance of non-being comes the acceptance of time. Sartre emphasizes the temporal dimension of human existence more than either Kierkegaard or Jaspers since he sees no refuge in eternity. Man is a temporal being, a process of self-development. There is no enduring individual who undergoes change from the past through the present into the future. We make our lives, creating them from moment to moment. Thus we negate our past as we create our present and negate our present as we create our future. But the present itself, as the mathematical limit between past and future, is in itself negation. Thus Being and Non-being continue their metaphysical dance and indeed the key to Sartre's type of existentialism lies in that dance. One might in fact, without more distortion than is always present in such paraphrases, say that for Sartre the creativity of negation solves the "riddle of the universe." Non-being negates itself and Being is born; the self negates itself and thus the past turns into the future; the person is forced to choose and negates a possibility, thus creating a reality; through anguish before a situation which gives us no information, we know ourselves and our freedom.

If this were simply a dialectical feat, it would be unworthy of discussion except as virtuosity. But the protests against Sartre which have arisen are eloquent testimony to the concreteness of his suggestions. He is a skillful dialectician to be sure, but what has impressed the western world is not his logic-chopping but the application of his philosophy to the practical problems of life. This has appeared most forcefully in his plays, novels, and essays. He has composed dramas in which the anguish of choice is revealed in a tragic atmosphere and he has shown us in his novels the process of self-creation at work. He is one of those rare philosophers who have been able to take from the past its lessons and integrate them into a radically new philosophy. He has taken over from Kierkegaard the thesis that the whole experience of living, and not simply sensory perception, must be used as the basis for philosophy, from Hegel the dialectical process, from Husserl the technique of investigating "essences." But one suspects that it was his own imagination which gave him the primordial insight which he then fortified by his reading. One also suspects that much of the opposilion to his point of view comes from the burden which he puts on each man's shoulders. His philosophy permits no evasions from responsibility; we can neither turn to God nor to a determined causal order to palliate our sense of responsibility.

This may be "dreadful freedom," but it rests upon the acceptance of the world as a problem to be solved in action. Most problems, those which we are given in schools, are solved by the application of ritualistic procedures, the rules of the game. The problems of life can seldom be solved in that way, for there is always the likelihood that the future will not be a repetition of the past and that improvisation will always be needed. We must act and there is no book of rules to tell us how to act.

What Sartre overlooks is the impulse to ritualize life and thinking itself and thus to force the future into the mold of the past. What we usually call tradition is precisely the dead or dying patterns of thought and behavior. Like all habitual processes, these too have their compulsive force and we project our feeling of compulsion into the world itself, transforming it into something which we call the uniformity of nature. We forget that we achieve this uniformity by adopting methods of thought which make things uniform. One of the lasting contributions of the thirteen forms of pragmatism was the emphasis which they put upon novelty and the element of uncertainty in all life. But what the pragmatists never saw to the best of my knowledge was the impossibility of being prepared to meet the unknown through procedures constructed in order to meet the known. If they had given more thought to the implications of their own theory, they would have been less optimistic.

If we close our historical study with Sartre's existentialism, it is because we believe it to be a beginning, not an end. It is hard to believe that any modern philosopher will turn his back upon time, multiplicity, freedom, the existent for eternity, unity, determinism, and essences. There is, to be sure, a pronounced revival of Thomism at the present time which emphasizes just those things that existentialism makes light of. But Thomism is philosophy in the service of religion and, unless the principle of authority takes over completely, philosophy will continue, as in the past, to justify itself on the basis of evidence and reason. An historian would, however, be a fool to prophesy. We none of us have sufficient evidence to predict the future of anything except the movement of the planets, and no one knows what hidden and apparently insignificant causes are at work to introduce a future utterly different from anything which any of us imagine at the present time. It is more prudent to ring down the curtain on what we have before us.

Bibliography

Adkins, A.W.H. (1960). *Merit and Responsibility*. Oxford. An excellent treatment of Greek ethical thought before the fourth century, working from literary texts. Its conclusions may be somewhat overdrawn, though many critics seem to overreact, and insist on misunderstanding them. For judicious correction, see Lloyd-Jones (1971) and A.A. Long (1970).

Anton, John P and George L. Kustas (eds.) (1971). *Essays in Ancient Greek Philosophy*. Vol 1. Albany, New York: State University of New York Press.

Benson, Hugh H., editor (1992). *Essays on the Philosophy of Socrates*. New York and Oxford: Oxford University Press. A good collection of the most important articles published since Vlastos (1971a).

Bodnar, Istvan M. (2001). "Atomic Independence and Indivisibility." Ch. 7 in Preus (2001).

Coulter, J.A. (1964). "The Relation of the *Apology of Socrates* to Gorgias' *Defense of Palamedes* and Plato's critique of Gorgianic rhetoric." *Harvard Studies in Classical Philology*: 269-303. A criticism of Calagero (1957).

Couprie, Dirk L (2003). "The Discovery of Space: Anaximander's Astronomy." In *Anaximander in Context: New Studies in the Origins of Greek Philosophy*. Albany: State University of New York Press.

Devereux, Daniel T. "Separation and immanence in Plato's theory of forms." *Oxford Studies in Ancient Philosophy* 12, 63–90. Reprinted in Fine (1999).

Dicks, T.R. "Thales." *Classical Quarterly* 9 (1959) 294-309.

Everson, Stephen, ed. (1990). *Epistemology*. Companions to Ancient Thought 1. Cambridge: Cambridge University Press. An excellent collection of philosophically sophisticated essays on Ancient theory of knowledge.

Fine, John (1983). *The Ancient Greeks: A Critical History*. Harvard University Press. In my view, the best political history of Ancient Greece available.

Finkelberg, Aryeh (1999). "Being, Truth and Opinion in Parmenides." *Archiv fur Geschichte der Philosophie* 81, 233–248.

Goodenough, Ward H. (1990). "Evolution of the Human Capacity for Beliefs." *American Anthropologist* 92(3) 597-612.

Gracia, Jorge J.E. (1992). *Philosophy and Its History. Issues in Philosophical Historiography*. State University of New York Press. A sensible and thorough consideration of the issues by a practicing historian of philosophy.

Heidel, W.A. (1906). "The *dine* in Anaximander and Anaximenes." *Classical Philology* 1: 279-282.

Horton, R. (1970). "African traditional thought and western science." In Wilson (1970), 137-171. An abbreviated form of an article in *Africa* 37 (1967) 50-71, 155-187.

Kerferd, G.B. (1981a). *The Sophistic Movement*. Cambridge. Has become the standard treatment. The best general work. Shows more philosophical sophistication than Guthrie (1962-1981).

Kirk, G.S. (1954). *Heraclitus: The Cosmic Fragments*. Cambridge University Press. An outstanding study.

Lewis, Eric (1999). "The Dogmas of Indivisibility, On the Origins of Ancient Atomism." *Boston Area Colloquium in the Ancient Philosophy*, 1–21.

Long, A.A. (1970). "Morals and values in Homer." *Journal of Hellenic Studies* 90: 121-39.

Mandelbaum, Maurice (1976). "On the historiography of philosophy." *Philosophy Research Archives* 2.

Mansfield, Jaap (1999). "Sources." Chapter 2 in A. A. Long (1999), 22–44. A review of the sources for pre Socratic philosophy, sketching and documenting recent criticism of Diels's work.

Nozick, Robert (1993). *The Nature of Rationality*. Princeton University Press.

Nussbaum, Martha (1979). "Eleatic conventionalism and Philolaus on the conditions of thought." *Harvard Studies in Classical Philology* 83: 63-108.

Owen, G.E.L. (1960). "Eleatic questions." *Classical Quarterly* 10: 84-102. Reprinted in Furley and Allen II (1975), 48-81 and in Owen (1986) 3-26.

Preus, Anthony (2001). *Before Plato. Essays in Ancient Greek Philosophy VI.* Albany, New York: State University of New York Press.

Pritchard, Evans, ed. (1957). *Ancient Near Eastern Texts Relating to the Old Testament.* Princeton, New Jersey: Princeton University Press, 1957.

Rist, J.M. ed. (1978). *TheStoics.* Berkeley, Los Angeles, London.

Robinson, Richard (1953). *Plato's Earlier Dialectic.* 2d ed. Oxford. Ch. X: "Hypothesis in the Republic," reprinted in Vlastos (1971b).

Scott, Dominic (1999). "Platonic recollection." In Fine (1999). This is extracted from Scott's book, *Recollection and Experience: Plato's Theory of Learning and its Successors* (Cambridge: 1995), 3–80.

Sedley, David (1999). "Parmenides and Melissus." Chapter 6 in A. A. Long (1999), 113-133.

Vlastos, Gregory (1946). "Solonian justice." *Classical Philology* 41:65-83. Reprinted in Vlastos (1993) I.

White, Nicholas P. (1976). *Plato on Knowledge and Reality.* Indianapolis, Indiana: Hackett Publishing Company.

Wilcox, Joel (1994). *The Origins of Epistemology in Early Greek Thought. A Study of Psyche and Logos in Heraclitus.* Studies in the History of Philosophy, 34. Lewiston, New York: The Edwin Mellen Press.

Wilson, Brian R., ed. (1970). *Rationality.* New York, New York: Harper. A collection of essays bearing on the rationality of preliterate peoples and of their practices and beliefs. The pieces are chosen to represent the range of current views, and many show considerable philosophical as well anthropological sophistication.

Index

P

R

S

T

U

V

W